THE AMERICAN

1775-1783 REVOLUTION

THE NEW AMERICAN NATION SERIES

Edited by HENRY STEELE COMMAGER *and*
RICHARD B. MORRIS

David B. Quinn	DISCOVERY AND EXPLORATION.*
Wallace Notestein	THE ENGLISH PEOPLE ON THE EVE OF COLONIZATION, 1603-1630. TB/3006.
Charles Gibson	SPAIN IN AMERICA. TB/3077
Mason Wade	FRANCE IN AMERICA.*
Wilcomb E. Washburn	THE INDIANS IN AMERICA*
John E. Pomfret	FOUNDING THE ENGLISH COLONIES.*
Wesley Frank Craven	GROWTH OF THE ENGLISH COLONIES, 1660-1710.*
Jack P. Greene	THE ENGLISH COLONIES IN THE EIGHTEENTH CENTURY.*
Louis B. Wright	THE CULTURAL LIFE OF THE AMERICAN COLONIES, 1607-1763. TB/3005.
Lawrence Henry Gipson	THE COMING OF THE REVOLUTION, 1763-1775. TB/3007.
John Richard Alden	THE AMERICAN REVOLUTION, 1775-1783. TB/3011.
Richard B. Morris	CONFEDERATION AND CONSTITUTION.*
Henry S. Commager	CONSTITUTIONAL DEVELOPMENT, 1789-1835.*
John C. Miller	THE FEDERALIST ERA, 1789-1801. TB/3027.
Marshall Smelser	THE JEFFERSONIAN ERA.*
George Dangerfield	THE AWAKENING OF AMERICAN NATIONALISM, 1815-1828. TB/3061.
Francis S. Philbrick	THE RISE OF THE WEST, 1754-1830. TB/3067.
Glydon G. Van Deusen	THE JACKSONIAN ERA, 1828-1848. TB/3028.
Clement Eaton	THE GROWTH OF SOUTHERN CIVILIZATION, 1790-1860. TB/3040.
Louis Filler	THE CRUSADE AGAINST SLAVERY, 1830-1860. TB/3029.
Russel B. Nye	THE CULTURAL LIFE OF THE NEW NATION, 1776-1830. TB/3026.
Frederick Rudolph	CULTURAL DEVELOPMENT, 1830-1860.*
Bernard Schwartz	AMERICAN CONSTITUTIONAL HISTORY, 1835-1877*
Ray A. Billington	THE FAR WESTERN FRONTIER, 1830-1860. TB/3012.
David M. Potter	THE COMING OF THE CIVIL WAR.*
Richard Current	THE CIVIL WAR, 1860-1865.*
Frank E. Vandiver	THE CONFEDERACY.*
David Donald	RECONSTRUCTION.*
John A. Garraty	HAYES TO HARRISON, 1877-1890.*
Harold U. Faulkner	POLITICS, REFORM AND EXPANSION, 1890-1900. TB/3020.
Foster Rhea Dulles	AMERICA'S RISE TO WORLD POWER, 1898-1954. TB/3021.
John W. Ward	CULTURAL HISTORY, 1860-1900.*
Rodman Paul	THE FAR WEST AND THE GREAT PLAINS.*
George E. Mowry	THE ERA OF THEODORE ROOSEVELT, 1900-1912. TB/3022.
Arthur S. Link	WOODROW WILSON AND THE PROGRESSIVE ERA, 1910-1917. TB/3023.
Arthur S. Link	WORLD WAR I.*
Loren P. Beth	CONSTITUTIONAL HISTORY, 1877-1917.*
Max Lerner	AMERICAN CULTURE IN THE TWENTIETH CENTURY.*
Paul Murphy	THE CONSTITUTION IN CRISIS TIMES, 1918-1965*
John D. Hicks	REPUBLICAN ASCENDANCY, 1921-1933. TB/3041.
William E. Leuchtenburg	FRANKLIN D. ROOSEVELT AND THE NEW DEAL, 1932-1940. TB/3025.
John Hope Franklin	THE NEW SOUTH *
A. Russell Buchanan	THE UNITED STATES AND WORLD WAR II, Volume I. TB/3044.
A. Russell Buchanan	THE UNITED STATES AND WORLD WAR II, Volume II. TB/3045.
Alfred B. Rollins, Jr.	POST WORLD WAR II—Domestic Affairs.
Kenneth W. Thompson	AMERICAN FOREIGN POLICY SINCE 1945*
Clifford Lord	STATISTICAL VOLUME.*

* *In preparation*

THE AMERICAN
1775-1783 REVOLUTION

BY JOHN RICHARD ALDEN

HARPER TORCHBOOKS
The University Library
HARPER & ROW, *Publishers*
New York

To Verner Winslow Crane

THE AMERICAN REVOLUTION, *1775-1783*

*Copyright 1954, by Harper & Row, Publishers, Incorporated
Printed in the United States of America*

*This book was originally published in 1954 by Harper &
Brothers in The New American Nation Series edited by
Henry Steele Commager and Richard B. Morris.*

First HARPER TORCHBOOK *edition published 1962 by
Harper & Row, Publishers, Incorporated
New York and Evanston*

Library of Congress catalog card number: 53-11826

Contents

Illustrations

Maps

Editors' Introduction

A HALF century ago the House of Harper launched the *American Nation* series under the editorship of the distinguished historian, Albert Bushnell Hart. That series, ultimately completed in twenty-seven volumes, established itself at once as an authoritative synthesis of the historical scholarship of its day. In the last half century the exploitation of new and rich mines of source material, the deepening and broadening of historical investigations, the importunate advances of new points of view, have operated to make most of the volumes of the older series inadequate to the needs of our generation. It is for this reason that the House of Harper is once again launching a comprehensive co-operative survey of the history of the area now known as the United States, from the days of discovery to the mid-twentieth century. It is hoped that The New American Nation Series will perform for our generation the service that the original *American Nation* series performed for two earlier generations.

Professor Alden's volume on the American Revolution presents one of the momentous events not only in American but in world history. For the American Revolution was far more than a successful war through which a handful of colonials broke away from their mother country and won their independence. It was rather a great creative movement whose influence was felt throughout the Western world.

"The foundation of our Empire," wrote Washington in 1783, "was not laid in the gloomy age of Ignorance and Superstition, but at an Epocha when the rights of mankind were better understood and more clearly defined than at any former period, the researches of the human mind after social happiness have been carried to a great extent, the Treasures of knowledge . . . are laid open for our use, and their collected wisdom may be happily applied in the Establishment of our forms of Government." It is no exaggeration to say that the American Revolution did as much to clarify and define the "rights of mankind," to encourage the "researches of the human mind after social happiness," and to apply wisdom to the processes of government as any comparable epoch in modern history. Out of it came not only a new nation, destined to expand over an entire continent, but a new body of institutions and practices destined to spread over a large part of the globe. With prophetic truth could Washington observe that "with our fate will the destiny of unborn Millions be involved."

The American Revolution, like the American Civil War, has always exercised a fascination for scholars, foreign as well as American, because of the complexity of motives and of interests, the color and drama of the action, and the significance of the issues involved. Until a generation or so ago it was common for historians to interpret the Revolution, its causes and its conduct, as a struggle of liberty against tyranny; to extol the virtue of the Americans and the wickedness of the British—or at least of George III and his hapless Ministers; to interpret the history of the generation before the war largely in terms of the coming of the war itself; and to concentrate on the military and political history of the conflict. Within the last half century—the shift in view can be dated back to Moses Coit Tyler's *Literary History of the American Revolution* and Sydney George Fisher's *Struggle for American Independence*— there has come an increasing appreciation of the complexity of the issues that were involved, of the merits of the contest on both sides, of the importance of economic and social developments, and of the world-wide character of the struggle. The coming of the war is no longer attributed to those "repeated injuries and usurpations, all having in direct object the establishment of an absolute Tyranny over these States" nor is George III presented to us as Tom Paine described him—the "Royal brute of Britain." With British as with American historians the emphasis is rather on the problems of imperial organization, the clash of economic interest, the friction inherent in an unsystematic administrative system, the sectional and class conflicts within the American colonies, and the incompatibility of political principles and practices, English and American. Nor is the story now told so largely in military terms. No less important than the winning of independence were the establishment of a union, the working out of problems of western territories, the transformation of colonies into commonwealths, and the development of self-government and of democracy within the States. Nor is the story of the Revolution told as if it were something that concerned Americans exclusively; its impact on Britain and on Canada has commanded the liveliest interest.

The broad economic and social consequences of the American Revolution—some of which will be traced in subsequent volumes of this series—were essentially by-products of the struggle for political independence and the establishment of an American nationalism. The common purpose which animated the patriots was their insistence that all government is limited, and that even the sovereign is bound by law. Having united on this principle, Americans promptly divided on its applicability to their own political and constitutional systems. One group favored limiting the sovereignty regardless of where it might reside, another sought to enthrone the majority of the electorate as the supreme authority. If it can be said that this great issue, which in one form or another has agitated American politics down to our own time, was not finally settled by the Revolutionary generation, it can also be asserted that this generation provided the framework within which the terms of settlement were to be worked out.

Two world wars of the twentieth century have dramatized the momentous importance of the economy in warfare, of the relations of the military to the civil authority, and of creating the machinery for the conduct of war by a grand alliance. In simpler and more modest form all of these problems appeared at the threshold of our national history, and our experience in the struggle for independence illuminates the nature of these problems and the character of the solutions which are essential to survival. If it is clear that the Americans failed to organize their economic resources for the struggle for independence, it is equally clear that they recognized the need for curbing inflation and sustaining military production. Nor is it less significant that the patriots maintained the supremacy of the civil over the military and cemented a system of alliances that achieved their purpose without too great a cost.

Such matters as these, and many others, are judiciously evaluated by Professor Alden. Drawing upon historical collections unavailable to an older generation of scholars, he has given us a balanced account of the military conduct of the war, and integrated this with the important political, diplomatic, economic, and social developments of the war years.

HENRY STEELE COMMAGER
RICHARD BRANDON MORRIS

Preface

THE period of the War of Independence is one that has long attracted historians, among them several great American and British scholars and writers. Interest in that dramatic era has not slackened, and the stream of books and shorter studies dealing with it flows on. This brief account, it is hoped, contains the results of the best scholarship, both old and recent.

It will be observed that something like one-half of this volume is devoted to warfare. No apology is offered for emphasizing things military. They deserve in this volume no less attention than they have received. The author has also deliberately devoted more space to the British and European scenes than is commonly given in books concerning the era of the War of Independence.

A few words about the viewpoint of this book. During the last fifty years historians have demonstrated beyond doubt that the classic works upon the American Revolution are colored by American and Whiggish prejudices. The Loyalists, George III, British intentions regarding the colonies, the behavior of the redcoats at Lexington, and many other topics are now generally treated with far more objectivity than formerly. The writer does not quarrel with the revisionists—in fact, has himself participated in such revising. However, he believes that the thought and conduct of the American patriots are ultimately defensible, that the Declaration of Independence is in the last analysis justifiable.

The author must express his gratitude for helpful services to Mrs. Barbara Blank, Miss Mary Doak, Wilson G. Duprey, Mr. Gene E. Hamaker, Mr. James Mulcahy, Mrs. Mary Belle Richmond, Mr.

Colton Storm, and Miss Winifred Taylor. Professors G. W. Gray and James L. Sellers offered useful suggestions. Professor John L. Champe kindly gave much needed help in preparing illustrations. Mr. Arthur B. Carlson also generously assisted with respect to them. Professor John F. Roche verified citations and other details in the manuscript. The University of Nebraska supplied typing services.

The maps in this volume appeared originally in William M. Wallace's *Appeal to Arms* and Richard B. Morris's *Encyclopedia of American History*. Gracious permission has been granted for their use here.

Above all, the thanks of the author must go to Mr. Bernhard Knollenberg, who graciously consented to read the manuscript and who made many comments leading toward its improvement, and to the editors of the New American Nation series, Professor Henry S. Commager and Professor Richard B. Morris, who performed similar functions. The writer asserts exclusive claim to all the shortcomings that may remain.

JOHN RICHARD ALDEN

University of Nebraska

THE AMERICAN REVOLUTION

1775–1783

CHAPTER 1

Coming of the Revolution

AT THE middle of the third quarter of the eighteenth century Britain was the greatest of the great European powers. Triumphant on land and sea in the Seven Years' War then ending, she reigned over all the wide waters frequently traversed by Europeans and over a vast and growing empire. In the year 1763 no European navy, perhaps no combination of two European navies, could successfully challenge her fleets and her sailors. Gibraltar and Minorca, the keys to the western Mediterranean, were British properties; she dominated Bombay, Madras, and Bengal in India, and could reasonably expect to develop and to exploit the resources of that subcontinent without molestation from Europeans; small but valuable colonies on the west coast of Africa were hers; she had obtained lucrative economic privileges, if not territorial rights, on the coasts of Nicaragua and Honduras; and the British flag flew over the Bermudas, the Bahamas, Jamaica, Barbados, and other West Indian islands. On the mainland of North America British territory extended from the Atlantic to the Mississippi and from the Gulf of Mexico to the Arctic Ocean. British merchant shipping had outstripped all competitors; British commerce was by the standards of the time immense and profitable; having coal and iron, Britain was already making progress in the Industrial Revolution, well in advance of her European rivals. Continental rulers and peoples looked across the narrow seas for leadership.

By 1783 Britain had lost the bulk of her North American possessions, her most prized colonies. Having exhibited peculiar genius for empire-building, Britain was, astonishingly, the first of the great powers to be forced to acknowledge the political independence of colonials. The entrance into the contentious family of nations of the United States of America, formed from the very heart of the British Empire, was an event that few Europeans would have anticipated a generation earlier. Almost equally surprising was the fact that the newcomer came not in the trappings of monarchy but in the form of a republic, with institutions and ideals pointing toward political and social democracy. Hence, it was entirely fitting that, in the ceremonies accompanying the surrender of Lord Cornwallis, British musicians played "The World Turned Upside Down."

This sudden reversal in the fortunes of Britain and the rapid birth of the United States are attributable at least in a measure to antagonisms existing between Britain and several European states. It is not at all inconceivable that the Americans would have won their independence without either foreign allies or foreign aid of any sort. Yet European money and munitions and the entrance of France and Spain into the war of the American Revolution undoubtedly hastened, if they did not assure, British defeat and American victory. The intervention of the Bourbon kingdoms and of other states in the struggle was prompted hardly at all by sympathy with the Americans, but rather by the opportunity to strike at hated Britain and to profit from her difficulties. In her rise to wealth and dominance Britain had trampled upon the ambitions of her rivals, Holland, Spain, and France. Viewed after 1763 as a mortal enemy at the courts of Versailles and Madrid, Britain made no move to placate her foes and failed to build alliances with the states of central and eastern Europe which might have gained for her powerful friends in time of need.

These abrupt changes must also be ascribed in some degree to British remissness with respect to land and naval forces. Although the traditionally small army was somewhat larger after 1763 than it was before the Seven Years' War, its duties were far greater than before the conflict. Denuding the garrison forces in the home islands, Britain could not put fifteen thousand redcoats in the field in America in 1775. Britain's wooden walls were also neglected. In the day of danger, thanks in some part to the incompetence of the Earl of Sandwich, in larger degree to a desire to economize, the fleet was no more than equal to that of France. Neglected and ill equipped, His Majesty's ships in 1775 were frequently old, and at least some were rotten with age. Meanwhile France had reconstructed her navy. Britain would pay heavily in consequence and would be in jeopardy as she had not been since the sailing of the Spanish Armada.

Inadequate in diplomacy and indifferent to the armed services during the period 1763–75, Britain during the same span was also weakened by corruption and civil commotion. Morality in public affairs was at low ebb at the close of the Seven Years' War. It did not rise, perhaps sank still further, as George III purchased support in order to restore the royal power. Grievous though the results of bribery by the King were upon British public character, his long campaign to re-establish monarchical authority produced other and greater evils. A core of politicians seduced by cash and position came in increasing numbers to occupy Cabinet seats and other posts of authority, especially after 1767. Beyond the fact that they could be counted on to do the King's bidding, they seldom had marked qualifications for office. Nor was their master sufficiently gifted to compensate for their defects. Moreover, although George III was able during several critical years to influence and eventually to dominate both Cabinet and Parliament, there were those whom he would not and perhaps a handful whom he could not cajole or buy. As his purpose to rule as well as reign became evident, bitter opposition sprang up. Many enemies of the King would have been content to reduce the authority of George III to the proportions of that exercised by George II; others, especially after open fighting had begun in America, desired also to take further moderate steps toward political democracy. There were in Britain a very few who wished for a republic. Divided among themselves, the opponents of the monarch and his associates were unable to gain control of the House of Commons and the Cabinet during the fateful years 1770–82. Nevertheless, they were numerous, and Britain was seriously torn by domestic discord when unity was desirable for the defense of the home islands and almost indispensable to the preservation of the empire. Indeed, some of the enemies of the King in Britain looked upon the Americans who rose against the British government after 1763 as political allies, and even came to identify them, perhaps mistakenly, with their own cause.

Above all, the swift rending of the British Empire and the appearance of the American Union are to be explained by the mistakes of the British government in dealing with the American colonies after 1763, blunders which drove them into armed rebellion. For generations the inhabitants of these maturing colonies had been moving in the direction of home rule. After the close of the Seven Years' War, George Grenville, Charles Townshend, Lord North, the Earl of Hillsborough, George III, and others who wielded power attempted to stem, and even to reverse, this tide. They also tried, for the first time in the history of the mainland colonies, to extract from them a large revenue through taxation levied by Parliament.

During the years 1763–65 the ministry headed by George Grenville goaded the colonists into open revolt by a series of ill-advised measures. It undertook to restrict settlement on and speculation in the lands beyond the Alleghenies recently won from France; to maintain a standing army of redcoats of about six thousand men in America; to compel the colonists under certain circumstances to provide quarters, supplies, and transportation for segments of this army; to make permanent the offices of two royally chosen superintendents of Indian affairs who had largely taken over the management of Indian diplomacy, formerly handled by the colonial governors and assemblies; to renovate the customs service in America and to enforce the long laxly executed Acts of Trade; to expand restrictions upon colonial paper currencies, so necessary to the colonists if not always properly regulated by them; to lessen the trade between the colonies and the foreign islands of the West Indies by imposing a tax of threepence per gallon upon molasses imported from those islands; and to secure a revenue from America through the tax on molasses and, especially, through the famous Stamp Act.

The Grenville program was not intended to establish British "tyranny" in America. Parts of it were not even new, although the stamp tax, long used in England, was a complete innovation in the colonies. The motives behind the program were mixed. Grenville and his associates sought to build more effective defense against France, Spain, and hostile Indians; to prevent wars between the colonists and the Indians; to protect the interests of British sugar growers in the West Indies; to assure to the mother country the benefits of her Acts of Trade; to buttress and rebuild British authority in the colonies; and to compel the colonies to assume a larger part of the financial burdens of the empire. The colonists, however, discerned in the Grenville measures a pattern of "tyranny." They wished to settle and to exploit the trans-Allegheny West; they detested curbs upon their commerce; they did not desire to provide quarters, supplies, and transportation for the redcoats; they needed a larger circulation of currency; they believed that they were already contributing their fair share, directly or indirectly, toward the expenses of empire; they did not want British authority in the colonies revived or strengthened. They found a majority of the Grenville measures to be violations of colonial charters, well-established customs, and the rights of Englishmen. In brief, they were "unconstitutional."

The passage of the Stamp Act in the spring of 1765 was the signal for riot and resistance in the colonies. The Americans almost unanimously refused to pay the tax. It was impossible to sell the stamps, and the stamp collectors and others who tried to enforce the law were threatened with violence. The Stamp Act Congress denied the right of Parliament to levy an internal tax in the colonies, and several assemblies voiced American discontent in more emphatic terms. The colonists insisted that the detested law be repealed, and buttressed their demand by refusing to import British goods.

In the spring of 1766 King, Cabinet, and Parliament faced an American crisis. Many British politicians, including Grenville, had no doubts regarding the authority of Britain over the colonies or the wisdom of the measures earlier adopted. They called for coercion. The Marquis of Rockingham, who had succeeded Grenville as Prime Minister, believed that the Stamp Act was within the powers of Parliament, that it would be prudent to conciliate the colonists by its repeal. William Pitt, the most popular political figure in Britain, who supported the contention of the colonists that the tax was beyond the authority of Parliament, likewise demanded repeal. The law was accordingly rescinded. However, Parliament simultaneously passed the Declaratory Act, which asserted that its jurisdiction over America was unlimited. Britain, while rejecting in theory the constitutional position of the colonists, had yielded when it came to practical application.

A second Anglo-American crisis quickly followed. In 1766 the tax on West Indian molasses was lowered to one penny per gallon but was extended to cover molasses imported from the British islands as well as the foreign ones. The molasses tax thus became unequivocally a measure to produce revenue. The same year the New York legislature was "required" to execute the Quartering Act of 1765. In 1767, under the leadership of Charles Townshend, Parliament passed, with considerable enthusiasm, the Townshend Acts, which levied duties upon paper, lead, glass, paint, and tea brought into American ports and established a Board of Customs Commissioners at Boston. Townshend contended that the colonists had admitted external levies for revenue to be within the powers of Parliament. He proposed to use most of the proceeds of the tax to pay the salaries of royal officials in America, hitherto defrayed by colonial assemblies. When paid—and occasionally not paid—by assemblies, these men had often responded to pressure from the colonials. With their salaries assured, they would more effectively defend the authority of Britain in America.

The Americans, who had not conceded external taxation for revenue to be within the authority of Parliament, now saw a resurrected pattern of "tyranny." They proceeded to denounce the revenue act as "unconstitutional," to riot, and once again to curb the importation of British goods. British troops who went to Boston to protect the Customs Commissioners became involved in clashes with the townsfolk which led to the Boston Massacre on March 5, 1770. However, that very same day Frederick, Lord North, the head of a new ministry, called for the repeal of the Townshend duties, except for that upon tea. Parliament complied. Again Britain had bowed before the wrath of the colonists; but once again Britain, by maintaining the levy on tea, had asserted her constitutional right to tax. In America most consumers proceeded to use smuggled tea.

In 1773, largely as the result of mismanagement on the part of Lord North, a third Anglo-American crisis developed. North undertook to assist the East India Company, which was in financial distress, and which had seventeen million pounds of tea in its warehouses. The company had been compelled by law to pay heavy duties upon its tea in England and to dispose of it there. North pushed through legislation which relieved it of the English duties and permitted it to send its tea to America. The company was thus enabled to sell tea cheaper in America, even after paying the

Townshend duty, than could the smugglers who had been supplying the American market with Dutch teas without paying the Townshend tax. North offered a great inducement to the colonists: tea taxed but cheap. If they bought the company's tea, they could no longer effectively argue against the constitutionality of external taxes for revenue. They did not rise to the bait. They refused to permit the sale of the company's tea, whether by consignees or customs officials, and they did not stop short of violence. The Boston Tea Party both destroyed British private property and challenged British public authority.

For the third time King, Cabinet, and Parliament were confronted by resistance to imperial taxation and control. Twice they had temporized. In the early months of 1774 they chose not to yield, but to coerce. In the "Intolerable Acts" they undertook to make Boston pay for its party and to bring Massachusetts to heel. The acts closed the port of Boston until that town displayed due respect toward Britain, removed the capital from Boston to Salem, royalized the upper house of the Massachusetts legislature, limited town meetings, and arranged for the selection of jurors friendly to Britain. They also provided for the quartering of troops to be sent to the colony and made possible trials outside Massachusetts for persons accused of crime as the result of their efforts to enforce the acts. General Thomas Gage, commander in chief of the army in America, now made governor of Massachusetts and authorized to bring in troops to maintain order in the colony, moved at once to his new post. These imprudent steps were almost overwhelmingly approved in Britain.

Boston did not break, Massachusetts did not submit. Both the town and the colony refused to pay for the destroyed tea; instead they prepared to resist. The assembly issued an invitation to all the colonies to send delegates to a general American congress. When Gage sought to set up the new royally chosen council, mobs threatened the appointees, forced several to refuse to serve or to resign, and drove the remainder into Boston, where British troops were gathering. So violent was public feeling that Gage prudently abandoned all efforts to enforce the "Intolerable Acts" outside Boston. He established his headquarters in the town, concentrated more and more troops in it, and fortified the isthmus which then was the only connection between Boston and the mainland. At the beginning of September he sent out troops to seize powder belonging to the colony in storage outside town. The rumor that the British army was taking the field quickly spread through New England. Before it was known to be false, hundreds of armed colonists began to march toward Boston. It was obvious that the Yankees would fight, very likely that they would receive military help from the colonists to the southward. Gage made ready for battle, but at the same time did all he could to avoid hostilities in order that his superiors in London might have time to re-evaluate the situation. Without specific orders he refused to precipitate a conflict. Meanwhile, the First Continental Congress convened and undertook to assert and defend American "rights."

In the winter of 1774–75 the British government learned that America had become a powder keg. Blame for this situation must be attributed in far larger measure to the inadequacies of George III and British politicians than to the activities of the radical leadership in America. Failure of the British supporters of the post-1763 policy to sustain their program over the objections of those who urged conciliation produced vacillations between harshness and weakness which, in turn, stiffened or invited American resistance. Had the new policy been firmly and steadily pushed in the Stamp Act crisis, it is barely possible that American resistance might have been peacefully overcome. But wiser by far than a consistent course of coercion would have been the abandoning of the effort to turn back the colonial clock. An American policy based upon recognition of the maturity of the colonies and of their value to the mother country, together with an attitude of good will, might have postponed indefinitely the era of American independence. Neither George III nor any Cabinet member had ever been in America; they did not know the strength and spirit of the colonies, were unaware that they could not permanently be kept within the empire except upon their own terms.

Hence, the greatest blunder of the King, the Cabinet, and Parliament was their decision in 1775 to bring America to heel by armed might. In the final analysis George III himself was personally responsible for this decision. The dominance which he had gained in London and his limited understanding now involved Britain in a military conflict which she might well lose and one from which she was unlikely to gain enduring benefits through victory. With Europe as a whole hostile or coldly neutral, with a weakened navy, with a small army, with a large part of the people of the home island opposed to governmental policy, with Ireland restless, George III and his followers sought to conquer a colonial people in considerable part of English stock, separated from the home islands by a broad ocean. Moreover, in order to compel submission, they undertook to invade and to occupy the colonies. The extent of their folly was not generally known in Britain until France aligned herself with the Americans and the War of Independence widened into a struggle waged on four continents and their adjoining seas. However, shrewd British observers realized in 1775, and earlier, that the colonies, even without assistance from Europe, would not easily be overrun by British arms, and that it might prove impossible to break down their resistance.

The colonies lay three thousand miles beyond the Atlantic. The voyage across it required a month under the most favorable conditions and might consume two, three, and even four months. The distance and the smallness of sailing vessels created major difficulties in communications, and especially in transport, since British troops could not be expected to "live off the country" indefinitely. It seemed doubtful that Britain could gather sufficient manpower to overwhelm the colonists, even with the aid of those loyal to the King, since the American population, about two and one-half millions, was more than one-quarter of that of Britain. Besides, there was no strategic center, in fact no strategic centers, in America, the capture of which would give Britain victory. Communications within the colonies were poor. Flat and open country where warfare could be carried on in the European style was not common; and woods, hills, and swamps suited for operations by irregulars and guerilla fighters were plentiful. Even the American climate, with its extremes in temperature, favored the colonials, inured to it. Certainly they would be able to feed themselves as well as large armed forces. They could even produce rifles, muskets, shot, and clothing—in fact, the bulk of the military equipment required to wage war effectively. True, they possessed no great store of liquid capital. But it was not at all certain that the British nation, carrying a heavy national debt, could bear the economic burden of a long contest; and there could be no assurance that the colonists would quickly succumb to British arms. To be sure, the colonists, in order to carry on the struggle, would be forced to unify thirteen jealous governments, but the centralized British governmental machinery was notoriously inefficient.

When France and then Spain joined the Americans as open and military enemies of Britain, the question whether or not the colonies would remain within the British Empire was then and there decided. Thereafter, thoughtful men in British public life, if not George III himself, recognized that the colonists must either keep their independence or be induced to return to the empire. A government under the control of the King could neither cajole nor concede, and the war continued to final patriot victory.

CHAPTER 2

Road to Lexington

THE CLOUD of war hung over the Thirteen Colonies after September, 1774. On April 19, 1775, the cloud released its burden, and the struggle began, the conflict of arms which moderate Americans and British had alike feared and striven to avert. Ostensibly, the war which began in the chill of the dawn at Lexington was waged until the summer of 1776 in defense of American rights within the British Empire; thereafter, for independence. But a few Americans, including the astute Samuel Adams, were virtually advocating independence as early as the fall of 1774; still others were unwilling to resist the trend. By that time American revolutionary regimes had begun to appear, accompanied by violence against supporters of British authority and even against those who wished to remain neutral.

If the planters and yeomen of the Old Dominion were the first to rise in defense of American liberties at certain stages of the crisis, the merchants, fishermen, and farmers of Massachusetts never lagged in the rear. They were not awed by King, Parliament, or bishop; and the General Court and the towns of the northern colony were in the van of protest along with the Burgesses and the parishes of Virginia. The colony on the Chesapeake had its Patrick Henry, its Thomas Jefferson, its Richard Henry Lee, its Washington; Massachusetts gave forth Samuel Adams, John Adams, Joseph Warren, and James Otis. It was Massachusetts, exasperated by the British "Intolerable Acts" and by the presence of the British troops in Boston, which established the first revolutionary assembly, in

11

October, 1774. For more than half a year before the day of Lexington British authority in that colony hardly extended further than the range of the cannon of the army in Boston; meanwhile a Provincial Congress elected by the Massachusetts voters and unrecognized by royal governor Thomas Gage debated within a few miles of the redcoat lines, assumed the management of public finances, collected military supplies, provided for colonels and captains, arranged for the training of militia, and prepared for combat. In the winter of 1774–75 the example of Massachusetts was followed, at least in part, by several other colonies. Conventions and congresses without the blessing of crown or Parliament began to supersede assemblies sanctioned by law and custom; and the traditional assemblies continuing to function were neither stout nor reliable bulwarks of British power. Committees of American leaders chosen by the voters, by congresses, by conventions, or in other ways increasingly wielded executive authority, pushing aside one by one the servants of the crown in the royal colonies and those of the proprietors in Pennsylvania, Delaware, and Maryland.

The patriots, or "Whigs," as they often called themselves, were signally successful in enforcing the Continental Association. On December 1, 1774, the Nonimportation and Nonconsumption agreements of the First Continental Congress became people's law, though hardly the law of Blackstone. Citizens pledged themselves not to buy British wares; and locally elected committees, usually dominated by the men who were most ardent in the defense of American rights, saw to it that the pledges were not violated. The names of the few who refused to promise to conform and of those who promised but failed to keep their word were published in the newspapers. If a recalcitrant, seeing the light, abjectly apologized, he might escape further punishment. For the obdurate, however, there was ostracism so complete that all but the most obstinate bent before it. For the latter there was the final argument of force, exerted both to injure and to degrade. Americans in the eighteenth century were not unaccustomed to brutality in the everyday course of events. Physical violence was commonplace in the colonies, as in the mother country. Lynch law was still in the future, but the genealogist would have little difficulty in unearthing precedents from the era of the Revolution; in fact, the very term was derived from the overzealous activities carried on against the friends of Britain by a Captain William Lynch of Virginia.[1]

Although six Americans were slain in public tumults in the colonies between the Peace of Paris of 1763 and the onset of the War of Independence [2] and even though no defender of British authority lost his life during the same period, it is nevertheless true that the champions of American liberty were the first to appeal to violence. In 1765–66 colonists not convinced of the wickedness of the Stamp Act by the verbal arguments of their neighbors learned the truth through force or the threat of it. The British troops in Boston after 1768 were challenged with fists and rods as well as words—the Boston Massacre was in fact the outgrowth of a series of clashes between British redcoats and Boston workmen. In the summer of 1774 violence against vocal partisans of Britain—and against some who did not speak up—was widespread, but peculiarly evident in Massachusetts, where the Loyalists, even the most dignified and the most respected, suffered grievously. In the fall of 1774 and during the following winter attacks upon the Loyalists increased, although the prudent ones often managed not to attract the attentions of strong-arm patriots. Loyalists in areas where they were numerous and where they could resist were somewhat safer from unwelcome visits by mobs. But in general their plight was miserable. Richard King of Massachusetts, twice menaced by a mob, once in 1766 and again in 1774, broke under the strain and became insane. Many another Tory handled in barbaric fashion must have thought of himself as a potential tenant of some American Bedlam. The ferocity of fanatical patriots, extremely distasteful even to such a determined antagonist of British misrule as John Adams, was displayed most conspicuously in the practice of tarring and feathering. Those who advocated the dignity of man rode man upon a rail, showered him with manure, beat him, and coated him with tar and feathers. Nor was tarring and feathering really less inhumane in Charleston than in New York because a mob in Charleston thoughtfully washed clean the helpless object of its

[1] The origins of the term "Lynch law," long debated, have now been rather definitely settled. See Albert Matthews in Colonial Society of Massachusetts, *Transactions* (1927–30), pp. 256–271.

[2] The boy killed in Boston by customs informer Ebenezer Richardson in February, 1770, and the five persons who died as a result of the Boston Massacre.

wrath before sending him home.[3] Thousands of Loyalists became timid during that fall and winter, and remained timid. Others, mistreated beyond endurance, became bitter foes of American rights. So Thomas Browne, given the costume of tar and feathers by a mob in Augusta, Georgia, became a vigorous leader of Tory troops in the ensuing war and did not scruple to lead Indians against the Southern frontier.

Throughout the latter part of 1774 and the early months of 1775 Britain and America were moving toward armed struggle. Patrick Henry warned his more complacent fellow Virginians that "the next gale that sweeps from the north" would bring "the clash of resounding arms." Nevertheless, the prudence and patience displayed both by General Gage and by some of the patriots in Massachusetts postponed hostilities for many weeks. The slowness of communications between America and Britain served to put off still further the day of open fighting. Nevertheless, there never was any doubt, except in the minds of wishful-thinking Americans, that crown and Parliament would resort to force. The resistance of Massachusetts to the "Intolerable Acts," its establishment of a virtually independent government, the challenge to Britain by the First Continental Congress, and the economic warfare waged by the colonists against Britain could bring only one result. But the slow movements of sailing ships and also of British politicians prevented the news of the fateful decision of King, Commons, and Lords from reaching America until April 14, 1775.

If open warfare was not anticipated by most Americans, some nevertheless did what they could to make ready for it. In colony after colony militia awkwardly practiced military exercises, and patriots collected weapons and ammunition. In New Hampshire they raided the colonial arsenal. Patriot leaders calculated their chances of successful resistance against the forces of the British Empire and took heart from an essay published by Major General Charles Lee at New York during the winter before Lexington. Lee, a veteran British-born officer who had served in America and in Portugal during the Seven Years' War and who had had some

[3] Sydney George Fisher, who contributed fruitful and provocative interpretations of the Revolution, put great emphasis upon this ugly phase of it. *True History of the American Revolution* (Philadelphia, 1902), pp. 155–168.

experience in warfare in eastern Europe, had returned to America in the fall of 1773 and given his allegiance to the patriot cause. His essay, which was quickly reprinted, assured the patriots that they could withstand the British regulars and whatever mercenaries Britain might purchase in Europe.[4]

While the First Continental Congress was deliberating in Carpenter's Hall, there was talk in Philadelphia of setting up a continental army. In the following December "a gentleman of Philadelphia" predicted that such an army would be led by Israel Putnam, New England's hero, George Washington, and Lee, holding rank in the order of their names. Simultaneously Lee was quietly circulating a plan for the organization of American regiments and was seen drilling militia at Annapolis by a horrified British veteran.[5] Both Lee and Horatio Gates, once a major in the British army but more recently a Virginia planter, also a champion of American freedom, visited Mount Vernon between the close of the First Continental Congress and the opening of the Second. Lee was twice a guest of Washington during that period. That Washington, Gates, and Lee conversed at Mount Vernon about things military can hardly be doubted. Soon afterward Washington urged that the two Englishmen be given important posts in the Continental army.

Making ready for conflict in desultory fashion, the patriots, through the machinery of the First Continental Congress, made quite clear to the British government what they wanted Britain to do in order to put a peaceful end to Anglo-American quarrels. The Congress, meeting in Philadelphia on September 5, 1774, contained delegates chosen in various ways by all the colonies except Georgia. Among its members were George Washington, Patrick Henry, and Richard Henry Lee of Virginia; John and Edward Rutledge of South Carolina; John and Samuel Adams of Massachusetts; John Jay of New York; Roger Sherman of Connecticut; and John Dickinson of Pennsylvania. This very able and representative body undoubtedly spoke for most of the patriots. It drew up a Declaration of Rights, which demanded, not independence, but recognition by Britain of the liberties of the Americans based upon "the immutable laws of nature, the principles of the English constitution, and the

[4] J. R. Alden, *General Charles Lee: Traitor or Patriot?* (Baton Rouge, 1951), pp. 62–65.
[5] *Ibid.*, pp. 61, 68.

several charters or compacts. . . . " It called for the repeal or withdrawal of all the British laws and measures since 1763—from the decision to maintain a standing army in America to the Coercive Acts—which the colonists had found obnoxious. Since the First Continental Congress represented a broader cross section of colonial opinion than its successor, it is evident that at that date most Americans would have settled for a restoration of the *status quo ante* 1763.

The Congress sent the Declaration of Rights, a petition to George III, and an "Address to the People of Great Britain" to London. The Declaration merited the thoughtful and careful consideration of those in power but failed to receive it. As early as November 18, 1774, the King told Lord North that "the New England governments are in a state of rebellion, blows must decide whether they are to be subject to this country or independent." [6] George III had made up his mind, and he did not change it.

The Cabinet, except for North himself and the Earl of Dartmouth, almost automatically plumped with the King for coercion of the Massachusetts patriots and their Yankee neighbors. North and Dartmouth considered halfheartedly the possibility of reconciliation, and Dartmouth even entered into wasted negotiations toward that end with Benjamin Franklin, agent for several colonies in London. Neither the witty North nor the pious Dartmouth was willing to make any important concession, and both finally accepted a program of coercion. A new Parliament chosen toward the close of 1774 gave solid support to North's ministry and its royal master.

A decision to make use of the redcoats and the Royal Marines in Massachusetts was tentatively taken in Cabinet as early as January 25, and Dartmouth as Secretary of State for the Colonies incorporated it in a "secret" letter to General Gage dated the twenty-seventh. But the negotiations with Dr. Franklin seem to have postponed its transmittal; winter storms on the Atlantic apparently caused further delay; and it did not reach Boston until mid-April.

Meanwhile Lords and Commons continued to debate the American question. In the upper chamber the Earl of Chatham and Lord Camden urged a policy of conciliation; Edmund Burke, George Johnstone, the Marquis of Granby, and David Hartley

---

[6] Sir John W. Fortescue (ed.), *The Correspondence of King George the Third from 1760 to December, 1783* (6 vols., London, 1927-28), III, 153.

labored toward the same end in the Commons. It was all to no purpose. Only a few dozen votes could be marshaled against the proposals of the ministry and the King. Most of the Lords, who spoke for themselves alone, obstinately followed the King and his cohorts. Many members in the Commons had been bought by place or pelf, secretly and even openly, and were bound in honor or dishonor in any case to support George III and North. But there can be no question that heavy majorities in both houses were convinced of the necessity of force. That those majorities represented the will of the British people is by no means clear. Among the middle classes and poorer folk the war never became genuinely popular.[7]

Parliament, consistently turning down proposals by the Opposition, voted again and again to sustain King and Cabinet. An address to the throne declaring Massachusetts to be in a state of rebellion was introduced on February 2 and approved five days later. A bill closing the Newfoundland fisheries to New Englanders and restricting their overseas trade to Great Britain and the British West Indies was brought in on February 3 and was passed before the close of March. Soon afterward these weapons of economic warfare were directed against the people of six more colonies. A message from the Cabinet of February 10 requesting additional funds to increase the army also received approval. Solemn warnings by Opposition members, "patriots," as they were often designated in England, went unheeded. They contended that America might or would resist, and perhaps successfully, and that France and Spain would take advantage of Britain's embarrassment. Charles James Fox predicted "defeat on one side the water, and ruin and punishment on the other."[8] That fabulous incompetent the Earl of Sandwich, First Lord of the Admiralty, defended the policy of coercion with the assertion that the Americans were "raw, undisciplined, cowardly men. I wish instead of 40 or 50,000 of these brave fellows, they would produce in the field at least 200,000, the more the better . . . if they didn't run away, they would starve themselves into compliance . . . the very sound of a cannon would carry

---

[7] See Fred J. Hinkhouse, *The Preliminaries of the American Revolution as Seen in the English Press, 1763–1775* (New York, 1926); Dora Mae Clark, *British Opinion and the American Revolution* (New Haven, 1930).

[8] William Cobbett (ed.), *The Parliamentary History of England, 1774–1777* (36 vols., London, 1806–20), XVIII, 227.

them off. . . ." [9] John Wilkes, symbol of opposition to the King, spoke largely to ears that would not listen when he prophetically asked: "Who can tell, Sir, whether . . . in a few years the independent Americans may not celebrate the glorious era of the revolution of 1775, as we do that of 1688?" [10]

Having committed himself to force, North also extended to the colonists what purported to be the open hand of friendship. To the astonishment of many of his own supporters he pushed through Parliament his extraordinary Conciliatory Resolution of February 20. It really conceded little to the Americans. If a colony through its assembly should contribute satisfactorily toward the expenses of the common defense of the empire and if it should provide for the support of its own civil and judicial officers, Parliament, by this resolution, agreed not to try to levy taxes for revenue within its borders. Moreover, the proceeds of taxes gathered in such a colony incident to the regulation of trade would be turned over to it. The resolution was an impudent cheat. When it was challenged as promising to the Americans too much, North virtually admitted that in reality it yielded little. For the colonists to accept its principles meant to abandon their stand against taxation without representation. Had some colonies accepted while others refused, serious

---

[9] *Ibid.*, pp. 446–447. General James Grant also spoke contemptuously in the Commons of the military qualities of the colonists. Sometime before his departure from England in the spring of 1775, Benjamin Franklin heard a British officer boast at a private gathering that "with a thousand British grenadiers, he would undertake to go from one end of America to the other, and geld all the males, partly by force and partly by a little coaxing." Albert H. Smyth (ed.), *The Writings of Benjamin Franklin* (10 vols., New York, 1905–07), IX, 261. Slurring attacks upon the Americans as soldiers aroused the resentment of Franklin as early as 1759. He protested in three pseudonymous letters published in London newspapers in 1759, 1766, and 1774. In a fourth, similarly made public in February, 1775, he replied to Grant's speech. Verner W. Crane (coll. and ed.), *Benjamin Franklin's Letters to the Press, 1758–1775* (Chapel Hill, 1950), pp. 9–11, 54–57, 262–264, 279–282. In the letter of 1766 (pp. 54–57) he ironically asserted that two thousand Highlanders plus three or four thousand Canadians and a body of Indian auxiliaries could overrun the colonies from Canada. He proposed as commander an unnamed general, probably General James Murray. In 1776 Murray declared that he had long favored using Canada as a base for the major British offensive. On September 6, 1777— six weeks before the surrender of Burgoyne—Murray declared, "The native American is an effeminate thing, very unfit for and very impatient of war." *Report on the Manuscripts of Mrs. Stopford-Sackville, Royal Historical Manuscripts Commission* (2 vols., 1904–10), I, 370, 371.

[10] *Parliamentary History*, XVIII, 238.

disunity would have been created among them, a possibility North no doubt had in mind.[11]

Strangely, all the confident talk by counselors of the King about the inevitable victory of British arms was not shared by the military man on the spot, Thomas Gage. Ominous warnings kept secret from Parliament had been received from him. He had said in the late summer and fall of 1774 that the Americans would fight well; that it would require a year or two and a large army to conquer New England alone; and that estimates of men and means to subdue the colonies as a whole should be made and then doubled. But one wrong-headed official after another accused him of weakness and timidity. Gage was "too far gone to be recovered," declared the Earl of Suffolk; he should have suppressed the "riots" in Massachusetts, asserted Attorney General Edward Thurlow; said Solicitor General Alexander Wedderburn of the abusive tongue, he ought to have dispersed the "mobs" in that colony and to have confined the American leaders. Large forces would not be needed, believed these gentlemen; besides, Britain could not quickly send reinforcements in great numbers. The Cabinet, which had sent four hundred Royal Marines to Gage's assistance before the end of 1774, now arranged to ship him a few additional regiments, largely taken from garrison detachments in the home islands.

Choosing to believe that Gage had not been energetic enough and to discount his sober advice, the King's men urged his removal from command. In January the King proposed a plan whereby Gage would continue in office as governor of Massachusetts and Sir Jeffrey Amherst would assume control of the troops.[12] It was dropped, in part possibly because Amherst did not desire the appointment. Eventually it was decided to retain Gage, but to invigorate the Boston command by dispatching thither Major Generals William Howe, Henry Clinton, and John Burgoyne.

The reinforcements ordered by the Cabinet together with the troops already on duty in America, might have sufficed for the

[11] North conceded that the act was intended "to hold out those terms which will sift the reasonable from the unreasonable . . . distinguish those who act upon principle, from those who wish only to profit of the general confusion. . . ." *Ibid.*, p. 33.

[12] *George III Corr.*, III, 157, 168; *Royal Historical Manuscripts Commission*, Thirteenth Report, Appendix, Part IV, 501, Fourteenth Report, Appendix, Part X, 240.

maintenance of bases necessary for the prosecution of an effective
naval war against American commerce. Viscount Barrington, Secretary at War, conscious of Britain's military weakness, had urged
naval blockade as the cheapest and most certain method of reduc-
ing the colonists to obedience. But Barrington's superiors gave no
more heed to him than they did to Gage or to Adjutant General
Edward Harvey, who had said that conquest of America by marching soldiers meant many, many soldiers. The Cabinet seems to have
been convinced that American resistance could be erased with fewer
than ten thousand regulars, assisted by the Loyalists. To enlist some
of these it sent to the colonies Lieutenant Colonel Allan McLean
with instructions to raise a body of Scottish Highlanders, recent
emigrants thought to be as obstinately loyal to the House of Hanover as they had been faithful so recently to the Stuart dynasty.

It may be assumed that General Gage gave close attention to the
"secret" orders which reached him on April 14, along with other
papers, some bearing news of North's Conciliatory Resolution. He
could only conclude that the resolution was an attempt to deceive,
for his instructions from Dartmouth were quite explicit. Gage, said
the minister, had been too moderate. Reinforcements would soon be
upon the ocean. He was to move decisively without waiting for
them. Since the people of Massachusetts, Connecticut, and Rhode
Island seemed committed to "open rebellion" and "determined to
cast off their dependence upon the government of this kingdom,"
force should be opposed to force—and quickly. A smaller British
army acting while the Americans were still unorganized would have
better chance of success than a more powerful one employed after
they had organized. Gage was to arrest the leaders of the Massachusetts Provincial Congress, even if he believed their detention
would be the signal for an uprising of the patriots—"better that the
conflict should be brought on, upon such ground, than in a riper
state of rebellion."

A loyal soldier, Gage did what he could to carry out these orders.
There was little point in trying to arrest the leaders of the Massachusetts patriots, for even if some could be put under guard inside
the British lines others were almost certain to escape. Dr. Joseph
Warren was in town, and might easily have been trapped, but
Samuel Adams and Hancock were somewhere in the neighborhood
of Concord; and John Adams was completely out of reach. But the

seizure of a few leaders would never have cracked patriot resistance. Instead, Gage planned to send an expedition to Concord, where the patriots had been depositing military stores since February. He knew all about those stores, for he had spies among the patriots. He also realized that the Provincial Congress at Concord was recessing on April 15 and that the scattering delegates would be able to furnish little leadership at Concord. A body of picked men led by Loyalists who knew the country might be able to reach that village and to destroy the patriot supplies without opposition. Such a blow would be disheartening to the patriots. Should that bloodshed which the ministry evidently assumed to be inevitable come in the course of this expedition, the patriots might be put in the light of aggressors.[13]

For many weeks before receiving his orders from London Gage had been preparing for just such an expedition. On April 15 he relieved from routine duty his best troops, the grenadiers and light infantry, with the announcement that they were to practice some new military evolutions. No intelligent person in Boston was deceived; the suspicion of local patriots that these redcoats were preparing to invade the interior was quickly confirmed by the sight of newly repaired boats floating at the sterns of the warships of a British fleet under Admiral Samuel Graves in Boston Harbor. On the night of the eighteenth those boats carried the troops from Boston across the estuary of the Charles River to Lechmere Point, from which they trudged on in the small hours of the nineteenth to Lexington. The March of the Seven Hundred was led by Lieutenant Colonel Francis Smith; with him was John Pitcairn, major of marines and second in command, a highly respected officer who was very probably sent along because of his knowledge of the terrain. Smith had orders to seize and destroy the supplies of the patriots in and near Concord and not to permit the plundering of private persons.

Although Gage doubtless did all possible to prevent word of Smith's advance from spreading, the patriot intelligence service

[13] The "secret" dispatch is printed in Clarence E. Carter (ed.), *Correspondence of General Thomas Gage with the Secretaries of State . . . 1763–1775* (2 vols., New Haven, 1931–33), II, 179–183. It prompted Gage to send out the expedition to Concord. J. R. Alden, "Why the March to Concord?" *American Historical Review*, XLIX (1944), 446–454. On this point see also, by the same writer, *General Gage in America* (Baton Rouge, 1948), pp. 238–244.

carried the news before the British troops had even started out. Paul Revere, in his famous ride, reached Lexington about midnight and William Dawes arrived at the village shortly afterward. Revere warned Samuel Adams and John Hancock, who happened to be spending the night near the village, to flee, which they promptly did. En route to Concord Dawes, Revere, and Dr. Samuel Prescott, a young man who had joined them, were intercepted by the British, but Prescott managed to make his way into Concord with the tidings.[14]

The redcoats knew long before they reached Lexington that their march was discovered. Minutemen and militia scurried about through the dark night. At cold dawn when the six companies of the advance guard under Pitcairn came to the village they found Captain Jonas Parker and about seventy men lined up on the green in crude battle formation. What Parker expected to achieve cannot be told. He refused to let his men make a peaceful departure before superior force, but ordered them to stand their ground. If the British wished to march on, they could. If they wanted a war, they could have it then and there. Pitcairn rode toward the three ranks of Americans, telling them, profanely it seems, to lay down their muskets and disperse. When they failed to obey, he apparently ordered his men to surround them. Parker at length realized the rashness of his behavior and issued a command to retire. The Americans began to fall away, taking their guns with them. Some village Hampdens retired most reluctantly. Then a shot or shots rang out. Who fired first will probably never be known, nor whether the man was British or American. A few Americans blazed away; the regulars charged; and the farmers and villagers fled, followed by bullets as long as they were within range. Eight Americans were slain, ten wounded. One British private was slightly injured. Unknown to historians until the twentieth century was Pitcairn's report to Gage on the skirmish which began a great war. As he approached Lexington, he

. . . gave directions to the troops to move forward, but on no account to fire, or even attempt it without orders; when I arrived at the end of the village, I observed drawn up upon a green near 200 of the

[14] For accounts by Revere of his ride, see Elbridge H. Goss, *The Life of Colonel Paul Revere* (2 vols., Boston, 1891), I, 180–229.

rebels; when I came within about one hundred yards of them, they began to file off towards some stone walls on our right flank—The light infantry observing this, ran after them—I instantly called to the soldiers not to fire, but to surround and disarm them, and after several repetitions of those positive orders . . . some of the rebels who had jumped over the wall, fired four or five shott at the soldiers . . . and at the same time several shott were fired from a meeting house on our left—upon this, without any order or regularity, the light infantry began a scattered fire, and continued . . . contrary to . . . repeated orders. . . .

Contemporary and several later American accounts tell a different story.[15]

As the main British force came along, Pitcairn's men fired a volley and gave a great cheer. Smith must have foreseen more and greater troubles to come, but he had his orders and he obeyed them. On he went to Concord at a rapid pace. The patriots there, warned by Prescott, had carried off and hidden a part of the military supplies. The British destroyed as much of the remainder as they could, dumping into a pond flour afterward retrieved. Meanwhile more and more patriots gathered about Concord, and a body of three to four hundred finally attacked a British covering party at the North Bridge, forcing it to withdraw into the village after several men on both sides had fallen.[16] Perhaps the British troops were now concerned for their safety, but they were not again molested until they had begun their return journey to Boston.

The sixteen miles back to Boston proved to be a gauntlet. Hundreds of angry and embittered Americans, from Sudbury, from Billerica, from Reading, from Woburn, from every neighboring town, poured upon the British line of march. A mile from Concord they began to shoot at the regulars from the protection of stone walls, houses, barns, and trees, and from both sides of the road. Soon their fire was galling; before long it was deadly; and the redcoats began to slump to the ground in numbers. Flanking parties

[15] A scholarly analysis of the beginning of the fight at Lexington, based in part upon new evidence from British viewpoints, is given in Allen French, *General Gage's Informers* (Ann Arbor, 1932), pp. 47–69. The exact words used by Parker and Pitcairn cannot be given with any assurance, nor is it certain, as American historians once contended, that the first fire came from the British. For Pitcairn's report see *ibid.*, p. 53.

[16] For a discussion of the fighting at Concord in the light of new evidence, see *ibid.*, pp. 70–114.

put out by Smith also caused heavy casualties among the Americans, but many patriots were willing to risk almost certain death to get in a shot or two at the British, and Smith's command was in desperate straits when it reached Lexington. There it was rescued in midafternoon by a relieving force of twelve hundred men under Earl Percy prudently dispatched by Gage. Then more hundreds of patriots joined the fray, as Percy slowly retreated toward Boston. Percy also put out flankers, who gave protection to the main body by engaging the patriots, often in hand-to-hand clashes. There was bitter fighting, especially on the outskirts of Cambridge. At that point Percy's whole force was in serious difficulty but he evaded the attacks of a large portion of the patriots by altering his route and marching, not to Boston, but to Charlestown peninsula, where he was safe at nightfall beneath the protecting guns of the fleet and the cover of the army as a whole.

The losses of the nineteenth of April were heavy on both sides, the British 273, the American 95. The patriots had shown beyond doubt their ability to stand up against well-trained troops—they would later display aptitude in the European style of formal battlefield warfare. Another consequence of the day was the siege of Boston, for the New Englanders, more than fifteen thousand of them, promptly swarmed up to the land defenses of that town. Talk of reconciliation still continued, but the bloodshed of the running engagement greatly widened the gap between Britain and America, and the ferocity with which it was fought suggests that the participants already looked upon each other as alien peoples.

CHAPTER 3

Boston

FOR MORE than a year after Lexington and Concord the announced goal of the patriots remained the protection of their rights within the British Empire. They took the initiative militarily, investing Boston, seizing Ticonderoga, and invading Canada. The Second Continental Congress now assumed leadership of the patriots in the struggle and chose Washington as commander in chief of the Continental army. Not until the summer of 1776 was Britain able to mount major offensives against the colonists.

The news of Lexington and Concord spread rapidly through the colonies, particularly the American version of the events of the day. The truth was sufficiently tragic; the truth with some adornments supplied by frenzied excitement and partisan malice was almost hideous. Documentary evidence gathered and widely circulated by the patriot leaders of Massachusetts portrayed the British troops as brutal aggressors and plunderers (there was indeed much plundering by Percy's men),[1] who set fire to homes, slew old men and women, and smashed out the brains of children. The British version, spread about in part by General Gage, gave a different story. According to the British, the first bullet had been discharged by the patriots; the Americans were cowards, skulking behind trees, fences, and buildings, taking pot shots, and refusing to fight openly like men; they were also inhumane in their treatment of the British wounded, scalping them and gouging out their eyes. One of the embattled farmers, hardly more than a boy, had in truth slain a badly wounded soldier with a hatchet.

[1] *Diary of Frederick Mackenzie* (2 vols., Cambridge, Mass., 1930), I, 22.

The Massachusetts patriots won two victories in the spring of 1775, the military struggle of April 19 and the battle of propaganda which followed. They told the story of the day first, most frequently, and most effectively; and their version found wide acceptance in the colonies, where so many were predisposed to receive it without serious questioning. So effectively was the patriot version popularized that it was accepted for generations, even by historians. Adherents to the patriot cause in the other colonies were strengthened in their devotion to that cause; arguing that British aggression at Lexington and Concord was really an attack upon all America, they clamored for common action against the common foe. Waverers were won over; more and more the demand for liberty within the British Empire gave way to insistence upon independence outside of it. If a majority was not yet ready to take this last long step, a majority was apparently ready for war.

All through the spring of 1775 new companies of American militia formed, and older ones drilled with greater assiduity; the manufacture of gunpowder and the molding of bullets went on at a rapid pace; and new uniforms, simple or ornate, were to be seen in village and town. The last of a British detachment in New York City made ready for departure to Boston. That clever and urbane Tory editor of New York, James Rivington, hurried off to one of His Majesty's warships in the harbor; and the Earl of Dunmore, the last of Virginia's royal governors, similarly found refuge behind the guns of H.M.S. *Fovey*. When North's Conciliatory Resolution was submitted to the Revolutionary state congresses as an avenue to peaceful accommodation, it was everywhere summarily rejected on the ground that its real purpose was to divide and rule. Nor did the Second Continental Congress, which began its momentous sessions in the State House in Philadelphia on May 10, 1775, recognize North's proposal as evidence of a genuine desire to satisfy American demands.

The new Congress, elected for the most part during the preceding winter, contained delegates from all the colonies save Georgia, which was not officially represented until the following autumn. Many of the faces were familiar to Philadelphians from the Congress of the preceding year. Again the Adams cousins served as leaders of those who were most vigorous against Britain. Samuel, clever propagandist and shrewd manipulator of men in the councils of Massachusetts patriots, was not quite so potent in Philadelphia. John, too conscious of the faults of others and of his own merits, was earnest, honest, intellectually gifted, and endowed with moral courage. His great career had hardly begun. Present also was Benjamin Franklin, who had landed at Philadelphia just before the opening of the Congress and who served as a representative of Pennsylvania.

Now an old man with a body weakened by the wear of seven decades, Franklin, the most famous American, had come home and had been joyously welcomed. No American, and perhaps no Briton, had been more loyal to the British Empire than Franklin. Serving after 1757 in London as agent for Pennsylvania and other colonies, he had been the chief spokesman for America there. He had loved England and not a few of the English, and he had striven during two decades to foster concord and political justice within the empire. Wisely avoiding so far as possible the wilderness of constitutional theory and the swamps of legal precedent, Franklin had early recognized that the only sure foundation of that empire was the recognition by all concerned of the equality of the British citizen in New London and the British citizen of old London, of the various British dominions under the crown. Upon such a foundation the structure of empire might have withstood the trials of centuries. He had even envisaged the passage with common consent of the imperial capital across the Atlantic at the day when the preponderance of power in the British union should move to the New World. But the vision of most British men of public affairs was clouded; and after 1770 the King and his political coterie regarded him as a stranger and a spy. An early and ardent defender of the rights of the Americans, he was a prime target for British suspicion. The brutal castigation which had been inflicted upon him by Alexander Wedderburn in the memorable session of the Privy Council in the Cockpit early in 1774 had perhaps taught him the uselessness of attempts at persuasion in England. Tolerant, experienced, wise, he became before long the ally of the Adamses.

Washington was there, sober, dignified, not much given to debate. Tall, narrow-chested, large hipped, he was physically powerful at the age of forty-three. His countenance, though not handsome, was manly and imposing. He was cool and reserved, except among intimate friends. He would have been quite at home among

British squires in Sussex. Distinguished early in life by the favor of British officials and military men, such as Robert Dinwiddie, Edward Braddock, and Gage, he had been among neither the first nor the last in Virginia to go to the defense of American rights,[2] but had pursued a steady course. Washington was not disposed to push prematurely for independence. Once committed to it, he would not easily turn back.

The Virginia delegation also included Thomas Jefferson, who came to Philadelphia to replace Peyton Randolph. Tall, slim, red-headed, gray-eyed, freckled, he was only thirty-two and shy. No orator, he shone in conversation. His *Summary View of the Rights of British America* had already won for him a reputation for literary and polemical talent. Planter and scholar, he was no worshiper of outworn dogma or custom. Unafraid of change, seeking and optimistically hoping for improvement, he would not balk at independence or social revolution.

The leader of the conservative element in the Congress was John Dickinson of Pennsylvania. Wealthy, learned, judicious, and generous-minded, he wearied every nerve to obtain a reconciliation with Britain. Opposed to independence, he refused to vote for it and temporarily returned to private life after its declaration.

Among the delegates were many others of talent or repute, including John Hancock, the wealthy Boston merchant and associate of Samuel Adams, who succeeded Peyton Randolph as president of the Congress; Richard Henry Lee of Virginia, whose views were similar to those of Patrick Henry and Jefferson; and four conservatives—Edward Rutledge of South Carolina, James Wilson of Pennsylvania, John Jay of New York, and Robert R. Livingston of the same colony.[3]

Dickinson's efforts to turn the delegates toward reconciliation

---

[2] Curtis P. Nettels, *George Washington and American Independence* (Boston, 1951), chaps. 4–6, suggests that Washington moved to the forefront in 1774.

[3] John Adams' comments in his diary on his colleagues are often biting. He found Samuel Chase "violent and boisterous . . . tedious upon frivolous points"; Edward Rutledge spoke "through his nose, as the Yankees sing"; Roger Sherman's use of his hands in speaking was "stiffness and awkwardness itself"; and John Dickinson's "air, gait, and action" were "not much more elegant." He described Benjamin Harrison as "an indolent, luxurious heavy gentleman, of no use in Congress or committee, but a great embarrassment to both." Charles F. Adams (ed.), *The Works of John Adams* (10 vols., Boston, 1851–66), II, 422–423; III, 31.

failed. The friendly gestures made from Philadelphia in 1774 had
been ignored in London; blood had been shed; and the Congress as
a whole tended to widen the definition of American rights announced by its predecessor. If in the fall of 1774 a majority in
Congress wished merely to go back to the "good old days" before
1763, now most of the delegates, had they formulated their ideas,
would have demanded greater freedom within the empire than
America had in 1763; a small minority would not willingly have
accepted less than independence. The bulk of the delegates held
views between those of Samuel Adams and Dickinson. Early in July
Congress approved the Olive Branch Petition, a last effort to persuade Britain to reverse her policy. The petition begged George III
to protect the rights of the patriots against Parliament. It was reluctantly voted, and many delegates had no faith in it.

There was little of the spirit of truckling in the Congress. Most of
its members, valuing highly their British citizenship, regretted that
the dispute had brought open warfare. Clerks, cobblers, and plain
folk generally among the patriots may have believed the propaganda of their champions that the war would be short and would
inevitably end in victory. The men who deliberated in the State
House knew better, and were well aware that such a contest might
lead to defeat for their cause and the scaffold for themselves—and,
perhaps worse, after the mutual exhaustion of the parties, to the
triumph of their hereditary enemies, the Bourbon monarchs of
France and Spain. Nevertheless, and in spite of divisions among
themselves with respect to the goal, the delegates assumed the burden of leadership in the American cause. On July 6 in a "Declaration of Causes of Taking up Arms" they solemnly announced that
the American people had been offered two choices, "unconditional
submission to the tyranny of irritated ministers or resistance by
force . . . ," and that they had chosen the latter.

Something closely approaching an American government functioned in Philadelphia in the late spring and summer of 1775. The
Congress lacked legal authority to act, even such authority as it
might have received from the several colonial legislatures, but
Americans everywhere expected it to assume responsibility, and it
did. An appeal from Massachusetts asking the delegates to "adopt"
the army besieging Boston was granted. Arrangements were made

for the enlistment of additional troops. A military code was hastily promulgated. A postal service was set up under the direction of Franklin. Three boards of commissioners were appointed to deal with the Indians beyond the western frontiers.

Since it was soon apparent that money was indispensable to action, the Congress was forced to find it. After briefly considering the device of loans, it turned to a familiar colonial means of raising money, the printing of paper currency. Gouverneur Morris supplied the inspiration. Congress voted to issue two million dollars, and then another million, the bills to be redeemed by the several colonies, in proportion to population. It was then hoped that no more would be needed. Members were aware that such a currency was a doubtful expedient, but when no other method of raising sufficient funds could be found Congress was forced to print such bills in large quantities.

For the purpose of forming an American army, the delegates requested the colonies to raise specified numbers of troops. Colonels and officers of lower rank were to be chosen by the several colonies, higher officers by Congress, which also set up hospital and quartermaster services, a commissariat, and paymasters. Militiamen remained under the control of the several colonies.

Undertaking the vexing and awkward task of choosing the principal officers, the delegates readily agreed that there should be a commander in chief. But who should have that all-important post? New Englanders thought it should go to General Artemas Ward, who was, by appointment of the Massachusetts Committee of Safety, virtually in command of the army around Boston. It was evident, however, that Ward's abilities were hardly equal to the duties of that office. If we give credence to the later recollections of John Adams [4]—they are not always to be trusted—John Hancock wanted at least the pleasure of gracefully refusing the appointment. Hancock was patently unfit to command an army. Another conceivable candidate for the post, although he could not have expected to attain it, was Charles Lee. Lee's qualifications were by no means small. Intellectually gifted, exhibiting flashes of genius, Lee had seen more military service than any other man available; he was a serious student of warfare; though troubled with gout and "rheumatism," he was only forty-three years of age and otherwise

[4] *Ibid.*, II, 415–417.

hardy; he was believed to be ardently attached to the patriot cause; and he was popular among the members. But Lee had been born in England and had spent only a small part of his life on the western side of the Atlantic; he was passionate, whimsical, satirical, and unstable. His services might be almost indispensable, thought many delegates, but he would not do for commander in chief.[5]

In the end one candidate, Washington, stood out before his rivals. Washington had had more experience in command than any other American-born officer; of the same age as Lee, he was physically fit to bear great cares; he was obviously a sober and responsible person; and he had a deserved reputation for gallantry in combat. A moderate in politics, he pleased on that score those who feared to put the army in the hands of an enthusiast; a man of wealth and an aristocrat, he satisfied those who were alarmed lest the struggle with Britain bring social leveling; a Virginian, he had the support of many Southerners and also of those who believed that the selection of a Southerner rather than a New Englander would encourage harmony among the patriots. That he wore his old Virginia uniform in the State House as a broad hint of his availability is open to question; he would hardly have donned it except to indicate that he was ready to serve in some military capacity.[6] John Adams endorsed Washington; he was formally nominated on June 15, according to later recollections, by Thomas Johnson of Maryland; and the delegates honored him with a unanimous vote of approval. Refusing to accept more in the way of compensation than his expenses, he declared in modest phrases that he would strive to the best of his abilities to do his duty.

That the Congress did not err when it entrusted the leadership of the American forces to Washington is a verdict sanctioned by the scholarship and public opinion of generations. If at one time the military genius of Washington was too generously assessed, if he was once believed to possess character and personality without flaw, and if he now appears to have been human, something less than divine, he still towers above the other commanders, British or American, of the War of Independence. He never won a major

[5] J. R. Alden, *General Charles Lee: Traitor or Patriot?* (Baton Rouge, 1951), pp. 72–75.

[6] John Miller, *Triumph of Freedom, 1775–1783* (Boston, 1948), p. 61, asserts that Washington could not have been angling for the command.

victory over the main British army in the open field. He displayed little talent for training his men. Only half-educated, he was deficient in the military lore of books. He did not function without petulance or complaint; he sent many a message to Congress suggesting that his employers were not doing all that they could to furnish him with men, money, and supplies. He resented adverse criticism and tried to avoid responsibility for his mistakes. On occasion he displayed jealousy of his fellow generals. Cold and reserved, except to intimates, he could not gain widespread affection. But Washington could win and hold respect. Intellectually neither quick nor brilliant, he possessed solid reasoning powers. He committed many errors in his early years of command, but as campaign followed campaign they became fewer and fewer. The triumph at Yorktown was in considerable part his personal victory. His courage, his devotion to duty, his stubborn perseverance, and the dignity and steady loyalty which he gave to the cause, coupled with his other great qualities, made him almost irreplaceable. While it may be rash to assert that except for his leadership the American rebellion would have collapsed, it is difficult to believe that the American army would have had as good fortune under the management of Horatio Gates, Charles Lee, Philip Schuyler, Israel Putnam, John Sullivan, Henry Knox, Anthony Wayne, Nathanael Greene, or any other ranking American officer.

There was as much contention regarding the selection of Washington's immediate subordinates as there was with respect to the choice of the commander in chief. Some delegates, notably Thomas Mifflin of Pennsylvania, were inclined to insist that Charles Lee be commissioned senior major general and in effect second in command. The claims of Artemas Ward, however, seemed superior; and the selection of Ward was more politic. He was later described by Lee as better fitted to be a churchwarden than a general. Lee's name was then proposed for a commission as major general with rank immediately below Ward. Even though Washington favored the nomination, there was sharp opposition. Lee was granted the appointment by a heavy vote, in part at least because many delegates believed his military knowledge and experience would be almost invaluable to Washington and the army, at least until the Virginian and other high American officers should attain a respectable level of proficiency. In the distribution of plums and burdens

Horatio Gates was not omitted. Born in England, the son of an upper servant, he had managed to climb to the rank of major in the British army, had sold his commission when further promotion became seemingly impossible, and had emigrated in 1772 from England to the Shenandoah Valley, where he had settled upon a plantation called Traveller's Rest. No great man, he knew something about army business, and Washington, an acquaintance of twenty years, desired his assistance. He was made adjutant general with the rank of brigadier. Lacking genius, Gates was courteous, kindly, and convivial. It is not surprising that he, the servant's son, had become a thoroughgoing republican; it is much to his credit, in view of later events and of the variety of vicious charges leveled against him, that his fidelity to his new masters has never been questioned.

On June 23 Washington, Lee, and other Continental officers left peaceful Philadelphia for embattled Boston. Escorted from the city by a cavalcade of well-wishers, they rode on to New York City, where they were officially welcomed on the twenty-fifth. A few hours subsequently William Tryon, royal governor of New York, who by chance arrived in the harbor that same day, was accorded an equally cordial greeting. New York City was no patriot stronghold. The party of Americans moved on to New Haven, where the generals watched Yale College students drill, thence to Hartford and on to Cambridge, arriving at their destination early in July. They found an American army recovering from the shock of the savage fighting at Bunker Hill.

For the besiegers of Boston, the ten weeks preceding the arrival of Washington at Cambridge were disheartening. Lacking decent shelter, a steady flow of food supplies, and efficient leadership, the American army was in critical straits. Had Gage had under his command ten thousand men—half the force he had earlier declared to be requisite for military coercion—the patriot army might well have been destroyed, for it is doubtful whether it could then have withstood a large-scale attack. Happily for the Americans, Gage found it impossible to undertake even a limited offensive until June. Admiral Graves urged upon Gage the wisdom of an attack on the besiegers while Percy and his men were still on Charlestown peninsula. The admiral, realizing the necessity above all of holding Boston, pointed out to the general that American artillery placed upon Bunker Hill, Breed's Hill, or Dorchester Heights might harass both army and fleet and make Boston untenable. He suggested that Percy be ordered to garrison Charlestown peninsula and fortify the two eminences upon it. Percy should burn the village of Charlestown. Meanwhile Gage should drive the Americans from Roxbury, put that village to the torch, and throw up entrenchments on the hills of Roxbury. From them the approaches to Dorchester Heights could be commanded by cannon. The plan possessed merit, and Graves promised to supply seamen for service in the harbor so that Gage could use the bulk of his men in the operation. But Gage, no doubt correctly, rejected the scheme as too risky. Instead he brought Percy's detachment into Boston, improved the defenses he had established on Boston Neck, disarmed the citizens of the town, and waited for reinforcements. Toward the end of May these began to appear in numbers—infantrymen, marines, and dragoons. When by June 12 his army had been increased to about six thousand men, Gage felt strong enough to assume the offensive, but on a limited scale.

Meanwhile the patriot army was equally inactive. An American attack upon the British fortifications on Boston Neck would have been little less than suicidal for the assailants; and the cannon of the British fleet clearly barred an attempt upon the town by water. Moreover, if the besieged possessed discipline without numbers, the besiegers had numbers without discipline. Besides, possession of Charlestown or Dorchester peninsula and heavy artillery were indispensable to the capture of Boston, and the patriots had neither enough cannon nor a proper site upon which to place them. There were sufficient large-caliber guns in American possession after May 10 to drive the British from the Massachusetts capital, but they were far distant, on the western shore of Lake Champlain in Fort Ticonderoga. Seized by men from Connecticut, Massachusetts, and Vermont led by Ethan Allen and Benedict Arnold, the fort yielded as part of its rich military stores about one hundred pieces of artillery, including many heavy cannon and some mortars. But guns powerful enough to batter Boston from Bunker Hill or Dorchester Heights could not be easily transported, and no effort was made to move them eastward until the ensuing winter.

In refusing to assume the initiative after April 19 Gage may have been motivated by politics as well as by military considerations.

Attempts had been made in the spring of 1775 by Governor Jonathan Trumbull of Connecticut, the legislature of the same colony, and certain New Yorkers to negotiate an armistice. Although the overture of the Connecticut officials, censured by the colony's troops about Boston, proved fruitless, hope of reconciliation was still not abandoned by either side. However, on May 25 Generals Howe, Clinton, and Burgoyne landed from the *Cerberus,* bringing instructions of April 15 from the Cabinet to Gage. Drawn up after news of the establishment of the military depot at Concord had reached England, the instruction ordered the general to raid that depot. It was further proposed that he issue a proclamation offering pardon to all but the most dangerous leaders of the Massachusetts malcontents, who should be seized. These measures, wrote Dartmouth, might restore British authority in Massachusetts, but he placed no great reliance on them. Four days before Lexington the Cabinet again expressed its ultimate faith in force. "It is however," declared the Colonial Secretary, "to the exertion of the fleet and army, in support of the vigorous measures which have been adopted by His Majesty and the two houses of Parliament that we are to trust for putting an end to the present troubles and disorders, and it is imagined that by the time this letter reaches you, the army under your command will be equal to any operation that may become necessary." [7]

The major generals dispatched both to assist and to bestir Gage were a curious lot. Howe, senior among them, claimed to be a friend of the Americans, but had nevertheless agreed to serve against them. Sturdy, vigorous, taciturn, he was a fine soldier, a splendid executive officer. As a commander he might have been more proficient had he given more time to his military studies and less to the pursuit of women. Clinton was smallish, paunchy, and colorless, but thoroughly devoted to duty. On certain occasions he was to display both ability and energy. Yet his record, in part because of factors beyond his control, would be mediocre. He was obsessed with the conviction that his merits were undervalued. Handsome John Burgoyne, the junior general, had charm, vivacious worldliness, and a vaulting desire for fame. Like Howe, he was an

[7] Clarence E. Carter (ed.), *Correspondence of General Thomas Gage with the Secretaries of State . . . 1763–1775* (2 vols., New Haven, 1931–33), II, 193.

able executive officer without genius for independent command; unlike Howe, he was grandiloquent. In addition, he was a bit of an intriguer with a genuine literary flair. All three major generals were, like Gage, personally courageous. If Gage lacked the genius needed to break down the American rebellion, his subordinates, unfortunately for the hopes of King and Cabinet, could not make up for his deficiencies. Perhaps as able a trio as could be found in England in the higher ranks of the British army, they were not good enough for the tasks ahead. To his sorrow the modest Gage would lean heavily upon Burgoyne for literary help and upon Howe for military counsel.

Immediately after landing, the trio began to urge Gage to take the offensive, Burgoyne voicing a need for "elbow room." Gage acted. On June 12 he proclaimed martial law and announced an offer of pardon to all patriots who would return promptly to their due allegiance—Samuel Adams and John Hancock excepted. His proclamation, prepared for him by Burgoyne, was a compound of bombast and misstatements of fact. Among the patriots it aroused laughter rather than alarm. It also provoked a remarkably abusive open letter to Gage from the Reverend John Cleveland of Ipswich:

Thou profane, wicked monster of falsehood and perfidy . . . your late infamous proclamation is as full of notorious lies, as a toad or rattlesnake of deadly poison. . . . Without speedy repentence, you will have an aggravated damnation in hell. . . . You are not only a robber, a murderer, and usurper, but a wicked rebel: a rebel against the authority of truth, law, equity, the English constitution of government, these colony states, and humanity itself.[8]

But more important than his propaganda campaign, Gage laid down military plans which brought a vigorous reaction from the American army.

On June 12, or immediately thereafter, the British commander and his major generals decided to put the British army in motion, even though fifteen hundred of the red-coated reinforcements sent out from the British Isles were still on the ocean. The morale of the besieged troops was rapidly wilting as the result of idleness and a narrow, though not inadequate, diet. Activity might well boost their flagging spirits. An attempt to crush the American army could not

[8] *Essex Gazette,* July 13, 1775.

be seriously considered; the risk was too great. Even if a victory over the patriots could be achieved it would bring no strategic advantages, for the British army was too weak, even with the troops momentarily expected, to advance into the interior of New Eng-

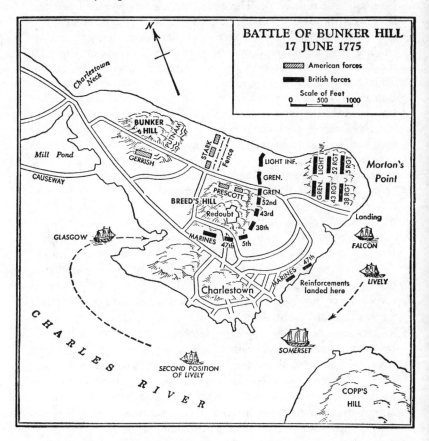

BATTLE OF BUNKER HILL
17 JUNE 1775

American forces

British forces

Scale of Feet
0   500   1000

land, where patriot sentiment ran high. It did seem strong enough to occupy and garrison Dorchester and Charlestown peninsulas, and thus to make Boston virtually impregnable. Accordingly the British generals undertook to place a detachment on Dorchester on June 18 and to send another as soon as possible to take post covering Bunker Hill and Breed's Hill.

The best-laid plans of the British in the War of Independence not uncommonly went agley, and this one brought no brilliant success. Somehow or other, possibly because Burgoyne was stupid enough to talk freely about it,[9] the scheme was known all over Boston by the fourteenth. The news then quickly passed the British lines, and the Massachusetts Council of Safety two days later was able to recommend to the American generals countermeasures, including an immediate occupation of Bunker Hill. Accordingly, in the evening of the sixteenth American militia traversed the narrow isthmus of Charlestown peninsula and moved up the slopes of Bunker Hill. Decently armed, that hill would have been more or less defensible so long as the mainland adjacent was in American hands. However, for some reason not surely ascertained, the militiamen trudged on to Breed's Hill, which was less elevated and more exposed to flank attacks by water. They labored through the night, erecting entrenchments. Their clanking and thumping noises were heard long before dawn by British sentinels across the water, and the high English officers gathered to consider the changed situation. There was no doubt that something should be done. Clinton, bursting for recognition, suggested that Howe be sent quickly with a large force to land on the tip of Charlestown peninsula and to assail the militia frontally, while Clinton himself with five hundred men disembarked in their rear from the Mystic River. This proposal involved risk, for Clinton's flanking force would have been exposed to attack from the mainland, a fact which Clinton and his colleagues seem not to have realized. However, with cover for his force by the cannon of light British vessels in the estuary of the Mystic, the risk could be minimized. But the other generals eschewed cleverness, and even persuaded Clinton that the most the situation required was forward movements from the tip of the penisula. It was agreed that Howe should execute them and that he should try to turn the American left flank along the shore of the Mystic.[10]

For the execution of so conventional and uninspired a plan, no British officer seemed better suited than Howe, but his execution of it was labored and unimaginative. Speed was desirable, if not essen-

[9] Allen French, *The First Year of the American Revolution* (Boston, 1934), p. 209.

[10] For an accurate account of the British plan and of Bunker Hill, see *ibid.*, pp. 211–267.

tial, but his men did not land on the peninsula until afternoon. Howe proceeded at a leisurely pace, taking victory for granted; he concerned himself as much with the problem of garrisoning the peninsula as he did with winning it. Finally, he ordered fifteen hundred men against the American position, endeavoring principally to turn the American left flank. But that flank had been strengthened while he dallied in Boston. The patriot musketry drove back the redcoats. Rebuffed on his right, Howe re-formed and staged a frontal assault. He personally led forward the British right; Brigadier General Robert Pigot, the left. The deadly fire of the outnumbered colonials under Colonel William Prescott beat back both assaults, with exceptionally heavy losses for the redcoats. Ill organized, awkward, and tired, the Americans—about 2,200 of them in all fought that day—had the advantages of position, and their hasty entrenchments served them well. Desperate, but reinforced from Boston by six hundred or seven hundred men, Howe once more advanced. Again the regulars were raked by punishing musket fire, but the militia lacked the powder to hold off the redcoats, who, relying on the bayonet, swept up into a central redoubt, which was the key to the American position. In the ensuing retreat of the colonials to Bunker Hill and thence to the mainland, they suffered heavy losses. General Warren was killed, his body left where it fell. Howe had gained Charlestown peninsula, but Gage had little cause for rejoicing. The patriots sustained casualties above four hundred, but Gage was forced to report more than a thousand for his army. Over 40 per cent of Howe's men were slain or wounded. Britain could not afford to buy many hills at such a price.

For all the sacrifice made in the encounter at Breed's Hill, one of the most sanguinary battles of the eighteenth century, the British were not relieved of concern over Dorchester Heights. Gage began to make arrangements for occupying those hills, but failed to issue the decisive orders, perhaps because he was led to believe that the Americans, lacking artillery, would not be able to make use of them. By July he had under his command in Boston all the troops dispatched from Britain. However, he made no further offensive gestures from "this cursed place," [11] nor did Howe, who succeeded him in command of the army on October 10. The King

[11] After the battle Gage expressed a wish that it be burned. *Gage Corr.*, II, 687.

and the Cabinet, for many months dissatisfied with Gage's behavior, decided to recall him immediately upon receipt of the ominous tidings of the battle of June 17. He was ostensibly ordered home to give advice upon the American situation; he would not return to the colonies, and he knew it. Howe was to have an opportunity to prove his talent, but not until 1776; he could accomplish nothing in the colonies with the forces available to him, and he could not even sail away because of lack of transports. He was compelled to stay in Boston until the end of the following winter, when he was ignominiously hurried away.

If the British suffered from boredom and bad diet within the beleaguered city, their opponents on the hills of the mainland faced equally serious problems. The Americans had extreme difficulty in securing ammunition and artillery; their army was torn by sectional dissensions and personal jealousies; discipline could with difficulty be maintained. Washington and his staff labored energetically to create a well-regulated army but made slow progress. During the autumn several thousands of the besiegers enlisted in the Continental forces and were pledged to serve until the end of the year 1776. The change brought perplexities and anxieties to Washington but no immediate improvement in the fighting quality of his officers and men. Once and again the Virginian considered an attack upon the British lines. To have tried it would have been a frightful mistake, one which he abstained from making.

At length the stalemate at Boston was resolved. Congress authorized Washington to bombard the town with artillery; in the winter Henry Knox went off to Ticonderoga under Washington's orders to fetch the necessary guns. By ingenuity and hard work Knox brought fifty-nine cannon and mortars to eastern Massachusetts. On the night of March 4 American working parties moved forward to Dorchester peninsula to throw up fortifications in that vital area so long left unoccupied. For a time the noise they made was covered by the roar of an exchange of artillery fire between Roxbury and Boston batteries; a fog even longer obscured them from Boston view. Numerous, well supplied, well led, and covered by a detachment of riflemen who had come up from the South to join the army, they toiled with amazing success. By the morning of March 5 the British could see formidable entrenchments and batteries. Moreover, fresh troops had been brought up to man them; the

American army as a whole was ready for action; and several thousand militiamen had been called up, ready to fight well on the anniversary of the Boston Massacre. Had Howe sent a detachment against the heights, Washington was prepared to make a general assault upon Boston. Howe realized that his army could not remain in Boston and that the fleet could not continue at its moorings in the harbor unless the Americans were driven from their new position. Artillery in Boston could not damage the American batteries on the heights; the American guns could level Boston. He ordered a detachment to prepare for an attack upon the heights. Happily for the men assigned to that task, a hurricane made their mission impossible and gave Howe an opportunity and an excuse to reconsider. He reconsidered, in council of war. The result was a decision to evacuate Boston and to remove to Halifax. The purpose of the British being made known to Washington, he entered into a tacit agreement to let them go peacefully. The regulars and eleven hundred Loyalists who could not or did not wish to remain in the town embarked. The evacuation took place on March 17, thus giving the Boston Irish of a later time two reasons to celebrate the day.

The departure of Howe and his men signalized merely the end of the preliminary stage of the war. Howe returned to the Thirteen Colonies in the summer of 1776, bringing a formidable invading force. The great American ordeal was still to come.

CHAPTER 4

Contest for Canada

THERE was not in 1774 or in 1775, nor has there ever been, a truly continental Congress in North America. The men who directed the American war effort during the War of Independence never represented more than the Thirteen Colonies. No delegates joined them from the British mainland colonies of East Florida, West Florida, Nova Scotia, and Quebec, or from the Hudson's Bay region, or from Bermuda, or from Jamaica or any of the other British possessions in the West Indies. It is likely that there were persons who sympathized with the American patriots in every British colony in the Western Hemisphere. But save in Nova Scotia and Quebec, they could not have been very numerous. Those who dwelt in the insular territories could not actively assist the patriots in any case, if for no other reason because they were isolated by British naval power. During the war New Providence (now Nassau) in the Bahamas was twice captured by the infant American navy; Prince Edward Island was also raided and its governor made captive. But there was no attempt to maintain control of those islands, nor any effort to enlist soldiers except on the American mainland and in Europe. It was not possible for the Americans to secure assistance from the scanty civilian populations of the Floridas, which were effectively dominated by British garrisons and ships until Spain made her late entrance into the conflict. Nova Scotia, too, failed to help the Thirteen Colonies, although many New Englanders had removed to that colony before the war. The transplanted New Englanders were in general neutral rather than pro-American or pro-British;[1] the royal navy secured Halifax from attack; and the arrival of large numbers of Tories in the province after 1776 confirmed its loyalty to the mother country. Outside of the Thirteen Colonies only one of the British possessions in the Western Hemisphere contributed importantly to the American cause. That was Quebec. In fact, early in the war it seemed likely to many patriots that Quebec would become a fourteenth colony—and state.

Quebec, or Canada, was under British military rule after 1760 as the result of the exploits of the army and navy under James Wolfe, Admiral Charles Saunders, and Jeffrey Amherst in the French and Indian War. The Peace of Paris of 1763 ceded the province to Britain. But though Canada then became legally British, its white inhabitants remained for many years French in sentiment. After the capture of the fortresses of Quebec and Montreal new settlers—sutlers, merchants, office seekers, and adventurers, from the British Isles and especially from the Thirteen Colonies—filtered into the valley of St. Lawrence. These "old subjects," as they were called to distinguish them from the French, or "new subjects," numbered only a few hundreds in 1775. The Gallic population was then possibly eighty thousand.[2] The American patriots counted upon friends and allies among both the "old subjects" and the "new subjects." In the end, however, most of the Canadians either gave their loyalty to Britain or remained quiescent. Paradoxically, Canada was to remain British because it was almost entirely French.[3] It was held within the empire because British statesmen, including George III himself, manifested after 1763 a more liberal attitude toward the Canadians than they did toward the American colonists to the south.

The soldiers and sailors who raised the banner of St. George in the St. Lawrence Valley did not bring in their baggage either the British constitution or representative government. After the Peace of Paris a theoretically civilian governor and other civilian officials assumed direction of the newly organized province of Quebec. The governor was nearly all-powerful, and the British regime was essentially as arbitrary as the French system which it replaced. Even

[1] John B. Brebner, *The Neutral Yankees of Nova Scotia* (New York, 1937), *passim.*

[2] Estimates range from 65,000 to 90,000.

[3] George M. Wrong, *Canada and the American Revolution* (New York, 1935), pp. 259–260.

though the first governor, General James Murray, was overly fond of bickering, the French inhabitants, accustomed to domination from above, were not especially discontented; and Murray was succeeded in 1766 by General Guy Carleton, who possessed qualities well calculated to placate those over whom he ruled. Irish-born in a family of soldiers, Carleton had early entered upon a military career and had climbed the ladder upon the bases of merit and the friendship of James Wolfe. Cold, reserved, even haughty, he was also honest and upright, courageous, just, prudent, and upon occasion generous, the almost perfect proconsul. He gave Canada as good government as an arbitrary regime would permit and soon gained the respect of the French, though hardly their affections. The "old subjects," accustomed to English liberties, he could not so easily satisfy, particularly after the passage of the Quebec Act in the spring of 1774.

The Quebec Act aimed to set up in Canada more or less enduring political institutions. Under its provisions Canada was to be ruled politically by a governor and council chosen by the crown; religiously, on the assumption that the province would remain French and Roman Catholic, by the hierarchy of the old Church. English criminal law was to supersede French; the feudal rights of the seigneurs of the old French aristocracy were confirmed; and the Church was empowered to impose and collect tithes from its faithful. The right to set aside all laws passed by governor and council was reserved to the British government, also the right to tax, except for purely local purposes. The act could hardly fail to satisfy the lords of the Church and of the land. The humbler French, the *habitants,* found little pleasure in the statute. The confirmation of the privileges of the seigneur brought them no benefit, but instead obligations they no longer wished to shoulder. Assured religious freedom, they were compelled to finance their Church, an obligation not always gladly borne. The peasants could find little in the act to persuade them that they should sacrifice their lives or properties for crown and Parliament. Some of the "old subjects" were also dissatisfied, and probably in greater degree. They found in the statute high favors to Frenchmen and papists, but for Englishmen they could discover neither representative institutions nor English civil law.

The Quebec Act, offering religious freedom to Roman Catholics in Canada at a time when Roman Catholics suffered from discrimination in Britain, was also intended to buttress the British grip upon the Thirteen Colonies. Its sponsors hoped to win bishop and seigneur, and through them the French generally. A loyal Canada with a militia that had proved its fighting qualities in days gone by might well check the ardor of New York and New England patriots. But while the hierarchy and the aristocracy were indeed won over, the act aroused little enthusiasm for Britain among the *habitants,* and none among the "old subjects." Nevertheless, the grant of religious freedom to the *habitants,* the influence of their Church and the aristocracy, their ancient feud with Yankees and Yorkers, and perhaps their own ignorance of the issues combined to keep most of them from joining the patriots during the first year of the war, a year that was critical for Canada. In general the humbler French would be neutral rather than active participants in the struggle between their former enemies.[4] Had they allied themselves with the colonists south and east of the St. Lawrence watershed, Canada might well have been the fourteenth state.

But Canadians, regardless of their preferences, could scarcely avoid entanglement in the struggle between the Americans and the British, for one or both antagonists were bound to bring the war to their land. The British could be counted upon to make use of Canada and its people to crush the rebellion; the Americans would surely seek allies in the St. Lawrence Valley and try to cover their northern frontiers. In 1775 an attempt on their part to conquer Canada was also to be expected, for the garrison force of redcoats on the St. Lawrence had been somewhat diminished by Gage in order to strengthen his army in Boston. Carleton, who was the commanding officer of the redcoats in his province as well as governor, had only three regiments of foot and three companies of artillery to defend it in the spring of 1775; and one regiment and one company of artillery were stationed in the Great Lakes country, where

---

[4] The text of the Quebec Act may conveniently be consulted in Peter Force (ed.), *American Archives* . . . , Fourth Series (6 vols., Washington, 1837–46), I, 216–220. For discussions of the intentions of its sponsors and of its effect upon the attitudes of the French toward Britain, see Wrong, *Canada,* pp. 228–259; R. Coupland, *The Quebec Act: A Study in Statesmanship* (Oxford, 1925), *passim;* A. L. Burt, *Old Province of Quebec* (Minneapolis, 1933), pp. 177–209; Charles Metzger, *The Quebec Act: A Primary Cause of the American Revolution* (New York, 1936), *passim.* The present writer has accepted the interpretations of Professor Burt.

they could offer no assistance toward the defense of Montreal and Quebec. They were, in fact, badly needed at Detroit and Niagara.[5] Carleton hoped for reinforcements from England, but none came until the spring of 1776. A series of delays along with a severe storm conspired to put off their arrival in time to participate in the campaign of 1775.

The Americans moved first. In the fall of 1774 the First Continental Congress sent an address to the Canadians urging them to make common cause with their fellow colonials. Although many Americans had bitterly condemned the Quebec Act because of its concession of religious freedom to Roman Catholics, although they had even included it among the "Intolerable Acts" of that year, the Congress now informed the Canadians that they were suffering from tyranny and invited them to send representatives to the Second Continental Congress.[6] This appeal had no discernible result, if for no other reason because Carleton prevented its circulation. In February, 1775, however, the Boston Committee of Correspondence, under the leadership of Samuel Adams, it is believed, sent a secret emissary, a lawyer named John Brown of Pittsfield, to the St. Lawrence. Brown made his way in the depth of winter to Albany and thence by way of Lake Champlain to Montreal. There he established contact with many of the "old subjects." Many of these were merchants, most numerous at Montreal, although a few were to be found scattered along the Lake Champlain-Richelieu River waterway and others at Quebec. Several of the "old subjects" quietly assured Brown that their sympathies lay with the patriots, that the bulk of the French population would do nothing toward the defense of the British regime, and that Carleton could then expect little aid, if any, from the Canadian Indians. Sending back to Massachusetts an optimistic report in March, 1775, Brown also urged an American attack upon the British garrison at Ticonderoga as soon as hostilities should begin. He reported that the Green Mountain Boys had pledged themselves to capture the weakly defended fort, which contained large military stores, including cannon. The seizure of Ticonderoga and of its weaker sister post of Crown

---

[5] The 7th and 26th regiments were based upon Montreal and Quebec; the 8th was stationed in the lake country.

[6] The address was voted on October 26. Worthington C. Ford *et al.* (eds.), *Journals of the Continental Congress. 1774–1789* (34 vols., Washington, 1904–37), I, 105–113.

Point, as the American agent hardly needed to point out, would open a path for an American expedition to the St. Lawrence. Departing from Montreal, Brown left behind him a network of communications between Canada and the Thirteen Colonies.

John Brown's mission was followed promptly by American action. Gage and Carleton had long before realized the military importance of retaining control over the Lake Champlain route, but Gage had lacked funds to restore the ruined works of the two forts and had too few troops properly to defend them. In March, 1775, Gage warned Captain William De la Place, commandant at Ticonderoga, to guard against a surprise assault. He did nothing more to protect the great passageway until the day of Lexington and Concord, when he sent off to Carleton a message urging him to send the 7th regiment without delay to Ticonderoga or Crown Point. But Gage's advice to De la Place was given insufficient attention, and his letter to the Canadian governor arrived too late to accomplish its purpose.

After the outbreak of warfare in Massachusetts many a patriot turned to thoughts of assault upon Ticonderoga and Crown Point. Among them were two Connecticut officers later accused of treason against the United States, Samuel Holden Parsons and Benedict Arnold, the one doubtless innocent, the other only too guilty. Parsons, returning home from the siege of Boston to go recruiting, met Arnold en route to Cambridge. Determined to secure for the American army the cannon stored at Ticonderoga, they then went their different ways. At Hartford Parsons organized and sent northward toward Ticonderoga some Connecticut troops, who enlisted the doughty John Brown and some forty men at Pittsfield. By May 7 the Connecticut and Massachusetts men were at Castleton, where their leaders conferred with Ethan Allen, in command of a body of Green Mountain Boys, who was likewise meditating the capture of "Ti." Shortly afterward Arnold, having done some effective talking at Cambridge, also appeared at Castleton, carrying a colonel's commission from the Massachusetts Committee of Safety and orders from the same body to seize the fort and its cannon. He had been authorized to gather four hundred men for these purposes but had hurried forward almost alone to the scene of action, leaving his subordinates to collect his troops. Never modest, Arnold insisted that he be accepted as commander of all the groups engaging in the project. His claim was heatedly contested, but Allen and Arnold, after some confusion, were recognized as joint commanders. Early in the morning of May 10 approximately eighty Americans made their way across Lake Champlain, surprised the garrison of Ticonderoga, rushed through its almost undefended walls, and secured the surrender of De la Place and forty-odd redcoats, about half of whom were unfit for service of any sort.[7] Not a shot was fired, and a handful of British regulars at Crown Point capitulated to Allen on the following day. Shortly afterward Arnold, now joined by some of his own men, took a British post at St. John's, on the Richelieu River. Exposed there to British counterattack, Arnold then prudently retreated, but Allen reoccupied St. John's and was promptly driven out of it by a force of redcoats. Nevertheless, the New Englanders had cheaply won Ticonderoga, with its almost priceless cannon, and the control of Lake Champlain.

Thus in May, 1775, Canada was opened to invasion from the south. That same month Jonathan Brewer of Massachusetts projected a march through Maine against Quebec fortress by way of the Kennebec and Chaudière rivers. Brewer even began to collect troops for the purpose, but Massachusetts leaders frowned both upon the scheme and upon Brewer. Shortly afterward Arnold pressed eagerly for an early advance in force from Ticonderoga to the St. Lawrence. Brewer's proposal was quite feasible in summer; and the two expeditions might easily have taken Montreal and Quebec. On May 29 the Second Continental Congress, after re-

[7] Vermont tradition of the capture of the fort has it that Allen was in command, also that Allen first demanded surrender of the fort from Lieutenant Jocelyn Feltham with the words, "Come out of there, you damned rat," or an equivalent. Allen seems to have repeated his demand several times. Four years afterward he wrote that he made his surrender demand "in the name of the Great Jehovah and the Continental Congress." John Pell, *Ethan Allen* (Boston, 1929), p. 85, accepts both the Vermont tradition and Allen's statement. It seems clear that Allen and Arnold entered the fort together, and that both men called upon Feltham, who was not dressed to receive visitors, and then upon De la Place to give it up. Since Allen was a deist, and for other reasons, it seems likely that his later recollection of his summons was inaccurate. Moreover, Feltham, describing the incident only one month later, said, "Mr. Allen . . . told me . . . that he must have immediate possession of the fort and all the effects of George the Third. . . . Those were his words." For Feltham's account see Allen French, *The Taking of Ticonderoga* (Cambridge, Mass., 1928), pp. 42 ff. The same author's *First Year of the American Revolution* (Boston, 1934), Appendix 14, pp. 733–734, analyzes in scholarly fashion the evidence regarding this incident.

ceiving the news of the fall of Ticondegora and Crown Point, voted a second address to the "oppressed" Canadians, urging them to join the patriots.[8] On June 1, however, it decided that the forts should be evacuated and that the captured cannon should be removed to Albany.[9] Some members did not wish to wage offensive war, lest the door be closed to reconciliation with Britain. Late in June Congress reversed its course again and finally ordered General Philip Schuyler to advance toward Montreal, which he was to seize along with other parts of Canada, if "it will not be disagreeable to the Canadians."[10]

The dilatory tactics of Congress were matched by those of Schuyler, who spent almost two months in preparation for the expedition. He faced, to be sure, a host of difficulties. He had trouble enlisting enough men and even greater trouble equipping them; he was compelled to build boats to carry his army, was handicapped by a shortage of gunpowder, and was grievously hampered by provincial and personal jealousies among officers and men. In addition, he had reason to be apprehensive that the Iroquois warriors, most of whom were under the influence of the Tory Johnson family, would attack the New York frontier in his absence. In the end his army was ready to move, and the neutrality of the Six Nations was temporarily assured. But Schuyler had performed too slowly at a time when speed was paramount. He made too much of his vexations; he was by turn petulant and then overly patient. He lacked both the physical vigor necessary to do his duties and to win the confidence of his men and any real enthusiasm for the northern invasion. Not until both Washington and Brigadier General Richard Montgomery, Schuyler's second in command, insisted upon action did his army of seventeen hundred men move forward. Writing from Cambridge, Washington informed Schuyler that he was sending an expedition against Quebec by the Kennebec-Chaudière route, and argued that Schuyler must execute his assignment—the British could not defend both Quebec and Montreal at once and at least one would fall.[11]

[8] The address is conveniently reprinted in Henry S. Commager (ed.), *Documents of American History* (New York, 1934), pp. 91–92.

[9] *Continental Congress Journals*, II, 74–75.

[10] *Ibid.*, p. 109.

[11] John C. Fitzpatrick (ed.), *The Writings of George Washington* (39 vols., Washington, 1931–44), III, 437–438.

Learning of desperate efforts on the part of Carleton to prepare Canada against invasion, Montgomery led the American van up Lake Champlain early in September without orders from Schuyler. On the fourth Schuyler joined his subordinate on the lake, and the American army proceeded to the Ile aux Noix at the source of the Richelieu River. There Schuyler remained, accomplishing nothing, until September 16. Then a combination of ill health and despondency caused him to turn southward toward his headquarters, leaving Montgomery in command. Thereafter he confined himself to sending supplies and reinforcements to Montgomery.

Had Richard Montgomery been given command of the expedition against Montreal from the beginning the story might well have been different. An Irish-born soldier, he had served in the British army in the French and Indian War, resigned from that army, and migrated in 1772 to New York, where he married into the powerful Livingston clan. As a redcoat, Montgomery had held no rank higher than captain. Yet he was energetic and bold, a splendid if somewhat theatrical commander and a devoted patriot. Had Montgomery been able to advance down the Richelieu in August, the objectives of the campaign might well have been realized.

As it was, American inactivity after the fall of Ticonderoga and Crown Point gave Carleton the time he so desperately needed if Canada was to remain in British hands at the end of the campaign. In the spring of 1775 Carleton began strenuous efforts to meet the threatened American invasion. He called upon both the "old subjects" and the "new subjects" to volunteer for service, but his appeals elicited meager response. With the assistance of several seigneurs, he tried vainly to raise the Canadian militia. Bishop Briand, the chief dignitary of the Church in Canada, called upon the French to support Carleton and ordered the rites of the church withheld from those who should aid the patriots. But even Briand's efforts had little net result, and it became apparent that the *habitants* were as likely to join the Americans as the British. Gravely concerned, Carleton continued his preparations as best he could. Proclaiming martial law on June 9, he moved his scanty forces of redcoats to cover Montreal, where he himself assumed command, made ready for defense of the forts at St. John's and Chambly, and at St. John's pushed the building of two vessels of war with which he hoped to regain control of Lake Champlain. He was able to secure the services of the crew of the British brigantine *Gaspée*, which wandered into the St. Lawrence. Allan McLean, coming from England by way of New York, turned up in the very nick of time [12] and raised a small body of veteran Highlanders to assist Carleton. The general might also have obtained valuable support from the Canadian Indians. Gage urged him to enlist the savages, but Carleton had little faith in the fighting abilities of red-skinned warriors and was repelled by their atrocities against women and children. He enlisted only a few; and even these proved more of a nuisance than a help.

Immediately after Schuyler's departure Montgomery invested Fort St. John's, on September 18. His army was wasting from disease, but reinforcements were coming and American advance agents in Canada, John Brown, Ethan Allen, and the "old subject" James Livingston, all urged him on. The fort, made of wood but stoutly built to resist cannon, was cut off from Montreal. Within it, however, were about five hundred British regulars and one hundred Canadian volunteers, the bulk of Carleton's forces, under the command of Major Charles Preston, a courageous officer, who was supported by an armed schooner lying in the Richelieu. The fort could not be carried by assault; nor with his weakened forces could Montgomery mask it and proceed northward. He was compelled to begin siege operations, which he could not push effectively during many weeks for lack of cannon, powder, and obedient troops. Finally, on November 2, with his fortifications and quarters almost in ruins, his supplies of food almost exhausted, his schooner at the bottom of the river, and with no hope of relief, Preston abandoned the struggle. He had delayed Montgomery fifty-five days and had, perhaps, saved Canada for Britain.

Held up at St. John's, Montgomery sent out parties under Ethan Allen and John Brown to the St. Lawrence to scout and to enlist Canadians. Allen and Brown, chancing to meet below Montreal, discovered that together they had 330 men, mostly French. Brown proposed an attack on Montreal, and Allen agreed. Brown with two hundred men was to cross the St. Lawrence above the city, Allen with the remainder below it. They were to launch simultaneous assaults on September 24. For reasons unknown Brown failed to get over the river. Allen succeeded, only to be confronted

[12] See p. 20.

by a superior force of British regulars, Canadians loyal to Britain, and Indians who came out from the city. For lack of boats his retreat was cut off. After a sharp but unequal fight, most of his men fled, and he was forced to surrender.[13] However, on October 19 Fort Chambly and eighty-three British regulars were captured by a mixed force of Americans and Canadians.

The obstinate stand made by Preston gave Carleton more precious time. The British governor was unable to muster enough strength at Montreal to come to the assistance of his valiant subordinate; and British prestige sank so low after the fall of St. John's that Carleton could not defend the city which Anglo-American armies had won fifteen years earlier after the utmost sacrifice. Its inhabitants made it clear that they would not fight against Montgomery, and they opened the city gates to him on November 13. However, Preston had presented to Carleton a formidable ally, General Winter, who brought with him ice, snow, sleet, and chill winds. Fleeing down the river with a little fleet of eleven ships and a few score of regulars, Carleton was intercepted en route to Quebec. Fleet and redcoats fell captive to jubilant American pursuers, but Carleton escaped and with a few attendants made his way to temporary safety in the great fortress. Weakened by winter and by the loss of several hundred men who went home, some with and some without official leave, Montgomery stopped almost two weeks at Montreal to refit and reorganize; then, leaving behind a substantial garrison, he floated down the river with more than three hundred men. Homesick but desperately determined,[14] he hurried forward to make a junction with a larger American force under Benedict Arnold which was already camped before Quebec.

Almost simultaneously with the American advance on Lake Champlain about eleven hundred patriots under Benedict Arnold began to move against Quebec by way of the Kennebec and Chaudière rivers. Washington personally organized this expedition,

---

[13] For an account of this enterprise see Justin Smith, *Our Struggle for the Fourteenth Colony* (2 vols., New York, 1907), I, 380–394.

[14] Although Montgomery displayed superb devotion to duty, he thought himself unequal to his command and asked three times in November and December to be relieved. Jared Sparks (ed.), *Correspondence of the American Revolution; Being Letters of Eminent Men to George Washington* . . . (4 vols., Boston, 1853), I, 481, 491; Montgomery to Robert R. Livingston, Dec. 17, 1775, Robert R. Livingston MSS, in the New York Public Library.

placed Arnold in command, and gave that intrepid man seven companies of New England troops and three of Pennsylvania and Virginia riflemen to execute it. These men, taken from Washington's own army, marched from Cambridge just before September. Had they left a month earlier, perhaps even a week earlier, Quebec

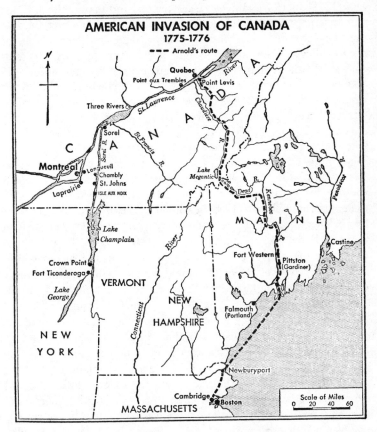

must have been theirs. On September 25 Arnold and his followers began to push up the Kennebec, walking along its banks and driving hastily built bateaux against its current. The boats, built of green timber, soon opened leaks; food supplies quickly became damaged; and the rough work of poling and portaging became utterly exhausting. Within three weeks the little army was on short rations. Weary and discouraged, the officers of the three companies forming the rear voted to turn back and led their men southward to safety and to obscurity. The remainder trudged, swam, climbed, and crawled over the divide between Maine and Canada. Arnold was dauntless, and he had heroic support from Aaron Burr, Eleazer Oswald, Daniel Morgan, Dr. Isaac Senter, and many others. Colds and dysentery created havoc; flour moistened with water became the standard diet, and then boiled leather; and every mile of progress beyond the divide brought new torture to body and soul. James Melvin in matter-of-fact language recorded his sufferings: "Rained all last night and this day. . . . Marched through hideous woods and mountains. . . . The company were [went] ten miles, wading knee-deep . . . one man fainted in the water. . . . Here a boat was stove, with four men, and one man drowned. . . . They agreed to part and the heartiest to push forward as fast as they could. . . . I was not well, having the flux. We went twenty-one miles." [15] On October 30 Arnold and an advance party reached the first French house on the Chaudière and hurried food back to their suffering fellows. The bones of perhaps two or three score were left in the woods, but the remainder, gaunt scarecrows, came on into the French settlements. The *habitants,* softened by pity, sympathy for the patriot cause, and gold, gave all the succor within their power. By November 10 Arnold with some five hundred more or less effectives had reached Point Levis on the bank of the St. Lawrence opposite Quebec. A storm and lack of boats held him to the south shore for three days. By the morning of the fourteenth he was camped on the Plains of Abraham and considering assault.

Unhappily for the Americans, Arnold had come too late. Had he been able to cross the river immediately, he might easily have carried the city. Then Allan McLean, with eighty troops he had raised, was absent on a futile march to relieve Fort St. John's; the French townsmen were restless; there was only a handful of regular troops and British marines within the walls. Hector Cramahe, lieutenant governor of the province, who was frantically trying to put the city in a posture of defense, was in despair. While Arnold

[15] Andrew A. Melvin (ed.), *The Journal of James Melvin* . . . (Portland, Me., 1902), pp. 47–53. Many members of the expedition managed to keep journals. Kenneth Roberts has published a collection of them in *March to Quebec* . . . (New York, 1938).

waited helplessly on the south bank, however, McLean and his men slipped into the city by water. Determined to resist to the uttermost, McLean promptly assumed responsibility for its safety. Calling into service all the able-bodied British in the city and three hundred Canadians, he collected altogether about thirteen hundred men. Included among them were perhaps one hundred red-coated regulars; Royal Marines and seamen from war and merchant vessels in the harbor; McLean's own volunteers, almost two hundred; a few artillerists; and many British civilians of one occupation or another. This motley garrison, though largely inexperienced, was well armed, well clothed, and stationed behind strong walls. On November 16 in council of war McLean, Cramahe, and other British officials pledged themselves to defend the city to the last extremity. McLean cleared the walls by burning down outlying houses, and twice drove off by cannon fire a messenger from Arnold demanding surrender. For several days the Americans occupied themselves by sniping at British sentries. Then, in the belief that he could not carry the walls, Arnold withdrew up the river to effect a union with Montgomery. As he did so, Carleton passed by on the river and made his way into the city.

On December 2 the two American commanders joined forces twenty miles above Quebec. By that time Arnold had 675 hardy followers available for service. Montgomery, who assumed command, could therefore muster about one thousand men, most of whom he was able to clothe in captured British uniforms. He immediately ordered his men to march against the King's in Quebec, which was again invested by December 5.

The little American force which encamped before Quebec was splendid in quality but almost doomed to failure. The sturdy walls of Quebec could defy the light artillery which Montgomery could bring to bear against them; the garrison within was well supplied for a siege, indeed, better prepared for one than the Americans; and the defenders, more numerous than the assailants, had acquired a superb leader. Guy Carleton never was given much opportunity during the War of Independence to display his talents as a commander of a large army in the open field. Perhaps he lacked sufficient dash and aggressiveness and, had he been given the chance, would have accomplished little more than Howe, Clinton, or Burgoyne. But for his task at Quebec he possessed every qualification. He had the traditional courage and tenaciousness of the veteran British soldier; he was cool and even cold in time of peril; [16] and he inspired respect and confidence alike among officers and men. Prudent and cautious, he did not make Montcalm's mistake: he did not rashly venture beyond the walls of the city and risk all in open battle on the Plains of Abraham. He chose to defend, and that most obstinately. He drove the disaffected from the city, built additional fortifications, sternly held his men to their duties, and waited for the American assault.

When Carleton refused even to receive his demands for surrender, Montgomery bombarded the city with his light artillery. The British responded with heavier guns, and it quickly became apparent that Quebec must be carried by storming, if at all. Moreover, as American enlistments were expiring, the attempt could not be long delayed. Montgomery laid plans for a night assault on December 27, but a deserter carried the news to the British, who were ready to meet it. As the night was clear and there was no hope of surprise, Montgomery decided to wait for a storm which would reduce visibility. It came on December 30, when the American plan was put into effect in driving snow and darkness. Two feints were made toward the upper part of the city in the hope of misleading the British, who could not cover all the long walls in strength. Meanwhile Montgomery in person led a detachment of New Yorkers forward against the west wall beside the St. Lawrence while Arnold drove against the eastern defenses beside that stream. If successful, they planned to meet in the lower part of the city and then reduce its remainder. The British were puzzled for a time, but when Montgomery and his followers entered a narrow pass before a watchhouse garrisoned by fifty defenders, they were cut down by heavy artillery and musket fire and many fell, including Montgomery himself. Without his leadership, the remains of Montgomery's force despairingly withdrew.

[16] See the praise of Carleton by Henry Hamilton, who observed Carleton's behavior at Montreal, in *Michigan Pioneer and Historical Collections*, X (1908), 267. Allan McLean later claimed that it was he, not Carleton, who saved Quebec. Mrs. E. S. Wortley (ed.), *A Prime Minister and His Son* (New York, 1925), p. 106. It is probably true that the exertions of both men were indispensable for the successful defense of the city.

Arnold's attack was hardly more fortunate. He and his men were seen as they approached and were subjected to a galling fire. They broke through an outer defense, but Arnold was wounded and had to be carried off. Daniel Morgan, who assumed command, hesitated for a few minutes before attempting the second and last barrier, giving the defenders an opportunity to recover from confusion and to bring up reinforcements. When he did move forward, he was bloodily repulsed in savage fighting; and when two sortie parties sent out by Carleton cut off his retreat, he and the bulk of his men were compelled to surrender. The Americans had failed; their army was cut in half, their leader dead.

Benedict Arnold refused to admit defeat. Even though Carleton's men far outnumbered his own, he continued the blockade of the city and begged for reinforcements and a veteran general, preferably Lee, to resume the assault.[17] American reinforcements came in very slowly from Montreal, and Carleton could have driven off the patriots. He would take no risk, however, since he expected to be strengthened by troops from England in the spring. Arnold, his injury preventing active service, was succeeded by General David Wooster, who was superseded in turn by General John Thomas. Neither Wooster nor Thomas ventured an attack. There was therefore little fighting for several months. On May 6 a British fleet reached Quebec from England, carrying ten companies of regulars and Royal Marines, the vanguard of larger forces soon to appear. At that time there were almost three thousand patriots before its walls. They were suffering from smallpox, mutinous spirits, and expiring enlistments. Thomas retreated toward Montreal, followed in leisurely fashion by Carleton and John Burgoyne with several thousand British regulars.

The Americans might conceivably have held out at Montreal. But smallpox continued to ravage their army. General Thomas was among the many who died from it. The *habitants* refused further assistance to the American cause. The famous commission consisting of Benjamin Franklin, Samuel Chase, Charles Carroll of Carrollton, and Father John Carroll, sent by Congress to win their affections, had labored in vain. The Americans had no hard money. General John Sullivan, Thomas' successor, ordered a retreat from

[17] *American Revolution Corr.*, I, 118, 156.

Montreal, and before the close of June the American army was out of Canada.[18]

Had the patriots captured Quebec they might with the support of the French Canadians have held Canada against British counter-attack. In all likelihood, however, the British, with their overwhelming naval superiority, would have regained control of the province. Besides, had the Americans been able to hold it with the help of the *habitants,* France as its ancient owner might have demanded the return of the colony. Nevertheless, the sacrifices of the defeated patriots were not in vain. Their northern offensive increased and complicated the military problems of the British and prevented a southward thrust along the Lake Champlain-Hudson waterway until the fall of 1776. Then Arnold, completely recuperated, brought Carleton's advance to a halt, further postponing a British march to Albany and New York. If nothing else, Montgomery, Arnold, and the northern American army had won time, and a British offensive from the north which might have succeeded at the start of the conflict was doomed to disaster when launched at a later day. Furthermore, the presence of the Americans on the St. Lawrence convinced the British government that Carleton's services were needed there. As a result, when Gage was superseded, Howe, Carleton's inferior in rank and efficiency, was given the supreme command in the Thirteen Colonies. Had Carleton occupied that post, the American rebellion might not have blossomed into a revolution.

[18] Professor A. L. Burt in "The Quarrel Between Carleton and Germain: An Inverted Story," *Canadian Historical Review,* XI (1930), 211, censures Carleton for not intercepting the Americans on the Richelieu.

CHAPTER 5

Britain Declares War

WITH every skirmish of 1775 between the redcoats and the patriots the chances of reconciliation between Britain and America diminished. Nevertheless, at any time before the end of that year the British government could have obtained both peace and the preservation of the empire by giving to the patriots generous guarantees of their rights. Such guarantees were not offered. Although many persons in Britain urged that concessions be made to the Americans, the government clung to its policy of coercion.

Thanks to Yankee enterprise, the patriot version of the shocking news of Lexington and Concord was known in London by May 29, 1775, two weeks before the arrival of General Gage's official account.[1] To some the reports from America spelled catastrophe; a few persons harboring high notions of imperial power were doubtless elated, for now that power would probably be invoked in the fullest possible measure; most thinking Englishmen were no doubt perplexed. Members of the ministry were deeply disappointed that the resort to the *ultima ratio* had at least temporarily failed. For this result King and ministers could logically denounce only themselves. They had appealed to force when they lacked force. They now pretended that the consequences of the expedition to Concord were not unfortunate. If they were, the fault was in Gage—he had

---

[1] Clarence E. Carter (ed.), *Correspondence of General Thomas Gage with the Secretaries of State . . . 1763–1775* (2 vols., New Haven, 1931–33), II, 198–199; Peter O. Hutchinson (ed.), *Diary and Letters of . . . Thomas Hutchinson . . .* (2 vols., London, 1883–86), I, 455–457.

bungled, acted without orders, or inefficiently executed them. Among them there was again much talk of recalling Gage because of his supposed incompetence. And Gage was almost surely to be a scapegoat, although the decision regarding his fate was postponed for some weeks.[2]

However doubtful the King might be regarding Gage's future, he was not uncertain about the need of crushing the American "rebellion." To deal with his insolent subjects he now urged powerful reinforcements for America. His ministers followed his leadership, but they could not readily produce either the redcoats or the ships and sailors desired by their master. The garrison troops stationed in the home islands were few, and it was unlikely that numerous recruits could speedily be secured in England. A national draft of men in mass was a measure unknown before the French Revolution. Meeting on June 15 and again five days later, the King's advisers decided to send to America six regiments from Gibraltar and Minorca; enlist Scottish Highlanders for overseas service; send more Royal Marines, to be raised in Ireland; augment the regiments already beyond the ocean by drafts from regiments at home; ask Carleton for two thousand Canadians; and commission additional frigates and naval transports. The army in Boston was too little in 1775 to conquer New England. Even with the reinforcements proposed by the Cabinet it would be too little in 1776 to subdue all the patriots. Thus in mid-1775 the military outlook for Britain was gloomy and the news of Bunker Hill brought no comfort. It became increasingly obvious during the latter part of the year that she must buy thousands of mercenaries if she was to wage war on land effectively.

The military problem which King and Cabinet undertook to solve was formidable enough, even had the people of the British Isles been far wealthier than they were. Britain, to be sure, possessed great financial resources, but the national debt of £136 million was enormous for that time. The interest upon the debt was heavy, the costs of a governmental system permeated by corruption and inefficiency were not small, and taxes were high when compared to levies a generation earlier. No reduction had been made in the debt since the Seven Years' War, which had been a major factor in its rise. It was doubtful that the nation could carry on another ex-

[2] J. R. Alden, *General Gage in America* (Baton Rouge, 1948), pp. 278–282.

pensive conflict without slipping into bankruptcy; and it was obvious that France and Spain might attack a Britain heavily involved in warfare with her colonists.

Moreover, public sentiment in the British Isles was not uniformly in favor of using arms against the Americans. The Roman Catholic Irish, long abused by their conquerors, sympathized with the Americans. British merchants and manufacturers were divided in their opinions, but at least a large minority among them opposed a war which would seriously damage their trade with America and which would prevent, perhaps for years, the collection of large debts owed them by the colonists.[3] Nor were the men of commerce who were opposed to war against the colonists moved only by economic interest. There were many in England and some even in Scotland who recognized George III as a would-be tyrant, who believed that subjugation of the Americans would encourage the King to strike at British liberties, and who saw the Americans as allies in a common struggle against arbitrary rule. They included merchants, artisans, noblemen, scholars, soldiers, and sailors. Englishmen who wished for the restoration of peace and who were willing to make concessions to the colonists in order to achieve it were perhaps as numerous as those who insisted upon their submission. A few preferred an independent and friendly America to one conquered, subordinate, and sullen. Opponents of the use of force were not silent. In June, 1775, John Horne Tooke and others went so far as to take up a collection in London for the benefit of the widows and orphans of the Americans "murdered" by the King's troops at Lexington. Tooke went to jail for his impudence, but there was no way to punish Lord Effingham, an army officer who publicly announced that he would not serve against the colonists, or Augustus Keppel, of the royal navy, who refused to fight against the Americans.

King and Cabinet might well have explored the possibility of reconciliation, and the arrival of the liberal-minded Richard Penn, former governor of Pennsylvania, in England in August with the Olive Branch Petition gave them an opportunity. Penn, however, was at first refused audience; and when Lord Dartmouth finally condescended to accept the petition, Penn was told that there would

[3] On the attitude of the merchants and manufacturers toward the early years of the war see Dora Mae Clark, *British Opinion and the American Revolution* (New Haven, 1930), pp. 87–118.

be no reply. The government would not discuss terms with the
"illegal" Continental Congress, it would bargain only with the
colonies individually; in effect, it would not negotiate. Almost
simultaneously, on August 23, the government gave public evidence
of its determination to wage war, issuing a royal proclamation which
referred to "an open and avowed rebellion" in America and asking
for information which would help to secure the punishment of those
both there and in England who transmitted news and advice across
the water.[4]

It was possible, of course, that Parliament, which convened on
October 26, would insist upon steps toward reconciliation. That
body numbered prominent critics of the King and his ministers
among its members. The Whig faction led by the Marquis of
Rockingham and including Edmund Burke and Sir George Savile
vigorously denounced the royal decision to wage war upon the
colonists. Although Pitt was too feeble to fulminate, most of a small
body of politicians who had long followed his leadership, particularly Lord Shelburne and Lord Camden, also condemned it. The
Rockinghamites and the Pittites received support from the Duke of
Grafton, whose disgust with governmental measures had driven him
to resign from the ministry and to enter into Opposition; from
Charles James Fox, that extraordinary young man whose rhetoric
and wit made him a power in himself; and from John Wilkes, who
spoke for a small Radical element. However, these groups and individuals, even when united, constituted a decided minority; and
there were among them old enmities, clashing ambitions, and
divergences in thought upon both domestic and colonial questions.

The Whigs and Radicals continued their assaults until the session
of Parliament came to an end late in the spring of 1776. They made
much of petitions from London and Bristol in favor of reconciliation. In November, Burke presented a bill to end the dispute with
America. It proposed renunciation by Britain of the right to tax the
colonists for revenue, repeal of the Coercive Acts and the Townshend tax on tea, and pardon to all Americans who had participated
in rebellion. It was defeated in the Commons by a vote of 210 to
105.[5] The Opposition insisted that subjugation of the Americans

---

[4] Benjamin Franklin Stevens (ed.), *Facsimiles of Manuscripts in European
Archives Relating to America* . . . (26 vols., London, 1889–95), V, No. 459.
[5] William Cobbett (ed.), *The Parliamentary History of England, 1774–1777*
(36 vols., London, 1806–20), XVIII, 978–82.

was difficult, even impossible. Grafton asserted that Britain "must be ruined by prosecuting this unnatural war," that victory would be more calamitous than defeat, for the "liberties of America once gone, those of Britain will not long survive them." [6] Henry Seymour Conway, an army officer, claimed that the Americans would prove to be equal, man for man, to the British regulars, their ardor compensating for superior British discipline.[7] Wilkes and David Hartley contended that a military victory, if achieved, would mean nothing, that the colonists could not be kept permanently in subjection, even by large garrison forces. Wilkes declared that the population of Britain was smaller than it had been in 1692, that the Americans doubled in numbers every fifteen or twenty years—his estimates were inaccurate, his logic sound. He called for the impeachment of the ministers responsible for the measures taken in the preceding winter "which have lost half our empire." [8] To which North responded by saying that a Parliament containing one Wilkes had one too many.[9] He attempted no reply to the prophetic eloquence of Hartley: ". . . You may bruise its [America's] heel, but you cannot crush its head. . . . The new world is before them. . . . When the final period of this once happy country shall overtake ourselves . . . may another Phoenix rise out of our ashes." [10]

The Opposition also maintained that France and Spain would not fail to attack a Britain engaged in a struggle with her colonists. Hartley and George Johnstone had already made that prediction, in May; and North had scoffed.[11] The warning was repeated by Lord Effingham, Grafton, the Duke of Manchester, and Conway. North and his ally, Viscount Townshend, ridiculed it.[12] The danger was too obvious to escape recognition by the Prime Minister, but he (or George III) chose to minimize it.

The King and the Cabinet refused to heed the warnings of their political enemies, and they discounted petitions from London, Bristol, and other places which begged for a reversal of policy. Supporters of the King claimed that many merchants who had signed

[6] *Ibid.*, p. 962.
[7] *Ibid.*, p. 998.
[8] *Ibid.*, pp. 1010, 1012.
[9] *Ibid.*, p. 1013.
[10] *Ibid.*, p. 1105.
[11] *Ibid.*, pp. 624–626.
[12] *Ibid.*, pp. 1208, 1213–1214, 1252–1253, 1257–1258, 1358–1360.

such documents did so under American pressure. They asserted that the petitioners, if not dupes of the Americans, were themselves disloyal malcontents. They made much of other petitions, some of them inspired by government, which supported the policy of coercion. Power sufficient to subdue the colonists was available,[13] they insisted. National honor and the preservation of the empire required that it be employed.

Privately Lord Barrington continued to concede the impossibility of military reconquest, and North to doubt the wisdom of using force, but outwardly the servants of the crown were firm and determined. George III would tolerate no weakness; he insisted upon military compulsion; and those who disagreed obeyed their obstinate master. It was almost true, in Shakespeare's language, that the King

> . . . having both the key
> Of officer and office, set all hearts i' the state
> To what tune pleas'd his ear . . .

So great had become his influence, through bribery and manipulation,[14] that his will alone might have been sufficient to gain Parliamentary sanction for coercion. Because the suffrage was severely limited and because districts sending members to Commons had little relation to population, a general election in eighteenth-century Britain did not express the popular will. It was rather "an occasion for a readjustment of interests and a redistribution of favors." [15] In the time of George I and George II the Whig nobility had divided the plums; by 1775, however, George III was the chief dispenser. In Parliament after the election of that year were seventy peers occupying government offices and 170 members of the Commons

[13] Lord George Germain declared on November 16, 1775, "Such forces as are necessary . . . will not be wanting." *Ibid.*, p. 990.

[14] How George III brought pressure upon members of the Commons is illustrated by a note from him to Lord North of March 12, 1772. "Lord North's attention in correcting the impression that I had that Col. Burgoyne and Lt. Col. Harcourt were absent yesterday is very handsome to those gentlemen, for I certainly should have thought myself obliged to have named a new governor in the room of the former, and to have removed the other from my Bedchamber." Sir John W. Fortescue (ed.), *Correspondence of King George the Third from 1760 to December, 1783* (6 vols., London, 1927–28), III, 328–329.

[15] William T. Laprade (ed.), *Parliamentary Papers of John Robinson 1774–1784, Publications of the Camden Society,* Third Series, XXXIII (London, 1922), xvii.

holding either offices or public contracts.[16] George III's personal following, the King's Friends, was numerous. Moreover, the Anglican clergy and the independent country gentlemen, who were greatly overrepresented in Parliament, usually saw eye to eye with the King.[17] Many a lord and commoner at Westminster who owed little or nothing to the King honestly, if mistakenly, gave hearty adherence to the policy of the crown. To do them justice, many of the King's Friends followed royal leadership from conviction as well as from interest. There is no reason to believe that men such as Lord Mansfield and Lord George Germain were moved exclusively by a desire for pelf.

In any case, Parliament gave its approval to the measures sponsored by government by steady majorities of two to one. The King's Speech condemned the American "authors and promoters of this desperate conspiracy. . . . They meant only to amuse, by vague expressions of attachment to the parent state, and the strongest protestations of loyalty to me, whilst they were preparing for a general revolt. . . . The rebellious war now levied . . . is manifestly for the purpose of establishing an independent empire." [18] The Americans must be brought back to their allegiance by armed might. Although it was heatedly denounced by the Opposition, the King's Speech was approved by heavy majorities in both houses. On November 20, 1775, North brought before the Commons a Prohibitory Bill, which passed into law in similar fashion. On paper at least, the measure established a complete naval blockade of America, authorized the seizure of American goods whenever found upon salt water, and called for the forcible enlistment in the royal navy of merchant sailors captured in American vessels. In effect, both King and Parliament had now given their answer to the Olive Branch Petition—Britain would wage war with all the strength at her command. Their reply could have only one result—to force hundreds of thousands of Americans who had wished for no more than

[16] *Ibid.*, pp. 12–17.

[17] Thomas Hutchinson noted in his diary on November 9, 1775, "All the independent landed interest of the kingdom vote with government, in what relates to America." *Hutchinson Diary*, I, 555. On the attitude of the country gentlemen in the early years of the War of Independence see also Clark, *British Opinion*, pp. 135–142, 244.

[18] *Parliamentary History*, XVIII, 695–696.

what they considered their rights within the empire to take the road to independence.

Appealing once more to arms, the British government could not deny itself a trifling gesture toward accommodation. The Prohibitory Bill also empowered the crown to send to America commissioners who might inquire into grievances and grant pardon to patriots who had discovered the error of their ways and repented.[19] In the following spring Richard, Admiral Viscount Howe was ordered to the command of the British fleet in American waters and was appointed as one of the commissioners. His younger brother, General William Howe, was chosen as the other. They were given power to bludgeon, but hardly to bargain, although it was long before the patriots learned for certain that the olive branch carried by the brothers was in reality a yoke.

The Prohibitory Bill was by no means the last of the measures of King and Cabinet calculated to alienate the Americans. While Parliament debated, the ministry strove desperately to procure on the European continent the troops they could not obtain in Britain. It had become apparent that the forces decided upon in June were insufficient for the task of conquering America and equally clear that there was little enthusiasm to enlist in the armed forces on the part of Britishers at home. The government sought everywhere to purchase troops. They tried to buy the services of a Scottish brigade in the pay of The Netherlands and were refused.[20] They approached Catherine the Great, who had just made peace with the Sultan of Turkey after a six-year war and who had available tens of thousands of veterans. But "Sister Kitty," as Edward Gibbon called the Empress, after seeming to listen with interest to the first British overtures, in the end returned a rude and contemptuous negative.[21] Finally, in the winter of 1775–76, they found a sympathetic hearing among the despotic rulers of the little states of western and southern Germany. Six of these small monarchs, greedy for British cash, were

[19] The fact that Lord George Germain, whose attitude toward the Americans was the same as that of the King, was actually offered similar powers in October, 1775, testifies to the political ineptitude of the ministry. He could not possibly have succeeded in such a mission. Gerald S. Brown, "The Policy of Lord George Germain Toward the American Revolution, 1775–1778" (Ph.D. thesis, University of Minnesota, 1948), pp. 56–59.

[20] Sir George O. Trevelyan, *The American Revolution*, Part II (2 vols., New York, 1903), I, 41–42.

[21] *George III Corr.*, III, 275–276.

willing, and in some cases eager, to sell soldiers. One after another they entered into agreements by which they received large sums in cash and other concessions in return for stipulated numbers of troops. Eventually they furnished almost thirty thousand men to the British army. The Landgrave of Hesse-Kassel personally sold seventeen thousand—hence the use of the word *Hessian* to describe all the German soldiers. Prince Charles of Brunswick supplied almost six thousand; the rulers of Hesse-Hanau and Anspach-Bayreuth each approximately twenty-four hundred; and the princes of Waldeck and Anhalt-Zerbst each about twelve hundred.

Britain was to spend millions of pounds for the services of these mercenaries and for the enrichment of the princelings who bartered over them, particularly the Landgrave of Hesse-Kassel. The German troops sometimes received good pay, and sometimes not, for exposing themselves to hardship, disease, and death in a distant quarrel which was not their own and which they could hardly understand. Britain gained from her bargains some regiments of veterans, others of mediocre caliber, and some of downright poor quality, with ranks filled by cajolery and impressment. Though the Germans were indispensable additions to the numerical strength of the British forces in America, their regiments were not nearly as dependable as those of the redcoats.[22]

The use of foreign mercenaries reaped a harvest of hatred in America. According to contemporary European standards, to be sure, it was normal practice to employ mercenaries against foreign enemies, but the hiring of them by Britain seemed irrefutable proof to the colonists that they were to be treated as foreigners. The news of the coming of the Hessians greatly increased colonial enmity against the British government, and even against the British people, and gave added impetus to the fateful Declaration of Independence.

The dealings of George III and his aides with the German dukes and princes were bitterly assailed in Parliament in the early months of 1776 by the Whigs and Radicals. In the course of the debates

[22] The most complete study of the German mercenaries in the War of Independence is that of Max von Eelking, *Die Deutschen Hülfstruppen im nordamerikanischen Befreiungskrieg, 1775–1783* (2 vols., Hanover, 1863), translated by J. G. Rosengarten as *German Allied Troops in the North American War of Independence, 1775–1783* (Albany, 1893). Edward J. Lowell, *The Hessians and the Other German Auxiliaries of Great Britain in the Revolutionary War* (New York, 1884), is also useful.

over the treaties of "alliance" which consummated some of these transactions Fox delivered a moving panegyric in memory of Richard Montgomery; and in the upper house the Duke of Richmond, Fox's uncle, who had gallantly served at Minden in 1759, hotly attacked the policy of the crown and defended the patriots, but to no avail. Parliament was then even more firmly under the domination of King and Cabinet than it had been in the closing months of the preceding year. On November 10 Lord Weymouth had joined the ministry, and he now spoke effectively in the Lords in behalf of the measures of the crown. On the same day Lord George Germain had also entered the Cabinet, as Secretary of State for the Colonies. Germain, like Richmond, had been on the battlefield of Minden in Germany in the last war. Repeatedly disobeying orders to lead a cavalry charge, for a reason or reasons even now mysterious, he had been accused of cowardice and had asked for a court-martial, which found him guilty and declared him "unfit to serve His Majesty in any military capacity whatever." Germain was quick to defend his own honor, was arrogant, obstinate, but not without talent. A firm believer in coercion, he infused new energy into the Cabinet and ably supported North from the Treasury bench.[23] In both houses crown majorities mounted to three to one.

Though unable to hold a commission in the army, Germain as Colonial Secretary was nevertheless largely responsible for military operations in America. Exhibiting great energy, he hurried across the ocean regiment after regiment, well equipped and commonly well trained. Ten thousand of these redcoats and Hessians were dispatched to the assistance of Carleton in Canada, to drive the patriots from that colony, to move southward toward Albany, and to "contribute to the success of the army under General Howe." [24] Howe was continually reinforced until by the fall of 1776 his army had reached a total of 34,000 men. He was instructed to seize New York City and to break down American resistance in its vicinity and in New England. Since Howe could hardly move until early

[23] Brown, "Germain Policy," *passim,* offers a relatively favorable view of Germain's conduct at Minden and of his management of the war. Professor Brown criticizes Germain for his lack of understanding of colonial political problems. See also Brown's "The Court Martial of Lord George Sackville, Whipping Boy of the Revolutionary War," *William and Mary Quarterly,* Third Series, IX (1952), 317–337.

[24] Brown, "Germain Policy," p. 159.

summer, Henry Clinton was temporarily detached from the main army and given three thousand troops in order to strike at the Southern colonies. It was hoped that Clinton's army, together with a supporting naval squadron under Sir Peter Parker, would establish contact with pro-British elements in the Carolinas and accomplish something useful before their services were required to the northward. Germain overestimated the numbers and the zeal of the American Loyalists, undervalued the numbers and power of the patriots.

Given proper strategy and sound tactics, the troops, sailors, ships, artillery, money, and paraphernalia of eighteenth-century warfare massed by the British government for the campaign of 1776 might nevertheless have been sufficient to break down American resistance. The royal navy could not be seriously challenged, although American privateers could and did seize supply vessels, wounding British pride and capturing matériel badly needed by the patriots. The royal infantry, the backbone of the army, was, to be sure, uneven in quality, but the army contained more than forty regiments organized before the Seven Years' War, many of them nourishing traditions of valor upon battlefields such as Blenheim and Fontenoy. In fighting on open fields both the redcoats and the Hessians were man for man superior to the patriots until the Americans had acquired experience and discipline. The best British regiments—like the 20th, the 21st, and the 44th—were inferior to none in the world in formal conflict on unobstructed ground.

The redcoat in the ranks, it is true, was often an impressed vagabond, a bit of flotsam or jetsam thrown up by British economic tides; commonly he was a simple country boy overpersuaded by smooth talk and gin to volunteer; not infrequently he was a soldier because he preferred military service to imprisonment or execution for crime. Nevertheless, the British private, if physically smaller than his patriot counterpart,[25] was sturdy and courageous. Moreover, he was often a veteran of many years, a professional fighting man, his regiment a large part of his life. He was thoroughly drilled in the

[25] A Hessian after Burgoyne's surrender commented that "nature had formed all the [American] fellows who stood in rank and file so slender, so handsome, so sinewy, that it was a pleasure to look at them, and we were all surprised at the sight of such a finely built people. And their size! . . . English America excels most of Europe in respect to the stature and beauty of its men." Roy W. Pettengill (ed.), *Letters from America, 1776–1779* (Boston, 1924), p. 111.

evolutions used in European warfare, highly disciplined, and obedient. His musket, no weapon for sharpshooting, was efficient enough at short range, and at closer quarters his bayonet was terribly effective. British noncommissioned officers, chosen, of course, from the ranks, were skilled in their duties.

Commissioned officers in the British regiments were also efficient, despite vicious practices in recruitment and a complete lack of formal training. The private soldier could not win a commission by valor. The lowest, that of ensign, and all subsequent higher ones to the rank of colonel were ordinarily purchased. Young men—and boys—of families possessing money and influence accordingly secured these much desired appointments, often without the slightest inquiry into the fitness of those chosen.

Promotion for merit alone was rare,[26] and officers of the Guards stationed in England were often advanced before those doing duty with regiments stationed outside the British Isles. In consequence James Boswell sought an appointment in the Guards in the hope of securing preferment without undergoing all the hardships of military life. He was not singular in soliciting such a commission; others with more powerful and energetic friends succeeded where he failed. Such a system [27] produced officers like the rascally Mr. Wickham of Jane Austen's *Pride and Prejudice* and the stupid George Osborne of Thackeray's *Vanity Fair*. But prototypes of Thackeray's William Dobbin and Colonel Newcome served as well. The officers came frequently from good and even great families; some of them were born and bred to the colors. They were often graduates of private schools such at Eton and Westminster, and at least occasionally of British universities. There was no national institution for training either infantry or cavalry officers. Not overly versed in military theory, the regimental officers were generally proficient through long practice.

The principal deficiency of the British army was to be found in the quality of its general officers, most of whom, in the war against

[26] In *Advice to the Officers of the British Army* (London, 1783), p. 48, an anonymous author offered satirical advice to adjutants: they should be attentive, but not too attentive, to a general's "girl." The admonition was not out of place with respect to America, since Generals Howe, Clinton, and Burgoyne had mistresses in America.

[27] Described in Eric Robson, "Purchase and Promotion in the British Army in the 18th Century," *History*, XXXVI (1951), 57–72.

the patriots, were better fitted to be colonels than field commanders. The men in the highest echelons were with few exceptions steady, methodical, cautious, and fundamentally unimaginative. Except for Lord Cornwallis and Burgoyne, they were unwilling to assume great risks in order to achieve decisively—and Burgoyne possessed other faults, including an inordinate vanity and a romantic temperament, which brought him defeat and humiliation. Had James Wolfe held the supreme command in America during the early years of the war, the resistance of the patriots might have been beaten down by swift and daring strokes; Cornwallis might have performed almost as brilliantly; the leadership of a Benedict Arnold might have brought success to British arms before the Americans had learned to fight in formation. Gage, Howe, Clinton, and Carleton were not incompetent, but there was among them no Turenne and no Napoleon. Nor was there genius in the supreme command at London. Germain did not possess it. Jeffrey Amherst, Britain's most trusted general officer, who gave occasional advice to the Cabinet after 1775, had few gifts, if any, beyond those of the British commanders in chief in America.

The plan of campaign for 1776 revealed obvious defects in British strategy. The navy, with very little help from the army, might eventually have brought the war to an end by tightly blockading the coasts of the Thirteen Colonies. Gage had proposed such a plan, and General James Grant as well as Barrington had favored it.[28] Had the colonists been confronted with continuing economic distress rather than invasion and bloodshed they might well have chosen to abandon the struggle, to compromise. The cost of a blockade would have been low in men and money. However, having decided to employ the army in major operations, the British should have struck as powerfully and as quickly as possible at precise objectives, the attainment of which might end the war. It was generally recognized that their chances of success would decrease as the patriots acquired experience in large-scale warfare, and that time would render ever more likely the entrance into the conflict of Britain's old enemies, France and Spain. Assuming the necessity of

[28] Alden, *Gage in America*, pp. 219–221; Barrington to Gage, Jan. 3, 1775 (private), General Thomas Gage MSS, in William L. Clements Library, University of Michigan; Grant to James Wemyss, Dec. 16, 1774, Alexander Wedderburn MSS, I, in William L. Clements Library, University of Michigan.

land campaigning, the plan which they adopted had some merit. However, Canada was a poor base from which to invade the Thirteen Colonies. Regaining control in that area would involve perhaps five thousand men. But the remainder of those who went to the St. Lawrence should have been added to Howe's army. Moreover, it was unwise to risk a serious setback in the South for possible small gains, and the troops under Clinton should likewise have been destined only for service under Howe. He would thus have been assured of overwhelming strength in his movements against New York and New England. With Carleton making gestures toward a southward advance, with Howe moving rapidly, the patriots would have been exceedingly hard pressed. Carleton would not have been in danger of isolation and destruction, and the conquest of New York would have been a virtual certainty, the subjugation of New England, the area of greatest patriot strength, highly probable. Once the Yankees were beaten, the middle colonies, where the patriots were proportionately least numerous, would probably have offered only weak resistance. The collapse of the American cause in the South must soon have followed. The patriots could well rejoice that the British did not concentrate all possible strength under Howe, and that this commander was notoriously averse to moving fast or taking major risks.

CHAPTER 6

Independence Proclaimed

IN THE fall and winter of 1775 and in the early months of 1776 news traversed the ocean that Britain would try to solve her difficulties with the colonials by force and more force; and the patriots, bracing themselves for a great struggle, reconsidered the goals for which they were fighting. On July 2, 1776, after much debate and soul searching, they announced the secession of the Thirteen Colonies from the British Empire and the birth of a new nation, the United States of America.

It was often argued by supporters of Britain in the troubled years between the close of the French and Indian War and the day of Lexington that resistance to British measures was motivated, in part at least, by a desire for independence. Royal Governors Francis Bernard and Thomas Hutchinson of Massachusetts had on several occasions accused the opponents of British policy of plotting separation from the empire. To be sure, the assertions of Bernard and Hutchinson and of others who shared their belief should not be accepted as cool statements of truth from impartial witnesses. Nevertheless, there were some American leaders and American plain folk who wanted independence before April 19, 1775, but they were few in number. A far larger group of persons favored some kind of dominion status under the crown, and rested their case on rights which they claimed were their due as Englishmen.

Lexington, Concord, Bunker Hill, and minor military clashes in the summer and fall of 1775 abruptly changed the political objectives of the struggle and accentuated the cleavage between Briton and American. Especially among the patriots of New England, who first met their "cousins" face to face in desperate combat, did the conviction arise that the British people were their bitter enemies rather than merely antagonists in a family quarrel. Sentimental attachments to the mother country began to snap. The fighting New Englanders were now tempted to demand, not merely freedom from Parliamentary interference in their domestic affairs, but severance of all political ties. Jerseymen, Marylanders, and Carolinians began to look upon the people and rulers of Britain as unnatural relatives, if not foreign foes. They, too, enlarged their concepts of American rights and learned to contemplate without horror separation from the parent country. Nevertheless, a large majority among the Americans clung for many months after Lexington, at least ostensibly, to hope of reconciliation. Many continued to believe that Cabinet and Parliament might yet reconsider, repent, and even fully recognize colonial "rights"; that the King was less hostile toward the patriots than his associates in government and that he might use his influence toward a negotiated settlement; that an aroused British public might force a reversal of policy in London; that the Olive Branch Petition would be accepted by not unfriendly hands.

It is less than fair to stigmatize as hypocrites patriots like Samuel Adams and John Adams who openly wished for independence in the summer and fall of 1775. How about that far more numerous group of "Whigs" who continued to assert their loyalty to the empire while they fought against Britain? If they were sincere in their protestations of fidelity to the empire, it has been frequently asked, how could they possibly have become converted to complete separation in the space of a twelvemonth? Yet in voicing loyalty to a British Empire constituted according to their own desires, one in which America would possess at least a thoroughly safeguarded home rule, they engaged in no deceit. Should Britain refuse to yield to their demands, they viewed independence as the only alternative, but did so with profound misgivings. Their attitude was consistent with their demand for their "rights," within or without the empire, as fate would determine. In their devotion to their "rights" they were in agreement, of course, with the Adamses and those other patriots who were convinced that their liberties could not be secure under the British flag. The "Whigs" were quite united with respect to their ultimate goal; they differed regarding means toward attaining it.

To the patriots debating among themselves the issue of freedom within or outside the empire came, late in 1775 and early in 1776, news of the royal proclamation of August 23,[1] reports that hired German soldiers would be employed against them, and word of the King's Speech. It was now evident to all that Britain intended to wage war, perhaps without restraint. Those Americans who had already committed themselves to independence described the measures as proof that Britain looked upon the colonists as a foreign people, against whom it was proper to send brutal mercenary troops. Many patriots not hitherto convinced of the necessity of separation now were reconciled to the break. Notable among them was Washington, who urged that independence was the great objective of the war. Early in 1776 he declared that "I have never entertained an idea of an accommodation, since I heard of the measures, which were adopted in consequence of the Bunker's Hill fight." [2] Another was Charles Lee, who later changed his mind. The King's Speech and the "infamous plans adopted by a venal ministry" meant to George Lux of Baltimore in January, 1776, that "all hopes of an accommodation is now lost. . . ." [3] To many waverers the subsequent news of the passage of the Prohibitory Bill was the final straw. They argued that crown and Parliament had cut off the colonists from the empire, and that a declaration of independence by the patriots would merely confirm the decision of the British government. It "makes us independent in spite of our supplications and

[1] The proclamation reached Philadelphia on October 31, the King's Speech on January 8, 1776. William Duane (ed.), *Passages from the Remembrancer of Christopher Marshall . . .* (Philadelphia, 1839), pp. 56–57, 62. Although the statement has received very little attention from historians, Richard Henry Lee asserted in November, 1775, that "The proclamation that followed the receipt of so humble a petition has determined the councils of America to prepare for defence with the utmost vigor both by sea and land." James C. Ballagh (ed.), *The Letters of Richard Henry Lee* (2 vols., New York, 1911–14), I, 161.

[2] John C. Fitzpatrick (ed.), *The Writings of George Washington* (39 vols., Washington, 1931–44), IV, 321. Early in January Washington commented bitterly upon the King's Speech. On January 31 he referred to "the sound doctrine and unanswerable reasoning" of Tom Paine's *Common Sense. Ibid.*, pp. 210, 219.

[3] *The Lee Papers, Collections of the New York Historical Society for the Years 1871–74* (4 vols., New York, 1872–75), I, 239.

entreaties," declared John Adams.[4] Joseph Hewes of North Carolina in consequence asserted that "nothing is now left but to fight it out." [5]

Chiefly influential in leading the patriots toward formal separation was Thomas Paine, whose *Common Sense* came anonymously from the press in January, 1776. Resident in the colonies less than two years, Paine had come from England with a recommendation from Benjamin Franklin. Of humble birth, ill educated, Quakerish in antecedents, he had been a failure in business, in marriage, and in life. He had little reason to love the *status quo* in England. He had become a deist, a devotee of liberty in general, and a despiser of monarchy in particular. A gifted writer and propagandist, he now burst like a meteor into the arena of public affairs. In phrases at once eloquent and passionate, Paine denounced the masters of his native country and their policies and pleaded for an American proclamation of independence.

Paine advanced no new arguments, as the jealous John Adams long afterward asserted. But his language, suffused with both reason and emotion, carried extraordinary appeal. Moreover, he struck convincingly at one of the greatest obstacles to separation, American veneration for royalty. If the patriots insisted upon a complete divorce from Britain, they could hardly establish other than republican institutions; and republicanism to many of them was unhallowed by either precedent or practice. Paine savagely tore away the romantic veil about royalty in general and George III in particular. Kings were usurpers of power and tyrannical in its exercise, men, and no more than men, "the first of them nothing better than the principal ruffian of some restless gang"; the later ones, claiming the right to govern because of heredity, were rascals also. "Of more worth is an honest man to society, and in the sight of God, than all the crowned ruffians that ever lived." George III, as well as Cabinet and Parliament, was a cause of America's woes. He was responsible, with others, for loosing upon the colonials Indians and Negroes along with the redcoats. He should be disowned, and the patriots should set up republican forms based upon the consent of the governed, for their own sake and in the cause of mankind, which

[4] Edmund C. Burnett (ed.), *Letters of Members of the Continental Congress* (8 vols., Washington, 1921–36), I, 406.
[5] *Ibid.*, p. 401.

might find safety and inspiration in a kingless and free America. "The blood of the slain, the weeping voice of nature cries, ' 'TIS TIME TO PART.' "

O! ye that love mankind! ye that dare oppose not only the tyranny but the tyrant, stand forth! Every Freedom hath been hunted round the globe. Asia and Africa have long expelled her. Europe regards her like a stranger, and England hath given her warning to depart. O! receive the fugitive and prepare in time an asylum for mankind.

Common Sense had an enormous circulation, 120,000 copies being printed within three months.[6] It caused a sensation throughout the colonies, and it has been described not infrequently as the determining factor in the debate over independence. The pamphlet no doubt did decisively alter the opinions of some of the less sophisticated "Whigs."

However magnificent may be the magic of words, violence commonly has greater effect upon the minds of men; and it seems likely that the known determination of the British to crush the rebellion and their actions in America toward that end had greater effects in the early months of 1776 than Paine's propaganda.[7] The depredations of Lord Dunmore on the coast of Virginia, attempts on his part to enlist Negro slaves in the King's service, his scheme to bring Ohio Valley Indians down upon the western frontier of the Old Dominion, and open fighting between Dunmore's motley following and the patriots provoked the Virginia "Whigs" to seek freedom outside the empire. A vain rising of the Loyalists in North Carolina in February, 1776, similarly drove the patriots of that colony toward independence; and when they learned that Parker and Clinton were joining forces off their shores, presumably to attack them, they officially authorized their delegates in the Continental Congress to vote for separation. The burning of Falmouth (now Portland), Maine, by Admiral Graves' sailors and the defeat and death of Montgomery likewise impelled the Yankees toward

---

[6] According to Paine's biographer Moncure Conway. Philip S. Foner (ed.), *Complete Works of Thomas Paine* (2 vols., New York, 1945), I, xiv, states that almost half a million copies were sold soon after publication.

[7] Charles Lee asserted in February, 1776, that *Common Sense* undoubtedly operated "most powerfully on the minds of the people" but that its effects were "trifling comparatively." He claimed that British leaders by their "last acts" had "given the coup de grace to dependence." *Lee Papers*, I, 325.

independence. It was hardly a coincidence that the colonies in which British forces operated or immediately threatened were the earliest to insist upon leaving the empire, whereas the middle colonies, which were not attacked until July, 1776, were more reluctant to take the fateful step.

With the appearance of *Common Sense* the conflict over dependence versus independence, hitherto not much discussed officially or even openly, became public and bitter. Every conceivable argument was employed on both sides. Those who were opposed to separation made much of the generosity of the mother country toward her progeny. To be sure, Britain at the moment was hardly acting the role of the sympathetic parent, but British severity might soon be replaced by British loving-kindness. They pointed out that no other European nation had been so liberal in its treatment of its people beyond seas, that the Americans had been permitted largely to conduct their own domestic affairs, that their personal rights as British subjects had been generally respected, that they had enjoyed substantial religious freedom. If American manufactories and American commerce had been restricted to the benefit of residents of the "old country," had the colonists not prospered exceedingly? At the worst, continuance under the British flag would lead to minor and not major diminution of American rights. Independence, on the other hand, might bring in its train far greater evils: social leveling, the weakening of property rights, a mob regime, even continental anarchy. It was not at all certain that the colonists could create stable and responsible governments to replace those which would be destroyed. And further, should the Anglo-American war not end soon, France and Spain, whether as pretended friends or declared enemies of the colonists, would intervene and perhaps subject them to the rule of their Most Christian and Most Catholic Majesties. The risks of a declaration of independence were vast; it would be better to abandon the thought, or at least to wait until a more propitious time. To cautious and propertied "Whigs" such arguments were often conclusive, and they were buttressed by sentimental loyalties.

But the advocates of separation produced even more compelling appeals to reason and to passion. The "rights" of Americans could not, they contended, be rendered inviolate within the empire. Should Britain promise to respect them and American arms be set aside, Britain would very likely resume her tyrannical measures, perhaps at a time when America was seriously disunited and ill prepared to resist. What guarantees against such an event could be found, they asked; and there was no ready answer, since it was idle to speak among "Whigs" of the good faith of Britain. American "rights" would be assured under American governments; such governments, respectable, responsible, and enduring, could be established, and some sort of American union as well; anarchy and mob rule were the merest creatures of fancy. An independent America would be free to manufacture, and to trade as it wished with all the world. Those who demanded independence admitted the risk of conquest by the Bourbons. Risks, however, had to be taken, and this one was minor. Indeed, if American "rights" were to be preserved, the patriots must obtain help from France. French guns, powder, and livres were essential to successful resistance against Britain. To secure aid from Louis XVI independence must be declared. That monarch had to be convinced that the Americans would not abandon the struggle immediately after France had committed herself to assist the rebellion within the domain of her old antagonist. We must, cried the champions of separation, assert our independence, make an American union of American states, and seek aid and alliances in France and Spain. Less than a final rupture with Britain, they declared, and with telling effect, would render vain the sacrifices of the American homeless, wounded, and slain. To patriots now realizing, perhaps for the first time, that British Americans and Britons were not one and the same people, such contentions were convincing.[8]

While the great debate moved toward its momentous conclusion, political ties between America and Britain continued to snap, one by one. Popularly chosen assemblies replaced the colonial legislatures, or usurped their powers; and executive and judicial officers became American rather than imperial. What may be called state governments appeared in each of the Thirteen Colonies. Moreover,

[8] Curtis P. Nettels, in *George Washington and American Independence* (Boston, 1951), chaps. 7–16, cogently argues that Washington as commander in chief by word and deed exercised great influence in the making of the decision to assert independence. Possibly he has overestimated the role of Washington in that connection. Certainly the commander in chief and other high American officers, including Lee, Gates, and Greene, brought pressure directly and indirectly upon political leaders.

those governments, one by one, began to authorize the representatives they sent to Philadelphia to vote for a general American declaration of independence. The Massachusetts delegation was apparently clothed with such power by instructions given to it in January, 1776, and the delegations of South Carolina and Georgia by mandates of March 23 and April 5 respectively. On April 12 that of North Carolina was specifically given permission to vote for separation. The Virginia Convention on May 15 ordered its delegates in the Continental Congress to propose a resolution asserting independence and counted upon the support of the solid New England delegations. In the meantime Congress itself had taken many strides toward separation. It had opened American ports to all the world save Britain on April 6,[9] had advised the several colonies on May 10 to maintain or establish governments without the authority of the empire.[10] On the very day when Virginia committed herself to the final step it urged the destruction "of every kind of authority under the . . . crown." [11] Nevertheless, it hesitated to cut the last tie.

The delegates of the Second Continental Congress in the Pennsylvania State House heard Richard Henry Lee formally propose on June 7 a resolution calling for a declaration of independence, an American confederation, and attempts to secure alliances with the powers of continental Europe.[12] That part of the Lee resolution asserting independence was promptly debated, on June 8 and again three days later. On June 11 a committee consisting of Thomas Jefferson, John Adams, Benjamin Franklin, Roger Sherman, and Robert R. Livingston was chosen to prepare a draft of a formal declaration, but adoption of the measure itself was necessarily postponed. It was generally agreed that the Congress should act for all the colonies—and all their people; and it was obvious that unanimity was highly desirable. Many delegates, especially men of the five middle colonies from New York to Maryland, held back. Their leaders, including James Wilson, John Dickinson, and Robert R.

[9] Worthington C. Ford *et al.* (eds.), *Journals of the Continental Congress, 1774–1789* (34 vols., Washington, 1904–37), IV, 258.
[10] *Ibid.*, p. 342.
[11] *Ibid.*, pp. 357–358.
[12] *Ibid.*, V, 425.

Livingston, argued that such action was premature.[13] Further debate was deferred until July 1. Before that day arrived New Jersey imprisoned its last royal governor, William Franklin, Maryland ordered its last proprietary governor, Sir Robert Eden, to depart, and both colonies gave their delegates power to act; Delaware renounced all external authority and by implication freed its representatives of clogging instructions; and a new patriot Provincial Conference in Pennsylvania, displacing the old assembly of that colony, sanctioned separation. When the contest was resumed, Dickinson again urged delay. With the delegates meeting as a committee of the whole, only nine colonies voted for the measure, as South Carolina, Pennsylvania, Delaware, and New York withheld approval. But the end of the struggle was near. That same day the Carolinians announced that they would not stand against the general will. On July 2 the appearance of a new delegate from Delaware, Caesar Rodney, and abstentions by members from Pennsylvania, including Robert Morris and Thomas Willing, altered the votes of those colonies. Accordingly the delegations of twelve of the Thirteen Colonies, with that of New York abstaining but approving, decided "That these United Colonies are, and, of right, ought to be, free and independent states; that they are absolved from all allegiance to the British crown, and that all political connexion between them, and the state of Great Britain is, and ought to be, totally dissolved." [14]

At long last the patriots, setting aside doubts and fears, at least for the moment, had pledged themselves to the creation of a new nation. "The second day of July 1776," wrote John Adams to his beloved Abigail, "will be the most memorable epocha in the history of America. I am apt to believe that it will be celebrated by succeeding generations as the great anniversary festival. It ought to be commemorated, as the day of deliverance, by solemn acts of devotion to God Almighty. It ought to be solemnized with pomp and parade, with shows, games, sports, guns, bells, bonfires, and illuminations, from one end of this continent to the other, from this time forward, forevermore." [15] A day in July, 1776, did indeed

[13] Edmund C. Burnett, *The Continental Congress* (New York, 1941), pp. 173–174.

[14] *Continental Congress Journals,* V, 507.

[15] Charles Francis Adams (ed.), *Familiar Letters of John Adams and His Wife Abigail Adams, during the Revolution* (New York, 1876), pp. 193–194.

become memorable to Americans, but it was, perversely, the fourth rather than the second day. On the fourth, with New York again abstaining—a New York state convention gave its approval on July 9—the Congress, after making some changes in its text, voted to approve that famous document, the Declaration of Independence, in which the patriots informed a candid world why they had undertaken to form the United States of America. Americans have celebrated the day on which the justification was approved, not the day of the deed.[16]

The author of the Declaration was, of course, Thomas Jefferson, whose flowing periods were not too seriously altered by his fellow committeemen, Franklin and John Adams.[17] Congress made somewhat greater changes, including deletion of phrases condemning the British people and the slave trade.[18] Adams, jealous of the repute of his early friend, later rival, and again the friend of his old age, declared years later that the Declaration said nothing new. "There is not an idea in it, but what had been hackneyed in Congress for two years before."[19] There was indeed no novelty in its thought, derived from John Locke and other political philosophers.[20] But there was genius in its eloquent, dignified, and melodious phrases, in a style superbly fitted to the content of the document. Who else

[16] The Declaration was engrossed and signed by delegates on August 2 and thereafter.

[17] Carl Becker, *The Declaration of Independence: A Study in the History of Ideas* (New York, 1922), pp. 135–171; Julian P. Boyd, *The Declaration of Independence* . . . (Princeton, 1945), pp. 16–31. Joseph Lewis, *Thomas Paine: Author of the Declaration of Independence* (New York, 1947), contends that the first draft of the Declaration was written by Paine. Mr. Lewis' thesis is untenable.

[18] Boyd, *Declaration of Independence,* pp. 31–38. It was considered improper to condemn all the British people, since so many among them were friendly to the patriot cause. Criticism of the slave trade would have offended many Southerners and even a few New Englanders.

[19] Charles F. Adams (ed.), *The Works of John Adams* (10 vols., Boston, 1851–66), II, 512.

[20] No substantial proof has yet been offered to support the notion that Jefferson's thought was influenced by that of Jean Jacques Rousseau. Paul M. Spurlin, "Rousseau in America, 1760–1809," *French-American Review,* I (1948), 8–16. For an evaluation of the impact on American Revolutionary political philosophy of English thinkers like Harrington, Sidney, Locke, and the juristic writer Blackstone, and of Continental writers, such as Vattel and Burlamaqui, see Clinton Rossiter, *Seedtime of the Republic* (New York, 1953), chap. 12.

among the patriots could have voiced their common thought in language so exalted and moving as that of Jefferson?

The Declaration was also, at least to most patriots, a convincing apologia for separation. Jefferson briefly and peremptorily denied that the British Parliament ever had the right to legislate for the colonies. Parliament was "foreign to our constitution, and unacknowledged by our laws," a body which had usurped authority. The colonials had really owed allegiance merely to the crown, and that only because they had freely offered it in exchange for protection from the crown. They, the governed, had entered into a solemn compact with the British monarch, their governor. Now the King, supported by a Parliament which voiced pretensions to a sovereignty it had never held, had violated that compact. He had withdrawn his protection; he had sought, and he was seeking, to subject the colonists to an "absolute Despotism." In consequence it was their privilege and their duty to declare the compact at an end and to enter into another or others which would safeguard their "unalienable rights," given to them by their Creator and including "life, liberty and the pursuit of happiness."

The long list of charges against George III, intended to prove that the King was a would-be tyrant, does not contain an accurate description of the conduct of the British ruler. George III was not the absolute ogre limned by the catalogue of his crimes. Criticism has been directed against the political theory of Jefferson and his colleagues. It has quite properly been asserted that their view of relations between America and Britain conflicted, at least in part, with the facts of history after 1607. Much has been said—far too much—to controvert that immortal proposition that "all men are created equal." In essence, nevertheless, the Declaration was politically sound and morally just.

The Declaration was joyously hailed by most of the patriots. Freedom was proclaimed at Philadelphia on July 8 amidst cheers of a great throng, the firing of cannon, and the ringing of church bells, and was announced to Washington's army on the following day. The Declaration was read in Boston churches, celebrated everywhere by illuminations, "elegant entertainments," and thirteen volleys of gunfire. A toast offered at one of the celebrations was: "May the freedom and independency of America endure till the sun grows dim with age and this earth returns to chaos." [21]

The Declaration clothed the patriot cause in a new nobility, and it offered a precise goal, the attainment of which would presumably bring public weal and private happiness. It was in itself a major step toward the achievement of independence. Giving a new dignity and appeal to the American cause, making possible large-scale foreign aid, it also committed the mass of the patriots almost irrevocably to separation. Once pledged, the patriot found it extremely difficult to retract and to accept less than absolute freedom. It is hardly to be doubted that many a defender of American "rights" after July, 1776, in moments of caution, discouragement, and despair, would have been willing to resume the ancient allegiance upon suitable terms. But "sacred honor," oaths of loyalty to the several infant states and to the United States, and the likelihood that accusation of treason and punishment would follow, discouraged attempts to return to the embraces of the mother country. [22] There were even some patriots who openly declared immediately after the proclamation of independence that they would prefer reconciliation with Britain, among them two prominent Pennsylvanians, Robert Morris and Joseph Reed. [23] Not many followed their example; and both Morris and Reed finally resolved to be satisfied with nothing less than complete separation.

There were many persons who were patriots before July, 1776, but Loyalists after that time—persons who had been willing to go far in defense of American "rights" but who could not or would not take the last long stride. Timidity, inborn loyalty to the empire, prudential thinking, family ties, official connection, and a host of other factors led them to renounce their association with their fellow patriots and to align themselves under the imperial banner. Accordingly the Loyalist party increased in numbers and power in the summer of 1776.

[21] John H. Hazelton, *The Declaration of Independence* . . . (New York, 1906), p. 269.

[22] If Philip Schuyler after Saratoga considered an attempt to organize a party in New York to work for reconciliation (as Major John Dyke Acland of the British army reported after a conversation with him) he must have weighed such obstacles. The Acland report is ably discussed in Carl Van Doren, *Secret History of the American Revolution* (New York, 1941), pp. 53–58.

[23] Hazelton, *Declaration of Independence,* pp. 226–228.

The Tories, of course, varied in their thoughts, emotions, and actions. There was no unique patriot mold, and there was no one Loyalist pattern. To be sure, two groups of Tories are easily distinguished from each other, those who, like Dr. John Joachim Zubly of Georgia, late and reluctantly gave their fealty to Britain, and those who, like the scientist Benjamin Thompson, would have chosen to support the mother country under almost any circumstances. Between the tardy converts and the always faithful, however, were Loyalists, no doubt more numerous than the combined wings of the party, whose opinions and sentiments evade easy classification. They might be bitterly hostile or actually sympathetic to American "rights"; they might or might not be moved by fear of democracy; they might be alarmed lest they lose office or social position under a new regime, and they might not; they might be adherents of Britain merely because their neighbors were, or because their neighbors were patriots; they might know and love the old country, and they might have small knowledge of and little affection for the home islands; they might be conversant with the issues of the day, and they might have given them only cursory thought. But in one thing they were alike, that they chose to support King and Parliament, not without hesitation but without prolonged agony of mind or heart.[24]

Nor can the Tories be easily described in terms of social status or economic condition. Some came from quasi-aristocratic families, like the Fenwicks of South Carolina, and others were the humblest folk. They were rich, like Joseph Galloway of Pennsylvania, and they were poor; they were large landowners, and they were middling and small men of property; they stood behind counters, and they possessed hands unwrinkled by trade or toil; they were well educated, like Samuel Seabury of New York, and they were illiterate; they were pious, as was the Reverend Jacob Duché, and again otherwise. Truth to tell, the Loyalists were of every station and every occupation. However, certain groups were proportionately more generously represented in the party than others. The Anglican clergy in the middle and Northern states stood almost unanimously under the royal standard; officeholders in the proprietary and royal

---

[24] Tory thought and attitudes are ably discussed in Leonard W. Labaree, "The Nature of American Loyalism," *Proceedings of the American Antiquarian Society,* New Series, LIV (1944), 15–58.

colonies, such as Attorney General James Simpson of South Carolina and Councillor Joshua Loring of Massachusetts, usually clung to their privileges and their bread and butter; great landowners, like Beverley Robinson of New York, and wealthy merchants, such as David Franks of Philadelphia, were numerous among the adherents of Britain; and Quakers, for example, Israel Pemberton of Philadelphia, were commonly Tories. Nevertheless, there is little reason to contend that the Tories were, in the average, much superior to the patriots either in social standing or in goods.

Nor can the Tories be simply labeled in terms of national background. Undoubtedly their English ancestors were more numerous than those of other origins. Prominent among the Loyalists, however, were Scottish Highlanders, especially clansmen who had been born in the mountains of North Britain. And many a Loyalist sprang from non-British forebears, Irish, Dutch, German, French, Swiss, Jewish, even Negro. Yet there was proportionately, perhaps, more British stock among the Loyalists than among the patriots, since the non-British elements could hardly be so strongly attached emotionally to the British Isles as those whose progenitors emigrated from England, Wales, and Scotland.[25] Certainly, recent British emigrants, although such famous patriots as Richard Montgomery, Horatio Gates, and Thomas Paine were latecomers, were commonly Loyalists, since they had not been long exposed to the American environment. Contrariwise, the Roman Catholic Irish who crossed the ocean toward the end of the colonial period remembered their ancient and contemporary grievances and tended to join Britain's enemies, even though the British were able to organize a Provincial Corps of Roman Catholic Volunteers.

The number of the Loyalists has been a matter of dispute, and must remain so, partly because there could be no counting of heads, partly because neutrals and near-neutrals were frequently classed as Tories both by the patriots and by their opponents. Certainly the Loyalists did not compose four-fifths or nine-tenths of the population of the Thirteen Colonies, as Joseph Galloway, one of their leaders, seems to have contended.[26] Nor were the Americans over-

[25] Alexander C. Flick, *Loyalism in New York during the American Revolution* (New York, 1901), pp. 31–36, analyzes the composition of the Tory party in New York.

[26] Julian P. Boyd, *Anglo-American Union: Joseph Galloway's Plans to Preserve the British Empire, 1774–1788* (Philadelphia, 1941), pp. 83–84.

whelmingly of the patriot persuasion, as John Adams claimed in 1780, when he was attempting to secure for Congress a loan from Dutch bankers.[27] Another estimate, which must be nearer to the truth, is that the American population was in equal parts Loyalist, patriot, and neutral.[28] This formula is popular in part, however, merely because of its symmetry; and it is to be suspected that the patriot element was larger than the others, both before and after 1776. It is likely (if the Negroes be excluded) that a substantial majority supported the patriot cause after the Declaration of Independence. Neutrals and near-neutrals can hardly have been so numerous as to form one-third of the whole population unless the Negroes be included among them.

The most informative evidence regarding the attitudes of the American people is to be found in data on military service. It has been estimated by one competent authority that fifty thousand Loyalists took up arms in behalf of Britain.[29] Another sets the figure at thirty thousand, probably a more accurate estimate. When it is recalled that the Tories seldom volunteered in the early years of the war, because they believed, or affected to believe, that the redcoats needed no assistance, these numbers are impressive. It has been asserted that there were more than eight thousand of them on British army rolls in 1780,[30] when not many more than nine thousand men were in Washington's army. However, Tory enlistments were then at their peak; and the figures do not take the militia into

---

[27] *Adams, Works,* VIII, 270.

[28] This estimate is also commonly, but erroneously, attributed to John Adams. The mistake appears as early as 1902 in Sydney George Fisher, *True History of the American Revolution* (Philadelphia, 1902), p. 229, which cites an estimate offered by Adams in 1815. However, Adams was then discussing parties with reference to the *French* Revolution. *Adams, Works,* X, 110–111.

[29] Claude H. Van Tyne, *The Loyalists in the American Revolution* (New York, 1902), p. 183. Such an estimate probably means little more than that of Emory Upton's calculation of the total number of Continentals and patriot militia who served, 395,858. Emory Upton, *Military Policy of the United States* (Washington, 1907), p. 59.

[30] Edward Channing, *A History of the United States* (6 vols., New York, 1905–25), III, 215–216. The figures given are doubtless too high. That offered by Germain is to be distrusted because he constantly exaggerated the strength of the British army in America. Moreover, the figures represent members on the rolls, not numbers ready for service. On September 1, 1781, Sir Henry Clinton in a return of the British army reports only 5,415 Loyalists in service. *Report on the Manuscripts of Mrs. Stopford-Sackville, Royal Historical Manuscripts Commission* (2 vols., 1904–10), II, 211–212.

account. It is a striking fact that British armies moving away from fortified bases were often in grave danger of being overwhelmed, not only by the American regulars, but by hordes of harassing militia. Late in the struggle Tories did flock to the royal standard in the deep South, but even then and in that area, where the King's followers admittedly were numerous, the partiot forces constantly were actually or potentially larger than the royal contingent.[31] In the immediate vicinity of New York City and in other small areas fighting Tories doubtless outnumbered fighting patriots. But British armies on the march, early or late in the war, generally acquired few recruits. On the other hand, and especially in great emergencies, patriot militia moved in large numbers to the support of the Continentals. So New England militia came forward to join Washington in March, 1776, and Philadelphians to his assistance in December, 1776, and Yankees by the thousands to the aid of Gates against Burgoyne in 1777. It cannot be seriously contended that the Tories were less warlike than their enemies, nor that their services were long unwanted by the British.[32] Hence it would appear that the patriot following was distinctly larger than the Tory party.

The Loyalists seem to have been in the majority, or at least stronger than the patriots, in several sections of the state of New York, including the western portion of Long Island, New York City, and Tryon County.[33] They were probably more numerous than the patriots in Philadelphia and southeastern Pennsylvania;[34] and they outnumbered their opponents in certain parts of the Carolinas and Georgia. They also formed an imposing part of the population in New Jersey, Delaware,[35] and Maryland. In New England and

[31] The forces led into battle in the South by Gates and Greene were uniformly larger than those they opposed.

[32] It is true that the British made greater efforts to form Tory regiments late in the war than they did in its early stages. However, there were three thousand Tories in organized units in Howe's army in 1777.

[33] Flick, Loyalism in New York, pp. 180–182.

[34] In 1777–78, even though many Tories in the area were Quakers, over three hundred of them in southeastern Pennsylvania and New Jersey enlisted in British service. Pennsylvania Magazine of History and Biography, XXXIV (1910), 1–8.

[35] Harold B. Hancock, The Delaware Loyalists, Papers of the Historical Society of Delaware, New Series, III (Wilmington, 1940), passim, claims that the Tories were more numerous than the patriots in that state, but that they were unable to assert themselves because of the presence among them of American troops. A patriot officer declared in May, 1776, that they formed "a vast

Virginia,[36] however, the adherents of the crown were rather small minority groups.[37] The largest and possibly the hardest cores of patriot strength were to be found among the planters and yeomen of the Old Dominion and the farmers, fishermen, traders, and mechanics of Yankeeland. Among them developed the most strenuous and most effective opposition to British measures before the war; in the war, the regions between the Potomac and the Dan and between the Kennebec and the Hudson were the patriot strongholds. Had the British attempted in the War of Independence to invade the heart of New England, we would perhaps now appraise patriot numbers and defensive military power in larger terms. On the whole, it would seem that the Tories, admittedly not so formidable in arms as the patriots, were also many fewer in numbers, and that the patriots, never pressed to their utmost military efforts, especially in New England, would not have been easily conquered, even though they had not received aid from France and Spain.

majority" in Sussex County. George Ryden (ed.), *Letters to and from Caesar Rodney, 1756–1784* (Philadelphia, 1933), p. 87.

[36] Only ninety-three persons from Virginia asked Britain for compensation for the losses in property they suffered as the result of the war. Only thirteen were natives of Virginia; all but fifteen had arrived there after 1760. Isaac S. Harrell, *Loyalism in Virginia* . . . (Durham, N.C., 1926), pp. 62–63.

[37] Robert O. DeMond, *The Loyalists in North Carolina during the Revolution* (Durham, N.C., 1940), p. vii, states that "North Carolina probably contained a greater number of Loyalists in proportion to its population than did any other colony."

CHAPTER 7

Long Island to Morristown

IT WAS one thing to assert independence. It was another matter to attain it. On the very day that the Continental Congress formally cut all ties between Britain and America, General William Howe and thousands of British regulars from Halifax landed on undefended Staten Island. Howe did not come to join in the celebration, but rather to persuade the patriots that they should pursue happiness under the aegis of the British Empire. Ten days later, on July 12, Admiral Lord Howe and a battle fleet reached Sandy Hook from England. There followed into New York Bay transports carrying redcoats, Hessians, and Dunmore's troops from England, South Carolina, and Virginia. Came, too, mountains of paraphernalia and foodstuffs. Ships continued to bring in men and supplies during the summer and fall, until General Howe could count about 34,000 well-equipped men under his command. With that force, vast for a British army in the eighteenth century, and with the aid of his older brother's fleet, he would put the patriots to the supreme test. As the younger Howe moved toward New York, he cherished no dream of easy and overwhelming victory, and the patriot Declaration did not reduce his tasks. Nevertheless, the months of most grievous trial for the patriots were about to begin. Fortunately for them, the British attack upon the Southern colonies had already failed.

Let us first follow Clinton and Sir Peter Parker, who commanded a fleet sent to co-operate with Clinton, in their Southern adventure. It had been hoped in England that the General and the Admiral

would receive powerful assistance from Carolinians loyal to the
crown and possibly some aid from diversionary attacks by the Creek
and Cherokee nations upon the frontiers of the Carolinas and
Georgia. The two tribes were pro-British and largely under the
influence of John Stuart, royal Indian superintendent in the South
after 1762; but Stuart, who operated after 1775 from St. Augustine and Pensacola, was for many months opposed to the use of the
savages, partly because his wife was held as a hostage in South
Carolina, partly because he was only too familiar with their cruelties
in warfare. While Stuart strove to preserve the influence of the
crown among his charges, he also desired that they remain neutral,
at least until they could be supplied with white officers and white
allies who might limit their barbarities.[1] As a result, most of the
Creeks remained quiescent. When the Cherokee, nursing old grievances against the backwoodsmen, independently took the warpath
in June, 1776, they moved too tardily and in too small force to help
Clinton and Parker.

Nor did the two British officers secure support from Southern
Loyalists. Clinton, traveling in leisurely fashion by sea from Boston
with a few scores of redcoats, did not reach the coast of North
Carolina, where the British were to gather, until the spring of 1776;
and Parker's fleet, which brought the bulk of the expedition's land
forces from England, straggled into the rendezvous after April 17.
While Clinton and Parker were still on the ocean, the numerous
Loyalists of North Carolina rallied prematurely to the royal standard. On February 5 General Donald McDonald called upon them
to rise. Hundreds of Highlanders recently come to the New World,
having now abandoned the lost cause of the Stuarts, responded to
the call; and with them came some of the old Regulators, nursing
their grievances against their low-country brethren since the battle
of the Alamance.[2] Collecting about sixteen hundred men, Mc-

[1] Philip M. Hamer, "John Stuart's Indian Policy during the Early Months
of the American Revolution," *Mississippi Valley Historical Review*, XVII
(1930), 351–366.

[2] Because governmental discrimination was practiced against back-country
people in North Carolina, particularly because tidewater officials in the uplands
charged excessive fees for public services, the back-country settlers resorted to
force to secure redress of their grievances. For the political ideas of their
leader, Hermon Husband, see W. K. Boyd (ed.), *Some Eighteenth Century
Tracts Concerning North Carolina* (Raleigh, 1927), pp. 193–392. The Regu-

Donald marched toward Wilmington to establish liaison, weeks before the arrival of the British contingents. The North Carolina patriots rose to the occasion. A thousand of them hastily gathered behind a bridge over Moore's Creek, which the Loyalists were compelled to cross in order to reach their destination. On February 27, 1776, the Highlanders tried to storm the bridge, but the patriots, led by Colonel Alexander Lillington, an unsung hero, drove them back with heavy fire from artillery, rifles, and shotguns, and then counterattacked, killing or capturing more than half of the Scots and routing the remainder.[3] This splendid little victory of the North Carolinians chilled the ardor of their Loyalist neighbors for several years.

Disappointed by the suppression of the Tory rising, Clinton and Parker loitered off the shores of the Carolinas for weeks, partly because they were obliged to await the arrival of delayed vessels, partly because they did not quite know what to do. The Cabinet, learning of the battle of Moore's Creek Bridge, hastily sent out word to abandon the whole enterprise, unless some great advantage could be gained, but the order reached the British commanders too late to affect their actions. They resolved to attack Charleston, principal city and seaport in the South. On June 4, 1776, the British warships and over thirty transports loomed beyond the bar across the entrance to its harbor and brought panic to the city. John Rutledge, the patriot executive of South Carolina, frantically girding for defense of his capital, was quite unprepared to meet a swift onslaught. He placed his slender hopes of successful resistance upon a fort upon Sullivan's Island on the northern side of the channel leading from the bar to the quays. However, this fort, commanded by Colonel William Moultrie and afterward named in his honor, was unfinished; nor were its works likely to be completed soon, for the provincial soldiers disdained physical labor, which was left to

---

lators, as they were called, were routed in the battle of the Alamance in 1771 by militia under the command of William Tryon, then Governor of North Carolina. They were kindly treated by Tryon's successor, Josiah Martin, and many of them supported the crown after 1775. At least a few joined the patriots. Probably the Regulators tended to favor the crown because their low-country enemies were patriots, but the relationship between the two conflicts has not been clearly established. Robert O. DeMond, *The Loyalists in North Carolina during the Revolution* (Durham, N.C., 1940), pp. 46-50.

[3] DeMond, *Loyalists in North Carolina*, pp. 94-96; Samuel A. Ashe, *History of North Carolina* (2 vols., Greensboro, N.C., 1908-25), I, 496-512.

Negro slaves. It was highly doubtful that the fort could withstand Parker's naval guns. Had it fallen, the scanty levies of South Carolina could not have prevented the entrance of the British regulars into Charleston; and the capture of the city, although it would by no means have ended patriot resistance in the Southern colonies, might have been seriously disturbing to the American cause.

The sight of the British ships at anchor off the bar threw Rutledge into despair. "For God's sake," he wrote to Charles Lee, begging for help, "lose not a moment." [4] Help was on the way from the winds, from North Carolina and Virginia, and from Parker's incompetence. The bar and contrary winds prevented Parker from entering the harbor for many days. Put ashore with hundreds of regulars on Long Island, north of and adjacent to Sullivan's, Clinton was virtually helpless because he lacked small vessels to cross the channel between the two islands and because landing parties would be opposed by several hundred American riflemen under Colonel William Thompson. While Clinton fumed, Lee, to whom Congress, in response to appeals from the South, had assigned the defense of the Southern colonies, hurried into Charleston, followed by Continental troops from North Carolina and Virginia. Toiling incessantly toward a successful defense of the city, Lee infused determination into the American troops, who now numbered nearly six thousand men. With every passing day British capture of Charleston became more unlikely.

As it happened, the city itself was not assailed, for the British failed even to pass the fort on Sullivan's Island. Lee had no faith in the structure, but the South Carolinians insisted that an attempt be made to defend it. He therefore strove to complete it. Clinton proposed an infantry assault upon the island under cover of the guns of the ships, but Parker refused to consider it. He requested the general to threaten a diversion while the navy battered Moultrie and his small garrison into submission. Late in the morning of June 28 Parker sent three of his smaller vessels up the channel to bombard the fort from the west, while the major portion of his fleet, seven ships, including two of fifty guns, hammered at it from the south. In spite of Lee's efforts, the fort still lacked walls on its western side, and Parker's plan might have succeeded. Fortunately for the Ameri-

[4] *The Lee Papers, Collections of the New York Historical Society for the years 1871–74* (4 vols., New York, 1872–75), II, 53–54.

cans, two of the ships sent on the flanking maneuver were poorly piloted, ran against a shoal in the channel opposite the fort, fouled each other, and lay helpless in the water. Meanwhile Parker began an eleven-hour frontal bombardment. Moultrie responded slowly and intermittently with the few guns which he could bring to bear. Toward evening Moultrie ceased firing for a time, and the British expected surrender. But Moultrie was merely temporarily out of ammunition, and as soon as he received more from Lee he resumed the struggle. Meanwhile Colonel Thompson warded off two minor attacks from Long Island by Clinton. Surprisingly, Moultrie and his men suffered little from the vaunted cannon of Britain's navy, the palmetto logs of the fort softly embracing the British shot. On the other hand, the guns of the garrison caused increasing damage to Parker's ships and over two hundred casualties, including Parker himself, who lost the seat of his trousers. In disgust and dismay he finally ordered his ships to retire.[5]

Parker and Clinton lingered on in the harbor for days, hoping to make some stroke that would reverse the verdict of June 28, but the fighting ships were in poor condition, and supplies of food began to run low. At last the British commanders relinquished their dreams of conquest in the Carolinas and sailed off to New York to join the powerful forces gathering for the major attack upon the patriots. An expedition conceived in the hope of gaining important results at small expense had failed. The victory of Lee, Rutledge, and Moultrie, and that of Moore's Creek Bridge, followed by successful attacks upon the towns of the Cherokee in the summer of 1776, prevented any serious military threat to the South for more than two years.

In New York Harbor Clinton and Parker found General Howe far less confident of victory than he had been earlier. He had hoped to move in strength early in the year—before the patriots could organize effective resistance. Germain had given him more troops than he had asked, but it had proved impossible to put ashore a large force at New York in the spring. He had envisaged a rapid conquest of that city and an easy triumph over the Continental army, although he had anticipated lengthy and tedious "mopping

[5] There is a good brief account of the battle in Willard M. Wallace, *Appeal to Arms: A Military History of the American Revolution* (New York, 1951), pp. 91–96.

up" operations. With the passing months he had come to realize that, save for some bad mistake on Washington's part, the American army would be difficult to destroy. If Washington refused to hazard that army in combat, if he retreated inland and contented himself with keeping his force in being, Howe could see no way in which the Continentals might readily be crushed. In view of the short period of good campaigning weather at his disposal and in expectation of meeting serious opposition from the main American army, Howe reduced his objectives. Before his men moved from Staten Island, he came to the conclusion that he would capture New York City, then do whatever time and circumstance permitted. If the British army in Canada marched southward as far as Albany, he would, of course, try to co-operate with it.[6]

In General Howe's military thinking time was of the essence. Still he did not hurry. There was no sound reason why he should not have assailed New York City within a few days after the arrival of his brother's fleet. He then had sufficient strength to act, even though Washington had brought his Continentals from Boston and was moving heaven and earth to protect the city. Yet the British army remained quiet in their crowded cantonments in the bay until August 22. In part, possibly, this surprising delay was caused by efforts of the Howes to use their authority as peace commissioners.

Viscount Howe had officially spread the news of the appointment of the commission even before he touched land, and had made much of the pardoning power entrusted to his brother and to himself. He had not thought it necessary to tell the Americans that they were authorized, not to negotiate, but merely to accept submission. King and Cabinet had insisted that no concessions, except for a promise of personal safety, be offered the rebels. If they laid down their arms, governments existing before 1775, save for those of Rhode Island and Connecticut, were to be restored. Rhode Island and Connecticut were to be compelled to accept royal governors and councils.[7] Moreover, the Americans were to contribute toward imperial expenses under the terms of Lord North's Conciliatory

[6] Troyer S. Anderson, *The Command of the Howe Brothers during the American Revolution* (New York, 1936), pp. 119–124. The present writer has relied heavily upon Professor Anderson's excellent monograph for analyses of Howe's intentions and actions throughout the period of his service in America.

[7] Weldon A. Brown, *Empire or Independence: A Study in the Failure of Reconciliation. 1774–1783* (Baton Rouge, 1941), pp. 84–88.

Resolution. The olive branch tendered by the brothers Howe lacked foliage. Their inability to offer more than pardon for supposed offenses was so obvious that the Continental Congress actually assisted in circulating Lord Howe's first pronouncements to the end that all patriots might know the truth.

Not content with mere proclamations, the brothers attempted on July 14 to open discussions with Americans in high office. They sent into the patriot lines at New York a letter addressed to "George Washington, Esq. etc., etc." The Virginian refused to receive it, since the letter did not recognize his position as an American general. A few days later a British officer acting in behalf of the Howes succeeded in obtaining an audience with Washington. He explained, not convincingly, that "etc., etc." had been intended to cover all of the American leader's titles. He told Washington that the Howes were eager to reach an accommodation and that they desired to open negotiations. Washington observed that conversations would be to no purpose, since they were without power to propose anything beyond pardons. In any case, he could not reply to their overture since he lacked authority to deal with peace proposals.[8] When unfounded rumors spread through his army that the Howes had offered generous terms, Washington was forced to issue a denial.[9]

Nonetheless it is highly doubtful that the attempts of the Howes to parley seriously interrupted their preparations for battle in July, 1776. Nor does it appear that the delay of the British attack upon New York City enabled Washington more effectively to defend that place. Washington did, indeed, have time to brace for the coming struggle. Unfortunately, he could not materially increase or improve his ten thousand Continentals, the backbone of his army; and it was useless for him to try to make his works more robust. The city was indefensible; to endeavor to hold it was to invite entrapment. Early in 1776 Charles Lee had begun to throw up defenses against the day of British attack, but he had told the Continental Congress that the city could be used only as a battleground—it could not be made strong enough to withstand the British army and navy. The Congress, however, had urged Washington, if possible, to hold the

[8] *Ibid.,* pp. 111–112.
[9] *The Orderly Books of Colonel William Henshaw, October 1, 1775, through October 3, 1776* (Worcester, Mass., 1948), p. 223.

city. Believing that the British could be fended off, at least for a time, he had committed his forces to its defense. He was accordingly compelled to occupy Brooklyn Heights, from which Manhattan could be cannonaded, and thus to divide his army in two, with the East River between. That part of his army on Long Island was inevitably exposed to British assault, its line of retreat in danger of being severed by the British fleet. Even more serious, Washington could not prevent the British fleet from moving up the Hudson, because Forts Washington and Constitution, built on northern Manhattan and on the Jersey shore opposite in the hope of closing the river, were weak and incomplete. Had General Howe chosen to land a large flanking force on the northern end of Manhattan, Washington's army would have been lucky, even by the most rapid evacuation of the city, to make its escape across the Harlem River to the mainland.

In short, New York confronted General Howe with great military opportunities. Washington's army was far inferior to his own in quality, if not in numbers. Late in August the American General had over 33,000 men on paper, but two-thirds of these were militia, largely untrained and unreliable, in service for varying periods. Moreover, Washington's paper returns were well above the actual number of men ready for duty, perhaps no more than twenty thousand. Happily for the patriots, Howe was far less venturesome than his old commander at Quebec, James Wolfe, from whom he seems to have learned very little of the art of war. On August 22 he put his redcoats in motion, not up the Hudson, but toward the Americans on Long Island. Twenty thousand royal troops, with forty pieces of artillery, landed in perfect order at Gravesend Bay. During the night of August 26, having secured information regarding the American forces and entrenchments on the island, Howe sent his British and German regulars into action. He knew that the Americans had built a formidable fortified line on Brooklyn Heights between Wallabout and Gowanus bays, also that the major part of the patriot troops on the island were not within that line. Most of the eight thousand patriots stationed on the island by Washington had been placed along a ridge to the southward, in order to delay the expected British advance against the American fortifications. Moreover, because of shortcomings among the American commanders, particularly Washington and Israel Putnam, the left wing of the patriots on the ridge rested on thin air. Thanks to Tory informants Howe knew that the Jamaica Pass, by which the British

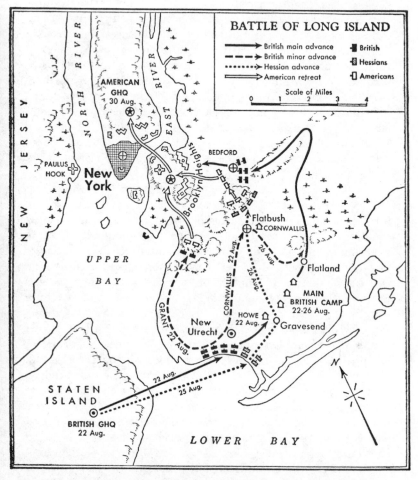

BATTLE OF LONG ISLAND

→ British main advance
⇢ British minor advance
⇢ Hessian advance
⇒ American retreat

■ British
◼ Hessians
◻ Americans

Scale of Miles

0   1   2   3   4

NORTH RIVER

EAST RIVER

NEW JERSEY

N

AMERICAN GHQ 30 Aug.

PAULUS HOOK

New York

Brooklyn Heights

BEDFORD

Flatbush

CORNWALLIS

UPPER BAY

Flatland

CORNWALLIS 22 Aug.

26 Aug.

GRANT 22 Aug.

New Utrecht

HOWE 22 Aug.

MAIN BRITISH CAMP 22-26 Aug.

Gravesend

STATEN ISLAND

BRITISH GHQ 22 Aug.

22 Aug.

25 Aug.

N

LOWER BAY

could march around that flank, was unprotected and unguarded. Howe made his battle plan accordingly. A detachment under General James Grant, who now had an opportunity to prove that the Americans could not fight, moved slowly northward along the shore of New York Bay against the patriot right wing. General

Von Heister deliberately pushed forward a second body against their center. Meanwhile, Howe personally led ten thousand men through the pass under cover of the night. In the morning of the twenty-seventh the valiant but incompetent Putnam, who had assumed the command on Long Island only a few days earlier, learned that his troops were being attacked, suddenly and almost simultaneously, in front and on the unprotected left flank. It was too late for Putnam to ward off the British blow. The American force on the ridge, outflanked and outnumbered, faced annihilation. The American left wing under General John Sullivan managed for a time to hold off Howe, but his defenses collapsed before bayonet charges. On the American right wing Maryland and Delaware Continentals under the Earl of Stirling fought gallantly and then desperately against Grant.[10] At length, after suffering two thousand casualties, the remains of Putnam's detachment found their way back to the entrenchments in their rear. Two American major generals, Sullivan and Stirling, together with a thousand other patriots, were captured by the British. British casualties numbered about three hundred.

Washington himself was at least partly responsible for the miserable choice of position for Putnam's men, and he did not redeem himself when the news of the British attack reached his headquarters on Manhattan. He promptly moved six regiments of reinforcements across the East River and personally assumed command within the patriot lines on Long Island. The reinforcements filed into the American entrenchments and were soon joined by the battle fugitives, who were closely pursued by the British. Both the reinforcements and those whom they were to reinforce were accordingly exposed to capture. The positions of the patriots could have been stormed, and their line of retreat across the East River was exposed to attack by Admiral Howe's ships. In spite of insistent urging from some of his officers, General Howe refused to let them attempt the American works. Giving too great weight to the risks and too little attention to the profits of overwhelming triumph, he adopted the dilatory tactics which were to characterize all his dealings with the patriots.

On the day after the battle Howe began cautious and conven-

[10] Christopher L. Ward, *The Delaware Continentals, 1776–1783* (Wilmington, 1941), pp. 30–41.

tional siege approaches. Almost simultaneously Washington realized the full extent of his peril. That day he actually brought over three more regiments from Manhattan, but one of these was composed of fishermen from Marblehead, a fact which suggests he was considering evacuation. By evening, following a council of war, he definitely decided upon withdrawal across the East River. That night the Marblehead men and others acquainted with watercraft manned numerous small boats and began to ferry militia and Continentals over the river. Rain and a stiff northwest wind made their task at first a difficult one, and it was prolonged until well after dawn. Since the storm and early morning fog hid the movements of the Americans, the British knew nothing about the retreat until it had been completed. Thomas Mifflin, who covered the evacuation with a rear guard, was not even forced to fight in order to execute his assignment. Washington had had the fullest co-operation from the elements, for wind and tide prevented Admiral Howe from entering the East River until the patriots were safely landed.

With his army collected on Manhattan, Washington was on safer ground but was far from secure. The patriots were still exposed to the danger of entrapment, their only feasible route of retreat being across a bridge at Kingsbridge leading to the mainland. Their morale was low, and the militia were departing for home by companies, almost by regiments. Those who remained had no great faith in Washington and his staff. "Would to Heaven General Lee were here is the language of officers and men," wrote a Delaware officer.[11] Strangely enough, although Washington more or less anticipated that Howe would now enter Westchester and strive to pin the Americans against salt water and the British fleet, he loitered for weeks on Manhattan. Fortunately for him, Howe also did some loitering—and when he did move, proved ineffectual.

Meanwhile Admiral Howe, hoping that the recent British triumph had taught the patriots the virtues of appeasement, again tried to enter into negotiations to end the war. He persuaded General Sullivan that he and his brother had larger powers than they had; and Sullivan was freed, with the understanding that he would

[11] George Ryden (ed.), *Letters to and from Caesar Rodney, 1756-1784* (Philadelphia, 1933), p. 112. On September 6 another officer wrote that Lee was "hourly expected, as if from heaven, with a legion of flaming swordsmen." Peter Force (ed.), *American Archives* . . . , Fifth Series (3 vols., Washington, 1848-53), II, 197.

go to Philadelphia to relay the news to the Continental Congress. Sullivan did so. The Congress, less impressionable than the General, appointed a committee to visit the Admiral and to discover what he had to say. The Congress made it clear that the Congress, and the Congress alone, must be recognized as officially representing the patriots. Franklin, John Adams, and Edward Rutledge accordingly conversed with the naval officer on Staten Island on September 11. The Admiral expressed a fervent desire for peace and hinted at gracious acts which might be expected from Britain when the rebels should submit. He limned a lovely picture, but he was forced to declare that he could not even deal officially with the Congress. The patriot leaders were not deceived by the suggestion that American grievances would be removed by the British government if the patriots would only lay down their weapons. They told the Viscount that they would settle for nothing less than independence, and the conference quickly adjourned.

While the Admiral conferred, General Howe made ready for battle. In anticipation of his next movement, the talented Nathanael Greene urged that New York City be evacuated and burned. If this advice, offered to Washington on September 5,[12] called for heroic measures, it was also sound. Greene would yield to the British a valuable position the Americans could not hold but would deprive them of cover for themselves and their supplies. Joseph Reed, Washington's Adjutant General, supported Greene. However, some of Washington's officers opposed the use of such strong medicine, and the Continental Congress had instructed the commander in chief not to injure the city—on the naïve assumption that, if lost to the British, it would be regained before much time had passed.[13] On September 12, Washington decided to withdraw from the city and to concentrate in the northern reaches of Manhattan. Before he could complete his arrangements, Howe took up the pursuit. Two large bodies of royal troops, protected by a naval bombardment, landed on Manhattan at Kip's Bay and Turtle Bay on the fifteenth. Overcoming feeble opposition, they pushed forward rapidly to the west and north. Patriot detachments

[12] George W. Greene, *Life of Nathanael Greene* (3 vols., New York, 1871), I, 212–213.
[13] Worthington C. Ford *et al.* (eds.), *Journals of the Continental Congress, 1774–1789* (34 vols., Washington, 1904–37), V, 733.

stationed to the south and west of Kip's Bay were in grave danger
of being surrounded, but they managed to evade the British thrusts.
Washington now took up position on Harlem Heights. The American retreat, "disgraceful and dastardly," as Washington called it,
had really been a rout. The next day a skirmish between a patriot
scouting party and the British advance guard brought on a series
of small encounters. These, known collectively as the battle of
Harlem Heights, were not decisive. However, the Americans fought
bravely and held their own.

In possession of New York City Howe remained cautious. He
occupied himself for four long weeks in building works to protect
the town, thenceforth to be the principal base for British operations
in North America. Meanwhile, his army stood still. Howe had concluded as early as September 2, immediately after his smashing
victory on Long Island, that the rebellion could not be crushed in
1776.[14] That conclusion should have led him to another: that he
should move as fast as he could during the year in order to complete
his task by 1777. Instead, he allowed day after day of good campaigning weather to pass while he threw up defenses against a weak
and retreating enemy. Washington, still in grave peril, also made
poor use of the early autumn. He remained of the opinion that he
could fight on Manhattan without too great risk [15]—until the British
troops were once more in motion. He strengthened his position on
Harlem Heights and tried to buttress it by completing Forts Washington and Constitution on the opposite sides of the Hudson. He
still hoped to close the Hudson to the British fleet through these
forts, and chains, booms, and sunken ships strung across the river
between them.

On October 9 the British resumed the offensive. Admiral Howe

---

[14] British Captain W. Glanville Evelyn, ignorant of Howe's thought, wrote on
September 24: ". . . We expect that another grand stroke will take place
before winter, which will not only clear this island of the rebels, but probably
disperse the great numbers they have collected; which, once done, the game is
up. . . ." D. G. Scull (ed.), *Memoir and Letters of Captain W. Glanville
Evelyn . . . 1774–1776* (Oxford, 1879), p. 86.

[15] John C. Fitzpatrick (ed.), *The Writings of George Washington* (39 vols.,
Washington, 1931–44), VI, 197. On September 25 General Henry Knox asserted that the army was safe on Manhattan, that it could have held New York
had the Jamaica Pass been protected! Knox to John Adams, Sept. 25, 1776,
Proceedings of the American Antiquarian Society, New Series, LVI (1946),
217.

sent out frigates which pushed their way up the Hudson through the patriot obstructions, despite cannon fire from the American forts. Three days later the younger Howe, having made New York City secure, finally began to move into Westchester. Apparently his intention was merely to force Washington to leave Manhattan, but it was not unlikely that he would try to exploit the opportunity to pin the patriots against the Hudson. The American army's only feasible line of retreat, to the northeast, was immediately endangered. However, leading a large force through the East River and Long Island Sound, Howe landed his men at Throg's Neck rather than at a more suitable location to the eastward. Throg's Neck turned out to be a peninsula connected with the mainland only by a narrow causeway, an unpleasant surprise for the British General. Learning of the British advance, Washington sent a few riflemen and then two regiments to delay it. These defended the causeway, prevented the British from fording, and persuaded Howe to alter his plan. He then led his men farther up the Sound and landed near New Rochelle. The patriot commander had not ordered a general retreat when he was informed of Howe's maneuver, but the fumbling and ill luck of the British gave him time in which to reconsider his tactics. Charles Lee, who had been ordered to rejoin the main American army after his victory at Charleston and who had just appeared in the American camp, joined by other members of Washington's staff, strongly urged that the army fall back to the northeast to escape encirclement.[16] Washington took this advice, and the major part of the patriot forces, about fourteen thousand men, trudged off to White Plains, arriving just ahead of the British. The patriot army had slipped out of a cul-de-sac, and Howe had lost a splendid opportunity. Washington dug in near White Plains, occupying fairly strong ground. Howe brought up his men and on October 28 assailed a part of the American right wing on Chatterton's Hill. After stiff fighting, he carried the hill, but achieved nothing. Waiting briefly for reinforcements whose arrival brought his numbers up to twenty thousand, he prepared once more to advance. Then a heavy rain prevented action. Before he could attack, Washington prudently withdrew to an easily

[16] See J. R. Alden, *General Charles Lee: Traitor or Patriot?* (Baton Rouge, 1951), pp. 140–142, and references cited therein.

defensible position at North Castle. Perhaps Howe had again been too slow.

By November 1 the prospect had brightened for the patriots. Washington had eluded Howe and managed to maintain a fairly strong army in the field. Winter was coming on. Moreover, all was well on the New York-Canadian frontier. The northern American army, under the command of Schuyler and Gates, had a relatively easy time after its retreat from Canada. It dug in at Ticonderoga and prepared for a hard struggle. Guy Carleton and John Burgoyne pushed southward in the summer and early fall but could not move against Ticonderoga until they obtained control of the waters of Lake Champlain. Accordingly, Carleton constructed a fleet for service there. However, Benedict Arnold, his health restored, simultaneously built an American squadron. Many weeks passed while the carpenters plied their tools, and Carleton's ships did not sail down the lake until October. Outmanned and outgunned, Arnold nevertheless led out a "mosquito fleet" to battle. He fought skillfully, but was decisively defeated on October 11 and again on October 13 off Valcour Island. Although Arnold himself and most of his men escaped, his little navy was almost destroyed. Nevertheless, Arnold was the real victor, for his enterprise and bravery had effectively delayed the British. The cautious Carleton, in view of the lateness of the season, decided not to venture forward against Ticonderoga. The British did not try to reach Albany and the lower Hudson from Canada until the following campaign. A junction between Carleton and Howe in 1776 would probably have been fatal to the American cause.

Although all seemed well for the Americans on November 1, the seeds of disaster had been sown. When evacuating Manhattan, Washington had left behind at Fort Washington on the northern end of the island a garrison of almost three thousand men. He had placed another force of 4,500 at Fort Lee [17] across the Hudson. Howe was now between Washington and the fort named in his honor, which had open communication only with its counterpart on the Jersey side. Howe decided to take advantage of this fact, turned his back on Washington, and marched westward. The Virginian quickly concluded that Fort Washington had become the immediate British objective and that it could hardly be defended. He

[17] Fort Constitution had been renamed Fort Lee in October.

promptly warned Greene, who was stationed at Fort Lee and whose jurisdiction included Fort Washington, to abandon the latter post, at the same time instructing him to use his best judgment. Believing that the fort could be held, at least temporarily, without much risk, Greene took no steps toward evacaution to Jersey.

To deal with the awkward situation resulting from Howe's change of front, Washington also took the apparently desperate step of dividing his army. Leaving Charles Lee at North Castle with half of it to ward off a possible British thrust into New England and General William Heath with two thousand men at Peekskill to guard the Hudson, he led the remainder across that river and pushed down its west bank toward Fort Lee. He arrived there on November 13 and conferred with Greene and other officers about the predicament of the garrison across the river. He was inclined to order its immediate withdrawal, but yielded to Greene's insistence that there was no reason to hurry. Greene's bad judgment and Washington's irresolution cost heavily. While they debated, Howe brought up overwhelming numbers to attack the fort. Ill planned and incomplete, it could not resist. Moreover, through information obtained from a deserter who had served in it, Howe was perfectly acquainted with its defects. On November 16, while Washington and Greene looked on helplessly from Fort Lee, British and Hessian troops swarmed up to its outworks, driving its defenders before them. In the afternoon, since there was no chance to make a successful resistance or to slip across the river, Colonel Robert Magaw, the commandant, surrendered. Something like three thousand men with all their equipment and scores of cannon were thus lost. The American cause had suffered a near-catastrophe.[18]

Worse was yet to come. Acting with unaccustomed energy, Howe promptly dispatched Lord Cornwallis and twelve regiments across the Hudson by way of Yonkers. Cornwallis rapidly marched southward down the west bank of the river. The troops available to Washington in Jersey, dispirited and dwindling every day in numbers, could not hope to stand against him. Retreating in confusion, they fled to Newark, abandoning Fort Lee without a struggle.

[18] Responsibility for it must be placed upon Greene and especially upon Washington. Washington tried to put at least part of it upon Congress, and some of his admirers among historians have been misled by his statements. Bernhard Knollenberg, *Washington and the Revolution* . . . (New York, 1940), pp. 129–139.

Immediately after the middle of November Howe was once more faced by great opportunities. He could easily have dealt with Heath at Peekskill and with little trouble could have gained control of the lower Hudson. He could also have sent at the same time a large force into New England with a fair chance of beating down resistance in that area. Alternatively, he could have pursued Washington with vigor into the streets of Philadelphia, into the very laps of the Continental Congressmen, and beyond. He could have struck blows which might have brought the American Revolution to a halt. Howe's brain did not burn with such thoughts. Rather, he was thinking of going into winter quarters, in the conventional way, in an unconventional war. He favored order against celerity, and system against discomfort. It was not in him to push the sword to the hilt if the blade were clouded with frost. Setting aside what he would have called grandiose and dangerous schemes, he proposed instead to make ready for the next campaign. He therefore ordered Cornwallis to drive Washington beyond New Brunswick,[19] in order that a part of the British army could find winter quarters in eastern New Jersey. In addition, with the objective of mounting an expedition into New England in the spring, he made preparations to send a strong detachment to seize and hold Newport as a base. Accordingly Clinton and six thousand men sailed from New York for Rhode Island on December 1, accomplishing their mission with ease.

At Newark Washington believed his situation to be critical. Soon he thought it desperate, for he mistakenly believed the British would not stop short of Philadelphia. He did not know the mind of his opponent. On November 29 advanced British detachments under Cornwallis moved against Newark, and Washington fled to New Brunswick, with his enemies in hot pursuit. As Cornwallis drew near, Washington again withdrew, leaving behind a broken bridge over the Raritan. Stopped momentarily at the bridge, Cornwallis recalled that he had orders not to pursue the patriots beyond that town. Moreover, his men were tired, though hardly so exhausted as Washington's, and he was unnecessarily worried about the detachment under Lee, then crossing the Hudson. Accordingly, he halted to refurbish and to await reinforcements. When he again moved toward the southwest, Washington was forced to retreat across the

[19] Then known as Brunswick.

Delaware. However, the American general, with three thousand men, reached the relative safety of the west bank of the river. Then he assembled all the boats for many miles on both sides of Trenton, making a further advance on the part of Cornwallis difficult. Arriving at the river, Cornwallis decided to go into winter quarters. With Howe's approval he established outposts on the east bank, principally at Bordentown and Trenton, and an advanced base at New Brunswick. Howe fancied that this arrangement was a bit venturesome, inviting American attack, but safe enough nevertheless. The British were calling it quits for 1776.

Not so their opponent, who might well have been content to nurse his wounds and to prepare for battle in the spring. Washington's spirits had sunk low after the disaster at Fort Washington, and they had fallen still further during the subsequent retreat. While hundreds of Jerseymen pledged themselves to be thenceforth loyal to the King, and the Continental Congress prudently retired to Baltimore, his army dwindled away. Nevertheless the Virginian was thinking of taking the offensive, in an attempt to regain control of western New Jersey.[20] He had not yet displayed much of that Fabian genius for which he has been perhaps overpraised; he was now to play in masterly style the part of Metellus. Tom Paine helped to set the stage with the first number of *The Crisis,* which was read to the patriot troops: "These are the times that try men's souls. The summer soldier and the sunshine patriot will, in this crisis, shrink from the service of their country; but he that stands it *now,* deserves the love and thanks of man and woman."

Early in December Washington called for assistance from the northern patriot army, and twelve hundred troops marched southward from Albany to join him. He sent urgent appeals to Charles Lee to bring his men over the Hudson and across northern New Jersey. After some delay, probably necessary, Lee reached the neighborhood of Morristown on December 5. There he lingered for a week in the hope of striking a blow against Cornwallis' exposed line of communications, although Washington entreated him to proceed to the Delaware with all speed. On December 13, after having ordered the 2,700 men in his command to march toward the river, Lee himself was surprised and captured by a scouting party

[20] *Writings of Washington,* VI, 367–368.

of British cavalry at Basking Ridge.[21] However, John Sullivan, again in active service, assumed Lee's duties and rapidly marched into Pennsylvania. Washington also was strengthened in December by two thousand militiamen who were raised in Philadelphia and sent forward by Thomas Mifflin.

On December 20 Washington had above six thousand men available for duty, while in the vicinity of Morristown New Jersey militia

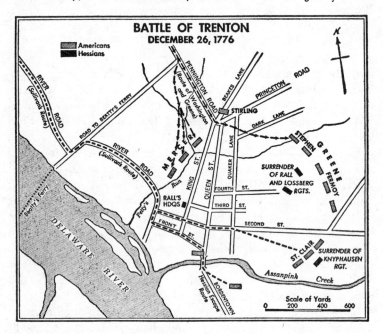

BATTLE OF TRENTON
DECEMBER 26, 1776

were assembling. The patriot commander felt sufficiently strong to attempt a series of surprise attacks against the British outposts along the Delaware.[22] Shortly afterward his arrangements were completed. Washington himself proposed to lead 2,400 men across the river at a ferry above Trenton in the night of December 25 and to attack its garrison, comprising fifteen hundred men, mostly Hessians, under Colonel Rall, near dawn of the twenty-sixth. His

[21] At the time many patriots thought the capture of Lee to be another very heavy loss. See Alden, *Lee,* pp. 159–160.

[22] On December 20 Washington even countermanded an earlier order to General William Heath to bring on reinforcements from Peekskill. *Ibid.,* p. 407.

plan was to move against it from the east and southeast. Meanwhile General James Ewing and a body of Pennsylvania militia were to pass the river below Trenton. Ewing was to prevent the garrison from fleeing southward toward Bordentown, where the Hessian Colonel Count Von Donop and two thousand more German troops had their headquarters. He was also to fend off Donop should he attempt to come to Rall's assistance. A further blow against Donop was to be struck by Colonel John Cadwalader, who was to cross the Delaware at Bristol with more Pennsylvania militia and to move toward Bordentown. If Trenton fell, the Americans were to converge on Donop with the help of a detachment of militia moving forward from Philadelphia under orders from Putnam, then military governor of that town.

It was a daring and splendid plan, and it was brilliantly executed, in part. Ewing and Cadwalader failed to move over the river, finding the cold and floating ice in the stream insuperable obstacles. However, the militia sent out by Putnam caught the attention of Donop, and he marched off from Bordentown to the southward, away from Trenton, in a vain effort to catch them. Rall was thus left without support. Washington carried out his own assignment perfectly. He managed to traverse the river, and his ragged men suddenly moved into Trenton in two columns at frigid dawn. Rall had been ordered to build fortifications against just such a contingency, but had failed to do so; he had received a warning that the Americans would attack him and he had ignored it. The appearance of the patriots so soon after the celebration of a German Christmas was for him untimely and unexpected.[23] He attempted to organize resistance, but it was too late. After brief fighting, in which the patriot losses were exceedingly small, five hundred royal troops fled toward Bordentown. The remainder were forced to surrender, among them Rall, mortally wounded. The Hessians who hastened off to Bordentown alarmed Donop, and he retreated toward Amboy.

On December 26 Cadwalader also reached the Jersey side of the

[23] The patriot soldier John Greenwood, who fought at Trenton, according to his recollections did not see "even a solitary drunken soldier belonging to the enemy." Isaac J. Greenwood (ed.), *The Revolutionary Services of John Greenwood* . . . (New York, 1922), p. 37. It seems likely, however, that the Hessians were in poor shape for battle because of libations during the preceding night.

Delaware and occupied Donop's headquarters. Some of Washington's generals were then in favor of further ventures, but the commander in chief, anticipating that the British would come up in force from New Brunswick, cautiously withdrew from Trenton across the Delaware. He might well have been content with his achievement, and prudence dictated that he should undertake no further offensive measures. However, Washington changed his mind and resumed the aggressive in the hope of striking further at the British detachments. Again pushing through the ice with great difficulty, on December 30 and 31, the Virginian reoccupied Trenton and collected there about five thousand men, including Cadwalader's force. His rashness almost cost him dear. Learning of Rall's defeat and capture, Cornwallis, who had gone off to New York, hurried forward from that town, collecting men as he went. On January 2 he entered Trenton with six thousand British regulars, and more were just behind him. As Cornwallis advanced, Washington withdrew to the southward behind Assanpink Creek. The Americans were now in great peril. They could not hope to retreat across the Delaware, for Cornwallis would hardly let Washington traverse that stream as he had traversed the East River. A flight southward along the left bank of the river would probably be equally in vain. It was not likely that they could hold their own in battle. Happily, the British commander, after unsuccessful preliminary attacks, decided to wait until the following day to strike a decisive blow. Before midnight Washington and his generals found the answer to their difficult problem. Leaving their campfires burning to deceive the British, the patriots quietly filed off in the darkness to the south and east, marched around the British army by a side road, and arrived at Princeton in the morning.

Cornwallis learned of Washington's maneuver when he heard firing in the direction of Princeton. He retraced his steps toward that town, too late to achieve anything. For a few moments the patriots were in serious trouble at Princeton, where they encountered three British regiments moving toward Trenton. One of these, under Lieutenant Colonel Charles Mawhood, made a bayonet attack which disrupted the American van. However, Washington personally restored order and finally drove off the redcoats.[24]

[24] For detailed accounts of the Trenton-Princeton operations see William S. Stryker, *Battles of Trenton and Princeton* (Boston, 1898); Leonard Lundin,

Washington momentarily considered making a further advance against the British base at New Brunswick, but his men were tired, and Cornwallis was at his heels. Instead he marched on to the hills of Morristown, where he could easily defend himself, could establish comfortable winter quarters, and could be on the flank of the British line of communications. Howe could not readily attack, nor could he maintain his advanced posts. Accordingly he withdrew his forces to New Brunswick and other stations to the eastward of that town.

The campaign of 1776 had ended, somewhat tardily according to the calendar. The main American army was still in being. After enduring a series of defeats, it had struck back in startling fashion and had reconquered West Jersey. The little victories of Trenton and Princeton, and the good fortune, splendid courage, and brilliant maneuvers of Washington, had infused new vigor into the patriot cause.[25] Howe had been proffered several chances to strike heavy, even mortal blows, and he had refused to seize them. He had lost face, and he was less confident of ultimate triumph than he was at the beginning of the campaign.

Cockpit of the Revolution: The War for Independence in New Jersey (Princeton, 1940), pp. 157–217; Alfred H. Bill, *The Campaign of Princeton, 1776–1777* (Princeton, 1948).

[25] The young Englishman Nicholas Cresswell wrote in his journal regarding the effects of Trenton and Princeton upon the patriots: "A few days ago they had given up the cause for lost. Their late successes have turned the scale and now they are all liberty mad again. . . . They have recovered their panic and it will not be an easy matter to throw them into that confusion again." *The Journal of Nicholas Cresswell, 1774–1777* (New York, 1924), pp. 178–180.

CHAPTER 8

Philadelphia Takes Howe

THE CAMPAIGN of 1777 opened auspiciously for the British. However, because of overconfidence, divided command, and poor communications, they blundered in their strategy. Burgoyne and William Howe, especially the latter, made tactical errors, and the patriots fought well. The result was disastrous for Britain. At the end of the year the independence of the United States seemed almost assured.

On November 30, 1776, immediately after the fall of Fort Washington, when Washington's army was threatening to disintegrate, Howe, now Sir William because of his triumph on Long Island, wrote to Lord George Germain recommending a plan for the next campaign. The new knight was not especially optimistic concerning the possibilities for the year 1777. He proposed to continue with the design he had developed upon taking command. He proposed placing eight thousand men in Jersey to hold off Washington, five thousand at New York City, and perhaps two thousand at Newport to protect his bases; he would send ten thousand up the Hudson to meet at Albany the Canadian army, which he expected to march southward, and to join forces at that town some time in September; and he would put another ten thousand in motion against Boston from Rhode Island. New England cut off and cut down, he would parade in power against Philadelphia in the fall, traverse Virginia in early winter, and stride through the far South in time to see the magnolias blossom in 1778. In a word, he would accomplish great deeds provided he had greater strength. His army had dwindled during 1776. He told Germain he would need fifteen thousand additional troops, knowing full well that the Colonial Secretary would be hard put to supply them. Perhaps more Germans and some Russians could be secured, the general suggested.

Howe could hardly have sent a better plan across the Atlantic. Moreover, its execution did not really entail the large reinforcements he sought. New England might have been reduced. Possibly Howe could have held the Yankees in subjection while staging a triumphant march toward Carolina, with or without the desired new contingents of Germans and Russians. But he failed to insist upon the execution of these measures. Only three weeks later he sent across the water to London an alternative plan containing startlingly different proposals.

Immediately before Trenton, when the fortunes of the patriots had reached their nadir, the British General placed in the mail a suggestion that an invasion of Pennsylvania be the principal business of his army in the next campaign. Convinced that patriot morale was rapidly deteriorating, that there was much affection for Britain in the City of Brotherly Love and its vicinity, and that the Pennsylvania Tories, once relieved of the incubus of the Continental army, could dominate their patriot neighbors, Howe drew for Germain a new design. On the assumption that he might have no more than nineteen thousand effectives, he would lead ten thousand into Pennsylvania; two thousand would remain in garrison on Rhode Island and double that number within the lines at New York City; and three thousand would be stationed on the lower Hudson, in part to serve as additional protection for the main British base, in part to "facilitate in some degree the approach of the army from Canada." [1]

Did Howe expect that this new plan would win the war in 1777, or early in 1778? Perhaps he did, for he sent off his second proposal only five days before Washington routed the Hessians at Trenton. Howe was unable to estimate patriot strength with any assurance, nor could he anticipate with any degree of accuracy what help he would get from England. Hence, he was probably trying to propose an alternative plan for employing nineteen thousand men rather than the full quota of 35,000 previously demanded. In any case, it

[1] Troyer S. Anderson, *The Command of the Howe Brothers during the American Revolution* (New York and London, 1936), pp. 218–220.

is obvious that his mind was unsettled, for he asked Germain for instructions while at the same time he indicated that his own operations might be dictated by "the exigencies of the moment." Moreover, it is apparent that in his thought there was a seed of disaster for Britain. The Canadian army advancing southward through the Lake Champlain-Hudson trough, although it might achieve little, would not be in great danger if the bulk of Howe's forces were moving on the Hudson and in New England. But this second plan would place only three thousand troops on the lower Hudson to "facilitate in some degree" the advance of their comrades from the north. The three thousand might, indeed, be of assistance to the Canadian army. Nevertheless, it was likely that the Canadian expedition would encounter difficulties in the northern wilderness, both because of transport troubles and because of American opposition in the woods of New York and Vermont. Howe should have postulated that the New Englanders, Yorkers, and Green Mountain Boys, relieved of fear of an advance in force on his part, might give the Canadian army a very bad time of it. He certainly knew that Montgomery's army traversing that same trough had suffered cruelly before reaching Montreal, and therefore that the geographical obstacles in the path of the Canadian army were formidable. Howe was giving insufficient attention to the fortunes of that army, which, to be sure, was not under his command.

When Sir William's first plan reached the imperial capital, it created something like consternation, since no one knew where to obtain fifteen thousand recruits. Moreover, Germain could not believe so many were needed, for he fancied that the end of the war was near. He therefore refused to sanction the plan. On March 3, however, he sent off to Howe his endorsement of the General's second plan.[2] Several weeks afterward he arranged to forward to Howe a copy of instructions to Sir Guy Carleton which informed Howe that the Canadian army would march toward Albany. He failed to insist that Howe take specific measures to co-operate with that army.[3] In addition, he was able to send only 2,900 troops to

[2] Germain to Howe, Mar. 3, 1777, Colonial Office, 5/94, Library of Congress transcripts.

[3] The sending of the instructions is mentioned in Germain to Howe, Apr. 19, 1777, *ibid.* See also *Royal Historical Manuscripts Commission, Report on Manuscripts in Various Collections,* VI (1909), 277.

New York to strengthen Howe, and 1,700 of these did not arrive until September.

Consenting to Howe's second plan, Germain, by that time aware of the resurgence of the patriot army under Washington, gave, like Howe, too little thought to the dangers which an advancing Canadian army would face with Howe marching the bulk of his forces to Philadelphia. Meantime, glory-seeker John Burgoyne had hastened back to England as soon as the campaign of 1776 had ended in Canada. Late in February he submitted to Germain a plan for a three-pronged attack to isolate New England. Under this plan he himself was to lead an army from Canada to the upper Hudson, an auxiliary force was to push eastward from Oswego, these forces to meet at Albany. This plan was also approved. Why did the King and the Cabinet allow themselves to be persuaded by Burgoyne? To be sure, such a movement had long been considered and approved—with Howe advancing northward in major strength. Germain probably calculated that the patriots could not withstand Burgoyne, and that the three thousand men Howe proposed to place on the lower Hudson would assure the safety of Burgoyne's army, should it need support as it drew near Albany. Overswayed, perhaps, by the assurances of the too-confident Burgoyne, Germain underestimated the problem of transport from Montreal to Albany and the great tactical advantages possessed in the trough by the defenders. It is hardly to be doubted that he also erred in appraising patriot power on the middle Hudson. Even so, had Howe carried out his second plan, had he sent three thousand regulars toward Albany, Burgoyne might have escaped disaster.

If Germain undervalued the peril to which the Canadian army would be exposed, he blundered even more seriously in measuring the benefits which would result from the execution of the plans of Howe and Burgoyne to which he vouchsafed his approval. Like Howe, he expected that the Tories of Pennsylvania would rise in numbers at the General's appearance and that they would be able to hold the patriot element in check, thus leaving the General free to move on to further conquests. Yet there was grave doubt that Howe could achieve anything decisive by driving into Philadelphia, if Washington's army remained in being as a fighting machine. It was also doubtful that British control of the Lake Champlain-Hudson line would mortally hurt the patriots. It has often been said that such control would have caused an immediate patriot collapse. However, the mere severance of communications between New England and the states to the southwest would have left the Yankees unconquered and defiant still. In time the separation of the New Englanders from their fellow Americans would have weakened the patriots seriously—but could Britain afford the time? And would it have been easy for the British to hold a line along the Hudson against American attempts to re-establish their communications, simultaneously carrying on major operations elsewhere? It might also be argued that there was no point in sending an army south-ward from Canada in order to cut the states in two. Patriot trans-port routes ran across the lower Hudson, not through Ticonderoga or Albany. A British advance in force from New York City up the river toward Albany would have been a cheaper and less dangerous way to achieve Germain's purpose.

Commonly it is asserted that the year 1777 was above all others critical for the patriots. Yet American military power, although the number of enlisted Continentals had diminished, was greater than in the preceding year, while the British were actually weaker. Had British strategy been better calculated, the patriots would have been subjected to a harsh test. It is not at all certain that the most effec-tive use of their might by the British would have brought them a decisive or even a favorable result. Through defective planning—and in some degree faulty execution—they failed dismally, and lost the war. In retrospect it would seem that the patriot cause was in direst peril in November and December of 1776, and that Trenton marked a momentous turning point, perhaps more significant than the change in the course of events which followed upon the British capitulation at Saratoga and the ultimate failure of Howe in Penn-sylvania.

Before Germain's letter of March 3 giving assent to Howe's second plan reached New York City, the British General sent off to London, early in April, *a third plan*. He now intended to leave in the New York City and Rhode Island bases 4,700 and 2,400 men respectively; he would place under Governor William Tryon three thousand Tories in the vicinity of his principal base, these to operate "upon the Hudsons River, or to enter Connecticut as circumstances may point out"; and he would personally lead eleven thousand regulars to Philadelphia, not across New Jersey, but by sea to the

head of Chesapeake Bay and thence northward by land.[4] In consequence, Howe did *not* order three thousand regulars to act offensively on the lower Hudson to "facilitate" the approach of Burgoyne, as Germain expected he would do. And he did *not* even put
the Tories in motion, although he promised Carleton—and Burgoyne—that he would try to do so.[5] Moreover, Howe and the main
British army were too far distant to help Burgoyne when he was
trapped in the northern wilderness. Howe erred seriously, and he is
not to be excused because he promptly wrote to Carleton to warn
the Canadian governor—and Burgoyne—of the change in his intentions. Neither could he offer in extenuation his later assurance to
Carleton that he would come to the aid of the Canadian army,
should Washington move toward Albany. Nor is he to be held
blameless because he, not he alone, but Germain, Carleton, and
Burgoyne as well, mistakenly believed the Canadian army could
advance independently in relative safety.

When Germain received Sir William's third plan, he apparently
realized that Burgoyne would receive little, if any, support from
Howe. He seems to have had some misgivings. On May 18 he
signed a dispatch which urged Howe to finish his business in Pennsylvania in time to "co-operate with the army ordered to proceed
from Canada. . . ."[6] The letter lingered in passage almost three

[4] Howe to Germain, Apr. 2, 1777, *ibid.*

[5] Howe to Carleton, Apr. 5, 1777 (confidential), *ibid.*

[6] Germain to Howe, May 18, 1777, *ibid.* The first detailed and sound
analysis of British strategy in 1777 was offered by Anderson in *Howe Brothers,*
chaps. 12 and 14. Professor Anderson disproved the assertions (1) that Howe
was ordered in the spring to lead his army up the Hudson and (2) that an
order to that effect was prepared but not sent from England because of
Germain's negligence. A careful and independent study of British planning
in Gerald S. Brown, "The Policy of Lord George Germain Toward the American Revolution, 1775–1778" (Ph.D. thesis, University of Minnesota, 1948),
pp. 165–219, reaches the same conclusions. To the weighty evidence adduced
by these writers in support of the thesis that Germain sent out to Howe in
April all the instructions he desired to transmit should be added rather conclusive statements from a document which apparently escaped their notice. In
1777 both Alexander Wedderburn and William Eden were in position to know
the business of the Colonial Office, and the following passages in a letter from
Wedderburn to Eden of September 10 are therefore illuminating. "That both
armys will succeed in some enterprizes I have no doubt, but while they act
without concert & the operations of the campaign are conducted without any
apparent plan, I doubt the efficacy of our successes to subdue the rebellion. . . . But surely the want of authority to direct the conduct of a general
[Howe] if the indecision of his own judgment makes it necessary to direct him;

months, possibly because it was not promptly mailed, and did not reach Howe until August 16, when that general was at sea en route to Philadelphia. He could not then alter his arrangements. He could not finish his task in Pennsylvania in time to send a force to meet Burgoyne. Nor could he immediately detach a part of his army and send it back to New York, for he needed all the strength he had to achieve his own objective. He left Burgoyne to his fate, assuming that Burgoyne could take care of himself.

The British strategy for the campaign was sadly defective. In considerable part the difficulty of communication across the Atlantic explains its faults. Another cause was the existence after the recall of Gage of a divided command in America. Had Canada been placed under Howe, he could hardly have failed to recommend a more profitable distribution of the British troops, and Burgoyne, the inveterate seeker of fame, would have had less opportunity recklessly to cajole for an independent status. Burgoyne and Germain must share responsibility for the British debacle. Yet Howe was perhaps more at fault than they. His shifting from plan to plan made a coherent British effort impossible. Moreover, he erred in substituting an expedition by sea into Pennsylvania for a concentrated assault upon New England. Why he did so cannot now be surely ascertained. It is likely that he was as jealous of Burgoyne as Burgoyne was of him and that he was not eager to do anything which might assist his junior up the ladder of military renown. He was probably misguided by Tories who assured him that the Pennsylvania Loyalists would flock to the royal standard when he should appear on the Delaware. He was not duped by Charles Lee, who as a prisoner proffered some dubious advice to Howe and who afterward claimed that he had hoodwinked the British General into taking the sea route to Philadelphia.

Although historians have commonly agreed that the year 1777 was that of greatest peril to the patriot cause, Howe did not expect after Trenton and Princeton to annihilate his opponents in one campaign. He hoped only that the close of 1777 would find Wash-

---

the giving unlimited power without any confidence; the rewarding misconduct are errors in systems that leave us no right to blame fortune." Benjamin Franklin Stevens (ed.), *Facsimiles of Manuscripts in European Archives Relating to America* . . . (26 vols., London, 1889–95), XVIII, No. 1682. If there was neglect concerning a dispatch, it was in connection with that of May 18.

ington's army weak, and New York, New Jersey, and Pennsylvania under British domination. He did not intend to attack Washington's army at all costs. He proposed to proceed slowly and methodically, taking as few chances as possible, for he knew that one major defeat might be fatal to British power in America. Washington's army, on the contrary, could be beaten once and again, and continue still to fight. Even so, Howe would have been wise to risk heavily to secure quick victory. He knew, or should have known, that he did not have then and would not have later, even with the help of the Tories, enough men to overrun area after area while simultaneously policing his conquests. But the Howe of 1777 was the Howe of 1776.

After making another vain effort in the early months of the year to open peace negotiations with members of Congress, this time through Charles Lee as intermediary, Howe made ready at his characteristically leisurely pace to take the field, and waited until June to begin operations, by which time he had about eighteen thousand men available for offensive action.

While Howe pondered plans for the campaign, the American army experienced a new birth. In the fall of 1776 the Continental Congress proposed to raise a vast force of 75,000 men, to be enlisted for three years or the duration of the conflict. It promised every recruit a bounty of twenty dollars and one hundred acres of land at the end of his period of service. Various states offered additional bounties. Fewer than a thousand of the Continentals promptly re-enlisted under the new system. Moreover, no new recruits joined Washington until spring, partly because some of the states offered better pay to soldiers for service at home than Congress gave, partly because of the dangers and especially the hardships to which Washington's Continentals were exposed during the campaign of 1776 and the following winter. The men at Morristown had suffered because of inadequate clothing, inconstant food supplies, and a pitiful medical department. Their lot was far more distressing than that of the British and Hessians at New Brunswick and Amboy, who also suffered. Washington was forced to commandeer food and clothing from New Jersey civilians. Men deserted him rather than joined him in the first months of 1777. But something like one thousand Continentals clung faithfully to him, and a larger number of militia helped to preserve the semblance of an army. Then came milder weather, and about eight thousand Continental recruits. By the end of May, Washington had on his rolls nine thousand regulars. Thereafter, although Congress was able to raise in all only 34,000 men in 1777, Washington's forces never lacked a hard core of veterans.

In the late spring of 1777 Washington had only nine thousand Continentals, but they were well-equipped Continentals. In addition, he could call upon the services of additional thousands of decently outfitted militia. Formerly the patriots had been forced largely to produce their own equipment or to seize it from the British. They had managed to produce in some quantity. The army had made valuable captures on land; the Continental navy and patriot privateers had brought into port many British vessels carrying military stores. The patriots had also managed to purchase supplies from French and Dutch merchants. Yet these sources had been uncertain, and the patriots had often lacked powder, clothing, blankets, and even guns. But now secret aid from France and Spain, sent through the agency of the charming Caron de Beaumarchais, had begun to arrive. In March the *Mercury* from Nantes landed in New Hampshire twelve thousand muskets, fifty tons of powder, and large quantities of cloth, caps, shoes, stockings, and blankets. Shortly afterward, the *Amphitrite* reached New Hampshire from Havre,[7] bringing ten thousand more muskets, more powder, cannon, tents, and other paraphernalia. During most of the ensuing campaign the men with Washington, seldom handsomely uniformed, were neither naked nor poorly armed.

Toward the end of May Washington led his new army from Morristown to a strong position on the heights of Middlebrook, where he hoped to thwart an advance by Howe toward the Delaware and Philadelphia. Howe was about to evacuate his troops from New Jersey preparatory to embarkation. Apparently his transports were not ready, for he now led his men forward from New Brunswick, hoping to entice his antagonist into battle upon conditions favorable to himself. Washington would not be snared. Sir William then prepared a second trap, withdrawing his troops hurriedly toward New York as if in disorderly retreat. The Virginian almost took the bait, left his prepared position, and followed in pursuit. Howe then suddenly struck at the left flank of the patriots

[7] Francis Wharton (ed.), *Revolutionary Diplomatic Correspondence of the United States* (6 vols., Washington, 1889), II, 314, 328.

with the intention of forcing them to do battle in relatively open country. In the nick of time Washington managed to slip back to Middlebrook. A disappointed Howe then withdrew to New York at the close of June.

But still Howe delayed embarking for Philadelphia. The great amphibious operation which he and his brother were about to undertake required much preparation. Moreover, Howe may have considered a last-minute change of plan. Except for Cornwallis, James Grant, and the Admiral, British officers in New York were bitterly protesting against the scheme. Henry Clinton (now Sir Henry), assigned to command at the British base, was especially forthright in opposition, insisting that Howe carry out his first plan. Howe may also have waited until he could learn what Burgoyne was doing and what Washington proposed to do. At length he was informed that Burgoyne was optimistically advancing and that Washington did not intend to go to the aid of the northern patriot army, but rather to defend Philadelphia. Finally, on July 23 the British armada of more than 260 ships carrying about fifteen thousand troops and all their baggage set sail. Before departing Howe assigned seven thousand men, almost half of whom were Tories, to Clinton for the defense of New York City. He did *not* instruct Clinton to assist Burgoyne.[8] So far as Howe was concerned, neither regulars nor Tories would take the offensive in the lower Hudson Valley. Clinton believed, not without reason, that the troops given to him were hardly more than enough to assure the safety of New York City. He was to conduct what he afterward called a "d—d starved deffencive." [9]

Spring and a part of the summer had gone before the British warships and transports sailed down the New Jersey coast, and summer was almost at an end before Howe's army again set foot on shore. The fleet reached Delaware Bay on July 29 and moved up toward the Delaware River as if to discharge its cargo. Sir William seems to have considered such a step seriously, probably in order more quickly to pursue Washington in the event that his adversary had started for Albany. He discovered, however, that Washington was near Wilmington. Besides, the Americans had erected defenses

[8] Howe to Germain, July 7, 1777, Colonial Office, 5/94, Library of Congress transcripts.

[9] Quoted by Jane Clark in *American Historical Review*, XXXV (1930), 554.

in the river. The fleet therefore turned about and made its way into the Chesapeake as originally planned. At the head of that bay the expedition began to disembark on August 25, an army weary and weak from a voyage in cramped quarters and seasonal heat. A few days later it began to push northward toward Philadelphia, and promptly found itself face to face with Washington's forces amounting to some eleven thousand men. Howe has been criticized for this move on the ground that the distance between his landing place and the Quaker City was ten miles longer than that between Philadelphia and New Brunswick. In justice to Howe it should be pointed out that by taking the longer route he avoided the difficulty and danger of crossing the Delaware in the teeth of the main American army. In any case, Howe now had an opportunity to retrieve his strategic errors by smashing Washington on the battlefield.

While the British fleet tossed about on the waters between New York Harbor and Delaware Bay, Washington was sorely puzzled. He was convinced that Sir William intended to move up the Hudson. He could hardly believe that the British general was en route to Pennsylvania, and he even sent a part of his troops toward Albany, in the belief that the British were trying to deceive him. Nevertheless, he moved the bulk of his men toward Philadelphia, suffering great anxiety lest he had erred in his arrangements.[10] When he learned that the British fleet was off the Delaware Capes, he concentrated near Wilmington. When the British sailed out into the Atlantic again, he and his generals concluded that the Howes intended to attack Charleston. He was "compeld to wander about the country like the Arabs in search of corn." [11] Receiving news of the British landing, he decided to fight rather than to keep out of reach. Washington refused to abandon Philadelphia to his enemies without a struggle.

After some preliminary skirmishing, Howe's army entered Kennett Square, Pennsylvania, on September 10 to find itself confronted by Washington, who had taken position on the rough and rugged

[10] He wrote to Gates on July 30, "Genl Howe's in a manner abandoning Genl. Burgoyne, is so unaccountable a matter, that till I am fully assured it is so, I cannot help casting my eyes continually behind me." John C. Fitzpatrick (ed.), *The Writings of George Washington,* (39 vols., Washington, 1931-44), VIII, 499.

[11] George W. Greene, *Life of Nathanael Greene* (3 vols., New York, 1867-71), I, 438-439.

northern banks of Brandywine Creek. With eight thousand Continentals and three thousand militia he dared Howe to do his worst. Anticipating a frontal attack, he placed a strong body of Continentals under Nathanael Greene at and above Chad's Ford, his center; another under John Sullivan to the westward, his right flank; and

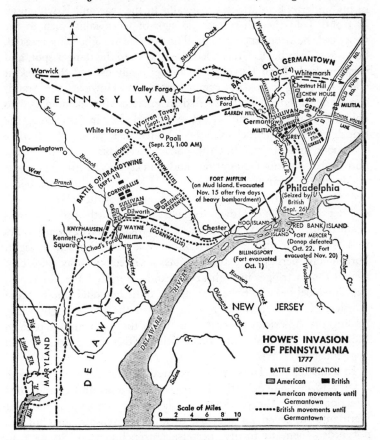

HOWE'S INVASION OF PENNSYLVANIA 1777

BATTLE IDENTIFICATION

American   British

---- American movements until Germantown

•••••• British movements until Germantown

Scale of Miles
0   2   4   6   8   10

a small force of militia, his left flank, to the eastward, where there were no good roads across the creek. Two brigades were held behind the center in reserve. Knowing Howe's fondness for flanking movements, Washington should have been thoroughly prepared for an advance around his right wing. On September 11 the British General sent about half his men forward under General Knyphausen to Chad's, where they amused themselves with desultory firing against the patriot center. Meanwhile, Cornwallis led the remainder to the westward, crossed the creek at unprotected fords well above the American right wing, and descended upon its rear in early afternoon. Washington received news of the flanking movement and rashly undertook to attack Cornwallis in the rear and Knyphausen in front. Told that there was no sign of Cornwallis' men to the westward, he dropped the plan. The American right wing resisted, but was driven back. Greene led the reserve to the danger spot, and was repulsed. Then Knyphausen rather easily crossed the creek at Chad's, driving the patriot center before him. However, the American army, although it finally fled in great confusion, managed to hold off its assailants until sunset. At nine o'clock in the evening the British refreshed themselves and celebrated their victory "with some cold pork and grogg," but the patriots were permitted to retreat northward without molestation, and quickly to re-form. Such was the battle of Brandywine, in which Howe's casualties numbered over five hundred, Washington's one thousand or more.[12]

After Brandywine Howe trudged slowly northward and was again confronted by Washington at Warwick Tavern, twenty miles west of Philadelphia. The Virginian was still disposed to fight. Fortunately, perhaps, for the patriots, a violent two-day rainstorm wetted the cartridges in both armies and compelled Washington to withdraw behind the Schuylkill River until he could obtain more powder. Howe then made a feint toward the patriot right wing, leading the American general to move to the westward. A path to Philadelphia was thus opened, and the British entered the city on September 25.

In Philadelphia, Howe posed as an all-powerful conqueror, with a view to emboldening the Pennsylvania Tories and causing disaffection among the patriots. He placed nine thousand troops at Germantown, seven miles away, to hold off Washington, but did not order them to fortify, because entrenchment might be considered a sign of weakness. Moreover, he kept three thousand grenadiers, his best troops, in Philadelphia.[13] Usually so prudent, he

[12] Washington's operations at Brandywine were carried on as if he were "in a daze," asserts Douglas S. Freeman, *George Washington* . . . (5 vols. to date, New York, 1948——), IV, 488.

[13] Robert F. Seyboldt (ed.), "Journal of the Proceedings of the Army under

was momentarily incautious, as he had been when he permitted the establishment of scattered posts in New Jersey the preceding year. His rashness might well have cost him heavily, especially because he had sent detachments to try to open up the Delaware River for the fleet. These could not be brought quickly into action against Washington.

The British line at Germantown, about three miles long, was well placed with reference to terrain. The left rested on the Schuylkill, and a fairly deep gorge covered its front. Nevertheless, Washington, learning of the weakness of the arrangements made by Howe, saw an opportunity to make a surprise attack. At dusk on October 3, his army advanced toward Germantown from its quarters near Skippack Creek, sixteen miles distant. Reinforced, the patriots again numbered about eleven thousand. They marched in four columns along four separate routes. The two columns on the flanks, composed of militia, were ordered to pass around the British line and to assail it from the flanks and rear; the others were to make frontal assaults. Washington's plan was daring and involved,[14] yet it almost succeeded. The militia failed to execute their assignments. However, the Continentals surprised the British advance guard at dawn and drove it back. Then, luckily for the British, both columns of the Continentals wasted some time in vain attempts to drive a part of the British advance guard from the Chew house, a stone structure about two miles from the royal lines. Finally both resumed their march in a heavy fog, leaving the fight at the Chew house to a masking force. Meanwhile, the main body of British and Hessians had been warned and hastily formed. The Continentals drove them back at one point and threatened to break through. At this critical moment Cornwallis dashed from Philadelphia with the troops stationed there, but was still at some distance when the tide of battle suddenly turned. Confused in the fog, patriots in one column fired upon the other. The sounds of the continuing conflict at the Chew house, which was successfully defended, led some of the patriots to believe that they would be surrounded. The Continentals fell back. Pressed by the royal troops, they finally fled in great confusion to

the Command of Sir Wm. Howe in the year 1777," *Proceedings of the American Antiquarian Society,* New Series, XL (1930), 87.

[14] It is described as "too intricate for inexperienced officers and imperfectly disciplined troops" in Sir John Fortescue, *A History of the British Army* (13 vols., New York, 1899–1930), III, 221.

their camp. Howe reported his casualties to be 535; the patriot losses were somewhat greater.

Still Washington was not unwilling to fight. Reorganizing, he took post toward the end of October at Whitemarsh and dared Howe to attack him. The British came out of Philadelphia, and the two armies were again face to face on December 5. But Washington's position was strong, and Howe returned to the city. The Americans then moved into winter quarters at Valley Forge, twenty miles away. Howe was now firmly in possession of Philadelphia, for the Delaware River had been opened to British shipping during October and November. In a series of actions beginning on October 6 Admiral Howe's fleet and detachments of royal infantry had captured three American redoubts on the river and rid its channel of obstructions placed therein by the patriots.

Had Howe captured Philadelphia—or had Philadelphia taken Howe, as Benjamin Franklin is reported to have said? The British General had reached his destination, but he had not attained his objective, for Pennsylvania gave him no joyous welcome and few more than three hundred Tory troops. In southeastern Pennsylvania he found numerous neutrals and some supporters of the crown. However, many of the latter were Friends, averse to carrying arms. They and other Pennsylvanians were commonly willing to sell him foodstuffs for hard cash. Remaining in Philadelphia until June of the following year, the British army was safe and not uncomfortable. Its presence enabled the Tories to assert themselves; they responded feebly. The presence of the troops—and the frolicking of both the British and the Germans at civilian expense—also steeled many a Pennsylvanian against Britain. A British officer thought that the faces and actions of most Philadelphians on the day of Germantown evinced their desire for a patriot victory.[15]

Before the end of October Howe knew that he had failed, and that Burgoyne had met disaster. He now had no hope that Germain would send him the numerous reinforcements he needed to carry on the war in the style which he desired. He submitted his resignation.[16] It was eventually accepted, and Clinton replaced him in May, 1778.

[15] G. D. Scull (ed.), *The Montresor Journals, Collections of the New-York Historical Society for the Year 1881* (New York, 1882), p. 462.

[16] *Report on the Manuscripts of Mrs. Stopford-Sackville, Royal Historical Manuscripts Commission* (2 vols., 1904–10), II, 83.

Howe was the only British commander who had a real chance to crush the American rebellion. He failed to achieve what many at the time expected of him—overwhelming victory. Frequently historians, ascribing tactical genius to Howe, and making little of his tasks and much of the powers of the British army and navy, have expressed surprise that his accomplishments were in the end so small. In the final analysis he achieved so little because he moved too slowly, too carefully, and too conventionally, and refused to take substantial risks. Had Washington's army been destroyed, American morale and the American cause might have collapsed in 1776, possibly in 1777. There can be no assurance, however, that the patriots would have quit the conflict or that they would not have raised new armies.

It has even been suggested that Howe failed because he did not wish to win. This curious thesis stems from the well-known fact that both the General and his brother had a sentimental tie with the Americans. However, their lack of personal rancor toward the patriots hardly supports the inference that they preferred American independence to subjection of the rebels upon the terms laid down by the King and his counselors. They stood first for maintenance of the empire, secondly for sympathy toward the erring colonists. Their personal reputations and sense of honor required that they do their best to put down the rebellion, and there is no good reason to believe that their political sentiments persuaded them to do otherwise.[17]

Nor is Sir William's lack of success to be entirely explained, as it was in his own day and since, by his devotion to alcohol, to gambling, and to his mistresses, one of them the beautiful Mrs. Joshua Loring, whose husband as British commissary of prisoners is said to have prospered by feeding the dead and starving the living. An English wag wrote in the spring of 1777:

[17] There is no reliable evidence that the Howes wished to offer to the patriots peace terms substantially more favorable than those sanctioned by George III and the British Cabinet in 1776. Their older brother George Augustus, the second Viscount Howe, was idolized by colonial troops with whom he served in the Seven Years' War. He was killed at Ticonderoga in 1758, and the colony of Massachusetts erected a memorial to him in Westminster Abbey. Richard and William valued the generous appreciation of their brother's merits displayed by the Americans.

> Awake, arouse, Sir Billy,
> There's forage in the plain.
> Leave your little filly,
> And open the campaign.[18]

Despite Howe's devotion to pleasure, to diversions not un-known to other commanders whose measures prospered, it would, perhaps, be more judicious to ascribe his failure equally to self-indulgence, to ignorance, and to lack of ability.[19] He merely fol-lowed British military traditions and practices. He lacked percep-tion, initiative, and boldness. He feared the seemingly dangerous disorganization which proceeded from rapid movements of an eighteenth-century British army. Disorganization would lead to a loss of fighting power, which might in turn bring defeat in battle. One such defeat could be fatal. To Howe it seemed wise to advance slowly and to be ready for conflict at any time; to assail American forces as opportunity and need dictated; and to win a succession of victories at the smallest possible cost, thus persuading the Americans of the futility of their efforts and of the expediency of negotiating with a generous victor. Howe's military policy was based upon routine, caution, and lack of insight. Unfortunately for him, as he himself early realized, successful execution of that policy required large forces and much time. Appreciating the fact that he might not be given either the necessary power or the requisite years, he never-theless clung doggedly to his erroneous concepts, and so perhaps un-intentionally insured American independence. Strange to relate, on the two occasions when he calculatingly dared, he fumbled—in defeat at Trenton and in fruitless victory at Germantown.

[18] James Boswell reports the General as saying in 1781, "A husband quite constant must be a cold companion not worth having, and the best is one who, after being away a while, likes his wife better than any other woman." Geoffrey Scott and Frederick A. Pottle (eds.), *Private Papers of James Boswell from Malahide Castle* (18 vols., Mount Vernon, N.Y., 1928–34), XIV, 229.

[19] In *The Journal of Nicholas Cresswell, 1774–1777* (New York, 1924), p. 257, Howe is described by a contemporary as "the great chucclehead." Cress-well's judgment is possibly too harsh.

CHAPTER 9

Surrender at Saratoga

WHILE Howe was winning indecisive victories in southeastern Pennsylvania, Burgoyne and his British expedition from Canada were defeated on the Hudson. Thirteen days after Germantown the soldier-playwright was forced to capitulate at Saratoga.

Burgoyne capitalized on a bitter quarrel between Germain and Carleton to secure this expedition for himself. The origins of the conflict between the Colonial Secretary and his subordinate are shrouded in mystery. It is certain, however, that by 1776 the two men cordially disliked each other. In August of that year, when nothing but praise was on British lips for the commander who had saved Canada, Germain undertook to deprive Carleton of opportunities to win new glories. He dispatched an order directing him to turn over to Burgoyne or some other officer the command of the British troops then moving southward toward Ticonderoga. His dispatch would have confined Carleton to garrison duty on the St. Lawrence. As it happened, because of bad weather the ship carrying the letter failed to reach Quebec and was forced to return to England.

Late in 1776 Burgoyne came to London with news that Carleton had gone no farther south than Crown Point—that the Canadian Governor, after securing control of Lake Champlain, had decided to withdraw rather than risk an attack upon the American army posted at Ticonderoga. Carleton's failure to invade New York caused disappointment in London. Perhaps he had been too prudent, although a setback at Ticonderoga at the beginning of winter would have been a severe blow to the northern British army. In any case, thoughts of the London military planners ran toward appointing a more aggressive general to lead the bulk of a northern expedition into the Thirteen Colonies. There were two candidates, Burgoyne and Clinton, each of them eager to distinguish himself, each desiring an independent command, and each with rather important political connections. Clinton, although he was a member of the Newcastle clan of Whigs and was senior in rank and a more experienced soldier, lost the contest. Perhaps he failed to secure the plum because Burgoyne had influential in-laws, perhaps because Burgoyne asked first and more persistently. Burgoyne arrived in London on December 9, and promptly gained audience with Germain and the King. On the thirteenth, while Clinton was en route to London from Rhode Island but still far to the west of Land's End, George III informed Lord North that Burgoyne might have the post. After Clinton reached England, he and his friends must have spoken earnestly into official ears, for Germain and the King agreed on February 20 that he should be chosen. Nevertheless, the final decision, taken at a Cabinet meeting in March, was in favor of Burgoyne. Since Clinton was made a Knight of the Bath less than a month later, supposedly as a reward for his services in the battle of Long Island, it may be inferred that he was given a consolation prize.

John Burgoyne, by scandalous rumor an illegitimate son of Lord Bingley, himself later a father without sanction by Church or state, acquired dignity and influence by eloping with and marrying a daughter of the great Stanley family. A cavalryman, a dandy, and a playwright, he was also a steady and convivial drinker, an inveterate and almost too successful gambler, and generally a bit of a rake. Handsome, courageous, and bold, he was a poseur and addicted to romantic rodomontade.

Yet Burgoyne was not without military talent and he anticipated most of the difficulties he later encountered, although he underestimated them. He expected to face an enemy in great force at Ticonderoga, to encounter other patriot fortifications to the southward, and to find roads in northern New York blocked by felled trees and broken bridges. Nevertheless, he proposed to force his way to Albany from the north and to join forces at or near that town with Lieutenant Colonel Barry St. Leger. According to a plan developed by Burgoyne and London officials, Burgoyne himself, with seven thousand regulars and Canadian, Tory, and Indian auxiliaries, was to push toward the old Dutch town from Lake Champlain, while St. Leger would create a diversion and advance toward the same objective with a smaller body of regulars, Tories, and Indians via Lake Ontario and the Mohawk Valley. Burgoyne was not promised aid from Howe in great force. However, according to his later statements, he assumed that Howe would mount at least a minor offensive on the lower Hudson.[1] At the close of the campaign it was understood that Burgoyne's army would come under the direction of Howe and that communications between Albany and New York City would definitely be established.[2]

Leaving London on March 27, Burgoyne reached Quebec on May 6. There he presented to Carleton a letter from Germain which insultingly informed the Governor of Burgoyne's appointment and specified in great detail precisely what Carleton should do to assist him. Burgoyne must have expected that the Governor would resent the rather shabby treatment given him and that he himself might feel the effects of Carleton's wrath. Sir Guy was certainly angry, and he sent off to Germain a contemptuous rebuke, along with his resignation as governor. Nevertheless, he gave Burgoyne a full measure of cooperation.

Early in June Fort St. John's on the Richelieu River was again a-throb with military activity.[3] There on June 14 the royal standard of Britain was ceremoniously raised aloft; there on the following day Carleton politely bade farewell and good fortune to Burgoyne, now surrounded by formidable though heterogeneous forces and possessing a fleet in control of Lake Champlain. Shortly afterward Burgoyne and his army began to move up the river and across the lake. Only three thousand regulars were left behind in Canada. Under Burgoyne were 6,700 rank-and-file infantry, British and German; 600 artillerymen; 250 dismounted German dragoons;

[1] John Burgoyne, *A State of the Expedition from Canada* . . . (London, 1780, 2nd ed.), pp. 22, 188–189.

[2] The substitution of Burgoyne for Carleton is doubtless explained in part by the fact that Carleton was superior in rank to Howe. Had Carleton reached New York, he might have claimed the supreme command in the Thirteen Colonies.

[3] Hoffman Nickerson, *The Turning Point of the Revolution* . . . (Boston, 1928), offers a good description of the Burgoyne campaign.

about 650 auxiliary troops, Canadians and Tories; and some 400 Indians. Altogether his army comprised some 9,500 officers and fighting men. Accompanying the troops were no fewer than 138 cannon, so numerous because it was expected that Ticonderoga would not surrender without a battering, and scores of women, the usual camp followers. A week later St. Leger, a veteran officer who was familiar with warfare in America, led about nine hundred regulars, well-trained Tories, and Canadian scouts westward from Montreal. On July 26, having collected almost one thousand Indian allies, he set forth from Fort Oswego toward Albany.

Before he left St. John's, Burgoyne read Howe's letter to Carleton stating that Howe would give him little and probably no help, unless Washington attempted to join the northern American army. Therefore, he should have been aware that he could count only upon his own forces and those of St. Leger.[4] Yet there is no indication that he was troubled at this stage.

Nor had Burgoyne suddenly acquired prudence or practicality. Sailing down the lake, he issued a most remarkable proclamation to the patriots. His and other British armies and the royal navy were trying to restore constitutional government, and also to protect the "general privileges of Mankind"! The patriots had set up "the compleatest system of tyranny that ever God in his displeasure suffer'd for a time to be exercised over a froward and stubborn generation." They were responsible for "arbitrary imprisonment, confiscation of property, persecution and torture, unprecedented in the inquisitions of the Romish church. . . . " He offered encouragement to those "whom spirit and principle may induce to partake the glorious task of redeeming their countrymen from dungeons and reestablishing the blessings of legal government." He wished to safeguard "the industrious, the infirm, and even the timid inhabitants. . . .," but would strike hard "by the blessing of God" at rebels. Moreover, although he was conscious of his own Christianity

---

[4] Burgoyne afterward asserted that for a long time thereafter he counted on co-operation from Howe. He claimed that he expected Howe to alter his plans as soon as Howe received instructions from Germain concerning the Canadian army. Burgoyne, *Expedition from Canada*, pp. 22, 188–189. Burgoyne's claim is not implausible but hardly exonerates him of all blame for the disaster which befell him. On July 11 he did not want help from Howe. He regretted then that his orders did not permit him to turn his march against New England, which he fancied he could easily conquer. *Ibid.*, pp. xxxviii–xxxix.

and sense of honor and of the King's clemency, none should think they could escape his wrath because of distance. "I have but to give stretch to the Indian forces under my direction, and they amount to thousands, to overtake the hardened enemies of Great-Britain and America. . . ." And so on. En route to Ticonderoga Burgoyne also addressed some bombast to the Iroquois warriors who accompanied him. These "brothers" were cautioned not to slay or to scalp old men, women, children, or wounded patriot fighting men. He likewise issued a general order to the army in which he blandly asserted that his Hessian mercenaries were as eager as his redcoats "to contend for the king, and the constitution of Great Britain, to vindicate law, and to relieve the oppressed." "This army must not retreat," he declared.[5] Few generals have been able to match Burgoyne's elegant and pompous clowning.

On July 1 Burgoyne began operations against Ticonderoga and found its garrison and the northern American army as a whole unprepared to resist. That army, like Washington's, had almost disintegrated during the preceding winter; at Burgoyne's approach it contained just above five thousand men, almost half militia. The problem of supplying even so small a force seemed to be almost insoluble, and the northern patriot forces were hard hit by troubles of command. Philip Schuyler had directed its fortunes until March. Then the Continental Congress had given his post to Gates. In May, however, the same body had removed Gates in favor of Schuyler. The northern army was troubled even more seriously by regional jealousy, for the Yankees and New Yorkers who composed it were on occasion almost as hostile toward each other as they were toward George III himself. Antagonistic in terms of national origins, religion, and social structure, they were also at odds because of the conflicting claims of New York and New Hampshire to the region of Vermont. To make matters worse, the Yankees hated and distrusted Schuyler as a New Yorker, a Dutchman, an aristocrat, and a snob. They admired Gates. Conversely, the New Yorkers were devoted to their leader and had little use for Gates.

In command of Ticonderoga when Burgoyne made his appearance was General Arthur St. Clair, once a British army officer. He

[5] Burgoyne's remarkable pronouncements may be conveniently inspected in Edward B. De Fonblanque, *Political and Military Episodes . . . Derived from the Life and Correspondence of . . . John Burgoyne . . .* (London, 1876), pp. 245, 489–92.

had 2,300 Continentals and 900 militiamen with him in the moment of crisis. Off to the south was Schuyler with two thousand patriots, too weak to offer much hope of relief. Then, too, Ticonderoga, though described on occasion as an American Gibraltar, was no unassailable citadel. Actually, in 1777 the patriots occupied two fortresses, the one on the western shore of the lake captured by Ethan Allen and Benedict Arnold two years earlier, another opposite on the eastern shore on Mount Independence, built in 1776, and some outworks as well. Between the major fortifications there was a boom designed to hinder the passage of the British fleet. Although much time and money had been spent in an effort to make the position impregnable, St. Clair could not hope to resist for very long. He did not have enough troops to man both fortresses, and it was doubtful that he could maintain even one against Burgoyne, especially since both could be cannonaded from Mount Defiance, a lofty and commanding eminence immediately to the south and west. The patriots—like the British and French before them—had neglected to fortify this hill. Perhaps St. Clair neglected it because he did not have enough men to defend it. He suspected the weakness of his position and was alert. As Burgoyne's Indians, Tories, and then regulars neared and opened a desultory fire, he concentrated in the two fortresses. He hoped for a few days that Burgoyne would stage a foolish frontal attack in the fashion of Howe at Bunker Hill. Instead, the British General sent artillerymen with cannon to the summit of Mount Defiance. It was time to depart, and St. Clair ordered evacuation and retreat in the night of July 5, the British entering the fortresses on the heels of the fleeing patriots.

So easy was the capture of Ticonderoga and its cannon, a task upon which Burgoyne had expected to spend much more than five days. The news of the victory of the British was joyously received everywhere by their partisans. It is reported that George III, waving a report of it, rushed into the dressing room of Queen Charlotte, when she was *en déshabillé,* shocked the ladies-in-waiting, and shouted, "I have beat them! I have beat the Americans." Burgoyne's name was on everyone's lips.[6] In contrast, the patriots were downcast, and John Adams talked of shooting a general who gave up his

[6] *Correspondence of Mr. Ralph Izard of South Carolina, from the Year 1774 to 1804 . . .* (New York, 1844), p. 333.

post without offering battle—*pour encourager les autres*.[7] Both sides exaggerated the importance of Ticonderoga. St. Clair had actually been prudent. Moreover, if he lost cannon and stores, his retreat was successfully executed. A small part of his garrison which he sent southward on Lake Champlain was pursued and attacked, but was finally rescued by an advanced detachment of Schuyler's men. The larger portion fled southeastward. Its rear guard was assailed by the British at Hubbardton, Vermont, and was defeated after a fierce fight, but the British victory was expensively bought. Although American losses were larger, Burgoyne's men suffered almost two hundred casualties, including thirty-five or more dead. He could not afford many such conflicts and still reach Albany. Most of St. Clair's Continentals lived to join Schuyler, and to fight on other days. Some of the American militia also returned to the fray.

After the fall of Ticonderoga the northern American army was both distracted and dispirited. Luckily for that army, Burgoyne, assuming triumphal entry into Albany, only seventy miles away, was in no great hurry. Moreover, he decided, for reasons not clearly ascertained, to move to Fort Edward on the Hudson by way of Skenesboro (now Whitehall) and Wood Creek rather than by the easier route of Lake George. He also made the mistake of taking with him fifty-two pieces of artillery, which made his progress infinitely slow. He was still further retarded by lack of horses, badly made baggage carts, and such superfluous equipment as his own silver plate, choice wines, and extensive wardrobe. Schuyler, doing everything possible to gain time, slowed down Burgoyne's advance by having huge stones rolled into Wood Creek, turning water across the British route, and felling thousands of trees across the wagon tracks that Burgoyne used. As a result, Burgoyne did not pass beyond Skenesboro until July 24. Five days later he reached Fort Edward. Shortly afterward his army moved forward another seven miles down the east bank of the Hudson, stopping at Fort Miller, just north of the Batten Kill. There Burgoyne remained until September 13, partly because of lack of supplies, partly because of increasing American opposition. Before he again gave the order to march Fortuna—and many of his Tory and Indian allies—had deserted him. By August 20 he knew that his situation was difficult, possibly desperate.

[7] Charles F. Adams (ed.), *Familiar Letters of John Adams and His Wife Abigail Adams, during the Revolution* (New York, 1876), p. 292.

It has often been suggested that Burgoyne's delay was unnecessary and fatal to his hopes. It may be, however, that his failure to
move forward merely postponed his final defeat for some weeks, for
the patriots were gathering to oppose him. Retreating before Burgoyne down the west bank of the Hudson to Saratoga, thence to
Stillwater, and again to the mouth of the Mohawk, Schuyler, who
from the time of his appointment had written almost despairingly to
the Continental Congress, sent off a series of gloomy dispatches to
his employers. Since he had failed previously to give a solid demon-
stration of a will to fight, which he may or may not have possessed, the men at Philadelphia became alarmed. At length the
delegates, who were fuming because of what they regarded as the
needless evacuation of Ticonderoga, once more, on August 4, gave
the command of the northern army to Gates.[8] Ten days later they
clothed him with something like dictatorial powers. On August 19
Gates reached Albany from Philadelphia. Thanks in part to the
efforts of Schuyler, the tide was already turning in favor of the
northern patriots.

Even as it retreated the northern American army gained strength.
Six hundred Continentals from Peekskill joined it and soon afterward two valuable officers, Major Generals Benjamin Lincoln and
Benedict Arnold, sent forward by Washington. Schuyler promptly
ordered Lincoln to direct operations in Vermont against Burgoyne's
left flank and communication lines. He performed useful service
there. Arnold was to achieve even more than Lincoln. Early in
August Schuyler had under him about 4,500 men, the majority
Continentals; a month later Daniel Morgan and five hundred riflemen reached Albany. Moreover, the New England militia were
slowly gathering and advancing toward Ticonderoga and the
Hudson. Nor were they coming to consume supplies for a week or
two and then suddenly vanish. The Yankee farmers and woodsmen
were determined to defend their homes. The news of the murder,
before the end of July, of innocent Jane McCrea by one of Burgoyne's Indians and of "Gentleman Johnny" Burgoyne's failure to
punish the slayer steeled them in their stand.

However, the honor of striking the first telling blow to the splendid dream of Burgoyne fell, not to the Yankees, but rather to the

[8] Bernhard Knollenberg, *Washington and the Revolution* . . . (New York,
1940) pp. 12-20.

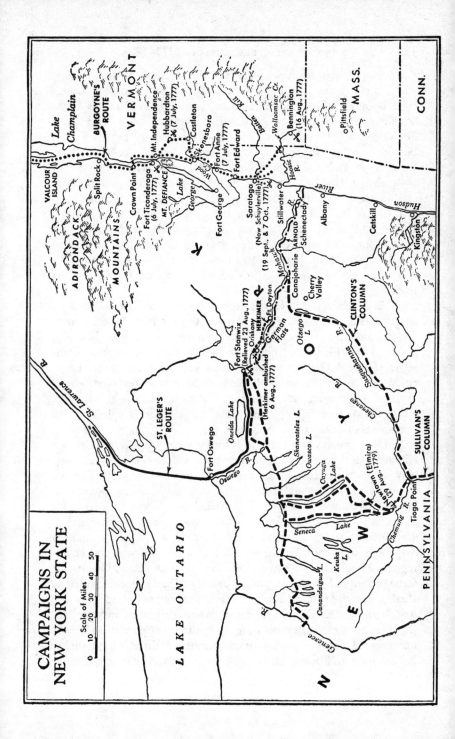

CAMPAIGNS IN NEW YORK STATE

Scale of Miles
0   10 20 30 40 50

defenders of the Mohawk Valley. The patriots of that valley, which held many Tories, dreaded the approach of St. Leger, both because of his Indian auxiliaries and because of his occasionally even more vengeful Loyalist contingent, but there was little faltering. In old Fort Stanwix, only recently renamed Fort Schuyler, which barred St. Leger from Albany, Colonel Peter Gansevoort and Lieutenant Colonel Marinus Willett, a pair of stouthearted Dutchmen, made ready in the spring and summer for the day of battle. Counting on the 450 Continentals who formed the bulk of its garrison, they refused to be unnerved by Indian raids and threats, steadily improved their fortifications, and stored munitions and foodstuffs for weeks of siege. Moreover, on August 2, just as St. Leger's force began to emerge from the woods, more than two hundred patriots bringing supplies entered the fort from the east.

St. Leger expected to capture the fort with ease. On August 3 he paraded before it all his forces, hoping to intimidate its occupants. They noted his Indians hideously undressed for war but also observed that his white troops were no more numerous than themselves. Colonel Gansevoort refused to surrender. Since St. Leger could not storm the walls of the fort, he surrounded and loosely invested it, simultaneously sending back more than two-thirds of his white troops to bring up some light cannon and supplies and to improve his line of communications.

At the moment when the British forces were thus divided, General Nicholas Herkimer and eight hundred patriot militia forced their way up the Mohawk in an attempt to relieve the fort. The besiegers, 250 whites and four times as many Indians, were thus exposed to danger of attack by overwhelming forces. Whatever his faults as a commander, St. Leger was courageous. He dispatched 400 Indians and a small detachment of Tory rangers to make a surprise assault upon Herkimer and his men. They took post covering two ravines six miles east of the fort, near Oriskany. On August 6 the patriot militia, accompanied by sixty friendly Oneida warriors, carelessly moved in column through the ravines. Suddenly the British Indians fired upon their rear guard, rushed it, and put it to flight. A second attack, this time upon the main patriot body, was unsuccessful, for the patriot militia formed a circle, found shelter behind trees and brush, and fought desperately. The struggle, interrupted by a rainshower, endured for hours. It was carried on hand to hand with musket, tomahawk, pistol, and knife. At length the Indians and Tories had their fill and withdrew toward their camp, leaving the militia masters of the field. The attackers carried off dozens of prisoners, and the patriots suffered two hundred other casualties, but the aggressors had lost almost as many as the patriots in slain and wounded.

Herkimer, mortally wounded, felt compelled to withdraw, and his men retreated down the Mohawk. Though they had failed to achieve their mission, they had held off their assailants and cast dread into the hearts of St. Leger's fickle red-skinned allies. They had also made it possible for the defenders of Fort Stanwix to strike for themselves. Informed by messengers from Herkimer of his approach, Gansevoort ordered Willett to lead 250 men on a sortie. Had Gansevoort moved out with the whole garrison, he might have routed St. Leger. As it was, Willett effectively raided the British camp, destroying quantities of supplies, and returned to the fort with little loss. At least for the time being St. Leger had been checked.

The tide of warfare in the North had begun to run against the British. St. Leger, now gathering all his forces around Stanwix, seemed less assured that he would ride a conqueror into Albany. While his savages burned and otherwise tortured their captives, he sent flag after flag of truce to Gansevoort, demanding the surrender of Stanwix. He claimed that Burgoyne was all-victorious, that the fort could not withstand him, and that it was best for the garrison to give up immediately. Should the patriots attempt further and vain resistance, he would be unable to prevent the commission of further atrocities by his forest brutes. Gansevoort, certain that the fort could be held for many days and guessing that St. Leger was bluffing, steadily refused all his demands, declaring he would fight to the last. He sat tight, and he sent Willett out through St. Leger's lines to seek help. Willett had not far to go, for he shortly encountered Benedict Arnold and a thousand Continentals coming up the Mohawk. These reinforcements were by no means premature, for St. Leger was beginning to make regular approaches to the fort.

Fortunately for the besieged within Stanwix, Schuyler risked dispatching an expedition to their assistance immediately after receiving news of the events of August 6. This step temporarily weakened the main northern army, but he guessed, correctly as events proved, that Burgoyne would not attack in the near future. Arnold volunteered for the command, and reached Fort Dayton by August 21. There he was joined by a few dozen militiamen. Even Arnold had his moments of cold caution. After a council of war, he decided to ask Schuyler for another thousand troops. Time, he believed, was on his side. Then he learned that Stanwix was really in grave danger. He marched forward on August 23.

Scenes of bloody conflict might well have been anticipated by Arnold's men, but they conquered without striking a blow. Prior to departing from Fort Dayton, Arnold, whose fertility in expedients was matched by his boldness in fighting, tried stratagem as a possible substitute for force. The patriots held prisoner two brothers, both Tories and one a half-witted fellow named Hon Yost. Arnold informed Hon Yost his life would be spared if he went to the British camp and told St. Leger's Indians that the patriots were at hand in overwhelming numbers, that they would do well to flee for their lives. Hon Yost leaped at the chance to save his life, and Arnold retained his brother as a hostage. The madman's clothing was then shot full of bullet holes, and he was sent off in the guise of an escaped prisoner. Accompanying him was a friendly Oneida, prepared to tell the same story; en route the two unlikely emissaries met several Indians, who joined them and agreed to help. Yost reached the British camp and related his tale, accepted at face value by the hostile braves because of their respect for any madman. One after another the Oneida and his associates stepped forward to repeat the same story. St. Leger scoffed, but his Indians grew alarmed. They had lost their blankets in Willett's raid; scores of their warriors had fallen at Oriskany; and they believed that St. Leger would place the burden of battle upon them. They began to depart in groups, and finally fled en masse, forcing the British commander to abandon the siege. Retreating helter-skelter, St. Leger's army dissolved.[9] He loyally tried to lead his white troops to the aid of Burgoyne but was forced to travel by way of Montreal and was unable to reach him in time. Arnold, his special assignment so easily executed, hastily rejoined the main American army, leaving the patriots in firm control of the lower Mohawk Valley. Thus ended the British effort to reach Albany from the west.

[9] St. Leger's report to Burgoyne on his misfortunes is printed in Burgoyne, *Expedition from Canada,* pp. lxxvii–lxxxiii.

1. GEORGE WASHINGTON

Painting by James Peale in Independence Hall, Philadelphia

2. BENJAMIN FRANKLIN

By David Rent Etter, after Martin, in Independence Hall, Philadelphia

3. George the Third

An engraving, courtesy of the William L. Clements Library, University of Michigan

4. The Battle of Lexington, 1775. (From a print of 1798, courtesy of The New-York Historical Society)

5. The Death of Montgomery, Quebec, 1775. (Painting by John Trumbull, courtesy of The New-York Historical Society)

I [George Washington Commander in Chief of the Armies of the United States of America] do acknowledge the UNITED STATES of AMÉRICA, to be Free, Independent and Sovereign States, and declare that the people thereof owe no allegiance or obedience to George the Third, King of Great-Britain; and I renounce, refuse and abjure any allegiance or obedience to him; and I do [swear] — — that I will to the utmost of my power, support, maintain and defend the said United States, against the said King George the Third, his heirs and successors and his or their abettors, affistants and adherents, and will ferve the faid United States in the office of [Commander in chief of armies] which I now hold, with fidelity, according to the beft of my fkill and underftanding.

[Sworn before me this at Valley Forge May 10th 1778 Sterling Major Genl]

G Washington

6. Washington's Oath of Allegiance to the United States. (Original in The Department of Defense, Washington, D.C.)

By His EXCELLENCY
Sir WILLIAM HOWE, K. B.
General and Commander in Chief, &c. &c. &c.

PROCLAMATION.

WHEREAS by my late Declaration bearing Date the 27th Day of August, 1777. Security and Protection was engaged to all Persons Inhabitants of the Province of PENNSYLVANIA &c. who, not guilty of having affumed legiflative or judicial Authority, may have acted illegally in Subordinate Stations: and confcious of their Mifcondunct, been induced, to leave their Dwellings, provided fuch Perfons would forthwith return, and remain peaceably at their ufual Places of Abode: and a free and general Pardon was promifed to all Officers and private Men then actually in Arms againft His MAJESTY, who might be willing to relinquifh the Part they had taken in the Rebellion, and fhould voluntarily come and furrender themfelves to any Detachment of His MAJESTY's Forces before the Day on which it fhould be notified that the faid Indulgence fhould be difcontinued. AND WHEREAS many of the Inhabitants of PHILADELPHIA, the Diftrict of SOUTHWARK, the NORTHERN LIBERTIES, and the Townfhips of MOYAMENSING, PASSIUNK and GERMANTOWN, who have acted in fuch fubordinate Stations, have remained peaceably at their refpective Dwellings, and many Officers and private Men have furrendered themfelves to His MAJESTY's Forces, or laid down their Arms and returned to their Habitations agreeable to the Purport of my faid Declaration: And it is both reafonable and neceffary that all fuch Perfons, as a Proof of the Sincerity of their Intentions to return to their Allegiance, and to partake the Security and Protection engaged, and the Pardon offered to them as aforefaid, fhould take the Oath of Allegiance to His MAJESTY: I DO therefore hereby require all Perfons within the Places aforefaid, who have acted in fuch fubordinate Stations, or have furrendered themfelves to His MAJESTY's Forces, or laid down their Arms and returned to their Habitations as aforefaid, and all others, not comprized in my faid Declaration, who have, in any wife, been aiding or abetting in the faid Rebellion, to repair to the Office in the City of PHILADELPHIA, appointed for the Purpose, and take the Oath of Allegiance to His MAJESTY:—And I do hereby declare that all fuch Perfons, who fhall fail to comply with this Proclamation, on or before the 25th Day of October, 1777, will be confidered as Perfons out of His MAJESTY's Peace, and treated accordingly.

GIVEN under my Hand, at Head Quarters in Germantown, this Firft Day of October, 1777.

W. HOWE.

By His Excellency's Command.
ROBERT MACKENZIE, Secretary.

7 Howe's Offer of Pardon to Philadelphians, October 1, 1777. (Courtesy of The New-York Historical Society)

9. A British Armchair Strategist, 1779: "Beg your pardon my Dear Sir—had it from my Lord Fiddlefaddle. He'd nothing to do but cut 'em off pass the Susquhanna and proceed to Boston possess himself of Crown point—then Philadelphia would have fallen of course and a communication opend with the Northern Army—as easily as I'd open a Vein." (Courtesy of The New-York Historical Society)

8. Recruits for the British Army in America, 1780. (From an engraving in the Phelps Stokes Collection, The New York Public Library)

11. The besieged Bostonians are shown in a cage suspended from the Liberty Tree, left to starve—the punishment dealt to slaves convicted of capital offenses. Their cries for assistance are being answered by men from Marblehead who offer them codfish in contribution boxes. (Courtesy of The New-York Historical Society)

10. A patriotic barber refuses to finish shaving his customer on discovering that he is Captain Crozer, commander of one of His Majesty's ships. This cartoon was once captioned, "The Captain in the Suds." (Courtesy of The New-York Historical Society)

12. A British jibe at Sir William Howe, from *Westminster Magazine,*
1779. (Courtesy of The New-York Historical Society)

13. Medals showing Light-Horse Harry Lee and John Paul Jones which
were ordered by the Continental Congress and made in France.

14. Cornwallis landing troops in New Jersey, November 20, 1776. (From the Emmet Collection, The New York Public Library)

15. The attack on Fort Washington outside New York City, November 16, 1776. (From the Phelps Stokes Collection, The New York Public Library)

16. JOHN HANCOCK

Painting by John Singleton Copley, Museum of Fine Arts, Boston. Lent by the City of Boston

17. ROBERT MORRIS

Painting by Charles Willson Peale in Independence Hall, Philadelphia

18. Thomas Jefferson, 1786

Engraved for Bancroft's *History of the United States* from the original portrait painted for John Adams by Mather Brown. (From the Emmet Collection, The New York Public Library)

19. John Adams

Painting by Charles Willson Peale in Independence Hall, Philadelphia

20. GENERAL THOMAS GAGE

Painting by Richard Wilson, courtesy of Henry L. Shattuck

21. LORD CORNWALLIS

From an engraving in the William L. Clements Library, University of Michigan

22. SIR HENRY CLINTON

From a contemporary engraving, courtesy of The New-York Historical Society

23. LORD RICHARD HOWE

Engraved from the painting by John Singleton Copley, courtesy of The New-York Historical Society

24. BENEDICT ARNOLD

From a contemporary engraving after a drawing by Pierre du Simitière

25. HORATIO GATES

Engraving from a painting by Gilbert Stuart. (From the Emmet Collection, The New York Public Library)

26. The *Phoenix* and the *Rose* engaged by American fire ships and galleys, August 16, 1776. (Engraving by D. Sevres from a sketch by Sir James Wallace, courtesy of the Phelps Stokes Collection, The New York Public Library)

27. The Battle of Princeton. (Painting by James Peale in the Princeton University Library)

28. JOHN RUTLEDGE

An engraving in the Emmet Collection, The New York Public Library

29. HENRY LAURENS, President of the Continental Congress. (From an engraving, of a painting by John Singleton Copley, in the Emmet Collection, The New York Public Library)

30. JOHN DICKINSON

Painting by Charles Willson Peale in Independence Hall, Philadelphia

31. NATHANAEL GREENE

An engraving in the Emmet Collection, The New York Public Library

32. "Evacuation Day." Washington's triumphal entry into New York City on November 25, 1783. (Lithograph by E. P. & L. Restein, courtesy of The Library of Congress)

The disastrous failure of the St. Leger expedition was followed by a serious defeat of part of Burgoyne's own army. Before the end of July that army was suffering from a lack of pack horses and was generally in need of provisions in order to press on to Albany. Informed that there were in Vermont oxen, cattle, draft horses, and saddlehorses (which could be used to mount his dragoons), General Baron von Riedesel, commander of the Germans under Burgoyne, urged his chief to send a raiding force toward the Connecticut River. After some hesitation the British General adopted the scheme—and bungled it. He chose Lieutenant Colonel Friedrich Baum to head the foray and placed under his command a motley collection of Germans, British marksmen, Tories, and Indians, over seven hundred in all. Originally Baum was ordered to proceed to Manchester. However, on August 11, the day of departure, Burgoyne was informed by a Tory that the needed animals, and flour as well, could be obtained at Bennington, that three or four hundred patriot militiamen were guarding the village, that the roads leading toward it were extremely bad, and that three thousand men should be sent upon the errand. Burgoyne saw several of his problems solved. He told Baum to march to Bennington but failed to give him more troops. Too confident, he assumed that the men already assigned to the expedition would suffice. Three days later, Baum, after struggling through rough and unfriendly country, was still some miles from Bennington when he suddenly came into contact with the advance guard of a body of New Hampshire militia led by Brigadier General John Stark. After repulsing Stark's detachment, he then found himself confronted by a large body of patriots, which he estimated at fifteen to eighteen hundred men, about four miles west of his destination.

By the merest chance John Stark was at Bennington at the right time. The New Hampshire legislators, rousing themselves to meet the enemy at their rear door, had voted on July 18 to raise a brigade of militia for two months' service. A resolute and experienced leader was easily found in the person of Stark, who had quit the Continental army because he had not been promoted with sufficient dispatch. Quickly collecting fifteen hundred men, a prodigious force for the small state of New Hampshire, Stark pressed westward in the hope of hitting at Burgoyne's long communication line. He and his volunteers had already reached Bennington when Baum appeared from the west. Since five hundred Vermont and Massachusetts men were also at the village, there were at Bennington in all some two thousand patriot militia, not the petty detachment that Baum had expected to face.

Baum prudently chose not to attack. He had been joined on the march by bands of Tories, but he was too weak to take the initiative. However, he imprudently decided not to retreat. He took a defensive position and set off a request to Burgoyne for reinforcements. Stark, determined to attack, also called for help, asking Colonel Seth Warner, who commanded 350 Continentals at Manchester, to hurry to his side. In a heavy rain on August 15, under orders from Burgoyne, Lieutenant Colonel Francis Breymann and 650 Hessians, burdened by artillery and military formality, made slow progress from the Hudson toward Baum's camp, while Warner moved more rapidly toward the same spot. The following afternoon Stark drove fiercely and in overwhelming force against Baum's variegated troops holding badly chosen positions, and routed them. Pursuing Baum's scattered command, he encountered and was repulsed by Breymann. Then Warner's men joined in the fray, Breymann ran out of ammunition, and Breymann took advantage of a covering night to flee back to Burgoyne.

The defeat of the royal troops at Bennington was a bitter blow to Burgoyne. Stark and Warner counted only about eighty patriot casualties. They had captured some seven hundred prisoners, while the slain and wounded of Baum and Breymann numbered about two hundred. Burgoyne had gained no horses and no supplies, but had lost a tenth of his army. Since he had been forced to leave a strong garrison at Ticonderoga, he now had with him no more than 5,500 regulars and 800 Tory and Indian auxiliaries. He still had cannon, some forty-two pieces. The patriots were steadily gathering to the eastward and threatening to cut his long supply line; before him was the northern patriot army, burgeoning rather than diminishing. It was now extremely doubtful that he could force his way to Albany.[10] On August 20 he sent off a report to Germain in

[10] It has been contended that there were many zealous Loyalists in the valley of the Connecticut River, that Burgoyne neglected to supply them with arms, that they could have covered his left flank and so saved him from final defeat. George B. Upham, "Burgoyne's Great Mistake," *New England Quarterly,* III (1930), 657–680. The argument has not been substantiated.

which he asserted that he would remain where he was or retreat to Fort Edward, were it not that his orders absolutely required him to push on across the Mohawk. He would run great risks, but he would try to execute his instructions. He was probably preparing an apologia for his own conduct in the event of failure.[11] Burgoyne was too reckless, too much of a gambler to be cautious. He would hardly have retreated, or even made preparations to fall back, unless his instructions had positively demanded that he do so. He still had some chance to achieve success. After spending a month collecting supplies, he moved his men across the Hudson to its west bank, on September 13 and 14.[12] In so doing, he virtually cut off his own chance of retreat and committed his army to victory or decisive defeat.

Before Burgoyne crossed the Hudson, Arnold's contingent and Morgan's riflemen joined Gates. Although Stark and his militia refused to serve beyond the two months for which they had enlisted, Gates by September 8 had more than seven thousand troops, the majority Continentals. He wisely decided to go forward to meet Burgoyne's expected attack, and he took position at Bemis Heights. There he occupied strong ground with the Hudson on his right and bluffs and woods on his left. His engineer, Thaddeus Kosciuszko, promptly laid out a plan of fortification, and his men immediately began to dig entrenchments. On September 18 Burgoyne encamped three miles to the north. He knew little about either the terrain or the disposition of Gates' troops, for patriot irregulars had driven his Indians and scouts within his lines. Nevertheless, he determined to attack. He ordered Riedesel with twelve hundred Germans to push forward along the riverside, Brigadier General Hamilton with an equally large force of British regulars to move into the woods to the right, and Brigadier General Simon Fraser with 2,200 regulars, Tories, and Indians to advance into the woods further to the right. He hoped that Fraser would envelop or, with Hamilton's help, break through the patriot left wing.

Burgoyne's scheme was ill chosen, particularly because the woods prevented easy communication between his three columns. To be

[11] Burgoyne, *Expedition from Canada*, pp. xliv–xlviii.
[12] Burgoyne's men were then apparently dependent upon a supply of pork. They were eating "Pork at noon, pork at night, pork cold, pork hot." Roy W. Pettengill (ed.), *Letters from America, 1776–1779* . . . (Boston and New York, 1924), p. 99.

sure, a frontal assault against the patriot entrenchments on the riverside was perhaps equally hazardous. In any case, the movements of the royal troops early in the morning of the nineteenth were observed by the patriots. Gates would have waited within his lines, but Arnold urged him to send a force forward into the woods on the patriot left. Gates agreed, and dispatched picked men under Morgan, who at Freeman's Farm came into contact with Hamilton's column (which Burgoyne himself accompanied). Morgan was driven back, but American reinforcements came to the scene. There followed hours of bitter fighting near and on the farm. Meanwhile, Fraser was off to the westward, out of touch with Burgoyne and largely inactive. Badly battered by superior numbers, the British center was about to break when Riedesel came up to its rescue. Forcing the patriots back from Freeman's Farm at dusk, Burgoyne held the field of battle. The patriots had suffered from British bayonet attacks and artillery fire, and their casualties were more than three hundred. On the other hand, American rifle and musket fire had been extremely effective in the forest; Burgoyne's losses were almost double; and his thrusts had been definitely halted.

The day after the battle of Freeman's Farm Burgoyne was disposed to resume the offensive, but his men were tired. On September 21 he decided to await a favorable opportunity, for he received word from New York that Clinton would soon lead three thousand men up the lower Hudson. Burgoyne hoped that Clinton's advance northward would create a diversion, perhaps persuade Gates to send a part of his army to protect the southern approach to Albany. The British troops dug in, and remained where they were for three weeks. During this period Burgoyne's situation changed from dangerous to critical.[13] Wisely refusing to divide his army to fend off Clinton, Gates merely ordered the garrison of Fort Stanwix to Albany. During this interval his forces were further augmented by New England and New York militiamen who poured into his camp by the hundreds. Gates was also strengthened by the efforts of Schuyler, who labored diligently at Albany to send him supplies.

[13] Baroness Riedesel, who had little affection for Burgoyne, afterward declared that he "spent half the nights in singing and drinking, and amusing himself with the wife of a commissary, who was his mistress, and who, as well as he, loved champagne." William L. Stone (ed.), *Letters and Journals Relating to the War of the American Revolution . . . by Mrs. General Riedesel* (Albany, 1867), p. 125.

Had he taken the offensive then, Burgoyne could probably have withstood an American attack. On the defensive he could have used his cannon to advantage. Gates sent out parties which bedeviled Burgoyne's men and made British scouting operations impossible; he continued to fortify his lines until they were almost impregnable; and he waited for his antagonist to move. He had every reason to believe that Burgoyne the gambler would eventually attack and that he would be repulsed.[14]

As late as September 27 Burgoyne was claiming that he could break through to Albany, although he doubted that his army could subsist there during the coming winter. Actually his situation was becoming desperate. His stores of food were so low that he was compelled to put his men on half rations a few days later, and he had had no good news from Clinton. His officers and his men were discouraged.[15] On October 4 in council of war he proposed to try again to flank the American left. His suggestion aroused no enthusiasm, and the next day Riedesel and Fraser urged, instead, that he retreat. Burgoyne characteristically regarded a withdrawal as ignominious. Instead, he determined to make a reconnaissance in force toward the patriot left wing on the seventh. If all went well, he would order a general assault against that wing on the following day.

On the seventh Burgoyne personally led fifteen hundred regulars and about six hundred Tories and Indians southwest from Freeman's Farm, leaving fewer than 3,500 men in his entrenchments. Ignorant of Gates' arrangements and even of the terrain, he halted in a wheat field, after advancing less than a mile, to take stock of the enemy's position. For a time he discerned nothing in the way of strong patriot units. Early in the afternoon, however, under orders from Gates, who had been accurately informed of the British movement, Continental infantry and Morgan's riflemen assailed him from the woods both on his left and on his right. Then a large body

---

[14] Gates informed his troops on September 26 that the British "must endeavour by one rash stroke to regain all they have lost, that failing, their utter ruin is inevitable." James P. Baxter (ed.), *The British Invasion from the North . . . with the Journal of Lieut. William Digby . . .* (Albany, 1887), p. 283.

[15] On September 24 bodies of the dead buried near the British camp became exposed as the result of heavy rains. The sight of them and the odor from them were not encouraging. *Ibid.*, p. 281.

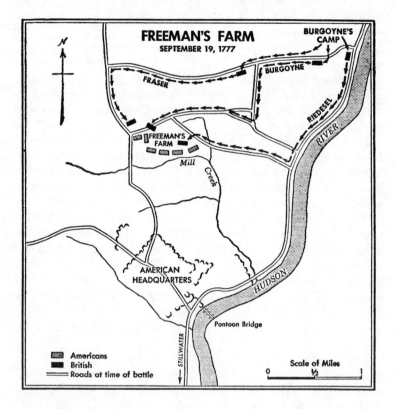

FREEMAN'S FARM
SEPTEMBER 19, 1777

BURGOYNE'S CAMP

BURGOYNE

FRASER

RIEDESEL

RIVER

FREEMAN'S FARM

Mill Creek

AMERICAN HEADQUARTERS

HUDSON

Pontoon Bridge

STILLWATER

Americans
British
Roads at time of battle

Scale of Miles
0   ½   1

of patriots attacked him frontally. Burgoyne's detachment was badly mauled, and was forced to fall back into the British entrenchments. The Americans sought to improve their advantage by storming the British lines. Arnold, who had quarreled bitterly with Gates and who was actually without command on that day, nevertheless took part in the American assaults and with his characteristic heroics inspired the patriots. He twice led detachments against the entrenchments on the British right flank. The second succeeded, but dusk prevented further action.

The second battle of Freeman's Farm spelled catastrophe for Burgoyne. While the patriots suffered no more than 150 casualties, the royal army counted about seven hundred killed, captured, and wounded. Among the slain was Breymann; mortally wounded was

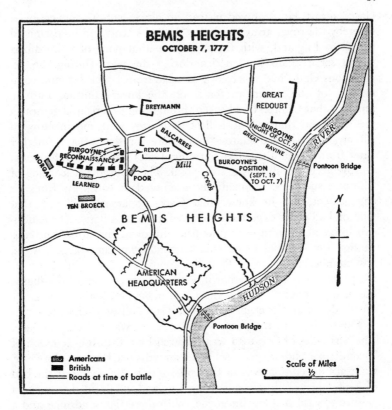

Simon Fraser. The British lines were now untenable, and Burgoyne withdrew the night after the battle. Retreating slowly, he took his stand two days later on strong ground surrounded by open country at Saratoga. He hoped Gates would be rash enough to attack him, but the American General merely followed at a distance, meanwhile sending out militiamen to prevent flight by Burgoyne to Ticonderoga. By October 12 Burgoyne knew that Clinton was moving up the Hudson. But Clinton seemed far away, and after a council of war Burgoyne decided to flee northward. It was too late, for his army was completely surrounded on the following morning. After another council of war he felt obliged to offer to surrender on honorable terms. Gates demanded unconditional surrender. On the fourteenth Burgoyne grandiloquently but courageously refused

Gates' terms. He proposed instead an agreement—a convention—whereby the royal army would lay down its arms and be permitted to sail to England, with the stipulation that none of its members would serve again in America during the war. During the negotiations Gates had received a message from Israel Putnam, commander of the American forces on the lower Hudson. Putnam reported that Clinton had broken through the American defenses on the river and that a British fleet and army were moving toward Albany, and warned Gates "to prepare for the worst." Another letter from Putnam was less alarming. Gates was worried, however, and he accepted Burgoyne's proposal. Then Burgoyne, learning of Clinton's successes, momentarily attempted to withdraw from his engagement. But he knew what Gates apparently did not, that Clinton had never expected to proceed so far as Albany. The American forces about him were now triple his own. He ratified the convention. On October 17 his once splendid army, now ragged, worn, and numbering no more than five thousand in all, laid down its weapons. Gates was generous in victory. Burgoyne entered Albany, but as a prisoner.[16] "This is the Lords doing and marvellous in our eyes!" declared Governor Jonathan Trumbull of Connecticut.[17]

The triumph of the patriots in the North was not yet complete. The surrender of Saratoga was followed by a British evacuation of Ticonderoga, no longer useful as an advanced base. Moreover, Clinton's expedition was in the end fruitless. Receiving at the end of September reinforcements from England, he decided to make a gesture toward helping Burgoyne. With three thousand men and a fleet he brilliantly broke through American defenses in the Highlands. Part of his forces reached Esopus (now Kingston) on October 15. They were too few, and perhaps too late as well,[18] and they

---

[16] Many writers have contended that credit for the American triumph should go to Schuyler and Arnold rather than Gates. They have placed faith in the statements of enemies of Gates. They have used him as a "whipping boy" to exalt Washington, and they have argued that his failure in the Camden campaign of 1780 proves his incompetence on the Hudson in 1777. While Schuyler and Arnold contributed to the patriot victory, the dictum of Edward Channing still stands: "*Prima facie* the verdict is for Gates; the burden of proof is on the other side." For his analysis see Edward Channing, *A History of the United States* (6 vols., New York, 1905-25), III, 276-278.

[17] Roger S. Boardman, *Roger Sherman* . . . (Philadelphia, 1938), p. 189. A British officer wrote, "It's true, it's pity, and pity is, it's true." E. A. Benians (ed.), *A Journal by Thos. Hughes* . . . (Cambridge, 1947), p. 26.

[18] Had Clinton arranged to withdraw the British garrison from Rhode

were quickly withdrawn to New York City in order to permit the sending of additional troops to Howe.

The Saratoga agreement was never carried out. Both the British and the Americans sought to break it. The prisoners violated it in minor ways, and Howe tried to arrange to ship the British troops to New York, proposing to use them immediately.[19] American leaders failed to keep the major pledge made by Gates, that the royal troops would be permitted to embark for England. They feared that Burgoyne's men would be assigned to garrison duty in Britain, thus releasing an equivalent number for service in America in 1778. Washington himself recommended that provisions be withheld from Burgoyne's men in order to delay their sailing.[20] The Continental Congress found various reasons why the convention should be nullified. Burgoyne's soldiers were finally sent off to Virginia, where they were treated as prisoners. There, largely because of desertion, the British army melted away. Burgoyne himself was allowed to return to England, to tell his tale of defeat and to try, not without some success, to place the blame for it upon Germain, upon Howe, upon anyone but himself. The news of his failure preceded him, causing consternation at the British court. It reached Paris early in December, was joyfully received there, and led Louis XVI and his ministers to recognize the independence of the United States of America and to take France into the war as the open ally of the patriots.

Island, he might have led five thousand men up the Hudson, enough to make a real attempt to rescue Burgoyne. He had not been authorized to take that step, but the emergency justified it.

[19] Howe to Clinton, Nov. 16, 1777, *American Historical Review*, XXXVII (1932), 722–723. Howe did not want the Hessians. He claimed that Washington had cheated him in an earlier exchange of prisoners and that the patriots owed him as many men as there were in Burgoyne's British contingents. Gates suggested to Congress that the convention troops be kept in custody until Howe entered into a satisfactory cartel for the exchange of prisoners. *Digby Journal*, p. 58.

[20] John C. Fitzpatrick (ed.), *The Writings of George Washington* . . . (39 vols., Washington, 1931–44), X, 10–11.

CHAPTER 10

Reformation in the States

WHILE the Continentals and militia fought against Britain, other patriots, assuming ultimate victory, remolded their political and social institutions. They created written constitutions both for the several states and for the United States; made careful provision for the protection of personal liberties; struck at religious privilege; assailed barbarous punishments for crime; moved haltingly in the direction of political democracy; redistributed land; and even ventured to attack the institution of Negro slavery. They initiated an "Internal Revolution" which continued beyond the war and exercised an enduring influence.

The War of Independence was hardly begun when the patriots began to try to form legal and permanent governments in the colony-states. Overturning regimes sanctioned by Britain, they were often forced for a time to govern through revolutionary and extralegal—if not illegal—conventions and committees. But they desired political institutions more stable, more ordered, and better calculated to preserve and enhance their own liberties, if not those of the Tories. Very generally, in part because of their long acquaintance with colonial charters, they looked upon the written constitution as indispensable. In the fall of 1775 John Adams developed a model constitution; early in 1776 Tom Paine proposed another. Even before Paine's model appeared, the New Hampshire patriots adopted for temporary use a written constitution which endured until 1784. The South Carolina patriots adopted a temporary constitution in March, 1776, one intended to be permanent in 1778. Two such documents designed for long use were actually promulgated before the Declaration of Independence, in Virginia and New Jersey, and six others before the close of 1777. Rhode Island and Connecticut continued in effect their colonial charters with minor revisions. Massachusetts similarly, but temporarily, operated its charter until 1780, when a carefully drawn basic document was put into effect.[1]

It is a striking fact that the early state constitutions were neither prepared by conventions especially elected for the purpose nor submitted to the voters for approval. In a few instances they were drawn up and declared in operation by legislative bodies chosen in elections in which constitution-making was not an issue. More commonly, they were conceived and declared in effect by legislators to whom the voters had entrusted the tasks of fashioning statutory and fundamental law. Thus even those who enjoyed the privilege of the ballot had little or no opportunity to voice their desires. This fact was a matter of concern to many patriots, including Jefferson, who insisted that any constitution intended to be more than temporary should be sanctioned by the voters.

That the basic law guaranteeing the rights of the individual and establishing the framework of state government might be adopted without ratification aroused the citizens of Massachusetts. When, in September, 1776, the towns of that state were asked whether they would permit the General Court to draft a constitution, Concord as well as other towns vigorously replied in the negative. Concord insisted that a prime purpose of such a document was "to secure the subject in the possession and enjoyment of their rights and privileges, against any encroachments of the governing part." If a General Court could mold a basic document, then another such assemblage could later alter it at will. Of what avail then a fundamental law? Accordingly Concord urged that a convention be specially elected to draw up a constitution and that the citizens of the state be given an opportunity to inspect and comment upon the result before it should be put into practice.[2] A mass meeting at Pittsfield proposed that a constitution should become valid only

---

[1] Allan Nevins, *The American States during and after the Revolution 1775–1789* (New York, 1924), contains a vast amount of information concerning these constitutions and about conditions in the states in general during this period.

[2] The Concord resolutions may conveniently be examined in Henry S. Commager (ed.), *Documents of American History* (New York, 1934), 104–105.

when approved by a majority of the voters. The General Court decided to draft such a document, which it submitted to referendum, but its handiwork was overwhelmingly defeated at the polls. In consequence the legislature called a state constitutional convention, which met in 1779–80 and which at least pretended to submit its product to the voters. More than a year earlier the first such convention had met in New Hampshire, but its work had been disapproved by the towns of that state. In 1783 another New Hampshire convention produced a document which received their consent. Massachusetts and her neighbor thus inaugurated the familiar and exceedingly important devices of the constitutional convention and the constitutional referendum. Further, since their method of constitution-making implied the supremacy of constitutions over legislative acts, the road was opened for the development of judicial review.

The Revolutionary state constitutions were often hurriedly drafted in the midst of other business, even by legislatures in flight before advancing British troops. In some cases there was little quarreling regarding their provisions, in others heated controversy. Nevertheless, on the whole, the work was amazingly well done, since the majority of the constitutions intended for permanent use remained in force for a generation or more.

On the surface, the new basic state laws were much alike. As a general rule, they contained a Bill of Rights; all provided for an elected legislature, usually consisting of two houses; all arranged for a governor (or president) elected either by the voters or by the legislature; all granted the suffrage only to property owners or taxpayers; and most of them gave at least lip service to the principle of separation of powers. But if the governments set up by these documents differed little in form, there were important variations in substance. In some instances these constitutions were devised by patriots who wanted little or no change beyond separation from Britain—by Conservatives; in others, they were composed by patriots who desired independence and alterations in the direction of political democracy and social equality—by Radicals; in still others, neither the influence of the Conservatives nor that of the Radicals was decisive.

In the main, the forms of government under the new state constitutions were patterned after those in vogue in the colonies before

1775, with elected governors and senates replacing governors and councils chosen by the crown or the proprietors. The substance was largely derived from the colonial experience of 150 years and from the doctrines of natural rights and compact so splendidly asserted in the Declaration of Independence, and again in the Massachusetts constitution of 1780. In the latter document it is declared that "The body politic is formed by a voluntary association of individuals; it is a social compact, by which the whole people covenants with each citizen, and each with the whole people that all shall be governed by certain laws for the common good";[3] and also, that "The people alone have an incontestible unalienable, and indefeasible right to institute government, and to reform, alter, or totally change the same when their protection, safety, prosperity, and happiness require it." [4] These ideas were derived from study of the writings of a galaxy of British and European political theorists, especially those of John Locke. From Locke, and perhaps more particularly from Montesquieu, came another concept of great importance, separation of powers among the branches of government in order to prevent any one of them from becoming dominant and tyrannical.

Although the makers of the first state constitutions quite uniformly subscribed to Lockeian principles, they did not agree with respect to their meaning and their application. The drafters quarreled little about statements inserted in the Bills of Rights guaranteeing trial by jury, the right of petition, freedom from self-incrimination, and other rights familiar to English law. They fought, and often bitterly, over provisions regarding religion, the suffrage, qualifications for office-holding, the powers of the governor as against those of the legislature, and other crucial issues. In fact, the Conservatives and the Radicals were seriously at odds regarding the political and social goals of the Revolution.

In essence, the Conservatives, though devoted to the ideal of independence, feared excessive change. In the seats of authority formerly occupied by royal appointees, they now wished to place the propertied, the educated, and the socially qualified. They despised and dreaded majority rule because they conceived the

[3] Francis N. Thorpe (ed.), *Federal and State Constitutions* . . . (7 vols., Washington, 1909), III, 1889.
[4] *Ibid.*, p. 1890.

humbler and less learned patriots to be incapable and even depraved. They opposed "mob rule" as leading to anarchy or dictatorship. Not a few of them defended established churches, feudal arrangements of primogeniture and entail, and privilege generally for the select and the superior. Had they been able to impose their will, the great planters, the wealthy merchants, and a portion of the clergy—the upper middle class—would have formed an American aristocracy and an American oligarchy. The Conservatives read their Locke as the British landed aristocracy and the British merchants read him after the Glorious Revolution of 1688. In the compact mechanics, small farmers, and slaves were not full and equal partners.

The Radicals refused to concede that the only great purpose of the patriots was separation from Britain. They would not admit that their rights—the rights of mankind—would be secured by the mere disappearance of royal and proprietary officials. To them Lockeian philosophy was a system of thought which sanctified neither rule by Britain nor domination by privileged Americans. They argued that all citizens were equal participants in compact. They were likely to look upon government as at best a necessary evil and to seek to limit its powers. They insisted that the suffrage should be generously granted, even that it should not be denied to any adult white male. They demanded just apportionment of legislative seats, so that the vote of the farmer and the frontiersman in the interior would have equal weight with that of the seaboard merchant and planter—tidewater areas were then frequently overrepresented. The Radicals would place power in the legislature rather than in the executive or the judiciary, since the legislature would be most responsive to popular will. Conceding that the wishes of a minority should be given thoughtful consideration, they were prone to insist upon majority rule.

Nor was Radical thought confined to things political. Enlightened "leftists" of the War of Independence demanded complete religious freedom; they inveighed against hereditary aristocracy and legal and customary arrangements which favored the eldest son at the expense of his brothers and sisters. They asked at least a modicum of free public education for the sons and daughters of all free men. They urged reform of civil and criminal law to prevent injustice and cruel punishments, and they assailed brutal treatment of prisoners. Some even attacked the institution of Negro slavery as inhumane and unwarranted either by Locke or by God. In short, many Radical leaders, and at least a portion of their followers, entertained views which may be described as liberal or progressive and as logical.

To be sure, all the Radicals were not occupied with altruistic designs for present and future improvement—they were not all Jeffersons. Some were shiftless, irresponsible, and unprincipled folk who found in the Revolution opportunity to evade payment of taxes and debts, to pull down to their own level envied neighbors, and to exalt themselves without resort to toil. Nor were all the Conservatives mere crass devotees of personal and class interests. A number, among them Henry Laurens of South Carolina, were troubled because they were fighting for the rights of man while continuing to hold Negroes in bondage. Many of them desired religious freedom. Indeed, many Conservatives were moderate men hardly to be distinguished from the milder Radicals. In fact, no hard and fast line can be drawn between Conservatives and Radicals. Within both groups there were infinite variations, and some individuals shifted from one camp to the other.

In the struggle between the Conservatives and Radicals the latter group possessed important advantages. The Tories, who in the main would have been natural allies of the Conservatives, were commonly excluded from public life and even from the ballot. Moreover, many men who had not been permitted to vote before the war had been allowed to help choose Revolutionary conventions and legislatures. These clung to the ballot as more permanent regimes appeared. The Second Continental Congress itself advised "a full and free representation of the people" in constitution-making; [5] and the influence of the new voters is to be discerned in the basic state documents. Inevitably, the majority of these suddenly enfranchised men joined the Radicals. In addition, the Conservatives, crying out against Britain, had come forth in defense of the rights of man and against taxation without representation, and had thus supplied their fellow patriots with ammunition which could be used against themselves. They could hardly deny the logic of the demands by the Radicals that the franchise be given to many of

[5] Worthington C. Ford *et al.* (eds.), *The Journals of the Continental Congress, 1774–1789* (34 vols., Washington, 1904–37), III, 319, 325.

those voteless in colonial days; nor could they easily counter Radical arguments for redistricting of seats in the legislatures. The interior regions, "the Old West," had long been so patently under-represented in the colony-states, especially in Pennsylvania, Virginia, and South Carolina, that the justice of those arguments was obvious. Yet in giving way to the Radicals on these points the Conservatives suffered serious diminution of their influence, not only because the new voters were inclined toward the Radicals, but also because "the Old West" was their stronghold. In sum, the Conservatives found it impossible to control the patriots as a whole and to insist that the only great goal of the war was severance from Britain.

Among the patriots were divisions along socio-economic lines. The small and tenant farmers, the frontier folk, and unpropertied people of the seacoast towns and cities tended to oppose the planters and merchants in the camp of the Conservatives. Class lines were not always clearly drawn, however. Jarring concepts were debated rather than settled by force; conflicting interests were compromised rather than decided by blows; and the Radicals found their most effective leaders among planters and certain merchants, lawyers, and other men of wealth, such as Jefferson, Richard Henry Lee, George Mason, George Wythe, Franklin, George Bryan, Thomas McKean, and Elbridge Gerry.

The influence of the Radicals may readily be discerned in the provisions of the new state constitutions concerning the ballot and qualifications for office-holding. Under these any taxpayer in Pennsylvania, Delaware, North Carolina, Georgia, and Vermont could vote. Any Virginian owning twenty-five acres of improved soil or five hundred acres of undeveloped land possessed the ballot. In the other states the suffrage was less generously offered to men who possessed either land or personal property in some quantity, or paid fairly substantial amounts in taxes. Very commonly, higher qualifications in the way of property or payment of taxes were required for members of the lower house of the legislature, still higher ones for membership in the upper house, and occasionally even higher ones for persons serving as governors. Office-holding was thus frequently reserved for men of means; no state conceded manhood suffrage; and plural voting on the basis of ownership of land was still possible in several states. But if political democracy had not been achieved, it is nevertheless true that the voting population was larger than it was in colonial days. Land was cheap, and the privilege of the ballot was often easily within the reach even of the poor. Since the Tories were usually disfranchised and since many sought safety in exile, there came a more or less permanent swing to the left in American politics.

The influence of the Radicals is also to be observed in the provisions of the early constitutions concerning the powers of the respective branches of government. While expressions of respect for the principle of separation of powers were freely offered, authority was usually centered in the legislature, and especially in the lower house. The Radicals feared strong executives and distrusted independent judiciaries. As a result the governor was given an effective veto only in Massachusetts, and he was in some states a mere figurehead. In several states judges were chosen by the legislature, and for very short terms. The Radicals believed, and not without reason, that the legislatures would be more responsive to the public will, particularly since they were also able in a number of states to require frequent elections. The political systems set up in states where the Radicals were dominant—for example, Pennsylvania, Virginia, and North Carolina—were accordingly ill balanced and not too efficient. They were, however, far more democratic than those established in states under Conservative domination—for example, Maryland.

Much redistricting in the direction of political justice and democracy is also to be found in these constitutions. In Pennsylvania the southeastern counties, almost absurdly overrepresented before 1775, lost their special and privileged position. In Virginia the Piedmont and Shenandoah regions received for the first time representation in accordance with their numerous population. Sectional favoritism was also eliminated in North Carolina. Concessions were made to interior folk in South Carolina and Massachusetts, although the Lowlands about Charleston continued for some years to hold a favored position. Frontier democracy was given larger opportunity to express itself, an opportunity which was not wasted.

The makers of fundamental law in the Revolutionary period also took long strides toward religious freedom. Before the war there was a relatively large measure of toleration everywhere in the Thirteen Colonies, but complete religious freedom nowhere except in Rhode

Island. In no fewer than nine colonies there were established tax-supported churches, enjoying privileges varying greatly from place to place. In New England, except for Rhode Island, the Congregational Church had the support of the state, while the Anglican Church was official in a few counties of New York and in all the colonies from Maryland to Georgia. It was usually difficult and sometimes impossible for a member of a dissenting sect to escape taxation for the support of the established church in his colony; and he who was attached to no religious organization could not evade it. Universally, save in Rhode Island (which in the eighteenth century restricted the political activities of Catholics and Jews), there were discriminations of one sort or another, relatively mild in Pennsylvania and Delaware, onerous in Congregational New England and Episcopalian Maryland and Virginia. Connecticut law still required church attendance; Roman Catholics could not hold office in Maryland.

The movement for disestablishment was facilitated by the fact that in no state were the Anglicans in a numerical majority. Except in Virginia, it was easy to reduce the Church of England to the level of other churches, for Presbyterians, Lutherans, Baptists, Roman Catholics, its own laymen, and deists (numerous among the leaders of the patriots) joined in the attack upon it. In Virginia, where the Anglicans formed perhaps half of the churchgoing population and included the bulk of the planters, there was a bitter struggle. However, Anglican clergymen in the upper South were distinguished for neither piety nor learning, and they were frequently Tories. Finally, the Church was definitely disestablished in the Old Dominion. The Congregational state churches in New England were less vulnerable; they lost some of their privileges, but were not deprived of all vestige of official sanction until the nineteenth century was well under way.

Disestablishment was, of course, not the equivalent of complete religious freedom, which was not attained in most of the states for some years. Thus New Jersey and the Carolinas continued to require that officeholders be Protestants; Massachusetts insisted that they declare themselves to be Christians; and Delaware demanded from them, and also from members of the legislature, that they declare their belief in the Holy Trinity. These and similar restrictions were soon to disappear. The trend was toward total religious liberty, with Jefferson and James Madison pointing the way in Virginia. In the Old Dominion the principle of toleration was incorporated in the Declaration of Rights of 1776. In the following year statutes requiring church attendance and the use of public money to support the Episcopal Church were repealed. The Episcopal Church fought bitterly against disestablishment and received powerful assistance from other Protestant sects, which desired that public funds be devoted to the maintenance of all the major Christian churches. Although the Episcopalian Church was deprived of all official status two years later, Patrick Henry, young John Marshall, and apparently Washington joined the ranks of those who wished to compel all citizens to help finance the Christian sects. Henry was able to mobilize a large majority in the assembly in favor of the scheme, but Jefferson, James Madison, and George Mason fought it persistently and imaginatively. At length the proposal was dropped, and the Statute of Religious Liberty, drawn up by Jefferson and sponsored by his friends, became law in 1786. In a long, rhetorical, and yet moving preamble the act condemned utterly all efforts to employ the power of government in behalf of any species of religion and affirmed that "truth is great and will prevail if left to herself. . . ." It was accordingly enacted "that no man shall be compelled to frequent or support any religious worship, place or ministry whatsoever, nor shall be enforced, restrained, molested, or burthened in his body or goods, nor shall otherwise suffer on account of his religious opinions or belief; but that all men shall be free to profess, and by argument to maintain, their opinion in matters of religion, and that the same shall in no wise diminish, enlarge, or affect their civil capacities." [6] Jefferson was justly proud of his contribution to religious freedom.

The Revolutionary generation, seeking to assert the natural rights of mankind, could not but be conscience-stricken when it considered the lot in America of some of the children of Nature's God, the Negroes, who composed one-fifth of the total population and half of that of South Carolina. Almost all of the Negroes were slaves. Generally they were held in mild subjection. Nevertheless, slavery

---

[6] The text of the law is readily accessible in *Documents of American History*, pp. 125–126. For the drafting of the act see Julian P. Boyd *et al.* (eds.), *The Papers of Thomas Jefferson* (6 vols. to date, Princeton, 1950——), II, 545–547.

then, as later, had its horrors, the worst of which was the traffic in human bodies between Africa and America. That brutal commerce had aroused indignation before the war, and the importation of slaves had been halted in Rhode Island, Connecticut, and Pennsylvania, but the British government and its representatives in the colonies had prevented the passage of similar laws in the royal colonies. When Britain and British officials could no longer interfere, American legislatures, with that of Delaware leading the way in 1776, undertook to put an end to the traffic.[7] During and immediately after the war the introduction from foreign lands of enslaved blacks was forbidden in all the states, save for South Carolina and Georgia. Even in the far South there was much sentiment in favor of such action, and importation was temporarily forbidden in South Carolina in 1787 and again in 1788.

The patriots did not content themselves merely with endeavors to destroy the oceanic slave trade. In the spring of 1775 there was formed at Philadelphia the first antislavery society in America, and many patriots, Conservative and Radical, including Washington, Jefferson, Madison, Patrick Henry, and Horatio Gates, were soon afterward urging the outlawing of Negro bondage. Economic interest, ignorance, feelings of racial superiority, and fear of the consequences of emancipation usually postponed or prevented action. Nevertheless, a few Negroes received their freedom in return for honorable military service in the war; and many thousands obtained it by manumission, made relatively easy by law in Virginia in 1782 and also by other states in the South. Moreover, Pennsylvania provided for gradual emancipation by a law of 1780; and statements of the Massachusetts Bill of Rights of the same year, including one which declared that "All men are born free and equal," were construed three years later by the highest court of that state to mean that slavery was outlawed. Certain other Northern states soon followed the examples of Pennsylvania and Massachusetts. Others did not act until after the close of the century. In the South, however, where there were both proportionately and absolutely many more slaves, sentiment began to swing after the war toward protecting that institution.

[7] The nonimportation agreement sponsored by the First Continental Congress included a pledge not to indulge in the trade and to boycott those who did.

If the patriots indirectly gave support to the concept of aristocracy by their failure to abolish slavery, they struck hard at that concept nonetheless. Provisions that there should be neither a privileged class nor hereditary offices were inserted in several of the first state constitutions. Two denied the legislature the power to create titles of nobility! Georgia even refused the privileges of voting and office-holding to persons claiming titles. Manorial rights and quitrents vanished. What was more important, the patriots demolished those twin props of landed aristocracy, primogeniture and entail. At the beginning of the war entailment, though forbidden in South Carolina, was more or less legal elsewhere. Primogeniture flourished in New York and the Southern colonies; in Pennsylvania, Delaware, New Jersey, and New England the eldest son received a double share in inheritance. With Jefferson and Virginia once again leading the way, these arrangements so well calculated to preserve family estates collapsed before the assaults of the reformers. By 1786 entails had been abolished or rendered innocuous in every state; by 1792 primogeniture had disappeared; indeed, by that time equality in intestate succession was universally established.[8] The results of these wholesale changes are difficult to measure, but in some areas they may have contributed to a more equitable distribution of land. Whatever the actual results, the social structure had been altered in the direction of equality.

The importance of redistribution of land, as Jefferson fully appreciated, can scarcely be overestimated. Ownership of soil brought relative economic independence, and with it advance in social and political status. More owners meant more democracy, social and political. Happily, redistribution proceeded during and immediately after the War of Independence, not only through the eradication of laws forcing and permitting concentration of ownership, but also through the abolition of British authority over the trans-Allegheny West and the confiscation of Tory property. The bars to westward settlement set up by the Proclamation of October 7, 1763, and later British restrictive measures vanished. Moreover, the great speculators in lands beyond the mountains, highly favored under the royal regime, found it somewhat more difficult to secure large grants from the state and federal governments at the expense of the

[8] See Richard B. Morris, *Studies in the History of American Law* (New York, 1930), chap. 1.

small farmer. Thus the path of the humble to landownership in the eastern part of the Mississippi Valley was made somewhat broader and smoother. To be sure, this result was hardly discernible until the war had ended and large-scale expansion beyond the mountains began.

The effects of confiscation of lands owned by Tories, however, appeared almost immediately. On November 27, 1777, the Continental Congress recommended that the states seize and sell the estates of Loyalists,[9] the proceeds to be used to finance the war. The idea of paying for the war in part at the expense of the Tories was a popular one among the patriots. Indeed, some states had already begun the process of confiscation. Now it was greatly hastened, and every state without exception declared Tory lands forfeited or at least subject to forfeiture. The result was a spate of sales of those lands which continued even after the close of the conflict. Whatever may be said about the treatment thus meted out to the supporters of Britain and the widespread corruption attendant upon such sales, many large estates were broken up and dispersed in smaller holdings among the patriots. In New York the lands of Tory James De Lancey became the property of 275 different persons; those of Tory Roger Morris went to nearly 250; and large tracts owned by Tories in the central and northern parts of the state were sold to poor farmers in quantities from one hundred to five hundred acres.[10] Since many of the Loyalists sooner or later went into exile (although some returned), it may be said that conservatism was permanently weakened both by their departure and by the fact that the less affluent were often enabled to acquire their properties and to move upward economically and socially.

If this analysis of change in the states accompanying and result-

[9] *Continental Congress Journals,* IX, 971.

[10] In North Carolina forty thousand acres belonging to Tory Henry Mc-Culloch were confiscated and sold in plots averaging two hundred acres. Robert O. DeMond, *Loyalists in North Carolina during the Revolution* (Durham, N.C., 1940), p. 180. It should be noted, however, that confiscated lands were often bought, at least in New York and Maryland, by merchants, army contractors, and Revolutionary leaders, men who already possessed land. Such speculators sometimes resold to poorer folk. Harry B. Yoshpe, *The Disposition of Loyalist Estates in the Southern District of the State of New York* (New York, 1939), pp. 115–117; Philip A. Crowl, *Maryland during and after the Revolution . . . , The Johns Hopkins Studies in Historical and Political Science,* Series LXI, No. 1 (1943), pp. 45–63.

ing from the war is already lengthy, it should nevertheless be recalled that the era of the Revolution brought increased pressure for more lenient treatment of debtors, for improvement in prison conditions, and for the revision and modernization of civil and criminal law. Certainly, education, in some part at least because of Revolutionary ferment, entered upon a new course. The concept of education at public expense received added impulse. In 1776 John Adams declared that "Laws for the liberal education of youth, especially of the lower class of people, are so extremely wise and useful, that, to a humane and generous mind, no expense for this purpose would be thought extravagant." [11] Jefferson, who was equally convinced with Adams of the values of education and of the desirability of spreading widely its benefits, proposed three years later that Virginia establish public schools for elementary instruction and remold the College of William and Mary into something approaching a university. Five Revolutionary state constitutions urged that provision be made for schools, in some instances specifically for free schools. It was apparent to many patriot leaders that the new American society in process of formation required diffusion of education, if for no other reason to the end that the less affluent citizens who were wielding influence in public affairs should be sufficiently enlightened to carry their burdens. Although the war temporarily interfered with the operations of schools and colleges, and although the proposals of Jefferson, and others like him, were temporarily set aside, the concept of a freer and more democratic educational system gained converts. Indicative of the future was the action of the legislature of Georgia in 1783 giving one thousand acres of land to every county for the support of schools.

[11] Charles F. Adams (ed.), *The Works of John Adams* (10 vols., Boston, 1856), IV, 199.

CHAPTER 11

Congress and Confederation

THE BRITISH subjects who lived on the mainland of North America definitely acquired the name "Americans" in the third quarter of the eighteenth century. The term was a useful one, making it easy to distinguish between them and the British at home. Its popularity did not rest on its convenience alone. That it was frequently and increasingly employed on both sides of the Atlantic after 1750 [1] attests both to the community of interest of the continental colonists and to the growing divergences from the British. Indeed, not long before Lexington, Hector St. John de Crèvecœur posed a meaningful question, "What then is the American, this new man?"

It would be idle to contend that the colonists had been cast in one rigid mold. There were very real dissimilarities between the Connecticut farmer and the Carolina planter, the Albany townsman and the tidewater Virginian, the Maine mariner and the Quaker merchant. The differences among the colonists were so marked that some contemporary observers believed it almost impossible to bring them together politically. Certainly the Albany Plan of Union had been very coldly received in 1754–55. Descended from disparate European stocks, the colonists exhibited variety and contrariety in religion; they were a product of diverse economic and social systems, of different climate and geography, and they were wedged apart by intercolonial strife over boundaries, lands, and trade. Intellectual and cultural contacts between colony and colony,

[1] It was used even before 1700.

164

though steadily increasing, were still relatively modest.[2] Commercial relations and travel by land were limited. There were colonists, especially Southerners, who were closer to the people of the mother country than they were to some of their fellows.

Nevertheless, the Americans were moving steadily in the latter part of the colonial period toward that community of sentiment which has been the basis of the modern national state. After all, in origins, except for the Negroes, they were not too sharply differentiated, since they almost universally had their roots in Britain and Europe west of the Elbe River. They were very generally Protestants. With minor exceptions (notably the Pennsylvania "Dutch") they spoke English, the mother tongue of the majority. All had been exposed to British cultural influences. Moreover, the impact of the American environment had in the main tended to make them alike rather than different. In the French, the Spanish, and even the Indians they had shared common enemies. Their association in the struggle against Britain after 1763 was a powerful cementing force, perhaps best evidenced first in the Stamp Act Congress and later in the Continental Congresses.

The War of Independence once again provided the colonists with a common danger and a common enemy. Virginians fought at Quebec and Saratoga; Delaware men marched to the defense of New York; New Englanders served at Brandywine and Germantown; and Marylanders moved to the defense of South Carolina. True, both the militia and the Continental troops exhibited on occasion sectional jealousy and distrust, but the Continentals, if not the militia, came to look upon themselves as American soldiers under the command of an American commander in chief chosen by an American government. It is difficult to believe that even one of them at the close of the war would have contended that he had been fighting for this or that truly "independent and sovereign" state, whether New Hampshire, Pennsylvania, or Georgia.

The war exercised similar though less influence upon civilian patriots. When Patrick Henry early in the struggle proclaimed himself an American rather than a Virginian, he was no solitary spirit. In October, 1775, the freemen of Botetourt County, in Henry's colony, declared that "when the honest man of Boston who has

---

[2] Michael Kraus, *Intercolonial Aspects of American Culture on the Eve of the Revolution* . . . (New York, 1928), *passim.*

broke no law, has his property wrested from him, the hunter on the Allegany must take the alarm." [3] Sectional and local suspicions and ancient antipathies did not promptly vanish, yet the patriot civilians became more united in sentiment. Washington's victory at Trenton was celebrated in Salem and Savannah. Both civilians and soldiers realized promptly that it was "Unite or die," and their leaders concluded that they might hang separately, should they fail to hang together. It was evident to all the patriots that their security, present and future, required them to give their loyalty to a central government. In turn, that central government furnished additional bonds of union, bringing the foremost patriots into intimate and more or less enduring association.

In some measure even the First Continental Congress exercised governmental powers. The Second Continental Congress, with its committees and administrative servants, was the central government of the United States down to 1781,[4] when the first national constitution, the Articles of Confederation, went into effect. The Congress declared the independence of the United States; appointed the commander in chief and higher officers of the Continental army; established the American navy and the marine corps; formed a diplomatic service; negotiated treaties with European nations and Indian tribes; organized a postal service; issued currency; and borrowed money. It even gave advice to the colony-states with respect to the making of their constitutions; and it drew up the Articles of Confederation.

It has often been said that the Second Continental Congress was little more than a council of ambassadors from the several states. One distinguished authority would have it that the Congress was "merely the central office of a continental political signal system." [5] It has been argued—without sufficient evidence—that the states were more important in the conduct of the war than the Congress was. It has been pointed out that some states asserted their independence through their own legislatures; that some were solemnly described in their constitutional documents as "independent and

[3] Hezekiah Niles (ed.), *Principles and Acts of the Revolution in America* (New York, 1876), p. 286.
[4] Edmund C. Burnett, *The Continental Congress* (New York, 1941), contains a thoughtful history of the congresses of the period 1774-89.
[5] Claude H. Van Tyne, *The American Revolution, 1776-1783* (New York, 1905), p. 188.

sovereign"; that one or two sent diplomatic representatives abroad; that a few attempted to borrow money in Europe; and that most of the Continentals were organized on the basis of states. Further, it has been noted that the actions of the delegates at Philadelphia were directed in part by the governments of the states which they represented, and that they were often specifically instructed with respect to questions before them. Thus the Declaration of Independence was not approved until most of the delegates were ordered or permitted to sanction it. In sum, it has been contended that in practice the states were almost all-powerful and the Congress extremely weak, also that the states were legally sovereign.

The scope of state sovereignty has been a matter of endless controversy. Suffice it to say that able historians have challenged that sovereignty and that the whole question is clouded in semantics. With regard to the fundamentally important matter of the location of power among patriot assemblages, it would seem that the Congress exercised a larger portion of it than some scholars have been willing to concede. The authority and the achievements of that body have been minimized both by defenders of states' rights and by those who would enlarge the fame of Washington at the expense of his employers. If it be true that many measures taken by the delegates required prior consent or later supporting action by the states, even in such cases the Congress was much more than an advisory council; and a very large number of basic decisions and policies were the product of the Congress itself, without state action or even consultation.

To be sure, the delegates who labored at Philadelphia, among other towns, did not always impress observers by their dignity and majesty. As time passed, they lost the services of Washington, Jefferson, Franklin, and John Adams. After the close of 1776 the greatest stars in the Revolutionary galaxy were not to be found among them, but shone in military camps, in European drawing rooms, and even at the state capitals. Several resigned from the Congress to accept state offices. Nevertheless, even at its lowest ebb Congress numbered some industrious men among its members.

After 1776 talent, integrity, and energy were not lacking in the Congress; genius was. Moreover, the body was riven by conflicting interests and by personal, interstate, regional, and ideological antagonisms. Its not infrequent errors in policy were matched by its faulty execution of its program. Members faltered in their tasks, were absent from duty at critical moments, and bickered intermittently on the floor and in committee. There was self-seeking among them. At times, especially in oppressive weather, so many delegates were absent that business was seriously interrupted. Voting was carried on by states, and the vote of a state was frequently omitted because it was insufficiently represented.[6] Even though the Congress deliberated in secret, its various shortcomings could not be long concealed from the public.

Too much has been said, perhaps, regarding the failings of the Congress. It was created in emergency, endowed with uncertain authority, and plagued by rapid changes in personnel. Hence it exhibited obvious defects lacking or less conspicuous in long- and well-established legislatures. Yet the delegates toiled almost incessantly, compromising most of their differences and striving rather generally for the common good. They were compelled not only to take part in deliberation and debate, but also as members of a myriad of committees to fulfill a host of executive functions, and some judicial ones. John Adams, not one to avoid duty, served on more than eighty committees. Not until 1781 was the burden of clerical and routine duties in great part lifted from the shoulders of the members of Congress by the creation of four executive departments.

The failures of the delegates have doubtless been overpublicized. They did not succeed in creating a stable currency; they made serious mistakes in military promotions; on occasion they gave Washington bad military advice; and they exhibited naïveté in the conduct of foreign affairs. But their record, when the difficulties to be faced are taken into account, is splendid rather than dismal. They did about all that could be done toward solving the problem of finances. They chose Washington as commander in chief and kept him in that office. They proffered him counsel both good and bad but generally permitted him freedom of action. If they displayed crudity and a measure of ignorance in dealing with foreign countries, nevertheless they and their representatives in Europe achieved the greatest diplomatic victories ever won by the United States. John Adams declared at the beginning of the war that the

[6] Burnett, *Continental Congress, passim.*

services of the patriot military men would be overvalued at the expense of civilian workers like himself. If the deeds of the Continental officers and men have not been excessively praised, too little credit has usually been given to the faithful in the Congress who struggled in adversity. Historians have at times been overly harsh in their appraisal of the delegates. They have condemned them for removing from Philadelphia to Baltimore as Howe's men moved across New Jersey late in 1776.[7] Should they recklessly have risked capture of the government of the United States?

The Second Continental Congress served for almost five years. Although the patriots were virtually unanimous after 1776 in desiring a central government based upon a written constitution, it was not feasible to put such a constitution into effect until 1781.

In the minds of the patriots independence and American union were virtually inseparable. The Second Continental Congress had hardly convened when some delegates began to talk of forming a confederation in order the better to defend American liberties. Soon Benjamin Franklin was displaying a plan called "Articles of Confederation and Perpetual Union." The majority of the delegates, rightly conceiving Franklin's scheme to be almost inextricably associated with independence, were against both the one and the other. The plan was circulated among the delegates. However, in the early summer of 1775 Congress declined even to enter any reference to the document in its journals; and two Revolutionary legislatures, those of New Jersey and North Carolina, which shortly afterward examined Franklin's proposals, rejected them. The North Carolinians were certain that "a further confederacy ought only to be adopted in case of the last extremity." In January, 1776, the Congress debated whether Franklin's plan should be considered, but the project was again set aside, since sentiment among the delegates was still opposed to separation. However, as the patriots increasingly turned to thoughts of independence, they also became converted to political union. Indeed, for various reasons union was slightly more popular than independence. When on June 7 Richard Henry Lee formally urged a declaration of independence, he also

[7] Typical is the statement, "Congress took fright, and retired to Baltimore," in John Fiske, *The American Revolution* (2 vols., Boston, 1891), I, 228. See also George A. Trevelyan, *The American Revolution* (New York, 1903), Pt. II, Vol. II, pp. 60–61.

called for the establishment of a confederation and for the con-
summation of foreign alliances. Thereafter it was generally assumed
that the Thirteen Colonies and their people had to be constitution-
ally united both to win and to preserve their independence. Thus
could be secured, Lee later asserted, "present strength, credit and
success" and "future peace and safety." [8] It was also assumed that
Congress must undertake to make a constitution to submit to the
states. The creation of a special convention for the purpose was not
even considered.

It need scarcely be pointed out that there was no unanimity
among the patriots in 1776, or at any later time, regarding the
nature of the union which was to be established. On June 12 the
Congress appointed a committee of thirteen, one from each colony,
to draft a constitution. The principal figures in the committee were
John Dickinson, Samuel Adams, Roger Sherman, Robert R. Livingston, and Edward Rutledge. Exactly one month later the draft
was completed and presented to the Congress for discussion and
action. It had been cast into good form by Dickinson, an acknowledged master of the pen; part of its content was derived from
Franklin's plan; part was drawn from the model of the Second
Continental Congress; Dickinson was probably more responsible for
its specific provisions than any other member of the committee,
even though he had left the Congress by July 4.

The Dickinson draft called for a one-house American legislature
composed of delegates chosen annually by the states, and for voting
in Congress by states. By express provision and by implication this
body was given large powers, with the notable and extremely important exception that authority to tax was reserved to the states.
Those powers, except in the area of taxation, could conceivably
have been construed to be as ample as those given to the central
government under the Constitution of 1787. Among them was
authority to settle boundary disputes between the states, to set limits
to states claiming lands westward to the Mississippi, and to form
new states "on the principles of liberty." The states were to contribute toward the maintenance of the common government in
proportion to population. These specific provisions, together with
the magnitude of the central power envisaged by the Dickinson

[8] James C. Ballagh (ed.), *The Letters of Richard Henry Lee* (2 vols., New
York, 1912–14), I, 308.

draft and the arrangement for voting by the states as equals, caused bitter controversy in Congress and led to prolonged debate among the delegates.

When the Dickinson draft was presented to Congress on July 12, speedy adoption was anticipated. Quickly printed and distributed among the delegates, it was discussed in committee of the whole for about three weeks after July 22, and again on August 19 and 20, when a revised plan was submitted to Congress itself. Meanwhile, optimistic belief that the instrument could be rapidly completed faded, to be replaced by fear of failure. Delegates from the states with larger populations were soon vehemently protesting against equal representation of the states in the proposed Congress and insistently demanding that representation be based upon numbers or upon financial contributions made to the central treasury by the states. Their colleagues from the states with smaller populations, anticipating domination by Virginia, Pennsylvania, and Massachusetts, strenuously clung to the principle of state equality as the only protection against such domination. There was also sharp disagreement as to the method of assessing the states' contributions to the central government. Delegates from areas where slaves were numerous contended that population was a proper basis only if slaves were not counted. Northern members urged that the slaves be included. When it was suggested that wealth was a more suitable criterion, hot dispute ensued over the possible modes of computing it.[9]

Perhaps no phase of the debate over the Dickinson draft was more bitter than that prompted by the proposal to give Congress authority to set westward limits to the states, to grant lands beyond those limits, and to make arrangements for the creation of new states. Massachusetts, Connecticut, Virginia, the Carolinas, and Georgia claimed by charter and other rights to extend to the Mississippi, and New York upon the basis of overlordship over the

[9] The Dickinson draft has been characterized as a document dominated by Conservative thought, which is represented as demanding a strong central government in 1776, as it did eleven years later. Merrill Jensen, *The Articles of Confederation* (Madison, Wis., 1940), chaps. 5–7, especially pp. 126–127, 163. But one should caution against overemphasizing the clash between Conservatives and Radicals over the making of the Articles of Confederation. Perhaps more stress should be laid upon the struggle between the representatives of the small and large states.

Iroquois and their possessions, asserted a pretension to vast lands lying toward the setting sun. By virtue of its charter of 1609 Virginia claimed not only Kentucky but also that vast region which was later known as the Old Northwest. Six states, New Hampshire, Rhode Island, New Jersey, Pennsylvania, Delaware, and Maryland, possessed neither sea-to-sea charter title nor shadowy suzerainty over an Indian confederacy. From the latter three, especially from Maryland, came powerful support for the phrases permitting Congress to set bounds to the so-called "landed" states. Delegates from these three insisted that, should the trans-Allegheny West be American territory at the end of the war, it would be as the result of common efforts in a common cause. Hence all Americans ought to have equal opportunity to settle in and to exploit the area. If the "landed" states were allowed to assert possession, their people would be given great advantage over others, since they would have easier access to and greater influence at their state capitals and county seats, where the lands would be granted or sold. Equal opportunity, the argument continued, could be secured in the immediate future only by placing the distribution of the lands beyond the mountains in the hands of Congress. There was justice in this contention, but less ground for complaint in another argument, that without central control over the West the population and wealth of the "landed" states would be increased at the expense of the others. Residents of the "landless" states would surely migrate in numbers beyond the Alleghenies into the interior of the "landed" states, but the only injury resulting would be to local pride.

The delegates from the "landless" states had a strong case, and they made the most of it, but it was morally weakened by the fact that the placing of Western lands under the control of Congress would favor the interests of numerous speculators in Pennsylvania and Maryland who had acquired stock in the Indiana, Illinois, and Wabash land companies. Largely on the basis of purchase from the Indians before 1775, the first of these claimed a vast tract south of the Ohio in what is now West Virginia, and the others great areas north of the Ohio in what is presently Illinois and Indiana. If the validity of Virginia's claims were upheld, these speculators could hardly hope to realize anything from their investments, for Virginia had not recognized the legality of their purchases from the Indians. Moreover, in view of the opposition of the Old Dominion's own speculators, it was very unlikely that Virginia would make any concession to them in the future. The Pennsylvania and Maryland speculators looked to the central government for more generous treatment, and were accordingly anxious to vest the territories in Congress.

Contrariwise, delegates from the "landed" states, especially Virginia, denounced the attempt to deprive them of a Western empire. They made much of their legal "rights," and denied that any substantial inequity would follow such recognition. Virginia delegates did what they could to expose the selfish interests attempting to invalidate their claims under the old charter. In rebuttal, James Wilson and Samuel Chase of the "landless" states reiterated their arguments, Wilson hinting that Pennsylvania might refuse to enter into a combination with her sister states unless her wishes were met. Since the Articles needed unanimous approval to go into effect, an impasse resulted.[10]

By August 20, a revision of the Dickinson plan was before the Congress, one which neither satisfied all the patriots nor could muster the required backing from the legislatures of all thirteen states. Delay was therefore inevitable. Moreover, Howe's offensive moves, initiated immediately thereafter, gave the delegates other food for thought. The flight of the Congress to Baltimore at the close of the campaign of 1776 provided further interruption. Not until April of the following year was the Congress able to resume discussion of the problem at Philadelphia. Then it was attacked with renewed vigor, and a decision to set narrow bounds upon the powers of the proposed central government was reached. But summer, absenteeism, and the approach of Howe on Chesapeake Bay prevented solutions to other questions. In September the Congress again took wing to escape Howe's army and found refuge in York, Pennsylvania. With the military fortunes of the United States seemingly at low ebb, a more effective union both to achieve greater efficiency and to gain foreign aid was believed to be more necessary than ever before. The delegates once more came to grips with the great issues still unsettled. There was a strong disposition to com-

---

[10] Thomas P. Abernethy, *Western Lands and the American Revolution* (New York, 1937), deals in detail with the influence of the trans-Allegheny West upon the course of the American Revolution, enlarging upon and superseding at some points Clarence W. Alvord's *Mississippi Valley in British Politics* (2 vols., Cleveland, 1917).

plete the constitution and to subordinate and override minority opinions. It was decided that voting in Congress should be by states, that contributions to the central treasury be made in accordance with the value of improved lands, and that no western boundaries should be set for the "landed" states. The Articles of Confederation were finished by November 15 and were then submitted to the states for approval. In an accompanying message the delegates acknowledged that the instrument could hardly be completely satisfactory to all, if indeed to any, but begged that local and special interests be jettisoned and that it be sanctioned for the general patriot good.

The Congress too optimistically hoped that the Articles would be ratified by March, 1778. The states were slow to act, and most of them clogged acceptance with conditions and amendments. In June every one of these was rejected by the Congress, which demanded and expected to obtain prompt and unqualified assent. That body was then permeated by a high hope that the union could be proclaimed before the second anniversary of the Declaration of Independence. But many long months were to pass before confederation was achieved. On July 8 the delegates of eight states formally signed the constitution on behalf of their constituents. Soon afterward two more states were officially committed. However, Maryland, New Jersey, and Delaware refused to concur, insisting that the instrument must give Congress the authority to lay down western boundaries for the "landed" states. The delegates appealed again to the "patriotism and good sense" of the dissentients, apparently not without result, since New Jersey and Delaware gave their signatures in the following winter. Maryland obdurately withheld her consent for another two years and was finally able to force a further revision of the Articles.

The uncompromising stand of Maryland's delegates impelled the Virginia delegation to propose in the late spring of 1779 the establishment of the union without Maryland.[11] Connecticut supported Virginia, but to many other states an incomplete union seemed as dangerous as none at all. Moreover, sympathy with Maryland's view upon the Western lands continued and even increased in other states. Even the assembly of Virginia, pursuing a line of thought

[11] Worthington C. Ford *et al.* (eds.), *The Journals of the Continental Congress, 1774–1789* (34 vols., Washington, 1904–37), XIV, 617–618.

proposed by Jefferson over three years earlier, hinted toward the end of the year that the Old Dominion might "at a future day" concede the wisdom of establishing new states beyond the mountains. In February, 1780, New York, urged on by Robert R. Livingston, Philip Schuyler, and Governor George Clinton, indicated its willingness to give up at least a part of its shadowy claim to Western lands, largely in order to cement the union. A special committee examining the Western problem recommended in July, 1780, that the Congress reverse itself and that it ask the "landed" states to make "a liberal surrender of a portion of their territorial claims" for the common good and security of America. The recommendation was adopted in the following September.[12]

Except for Maryland the response of the "landless" states to requests to abandon their special interests for the sake of union had not been ungenerous. Now the "landed" states, especially Virginia, were put to the test and were equally magnanimous. As early as November, 1778, Richard Henry Lee had suggested that Virginia should cede her claim to territory north of the Ohio River both for the cause of union and for the welfare of Virginia. He believed that too extended borders would lead to a loss of efficiency and even of democracy in Virginia. Jefferson harbored even more generous sentiments. Joseph Jones and James Madison,[13] Virginia delegates to the Congress in the summer of 1780, supported Lee and Jefferson. They urged the necessity of the cession [14] and also of the future formation of new states beyond the Ohio. On October 10 the Congress formally resolved that areas ceded by the "landed" states should be granted and settled under the direction of Congress and that new states fully equal to those existing should be located within them.[15]

Nor was the Virginia legislature lacking in liberality. Understandably sympathetic both toward the interests of some Virginia speculators in Western lands and toward the claim of Virginia soldiers to bounty lands, the legislature was not willing to see the region north of the Ohio selfishly exploited by the speculators of

[12] *Ibid.*, XVII, 86, 806–807.

[13] The statesmanlike work of Madison in connection with the thorny problem of Western lands is splendidly described in Irving Brant, *James Madison, The Nationalist, 1780–1787* (Indianapolis, 1948), chap. 11.

[14] Jensen, *Articles of Confederation*, pp. 225–234.

[15] *Continental Congress Journals*, XVIII, 915–916.

Maryland and Pennsylvania, and their associates. On January 2, 1781, that body agreed to cede to the union Virginia's trans-Ohio claims, subject to certain stipulations, including one which declared illegal and void all pretensions of private persons to ownership of soil beyond the river. The Old Dominion thus gave powerful impetus toward a solution of the problem of the West. Simultaneously Connecticut offered to give up at least a part of its claim to Western empire. It became apparent that all the "landed" states would sooner or later follow the lead of New York, Virginia, and Connecticut.

In January, 1781, the objections of Maryland on the score of Western lands had been largely met. To be sure, Virginia's offer was not too palatable to Marylanders like Thomas Johnson, Charles Carroll of Carrollton, and Samuel Chase, who held stock in the Illinois-Wabash company, recently formed from the Illinois and Wabash combinations. But personal interests could not be openly advanced as grounds for refusing to enter the Confederation, and there is little evidence of any deeply rooted opposition to entry. Indeed, Johnson now urged that Maryland ratify the Articles. The Chevalier de la Luzerne, French envoy to the United States, to whom the state was appealing for naval aid, also pressed for favorable action. Early in February the Maryland legislature authorized its delegates in Congress to sign the constitution.[16] On March 1, at long last, Congress was able to announce amidst public rejoicing the creation of a "perpetual" union.

Experience would reveal deficiencies in that first constitution of the United States. There was widespread feeling, even before Maryland finally gave its assent to the document, that the central government established by it could not function satisfactorily. Because of the time-tested virtues of the Constitution of 1787, it has been the fashion to judge its less durable predecessor severely. Yet the founders of the Confederation, in spite of their assertion that it was to be "perpetual," scarcely expected that their work would endure without change. Moreover, the Confederation was a very long step

[16] Upon the ratification by Maryland, see Kathryn Sullivan, *Maryland and France, 1774-1789* (Philadelphia, 1936), pp. 97-100; St. George L. Sioussat, "The Chevalier de la Luzerne and the Ratification of the Articles of Confederation by Maryland," *Pennsylvania Magazine of History and Biography,* LX (1936), 391-418; Jensen, *Articles of Confederation,* pp. 236-238.

toward the making of a more perfect union. Indeed, the much abused Articles, with a few amendments, might have served as a workable scheme of federal government for many years. In any case, the central government after 1781 had powers beyond those of the Second Continental Congress and powers based upon a solemnly ratified written constitution.

CHAPTER 12

The Bourbons Enter the War

THE MAKING and the ratification of the Articles of Confederation might have been merely a long exercise in political theory, had not France and Spain secretly helped the patriots before 1778, and had not the former become their fighting ally in June of that year. The entry of Spain into the conflict in 1779, sharply increasing Britain's difficulties, further assisted the patriots. The courts of the Bourbon princes at Versailles and Madrid now sought retaliation for the losses which they had suffered at the hands of Britain, especially in the course of the Seven Years' War. The Anglo-American war provided them with a long-awaited opportunity.

In 1761, in the midst of overwhelming defeat, Étienne-François, Duc de Choiseul, favorite of Madame de Pompadour and head of the French Foreign Ministry, began to rebuild French power in preparation for a war of revenge. He had won no laurels in the Seven Years' War, but now laid the keels for a new and powerful navy. After the Peace of Paris, he and other patriotic Frenchmen strove to build ships, to supply them with efficient artillery, and to man them with sturdy and experienced sailors. The result was the eventual restoration of French sea power and the development of a French navy which proved to be superior in all but numbers and morale to that of Britain. Choiseul and other Frenchmen also did what they could toward rebuilding that army which had achieved so little against Frederick the Great and Ferdinand of Brunswick. They improved the quality of the muskets and effected such minor reforms as the issuance of national uniforms, but could not force the replacement of higher officers chosen for family by others selected for merit. In consequence the army failed to keep pace with the navy. In addition, Choiseul's efforts to win friends for France among the powers of Europe, great and small, were crowned with a measure of success.

Choiseul shrewdly foresaw that Britain would alienate the affections of the Thirteen Colonies and that France might be able to take advantage of British mistakes in colonial policy. After 1764 he sent to America various secret agents, including the Baron de Kalb, to plumb colonial discontent, and he maintained an espionage service in England for that and other purposes. He hoped that the Thirteen Colonies would gain their independence and that they would divert their trade from England, in part at least, to France. Since he, with other French politicians of the generation after 1763, believed commerce to be the real basis of British strength, he calculated that such events would wound Britain almost mortally and bring wealth to France. Because he and his associates had no great desire to undertake to restore the shattered French empire,[1] they saw no good reason why France should not enjoy friendly and profitable relations with an independent America. Unhappily for Choiseul's plans, the reports of his agents were contradictory. Some informed him that the Americans were ready to revolt; others held such a move premature. By 1770 he had come to the conclusion that the colonial troubles of Britain were unlikely to cause her downfall for some years. He then undertook to support Spain in a bitter quarrel which had arisen between Spain and Britain over the Falkland Islands, expecting that war would follow and hoping that the two Bourbon kingdoms could subdue their old enemy. Unable to persuade Louis XV and the French ministry of the wisdom of this course, he was forced out of office.

That Choiseul in 1770 was willing to wage war against Britain in alliance with Spain is to be explained in part by the fact that Spain had also entered upon a period of reform and revival. While such a conflict would probably have ended in stalemate or defeat

[1] After 1763 Choiseul strove to develop the colonies remaining under the French flag, with little success and much expense. His failure provided an additional argument against attempts to regain or rebuild the French empire. See Carl L. Lokke, *France and the Colonial Question: A Study of Contemporary French Opinion, 1763–1801* (New York, 1932), pp. 15–62.

for the Bourbons, the Spanish government was not unwilling to risk it. Under the leadership of the benevolent despot Charles III, supported by able officials such as the Marquis Grimaldi, Count Aranda, and Count Campomanes, Spain was making rapid economic progress, and both her civilian and military officers were displaying unwonted ability and energy. At Madrid, too, there was keen desire to strike at Britain. Charles III and his advisers wished to safeguard the Spanish colonies in America, to regain Gibraltar and Minorca, and to obtain revenge. They were forced for lack of French support to bend before Britain in the matter of the Falkland Islands. They were the more eager, when opportunity came, to seek advantage from Britain's distress.

When the news came to France that Britain and the Thirteen Colonies had come to blows, the Comte de Vergennes occupied the Foreign Office. Although he was quite new in the ministry, having been appointed by Louis XVI after his accession to the throne in the preceding year, Vergennes was an experienced diplomat. His policies varied little from those of Choiseul,[2] but he was more cautious. Devoted to duty, gifted with a subtle intellect, unscrupulous when the needs of France seemed to require duplicity, Vergennes hovered on the fringe of greatness. He had feared that the crisis in Anglo-American relations might drive the North ministry from power and bring to the British helm the Earl of Chatham; further, that Chatham would be able to satisfy the Americans and that he would then once again lead the united forces of the British Empire against France and Spain. Hence, he decided to be most circumspect. As early as December, 1774, Americans in London, including no doubt Arthur Lee, had hinted to a French diplomat that the colonists might be interested in French aid, in the event that their quarrel with Britain ended in military conflict. Vergennes prudently avoided committing himself. But reports of Bunker Hill and of American determination to fight led Vergennes to believe that the opportunity so long hoped for by Choiseul had perhaps arrived. In September, 1775, he sent to Philadelphia a special agent, M. Achard Bonvouloir, to encourage the colonists and to intimate that they would be permitted free use of French ports. Almost simultaneously he entered into close association with

[2] Henri Doniol, *Histoire de la participation de la France, à l'établissement des États-Unis d'Amérique* (6 vols., Paris, 1884–92), I, 243–244.

Caron de Beaumarchais, a trusted French agent, who was eager to offer hidden help to the colonists for the benefit of France.

Whether Beaumarchais influenced Vergennes or Vergennes used Beaumarchais to execute a decision already reached by the Foreign Minister is not known. In any case, the two men worked hand in hand after the fall of 1775; and Beaumarchais, son of a watchmaker, self-made man, possessor of intellect, courage, comeliness, wit, and charm, was a very valuable helpmeet to Vergennes. In December, undoubtedly with the approval of the Minister, Beaumarchais wrote a letter to Louis XVI urging the young monarch to undertake to supply secretly munitions, and even cash, to the Americans. The King hesitated to strike clandestinely at a nation with which France was at peace. Beaumarchais emphasized that the chance to injure Britain seriously at little expense must not be ignored because of scruples laudable in private life but out of place in statecraft, and insisted that Britain's policy was to degrade and undermine France. As the winter passed Beaumarchais and Vergennes, who was encouraged to act by a report from Bonvouloir,[3] pushed their idea more and more strenuously, and they secured support in the French ministry. In March, 1776, Vergennes asked the Spanish government whether it would join in the project. The Marquis Grimaldi responded affirmatively and with a frank expression of hope that their aid might lead to the mutual exhaustion of both Britain and America.

Assured of co-operation from Spain, the French Foreign Minister formally laid the scheme before his colleagues. Its execution should be accompanied, he urged, by deceitful assurances of friendship to Britain. There should be no commitments to the Americans which would give Britain excuse to declare war upon France. He admitted that his proposals might bring such a declaration. France and Spain should therefore be constantly prepared for battle. Vergennes's plan contemplated the establishment of an American republic, or many American republics. Like Choiseul, he believed that American independence would cripple Britain commercially while at the same time assisting French trade. In support of his scheme he argued that the Americans, republican and weak, would not move against the French colonies in the West Indies. On the

[3] John J. Meng, "A Foot-note to Secret Aid in the American Rovolution," *American Historical Review*, XLIII (1938), 793.

other hand, he contended, perhaps without faith in his assertion, that there was real danger of an Anglo-American reconciliation and of an Anglo-American attack upon the French islands.[4]

There was opposition to Vergennes's project. The King saw in it both dishonorable conduct and potential disaster, and Turgot, his Comptroller General of Finances, shared his alarm. In a lengthy state paper[5] he vehemently insisted that war with Britain must be avoided, for it would ruin his grandiose designs for the renovation of the French economy and would drive the nation, already heavily in debt, into bankruptcy. He was opposed to such a conflict, whether to defend the colonies of France or to free those of Britain. He predicted that Europeans in America would in any case before long secure their freedom. If Britain should conquer the Thirteen Colonies, she could hold them only by force, thus weakening seriously her position with reference to France. Wisdom and morality dictated that France should remain at peace, declared the great Minister. However, Turgot very reluctantly consented to the giving of secret help to the Americans; the King's advisers, except for him, stood with Vergennes; and Louis accepted the view of the majority. On May 2 he directed that one million livres be turned over to Beaumarchais, who now became Roderigue Hortalez and Company and who undertook in the guise of a merchant to use the money to purchase and send munitions to the Americans. Beaumarchais was even permitted to buy royal ordnance from the manufacturers. The Spanish government promptly gave him another million livres.

So it was that France and Spain, before an agent of the Continental Congress reached French soil, and because their rulers saw the situation as capable of being exploited to their own advantage, determined to offer concealed assistance to the patriots. Using as capital the two million livres, to which France added a similar sum in the following year, Beaumarchais sent off the supplies to America which arrived after the end of 1776 and which hastened, if they did not assure, American independence. Later French subsidies and loans brought France's cash investment in the United States by 1783 to more than eight million eighteenth-century dollars. Since

---

[4] Samuel F. Bemis, *The Diplomacy of the American Revolution* (New York, 1935), pp. 19–20. The present writer has relied heavily upon this splendid work.

[5] *Œuvres de Mr. Turgot* . . . (9 vols., Paris, 1808–11), VIII, 534–604.

Beaumarchais's operations were essentially political and since he simultaneously tried to secure money for them from France, Spain, and the Americans, it is not certain even today whether the subsidies which he handled were entirely gifts, although they were so in the main. Beaumarchais and his heirs preferred to think of loans rather than gifts and long claimed that Congress had failed to pay 3,600,000 livres due to him. Finally, his heirs were paid by the United States, in 1835, 800,000 francs (the equivalent of livres) to settle the dispute. The validity of the claim may well be questioned, especially since the firm of Roderigue Hortalez and Company closed its activities with a small net profit. In any case the United States did not pay beyond their value for Beaumarchais's services.[6]

Happily for the patriots, assistance from Spain did not cease with the million livres granted in 1776. Spain soon prudently abandoned its connection with Beaumarchais, but found his counterpart in Don Diego de Gardoqui of Bilbao, and through him and her colonial officials contributed as much again in the form of cash and munitions. Spain also later lent to the patriots about $250,000.

It was well for the United States that the Bourbons decided, without being asked, to offer their help, for the patriots were unable to bring themselves to request it until months of fighting had passed. So long as there remained among them a widespread belief in the possibility of reconciliation, they could not and would not turn to France and Spain. Indeed, Congress would not even permit the patriots, save under special license, to trade with France and Spain until April, 1776, when American commerce was declared to be free, except with Britain. However, in November, 1775, after it had become evident that Britain would try to conquer rather than conciliate, Congress set up a "Committee of Secret Correspondence," the forerunner of the Department of State, to make contacts with "our friends in Great Britain, Ireland, and other parts of the world."[7] This body, later known as the Committee for Foreign

[6] On secret aid from France see Charles J. Stillé, "Beaumarchais and the Lost Million," *Pennsylvania Magazine of History and Biography*, XI (1887), 1–36; Elizabeth S. Kite, *Beaumarchais and the War of Independence* (2 vols., Boston, 1918), *passim;* and by the same author, "French 'Secret Aid' Precursor to the French American Alliance 1776–1777," *French American Review*, I (1948); 143–152; Claude H. Van Tyne, "French Aid before the Alliance of 1778," *American Historical Review*, XXXI (1925), 20–40.

[7] Worthington C. Ford *et al.* (eds.), *The Journals of the Continental Congress, 1774–1789* (34 vols., Washington, 1904–37), III, 392.

Affairs, immediately employed Arthur Lee as its agent in London and sought and obtained the friendly services at The Hague of Charles W. F. Dumas, formerly an associate of Benjamin Franklin. In March of the following year, as independence approached, it was chiefly instrumental in sending to Paris Silas Deane, a merchant of Connecticut, to try to buy munitions and other materials on credit and to discover whether the French government would assist the patriots.

Every step toward seeking foreign help was reluctantly taken. Only France and Spain could assist in major degree, and the Americans had looked upon them for generations as dangerous, papist, and inveterate foes. It was difficult suddenly to abandon traditional animosities, yet when it became apparent that the aid of France would be extremely valuable, if not indispensable to the winning of independence, the patriots were ready to embrace these old foes. Congress then gave its approval to Richard Henry Lee's proposal to seek "foreign alliances" along with others calling for independence and union. A committee "to prepare a plan of treaties to be proposed to foreign powers" was chosen on June 12, and reported on July 18.[8] The plan, drawn up with special reference to negotiating with France, was the basis of the famous Franco-American treaty of friendship and commerce of February 6, 1778, and of other later agreements to which the United States was a party. It was not immediately sanctioned by the whole body of delegates, and a few changes were made before it was approved on September 17.[9] Within the week following, Silas Deane, Franklin, and Jefferson were designated commissioners to the court of Versailles. Since Jefferson was unable to serve, he was soon replaced by Arthur Lee. Instructions were completed by Congress on October 16.

In order to obtain from Louis XVI French munitions and recognition of united American independence, Lee, Franklin, and Deane, characterized by one Loyalist as "fanatic, deist, and dunce," were empowered to offer privileges in commerce and to promise that America would never again acknowledge allegiance to Britain. In the event that France recognized the United States and as a result became involved in war with Britain, the commissioners were

[8] *Ibid.*, V, 433, 575–589.
[9] *Ibid.*, pp. 768–779.

authorized to give a pledge that the patriots would not make peace without giving France six months' notice. The patriot emissaries were instructed in addition to employ a few good military engineers and to buy or borrow from France eight warships of the line. They were ordered likewise to seek official recognition of the United States by other European governments and to propose commercial treaties to them. In December the "Secret" Committee gave the commissioners a powerful weapon: they should suggest to France that delay might lead the patriots to rejoin the British Empire. A month later Congress authorized them to offer territorial and other concessions to France and Spain in return for their entrance into the war—concessions at the expense of Britain rather than of the United States.[10] Meanwhile, Franklin had crossed the ocean, landing in France on December 6.[11]

While the Congress of the new nation was laying the foundation of its foreign policy, Vergennes, and apparently the French government, reached a tentative decision to declare war upon Britain, provided that Spain also entered the conflict. Turgot had been driven from office, and his restraining influence was no longer felt. Leaders at Madrid were eager to fight, but demanded as the price of action Minorca and Portugal. While Vergennes was willing in August, 1776, even to sanction an attack on Portugal in order to obtain the support of the Spanish army and fleet, he drew back when news came to Paris of the rout of the American army on Long Island. Clinging to the policy of secret aid, he decided that no further step should be taken until it was certain that the Americans would continue to fight in force and for some time. In accordance with that decision Vergennes cautiously watched events until July, 1777, when he again officially proposed armed intervention. He then urged the formation of a Franco-Spanish-American alliance, defensive and offensive, which would wage war until all the parties to it were willing to make peace. Louis XVI gave his approval, but Spain refused her consent. Charles III had now dropped plans for the conquest of Portugal; he had also acquired a new Foreign Minister, Count Floridablanca, who was more cautious

[10] *Ibid.*, VI, 1055.

[11] Soon afterward various emissaries were sent to other European courts, to Florence, Vienna, Berlin, St. Petersburg, The Hague. They accomplished very little.

than Grimaldi. Like his predecessor, he was opposed to American independence. He disliked republics and feared that the American one would serve as a dangerous example in both the Old World and the New. He also foresaw that an independent American nation might eventually prove to be a greater threat to the Spanish empire beyond the Atlantic than Britain had been. Floridablanca and Charles III therefore suggested Franco-Spanish mediation between Britain and the patriots, the result to be, they hoped, an uneasy truce between the contestants, one which would leave both weak— to the advantage of Spain, and France. Once more Vergennes retraced his steps. He found further reason for prudence in reports of Burgoyne's easy capture of Ticonderoga.

Nevertheless during 1777 Vergennes and France were moving toward the fateful plunge, with or even without Spain. Surreptitiously, yet almost openly, munitions and military supplies of all sorts left French ports for America, partly through the machinery set up by Beaumarchais, partly through the activities of genuine French merchants eager to trade with the patriots. Patriot vessels frequented French harbors, and American privateers brought their prizes into them. In fact, the patriot commissioners actually fitted out three warships in those ports. French officers, including the Marquis de Lafayette, crossed the ocean in numbers to join the Americans—often on leave of absence from the forces of France.[12] Well informed of these goings-on by Viscount Stormont, its ambassador at Versailles, and by a very efficient espionage service, the British government protested on several occasions, not vigorously enough to bring them all to an end, since Britain wished to avoid precipitating hostilities.

During 1777 Franklin achieved front rank as a diplomat. Since Silas Deane, if an adequate envoy, was less than single-minded in his devotion, and since Arthur Lee,[13] suspicious, quarrelsome, and cursed with a persecution complex, was temperamentally unfitted for his duties, Franklin promptly assumed the leadership of the American commission in France. In Congress before the end of 1775, and later in France, he declared that the patriots should no

[12] That Lafayette left for America with the approval of some French officials is well established in Louis Gottschalk, *Lafayette Comes to America* (Chicago, 1935), pp. 69–152.

[13] Deane and Lee are two of the patriot leaders whose careers have escaped close scholarly analysis.

more seek allies than a virgin should suitors; but he did not carry the principle to an extreme. Certainly he himself was neither naïve nor unsoiled after seven decades of a crowded life. He had had long experience in politics, was well versed in the wiles of mankind and a master of propaganda. He was also tolerant, witty, charming, and astonishingly adaptable. Moreover, Franklin was very well known in France as a scientist and as a philosopher. He could read the Romance languages, and could at least stammer in French. He was ideally equipped to serve as the representative of America. Learning of his appointment, the Marquis of Rockingham ruefully regretted that day in 1774 when the British Privy Council had vulgarly applauded Wedderburn's denunciation of the Philadelphian. To no avail, Lord Stormont spread it about that Franklin had fled to France because the American rebellion was collapsing.

Neither Louis XVI nor Vergennes received Franklin and his colleagues publicly for many long months. The Minister, however, consulted privately with them, and even helped "Poor Richard" to find outlets for his propaganda, giving assistance which the astute American publicist scarcely needed. Franklin was able to publish some very persuasive pieces, including a fictitious letter in which a German prince expressed the hope that the troops he had sold to Britain should sacrifice themselves as had the Spartans at Thermopylae—since a prince received added pay for soldiers slain! Officially without recognition, Franklin was decidedly in the favor of the French government. More important, he possessed or won the admiration and affection of powerful groups of men and women who molded public opinion in France.

Franklin was popular in France from the moment he landed. Well known for his experiments with electricity, believed to be the guiding force among the patriots, considered to be in the flesh the simple and virtuous man created by Jean Jacques Rousseau, his advent was hailed in Paris. He took advantage of every opportunity to create good will for America. A Mason, he fraternized with his fellows of the French lodges, and not without result. He associated freely with scientists and other scholars, winning favor even with Turgot. When it became apparent that he was thought to be a Quaker and that Quakers were in high esteem in France, he did not try to make public his real religious views. He dressed simply and modestly and permitted the French to draw their own conclusions. The followers of Rousseau, numerous among the middle classes and the nobility and even at the French court, believed that he and the Americans whom he represented were the unsophisticated and unspoiled children of Nature, of a new and glorious world. He took pains not to convince them to the contrary and carefully avoided artificiality and affectation. He dazzled the supporters of Voltaire with his intellectual gifts and philosophical wisdom and captivated the influential ladies of the French court by his gallantry and wit. Franklin became the rage among the scholarly, fashionable, and liberal elements, and as "Pater Patriae" created immense good will for the United States.[14]

Although sympathy for the Americans in 1777 permeated all classes in France and even official circles, there is little evidence that French policy was much altered, although Vergennes and those who wished to intervene openly in the Anglo-American conflict were doubtless encouraged so to act. As long as the news from America continued to tell of British advances and patriot setbacks, France would not move for fear that the patriot cause was collapsing. To many in France the capture of Philadelphia by Howe seemed to mark the beginning of the end. By November 24, however, it was known in Paris that Washington's army had performed creditably at Germantown and that the Baron de Kalb, who was serving with Washington, believed the patriots could drive the British into the sea.[15] Then on December 4 came the startling tidings that Burgoyne had capitulated.[16] The shattering blow dealt to British arms by the northern American army convinced even the most cautious Frenchman that the patriots would not readily submit;[17] the more acute concluded, and not without reason, that since Britain would almost certainly now offer the patriots concessions leading toward peace, France must move promptly if she

[14] Bernard Fay, *Franklin, the Apostle of Modern Times* (Boston, 1929), pp. 405–500, offering an impressionistic account of Franklin's French period, throws some light on French opinion of the sage. See also Carl Van Doren, *Benjamin Franklin* (New York, 1938), pp. 569–575, regarding Franklin's activities before the signing of the French alliance.

[15] Benjamin Franklin Stevens (ed.), *Facsimiles of Manuscripts in European Archives Relating to America, 1773–1783* (26 vols., London, 1889–95), VIII, No. 755.

[16] Richard Henry Lee, *Life of Arthur Lee* (2 vols., Boston, 1829), I, 357.

[17] The news of Germantown doubtless exercised minor influence upon French opinion; Saratoga was in itself an overwhelming argument.

moved at all. On December 15 and 16 Paul Wentworth, a British agent who had hurried across the Channel, informed Silas Deane that Britain was ready to offer generous peace terms. Was Vergennes told of these conversations? On December 17, without even waiting to discover whether Spain would join with France, the French Foreign Minister promised the United States formal recognition, a step certain to bring upon his country a declaration of war from London. In return, he asked a pledge from the American commissioners that the United States as an ally would not make a separate peace, a pledge which they gave.

Some weeks elapsed before the promise of Vergennes was fulfilled. He wanted assurance from Madrid that Spain would also enter the conflict. He urged the government of Charles III to act, and his plea was supported enthusiastically by Aranda, then Spanish Ambassador at Paris, but the Spanish ministry unanimously decided to maintain its official neutrality. The fact is that Spanish politicians were piqued because Vergennes had committed France without consulting them. Spain, they felt, was not yet ready for war. Above all, Floridablanca remained convinced that war to secure the independence of the American states would hurt rather than enhance the interests of the Spanish crown. Early in 1778 Vergennes learned that Charles III wished to avoid war. Almost simultaneously a crisis arose in central Europe because of the death of the Elector of Bavaria without a direct heir. It was likely that Joseph II, Holy Roman Emperor, would try to seize the Bavarian lands, that he would be opposed by Frederick the Great of Prussia, and that France, a defensive ally of Joseph, would become involved in their quarrel. Nevertheless, Vergennes was faithful to his promise.[18] On January 7 the French ministry and Louis XVI gave him their support. Accordingly, the texts of two treaties between France and the United States were prepared; and they were finally signed on February 6, despite receipt by Vergennes of a definite refusal from Spain to join in the war and despite renewed efforts by Wentworth and others to persuade Franklin and Deane to make peace with Britain.

The two treaties with France contained numerous provisions. By the terms of a Treaty of Amity and Commerce France officially

[18] The connection between the Bavarian crisis and French policy toward the patriots is ably discussed in Bemis, *Diplomacy,* pp. 70–74.

recognized the United States of America, and the two nations agreed to encourage trade with each other. The Treaty of Alliance carried far-reaching pledges. If France and Britain fell to blows before American independence was achieved, France and the United States were to be loyal allies and were not to lay down their arms until that independence was "formally or tacitly assured." Neither was to make a separate truce or peace without the consent of the other. France renounced forever all pretensions to the North American mainland east of the Mississippi and agreed to keep hands off the Bermudas, leaving the United States free to seize these territories. France was permitted to seize the British islands in the West Indies. Mutual guarantees were included. France guaranteed the independence and territories of the United States as they should be at the close of their war with Britain, the United States the existing possessions of France in the New World, together with such other territory as she might acquire as the result of participation in the war.[19]

The treaties of February 6 required, to be effective, the consent of Congress, which might have been refused, since the patriot representatives had exceeded their authority in their commitments to France. Nevertheless, while French officials were making hasty last-minute preparations for war, the French Ambassador in London notified the British government, on March 13, that Louis XVI had recognized the United States and had entered into a treaty of commerce with them. A week later the French King officially received Franklin, Deane, and Lee at Versailles. No doubt remained that Britain, though deeply committed in America, would retaliate with blows. The government, fully informed by the British espionage service regarding the course of Franco-American negotiations, reacted first by pressing its own efforts to negotiate with the Americans at Paris and beyond the Atlantic, and then, on June 17, with gunfire against French ships.

Dangerous though the situation of Britain was after she had been driven into war with France, it deteriorated still further when, in June, 1779, Spain entered the conflict. After France had taken the plunge, Vergennes continued his efforts to induce the Spanish

[19] The best texts of the treaties are to be found in David Hunter Miller (ed.), *Treaties and Other International Acts of the United States of America* (8 vols., Washington, 1931–48), II, 3–29, 35–41.

court to do likewise. In return he suggested all sorts of compensation, including Florida, Minorca, and even Jamaica. Floridablanca, desiring above all else the return of Gibraltar, refused to be enticed by Vergennes's offers. He hoped for many months to obtain Gibraltar, and perhaps Minorca, from Britain as the price of Spanish neutrality. Should the British refuse, he was prepared to fight. When it was apparent that Britain would make no concession to Spain, Floridablanca, after exacting a heavy price from Vergennes for Spanish military assistance, consented to the secret Franco-Spanish Convention of Aranjuez, in April, 1779. Simultaneously Spain sent an ultimatum to the Court of St. James offering mediation between Britain and the patriots on terms which George III and Lord North were certain to reject, and which they did in fact. Thereupon, in accordance with the agreement of Aranjuez Spain declared war.

The Treaty of Aranjuez was hardly a triumph for Vergennes. True, Spain promised to go to war by France's side, in the event that Britain turned down the ultimatum. In return, France was compelled to pledge that she would make no separate peace and that she would fight until Gibraltar was restored to Spain. In addition, France pledged all possible aid to Spain to wrest from Britain Minorca, Mobile, and other areas and privileges. Spain promised support to her ally's efforts to acquire territorial and commercial advantages in Newfoundland, Senegal, the East Indies, and elsewhere. It should be emphasized that Spain did not become the ally of the United States, that Spain did not even engage to recognize them, and that Spain offered such recognition only at the close of the war. The point should also be made that the obligations assumed by France at Aranjuez were to a degree incompatible with her prior commitments to the patriots. The unpleasant task of harmonizing the conflicting interests of Spain and the United States was left to Vergennes.

The list of Britain's open enemies was not yet complete. Vergennes managed to seduce other European states from their neutral course. From the beginning of the war Dutch merchants profited by selling munitions to the patriots; and St. Eustatius, the tiny Dutch colony in the West Indies, became the scene of a great traffic between the patriots and the European continent. Indeed, even British merchants sent to St. Eustatius goods which later reached

the American mainland. When Britain protested against the behavior of Johannes de Graaf, Governor of the little island, he was
recalled for investigation. Although it was evident that he had
encouraged trade helpful to the patriots and injurious to Britain, he
was exonerated nonetheless and ordered to return to his post.[20] Still
greater offense to Britain was offered by Dutch merchants after the
entrance of France and Spain into the war by carrying to those
nations masts and other naval supplies. Needled by the Duc de la
Vauguyon, French Ambassador at The Hague, the Dutch government turned down British demands that Dutch merchants cease
supplying Britain's enemies with naval stores. When The Netherlands finally prepared to join the League of Armed Neutrality and
to build a fleet to protect Dutch commerce, Britain sent to The
Hague in November, 1780, an ultimatum which was followed in
December by armed attacks upon Dutch shipping. The Netherlands
had finally joined Britain's foes. But the damage to Britain was inconsequential. As neutrals the Dutch had been able to hurt. As
belligerents they had no strength to strike, and their ships and their
colonies were exposed to attack. Admiral George Rodney promptly
captured and sacked St. Eustatius, closing off an avenue by which
the patriots had received large quantities of supplies.

At war with three European states, Britain was also confronted
after 1780 by the League of Armed Neutrality, which was
fomented and encouraged by Vergennes. The Baltic world after
1778 harbored much resentment against Britain because British
warships searched and seized neutral vessels carrying enemy and
contraband goods. Taking up a suggestion offered by Count Bern-
storff of Denmark and pushed by Vergennes, Catherine the Great
proposed in February, 1780, that the neutrals jointly adopt a series
of principles which would effectively protect their ocean commerce,
and that they bind themselves to carry them out, by collective force,
if necessary. Denmark and Sweden promptly agreed. Together with
Russia they also declared the Baltic closed to the warships of the
fighting nations. With the support of France and Spain the League
acquired adherents until, by 1783, all the major and most of the
minor European states had joined. As a result, and thanks in large

[20] John Franklin Jameson, "St. Eustatius in the American Revolution,"
American Historical Review, VIII (1903), 683–708.

part to Vergennes, Britain suffered isolation both military and diplomatic.

Thus, Britain's position after 1778 was perilous. Yet, though confronted with three major enemies, the United States, France, and Spain, it was still possible that her army and navy might retrieve some of the mistakes of her King and politicians.

CHAPTER 13

Stalemate in the North

NEWS of Saratoga, reaching London on December 2, 1777, caused panic among British officials who had hoped for major triumphs and who had expected nothing worse than minor victories from the campaign of 1777; and Howe's failure to crush Washington and his desire to be relieved of command neither alleviated their concern nor removed their confusion. Lord North, who had recently expressed a heartfelt wish "to get out of this d——d war" [1] and who knew a catastrophe when he saw one, began to talk of resigning. Nevertheless, the King and the North ministry soon evolved a shabby and ill-designed plan to meet a desperate situation. They proposed to offer concessions to the patriots sufficient to persuade them to make peace; to avert, if possible, French intervention; and to send a new and abler commander and reinforcements to America. None of the three parts of this program was successfully carried out.

Reconciliation with the patriots, if an alliance between them and France was to be prevented, required the most rapid action, to the end that Congress might be committed to peace and re-entry into the empire before receiving a French offer. At the very least it was essential that the terms of the British offer be fully known to the patriots before they formally allied with France. But British officials drew up their proposals in leisurely fashion and failed to present them to Parliament until February 17, 1778; and emissaries sent to America to lay them before the patriots did not leave England

[1] Reginald Lucas, *Lord North* (2 vols., London, 1913), II, 54.

until another two months had passed. Parliament, in session when the tidings of Saratoga arrived, actually recessed from December 11 to January 20 for the holiday season. Chatham, speaking in the House of Lords against a recess of six weeks in the midst of one of the greatest crises ever to face the British people, riddled the program and the behavior of the government. He urged that the attempt to conquer the patriots be abandoned, if for no other reason than because it was doomed to fail; he proposed that the most generous offer of peace within the empire be made to them by persons whom they did not hate and distrust; and he called for preparations for the war with France which could hardly be avoided.[2] The masterful Chatham was never more statesmanlike. Nor was he alone in his desire for conciliation, for the Rockingham Whigs joined in a sharp attack upon the ministry. To no purpose. Whatever were the private opinions of the supporters of the King and the North ministry—and many of them sympathized with Pitt—the King's political machine continued to run rather smoothly, and the Cabinet received its customary votes of confidence by majorities of more than two to one.[3]

When Parliament reconvened, the Opposition resumed its attacks. Charles James Fox, the Duke of Richmond, and the Rockingham group urged the recognition of American independence as a step toward better Anglo-American relations and as a measure to forestall war with France, while the Pittites supported the proposals of their leader, absent because of illness. But ministerial leaders would not even admit that there was genuine danger of war with France until February 17, when North finally conceded in the Commons that "it was possible, nay too probable" that France had recognized the United States.[4] Yet North knew at least as early as February 2, in part apparently because Silas Deane sold information to Paul Wentworth, that the French had made their decision.[5] Indeed, Dr. Edward Bancroft long afterward asserted that as a

[2] William Cobbett (ed.), *Parliamentary History of England, 1777–1778* (36 vols., London, 1806–20), XIX, 597–602, 741.

[3] *Ibid.*, pp. 590–592, 606–614.

[4] *Ibid.*, pp. 769, 774–775.

[5] That Deane in the later years of the War of Independence worked to preserve the British Empire is well known. That he sold Wentworth information at this time has recently been established in Carl Van Doren, *Secret History of the American Revolution* (New York, 1941), pp. 62–63.

result of his efforts the texts of both Franco-American treaties were in London within forty-two hours of their signature.

On February 17 North confessed to a dejected House of Commons that the war had gone badly and asked that Parliament give its support to an effort to save America for the empire by negotiation.[6] Parliament complied, passing bills which repealed the Townshend tea duty, the Massachusetts Government Act, and the Prohibitory Act, and authorized the sending of negotiators to America.[7] The adherents of the ministry were disgruntled; and the Opposition was unhappy but could not easily object to principles which it had earlier preached. Four days later, on March 13, George III was officially notified by the French Ambassador at London that France had recognized the United States; and after another four days Lord Stormont was called home. Conflict with France now seemed inevitable. Still the commissioners who were to go to America lingered in England, receiving instructions, making preparations, saying farewells. Finally, on April 16, they set out. The commission comprised the Earl of Carlisle, an attractive young nobleman; William Eden, an experienced diplomat; and George Johnstone, windbag, brawler, and former Governor of West Florida. With them went Sir John Temple and John Berkenhout, special agents who were to be used to cajole and if necessary to corrupt American leaders. Funds for bribery were made available. The Howe brothers were also to serve on the commission, which was authorized to offer much to the patriots, and in effect to concede home rule. It was authorized to deal with the Congress, with other patriot bodies, and with Washington. However, it was permitted neither to recognize American independence nor to withdraw British forces from the thirteen states. Moreover, any agreement into which it entered required the consent of Parliament.

Meanwhile, military instructions for the campaign of 1778 in America had been prepared, two sets of them. On March 7 orders

---

[6] *Parliamentary History,* XIX, 762–767.

[7] On February 18, David Hartley hurried off a letter to Benjamin Franklin to tell him of the change in British policy. "I hope in God that no fatal step has yet been taken between America and the Court of France. . . ." The Franco-American alliance had been signed, and Franklin described North's policy as "frivolous" and intended to drive a wedge between the new allies. Benjamin Franklin Stevens (ed.), *Facsimiles of Manuscripts in European Archives Relating to America, 1773–1783* (26 vols., London, 1889–95), VIII, Nos. 789, 793.

were signed by Germain appointing Clinton in the place of Howe and instructing him to spend the year ravaging the coast of New England, holding or abandoning Philadelphia as he should think fit. He would be sent large reinforcements. On March 21, however, after the open break with France, additional secret instructions to Clinton were signed by the King personally. According to them, Clinton was to evacuate Philadelphia, and, if need be, New York; if possible, he was to maintain control of Newport; he was to send an expedition to Georgia and to supply troops for an attack on the French West Indian island of St. Lucia. In sum, Clinton was to assume the defensive on the American mainland, except in the far South. Amusingly enough, Commissioner Eden, who carried the confidential orders to Clinton, was not told of their contents. The commissioners knew before departing that they could not order the British army to evacuate in order to persuade the patriots to deal with them; had they known that the army would ignominiously retreat at the very moment when they were to begin their work, they would never have left England.

Again and again during the four months after the receipt of the news of Saratoga North tried to resign. When it became evident that war with France could not be avoided, he begged George III to call the ailing Pitt back to Downing Street to assume the helm. A general cry arose for his return to power. But the King replied that he would abandon his crown rather than ask Chatham to serve as Prime Minister. Nor would he have Rockingham. If Pitt or Rockingham would serve under North, he would not object! The King, who had recently presented to North some thousands of pounds from public funds, appealed to North's sense of loyalty and duty, alternately entreating and commanding him to remain in office. After Chatham's famous last speech in the Lords on April 7, it was obvious that the great statesman's career was ending in final illness. Renewed pressure from his royal master led North to agree to stay in office; and that unhappy man continued to preside over an administration which he recognized as utterly unequal to its tasks.

While the British Parliament meditated upon new leadership and a new program and contented itself with a half-measure, Washington's army underwent the Gethsemane of Valley Forge. Howe's forces rested, well nourished, warm, and secure, in Philadelphia during the winter of 1777–78, but Washington's men, hardly more than twenty miles away, were tortured by cold, hunger, and disease. The encampment at Valley Forge lay in a region swept clean during the preceding campaign of cattle and grain. Worse, the commissariat established by Congress had broken down, and meat, bread, clothing, and blankets reached the army irregularly and in insufficient quantities. Shivering in their hastily built huts, the patriot soldiers underwent hardships greater even that those they had endured at Morristown. Many despaired of relief and deserted to their homes. Washington was forced to commandeer foodstuffs in order to preserve the semblance of an army. The Continental officers, who shared at least some of the hardships of the men and whose pay was too small to support them in a time of rising prices, were equally discontented. Many resigned, or threatened to resign, their commissions. At length Congress appointed Nathanael Greene to the post of Quartermaster General, and the energetic Greene saw to it that supplies were delivered to the army; at last Congress also undertook to placate the officers, by promising them half-pay for a period of seven years following the war, and to reward the men, by pledging to them a cash bonus at the close of hostilities.

That winter, despite the good news from Saratoga, was marked by dissension in Congress. There was no news for months from the commissioners at Paris, for their dispatches had been intercepted by the British navy. Moreover, the delegates were chagrined at the fall of Philadelphia. At least a few sought to find a scapegoat in Washington. Some delegates had long harbored the fear that Washington might attempt to make himself a dictator, and John Adams had actually once suggested that the higher army officers be annually elected. There was no doubt that Washington had acquired a strong following among the Continental officers, including Greene, Lafayette, the Earl of Stirling, Alexander Hamilton, and John Laurens. Now the Virginian was privately accused of incompetence. It was said of the man who was willing, perhaps too willing, to fight at Brandywine and Germantown—and afterward— that he was too much of a Fabius. Somehow or other he should have beaten Howe. The defeats which his army had suffered were contrasted with the victories won by the northern army, and a conclusion was reached that Gates the conqueror should replace Washington the failure. Whether any of the members actually pushed for the elevation of Gates to the supreme command is not and in all likelihood will never be known. James Lovell of Massachusetts may have; and possibly also Samuel Adams and Richard Henry Lee. Dr. Benjamin Rush, once but no longer a member of Congress, went so far as to propose the replacement of Washington by Gates as a remedy for the ills of the main American army.

It is unlikely that Gates ever had a real chance to win Washington's post. No one ventured to propose on the floor of Congress that Washington be removed. General Thomas Conway, Irish-born French officer who had joined the Continentals, said or hinted in a letter to Gates that he hoped Gates would supersede Washington. The fact was revealed, apparently by James Wilkinson, Gates' aide, while drunk. The subsequent behavior of Conway, Gates, and Wilkinson exposed them to ridicule from Washington's supporters, and it became patent that a drive to dismiss the commander in chief would surely fail. Because of his supposed offenses against Washington, Conway, a good though an imprudent officer, was challenged and gravely wounded in a duel by General John Cadwalader. Believing himself about to die, Conway wrote a gentlemanly letter to the commander in chief to express his "sincere grief for having done, written, or said any thing disagreeable to your Excellency." He recovered and returned to honorable service in the French army. The sinister phrase "Conway Cabal" immortalizes him, although there is no evidence that he was a major opponent of Washington or even that he was in close touch with members of Congress who are supposed to have desired the replacement of the Virginian by Gates.[8]

Despite a heavy toll of dead and maimed among the patriot soldiers at Valley Forge, the spring of 1778 saw a reinvigorated American army. News from abroad revived drooping spirits. Copies of the conciliatory acts passed by Parliament had been sent off to America in a belated attempt to persuade the patriots not to enter

[8] Edmund C. Burnett, *The Continental Congress* (New York, 1941), chap. 15, expresses the traditional view that there was a "plot" against Washington. However, Bernhard Knollenberg, *Washington and the Revolution* . . . (New York, 1940), pp. 65–77, points out in a cool and closely reasoned essay that evidence of a "Cabal" is almost completely lacking. L. H. Butterfield in his edition of the *Letters of Benjamin Rush* (2 vols., Princeton, 1951), II, Appendix 1, pp. 1197–1208, discusses relations between Washington and Dr. Rush and reaches the same conclusion.

into an agreement with France before the arrival of the Carlisle Commission. They reached New York in mid-April, and were zealously distributed by William Tryon, the royal governor. It was now evident that King, Cabinet, and Parliament were ready to make substantial offers in order to secure peace with the colonists. There must have been many among the patriots who were more or less willing to accept peace and autonomy within the British Empire,[9] but by 1778 such persons were in a minority. Goaded by the sufferings inseparable from war, exasperated by British brutal treatment of American prisoners, resentful of the depredations of Hessian and British troops, the majority of the patriots in 1778 would have settled for nothing less than independence. Moreover, distrust of the existing British regime was so thoroughly fixed in American minds that even those who would have been satisfied with autonomy questioned how far Britain was really willing to go and feared, not without cause, that attempts would be made to divide them. Above all, they were afraid that promises made to them when they were able to defend themselves would be broken when they no longer had weapons in their hands. Many patriots were disposed to refuse even to discuss peace terms until independence had been acknowledged. In effect, the British peace offer was virtually rejected before it was made. On May 2, a month prior to the arrival of Carlisle and his colleagues at Philadelphia, the Franco-American treaties were delivered at York by Silas Deane's brother Simeon. Two days later, Congress, setting aside some minor provisions, unanimously ratified both treaties. On May 5 Washington's army joyfully celebrated the momentous news.

Moving up Delaware Bay early in June, the Carlisle commissioners received the unwelcome news that, as the result of the

[9] William Eden asserted in June that there was at the close of May a strong party in Congress and an even larger one in the American army in favor of a negotiated peace. *Facsimiles,* V, No. 501. On June 4 Joshua Loring, Jr., British commissary of prisoners, conversed with Charles Lee, Daniel Morgan, and Alexander Hamilton at the American lines outside Philadelphia. The next day he reported that "all wished very much for peace. Morgan went so far as to say, that 99 in a 100, were of the same sentiment & wd. be glad to give up independency upon the terms offered by the acts, and that none (as he expressed it) but a few low dirty rascals who had got into the lead of affairs were for it. They were afraid however it was too late now. . . ." Edward H. Tatum, Jr. (ed.), *The American Journal of Ambrose Serle, Secretary to Lord Howe, 1776–1778* (San Marino, Cal., 1940), p. 305. Perhaps the Americans were pulling Loring's leg.

King's orders sent forward by William Eden, preparations to evacuate Philadelphia were already well under way. Sir William Howe had formally resigned his post to Clinton, had been given a magnificent farewell party, the famous Mischianza, and had sailed for England. In Philadelphia the commissioners found Clinton busily executing Germain's orders to take the British army back to New York. Now they could hardly threaten the patriots with attack by the redcoats. Infuriated because of the deceit practiced upon himself by his employers and shocked by their stupidity, Eden bitterly asserted that it was "impossible to see even what I can see of this magnificent country and not go nearly mad at the long train of misconducts and mistakes by which we have lost it." [10]

The disillusioned commissioners did what they could, formally requesting the Congress to begin negotiations. The Congress gave a rather clear-cut answer on June 17. It would not treat until American independence had been recognized or until the British military forces had been withdrawn. The commissioners could meet neither the one requirement nor the other. Sailing off to New York with the evacuating fleet, they despairingly continued their labors from that place until the following winter. Johnstone fumblingly tried to deceive, bribe, and flatter patriot leaders into bargaining, but his maneuvers were exposed and ridiculed. In August Congress refused to have anything further to do with the commissioners. Soon afterward Berkenhout turned up in Philadelphia in the guise of a physician seeking a new home. He conferred with Richard Henry Lee and Samuel Adams, to no avail. His real errand becoming suspected, he was jailed and sent back to New York. Later Temple turned up in the patriot capital and conferred cautiously with American leaders, but to no purpose. An appeal of October 3 addressed by the commissioners over the heads of patriot officials to the American people was no more effective.[11] The patriots had taken an irrevocable decision, that they would accept nothing short of independence.

On their voyage from Philadelphia to New York the Carlisle commissioners had much company, for they sailed with a vast fleet of transports carrying stores, three thousand Tories, and many

[10] *Facsimiles,* V, No. 500.
[11] The best account of the Carlisle commission is in Van Doren, *Secret History,* pp. 63–116. See also Weldon A. Brown, *Empire or Independence,* . . . *1774–1783* (Baton Rouge, 1941), pp. 205–290.

Hessians, escorted by Admiral Howe. It was impossible for Clinton to evacuate even his whole force by sea. He therefore sent off by water the least reliable of his Germans and those Tories who did not dare to remain in Philadelphia at the mercy of the patriots. Clinton himself set out by land for New York on June 18 with about ten thousand troops, marching across New Jersey. Washington promptly left Valley Forge in pursuit.

The patriot army which advanced eastward from Valley Forge was nearly as large as that of Clinton. It was an army improved by the labors of the highly publicized Baron von Steuben, who had begun to drill it in March; what was more important, it was well equipped and contained many veterans among both officers and men.[12] As it moved into New Jersey, hundreds of militia from that state took the field, attempting to harass Clinton. Since Clinton traveled slowly, the two armies converged at Monmouth Courthouse on June 28. Washington had held two councils of war to consider the wisdom of assailing the British. Charles Lee, recently returned to active service, along with all the other American officers, had advised against an all-out attack. Defeat in battle, a not unforeseeable result of such a conflict, might have vitiated the benefits of the French alliance and of the British retreat to New York. But Washington, although he also doubted the wisdom of engaging in a head-on clash, was more inclined to fight than many of his generals. He had decided to strike a partial blow at the British rear guard rather than permit Clinton to retire unmolested.

In the morning of the twenty-eighth Charles Lee led the attacking force of about 4,200 men forward across an open plain cut by three ravines and surrounded by woods. Washington followed in column at a distance of several miles. Near the courthouse Lee was confronted by the British rear guard, advantageously posted. The redcoats were soon joined by Clinton himself, who had sent on his baggage, was annoyed by militia assaults upon his flanks, and now prepared to cover his retreat by the classic remedy of an attack upon the patriot center. Clinton had with him six thousand men,

[12] Steuben's considerable services have commonly been overpraised. The army with which he worked was not a rabble in March or a perfect fighting machine in June. The traditional very high estimate of the value of his labors at Valley Forge appears in John M. Palmer's recent biography, *General Von Steuben* (New Haven, 1937), pp. 136–161. The studies of the adventurer-patriot by Friedrich Kapp and Palmer are by no means exhaustive.

foot and cavalry, the heart of his army. After desultory firing, Lee withdrew across the three ravines, in order to avoid being pinned against them, until his men reached high and easily defensible ground at the western edge of the plain. There Washington, coming up with the main body of patriots, assumed command of the American forces. When Clinton, following Lee, mounted two probing attacks, he was beaten off. At sundown both armies were exhausted by their exertions and by extreme heat. During the night, leaving his wounded behind, Clinton marched quietly eastward toward Sandy Hook and New York, which he reached without further difficulties.

The fighting at Monmouth was indecisive. The losses were approximately equal, about three hundred casualties on each side. Clinton obtained the fruits of victory in that his army was able to move on safely to New York. Washington had the pleasure of standing firmly against two attacks by British veterans and of claiming to hold the battleground. To Lee Monmouth brought humiliation. He exchanged sharp words with Washington on the field, and Washington implied that he had disobeyed orders. Lee demanded an opportunity to defend his behavior. Washington then formally accused him of disobedience of orders, unnecessary and shameful retreat before the enemy, and disrespect to the commander in chief. A court-martial, softening the accusations, found Lee guilty on all three charges and deprived him of the right to command for a period of one year. Eventually, after much debate, Congress confirmed the verdict. Later Lee angrily informed Congress he was in no mood to serve again, and he was formally removed from the patriot army. It is not certain that Lee deserved the treatment which he received. In any case, he took no further part in the war, dying obscurely in Philadelphia in 1782.[13]

The British retreat from Philadelphia was only the first of the military profits derived by the patriots from the participation of France in the war. Unprepared for a major naval conflict, Britain did not have sufficient power at sea in the spring of 1778 to match French fleets in the Atlantic and the Mediterranean. Fearing to

[13] The battle of Monmouth and the subsequent court-martial of Lee have been re-examined in detail in J. R. Alden, *General Charles Lee*, chaps. 13–16. Therein Lee appears in a more favorable light than in general histories of the War of Independence. That Washington on the field called Lee a "damned poltroon" is a myth.

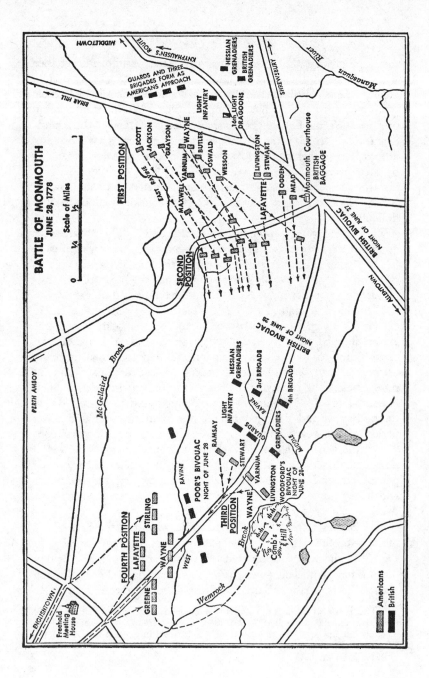

BATTLE OF MONMOUTH
JUNE 28, 1778

Scale of Miles

0   ¼   ½

Americans
British

weaken the defense of the home islands, the Cabinet permitted a French squadron of twelve ships of the line and five frigates under Count d'Estaing to sail unmolested from Toulon to America. After d'Estaing's appearance on the American coast a French fleet remained either off America or in the West Indies until the close of the war. While Britain was still renovating her navy, the ships of Spain became active. As a result, Britain's power on the seas was strained to the uttermost after 1779. Ships were needed to defend the home islands against a projected Franco-Spanish invasion; to supply and reinforce Gibraltar, long besieged by the Bourbons; to protect the British islands in the West Indies; to deal with a French squadron in the Indian Ocean; and to convoy merchantmen. In consequence the British navy could not establish its supremacy in all the theatres of water warfare. It was necessary in 1782 to surrender Minorca because it could not be reinforced, and the French were intermittently superior in force in the Caribbean Sea and on the coasts of the thirteen states. French sea power in the western reaches of the Atlantic made it possible for the patriots and their allies to attack British bases along the coast.[14]

French strength at sea also permitted a revival of patriot naval activities. Before the end of 1775 Washington had commissioned several craft, the majority of the states had outfitted war vessels, and the Congress had initiated *the* Navy and the Marine Corps. But all the American navies together, if for no other reason because they included no ships of the line, could not hope to cope with Howe's fleet. With many dozens of privateers and merchant ships carrying letters of marque, they had attacked with some effect British transports and merchant vessels. They had raided in the waters of the West Indies and of the Bay of St. Lawrence, and even in those surrounding the British Isles. It has been estimated that 342 British ships were captured between March and December, 1776, and 464 in 1777.[15] Early in 1778 something like ten thousand Americans were engaged in privateering. Nevertheless, the British had struck

[14] Two authorities on British naval history contend that the indecisive naval battle off Ushant between the British and French in July, 1778, spelled the loss of the colonies. See Sir Herbert W. Richmond, *Statesmen and Sea Power* (Oxford, 1946), pp. 149–150. A British victory at Ushant would hardly have assured triumph in America.

[15] Gardner W. Allen, *A Naval History of the American Revolution* (2 vols., Boston, 1913), I, 181–182, 289. The figures are at the best only approximations. They do not take into account recaptures by the British.

vigorously at the Amercian commerce destroyers, had managed to set up a workable convoy system in the Atlantic, to blockade quite tightly the coasts of the middle states, and to carry the British army without molestation from place to place along those coasts.

When their fleets were compelled to deal with those of France, and later of Spain, the British could not effectively blockade American ports, and American privateers multiplied. Over four hundred of them were operating in the latter years of the war, and they injured severely the British merchant marine and British trade as well. Before the war ended they had cost Britain something like two thousand ships, £18 million and twelve thousand captured sailors. The patriot navy, however, was permitted to dwindle away—ships cost money and the French had them—until it contained only two vessels by the end of the war. Yet it did not lack for glory, since John Paul Jones' capture of the *Serapis* with the old Indiaman renamed the *Bon Homme Richard* was a feat worthy of the highest naval traditions of the British themselves.

The presence of French warships in the western Atlantic forced Clinton to take the defensive. Had D'Estaing not loitered in his passage across the Atlantic, he would have arrived at the Delaware Capes in time to intercept the British evacuating Philadelphia by water. Since Admiral Howe's fleet was decidedly inferior to D'Estaing's, the French officer might have struck a decisive blow. He did not reach the Capes until July 8, by which time Howe had cast anchor at New York. Washington and D'Estaing then blockaded New York, and the Admiral considered attacking the British fleet, which contained only nine ships of the line, within Sandy Hook. Howe's fleet was far outgunned, since his largest vessels were 64's, while the French had six 74's, an 80, and a 90-gun ship. However, the British were more eager to fight against their traditional enemy than they had been to engage the patriots; Howe was undaunted, and his dispositions were skillful; and D'Estaing, discovering that his heavier ships could not pass the bar at the mouth of the harbor, failed to assault.[16] The capture of the main British

[16] A. T. Mahan, *Major Operations of the Navies in the War of Independence* (Boston, 1913), pp. 63-68, overemphasizes the danger to the British at New York at this juncture. Mahan contends that D'Estaing could have attacked successfully and that the city must then have fallen. Francis Vinton Greene, *The Revolutionary War and the Military Policy of the United States* (New York, 1911), p. 150, following Mahan, says that "Clinton's army—on Man-

base in North America was attempted neither now nor at any later time.

Temporarily abandoning all thought of investing New York, Washington and D'Estaing quickly turned their attention to the more or less isolated British garrison on Rhode Island. At the end of July General John Sullivan and D'Estaing moved against the island by land and sea. But General Robert Pigot, the British commander, stoutly resisted at Newport; and Howe, having received reinforcements from Halifax, came to the rescue. The British fleet was still decidedly inferior to the French, and D'Estaing sailed to attack him. A great storm interrupted the maneuvering for position of the two fleets, damaging and scattering both. Howe soon reappeared off Rhode Island, ready for further action, and Clinton led a relieving army from New York to Newport. D'Estaing, disillusioned by his experiences in northern American waters, moved to Boston to make repairs and then sailed for the West Indies in November. Sullivan, accomplishing nothing at Newport, withdrew to the mainland before superior forces. The Franco-American allies had posed two major threats and failed to carry them out. A period of mutual recriminations ensued.

The French navy, concentrating its American efforts in the Caribbean, failed to return in major force to co-operate with Washington for almost three years. Throughout 1779 the British dominated the waters adjacent to the American states, except for the coast of Georgia, where D'Estaing operated for a brief period in the fall of that year. News of the departure of D'Estaing from West Indian waters led Clinton to evacuate his exposed garrison on Rhode Island and to bring it to New York. In the summer of 1780 a French squadron and a French army of six thousand men under the Comte de Rochambeau took post at Newport. However, the

---

hattan Island and without ships—would have been caught like rats in a trap, and not a man would have escaped." But D'Estaing would hardly have conquered Howe without suffering losses. Indeed, the British Admiral, in spite of the odds against him, was confident of victory. William B. Willcox, "British Strategy in America, 1778," *Journal of Modern History*, XIX (1947), 111. Moreover, D'Estaing had to include in his calculations the naval reinforcements he knew to be en route from England to Howe. It should be added that the city was well fortified against assault by land, and that Clinton's army, including the garrison and all the troops evacuated from Philadelphia, was more powerful than the Franco-American land forces, Washington's army, and the four thousand French troops accompanying D'Estaing. Clinton would not have surrendered without trial by battle on terra firma.

British were strong enough to cover Newport from the sea without straining their naval forces. They were not again exposed to peril such as they had faced in the summer of 1778 until Admiral de Grasse sailed from the West Indies to Chesapeake Bay in 1781.

Washington was thus deprived of an opportunity to attack New York during the campaigns of 1779 and 1780. Had his army been superior to that of Clinton, he still could not have blockaded it effectively or have carried out a successful assault. The fact is, however, that his army, even after the appearance of the French regulars in Narragansett Bay, was numerically weaker than the British forces at New York.[17]

The Continental troops dwindled in numbers as the war progressed.[18] In part this decline is explained by the continuing hardships in the American service. Supplies of food and clothing remained inadequate. Pay, usually in the form of depreciated Continental currency, was low in buying power and, even more serious, highly undependable. Winter encampments brought suffering, that at Morristown in the bitter cold season of 1779–80 causing greater agonies than the stay at Valley Forge.[19] In January, 1781, dangerous mutinies broke out among Pennsylvania and New Jersey troops, in the course of which one officer was killed. These were put down only by lavish promises, much cajoling, and the threat of attack by faithful regiments.[20] Military life was not attractive to the patriots, especially when men prospered in civil pursuits and in privateering. Moreover, after the entrance of France into the war many soldiers felt that their services in the field were no longer necessary, even that victory was already assured. Such men as James Monroe and Alexander Hamilton considered themselves free to resign their commissions.

Even had Clinton assumed the offensive from New York after the British navy recovered control of the shores of the thirteen states,

[17] In the fall of 1779 Washington's paper strength was 27,000, that of Clinton almost 38,000. Clinton reported over 28,000 fit for duty; Washington could not have mustered half so many.

[18] Accurate figures for the number of Continentals in service year by year, which would permit close comparisons, are unavailable. The estimates presented by Henry Knox in 1790, in Walter Lowrie and Matthew S. Clarke (eds.), *Papers, Military Affairs*, I (Washington, 1832), 14–19, are obviously not trustworthy.

[19] Carl Van Doren, *Mutiny in January* (New York, 1943), pp. 18–19.

[20] *Ibid., passim.*

there was little reason to believe that much could be gained by marching against Washington. The British General would have been compelled to leave a large garrison in New York, and thus would have been able to put in motion forces no stronger than those of his opponent. Except for some stroke of fortune or a gross mistake on the part of Washington—neither to be expected—such an effort would probably fail. In fact, a defeat in the field could not be ruled out. Had Clinton concentrated at New York all the troops available in America, it is doubtful that he could have achieved major success. In any case, although he was instructed by Germain early in 1779 to make one effort to engage Washington,[21] Clinton's forces were increasingly concentrated in an effort to reconquer the Southern states, while simultaneously seeking to wear down resistance of the patriots elsewhere. To that end efforts were continued to corrupt patriot leaders, and destructive raids were constantly mounted. The new British policy, inspired in part by waning superiority to the patriots and the French on the mainland and in the West Indies, in part by hope of a Tory rising in the Southern states, began to take form in 1778 and crystallized the following year.

Efforts on the part of the British to win over influential patriots by persuasion and bribery began even before the war; and various minor Americans, in some cases secretly, in others publicly, had resumed their allegiance to the crown. In 1779 the Cabinet gave to Clinton the pardoning power which had been vested in the Howes three years earlier. In the spring of 1779, within a month after his marriage to the Tory belle of Philadelphia, Peggy Shippen, Benedict Arnold began a secret correspondence with Clinton which continued for sixteen months. It led to an agreement on the part of Arnold as commanding officer at West Point to turn over that important post to the British. Afterward Arnold claimed that he had never approved of the Declaration of Independence and that his treason was prompted by lofty motives. However, he bargained coolly and lengthily concerning financial rewards and other advantages in return for his services. His conspiracy was discovered before it could bear fruit. In September, 1780, Major John André, British Deputy Adjutant General sent out by Clinton to make final arrangements with Arnold, was captured in civilian clothes within

[21] Germain to Clinton, Jan. 23, 1779, Sir Henry Clinton Papers, in William L. Clements Library, University of Michigan.

the American lines on the Hudson and was executed as a spy. Arnold escaped to New York; and he and his family were generously compensated for his efforts. Although the patriots were shocked by Arnold's apostasy, their cause did not suffer. Nor were they injured by the unexecuted schemes of Clinton and his aides to seduce to the royal cause such patriots as Ethan Allen, Philip Schuyler, John Sullivan, and General Samuel Holden Parsons of Connecticut.[22] In the end the arts of corruption employed by the British proved even less effective than their arms.

More dangerous to the patriots were the continuing blockade of their coasts, the attacks upon their shipping, and the punishing raids by British regulars and Loyalist contingents. The royal navy and privateers struck savage and profitable blows at American maritime commerce, causing injuries almost as serious as those inflicted upon British trade by patriot vessels.[23] In the period 1778–81 General Charles Grey ravaged New Bedford and its vicinity, William Tryon made a destructive attack upon New Haven, and Benedict Arnold as a British commander plundered New London. A series of devastating invasions of Virginia began in the spring of 1779. These and other minor incursions caused heavy losses of property, aroused fear and panic in the areas overrun, and brought the war home to many patriots as never before. In most of these raids Tories participated. After the disastrous campaign of 1777 they came in increasing numbers to realize that they themselves must fight if the patriots were to be defeated. Now they were aligning themselves by the hundreds and the thousands under the royal banner. Both they and the British soldiers, who after the Franco-American alliance came to regard the patriots as national enemies, used the torch; and

[22] In *Secret History of the American Revolution,* Carl Van Doren has described the efforts of the British to persuade various Americans to leave the patriot camp. He fails to discuss the scanty evidence concerning the behavior of Joseph Reed in 1776–77. (Reed's fidelity to the United States seems well established in John F. Roche, "Was Joseph Reed Disloyal?" *William and Mary Quarterly,* Third Series, VIII (1951), 406–417.) In chaps. 6–16 Van Doren gives the best account of the Arnold conspiracy. He contends (pp. 200–202, 440), correctly it would seem, that Peggy Shippen Arnold was from the beginning privy to her husband's dealings with Clinton. The André-Arnold correspondence may be read in pp. 439–495.

It should be added that the fall of West Point to the British would by no means have brought an end to the war.

[23] Allen, *Naval History,* I, 289–290.

both were accused of brutality to civilians and the killing of prisoners.

The new policy pursued by Clinton soon brought results in the middle and Northern states. These successes, coupled with British victories in the South, of which more hereafter, have led American historians to speak of the "dark days of 1780." They have exaggerated the difficulties of the patriots.[24] Washington was not strong enough to attack New York, but he kept his army on or near the Hudson, and Clinton did not dare to assail him. Although Washington could not prevent British raids, he sent out General Anthony Wayne, who brilliantly stormed the British fort at Stony Point in July, 1779, and Light-Horse Harry Lee, who successfully attacked another British post at Paulus Hook [25] a month later.

Washington in addition was able to put in motion Continental forces and officers to assist in the defense of the western frontiers of the Northern states. New York and northern Pennsylvania had suffered cruelly at the hands of Tories and warriors of the Six Nations operating from the British post at Niagara. In 1778 they savagely raided the Wyoming and Cherry valleys. To deal with this menace Washington commissioned John Sullivan. In 1779 Sullivan led five thousand men toward Niagara. He failed to reach it, but he defeated his Indian and white enemies at Newtown and burned many Iroquois villages in central New York. Although the Six Nations and their Loyalist allies continued hostilities to the very end of the war, their long-waning military power was struck a mortal blow. To Pittsburgh also Washington sent assistance, toward the defense of western Pennsylvania and in the hope of mounting an expedition against the British base at Detroit. Detroit remained in the hands of the British, but their Indian auxiliaries north of the Ohio felt the weight of the long arm of the commander in chief. It was, to be sure, Virginia's George Rogers Clark who operated most effectively for

[24] In December, 1779, George III told Lord North, "I do believe that America is nearer coming into temper to treat than perhaps at any other period." Sir John Fortescue (ed.), *The Correspondence of King George the Third from 1760 to December, 1783* (6 vols., London, 1927–28), IV, 526. Patriot James Duane, accurately weighing the situation in May, 1780, looked forward to a happy end "of our arduous conflict. We have not experienced half the distresses . . . every contemplative mind must have expected." Edmund C. Burnett (ed.), *Letters of Members of the Continental Congress* (8 vols., Washington, 1921–36), V, 125.

[25] Now part of Jersey City.

the patriots in the Ohio Valley. He, too, was unable to reach Detroit, but in 1778 he occupied the French towns in the Illinois country and captured a British force under Lieutenant Governor Henry Hamilton after a desperate march to Vincennes early the following year.[26] Clark was unable to maintain ground north of the Ohio, but he took some of the sting from Indian attacks upon the new settlements in West Virginia and Kentucky, and he gave the United States a technical case for claiming the Old Northwest.

After the landing of the French army under Rochambeau on Rhode Island Washington once more revived the American dream of conquering Canada. Early in 1778 an invasion under the leadership of Lafayette was planned, but it was beyond the military potential of the patriots at that time. In the following winter the project was revived in Congress, with Lafayette pushing it, but Washington now advised against it, partly on the ground that France might demand the return of her ancient territory. Although Vergennes indicated no desire to recover Canada, the scheme was again dropped. Washington himself, his fears of French ambitions having abated, twice again considered a Franco-American descent upon Canada from the sea, only to abandon the design as impracticable.[27]

In essence, after the appearance of d'Estaing in American waters, the war in the Northern and middle states, moving into stalemate, became one of endurance. In that contest the patriots held their own; and there is little doubt that their powers were sufficient to carry on the struggle until a tired Britain should consent to independence. As it happened, British defeats at sea and in the South hastened the end.

[26] Recent research has somewhat revised the unfavorable reputation of "Hair-buyer" Hamilton. John D. Barnhart, *Henry Hamilton and George Rogers Clark in the American Revolution* (Crawfordsville, Ind., 1951), pp. 93–101.

[27] A. L. Burt, *Old Province of Quebec* (Minneapolis, 1933), pp. 246–247.

CHAPTER 14

The Home Front

ALTHOUGH large numbers of patriots rendered military service of one sort or another in the War of Independence, only a small fraction was in the field at any one time. Some areas of the thirteen states, such as the interior of New England, never felt the tread of British troops except as captives; and other regions, like Maryland, experienced little fighting. Civilian life went on, even in the immediate vicinity of the armies. The war was not total. Nevertheless, no one was unaffected. If there were proportionately few homes in which the loss of a father, son, or brother was mourned,[1] all were touched by economic dislocation and inflation.

The war inevitably brought wrecking and plundering of civilian property. The Howe brothers, hoping for Anglo-American reconciliation, displayed solicitude toward unarmed patriots and discouraged needless destruction and looting. Sir William, however, could not consistently restrain his men, and both British regulars and Hessians under his command pillaged and robbed, notoriously in New Jersey in the latter months of 1776—thereby converting many to the American cause. The raids carried out under Clinton's direction added official theft and desolation to the havoc created by

---

[1] It is impossible to estimate with accuracy patriot casualties. However, there was no battle in the war in which as many as five hundred patriots were slain. In February, 1778, Lord Barrington informed the Commons that the number of British killed in action up to that time was no more than twelve hundred. William Cobbett (ed.), *The Parliamentary History of England, 1777–1778* (36 vols., London, 1806–20), XIX, 721. Of course, deaths from wounds, disease, and hardship would form a large part of the totals.

private enterprise. Stock and grain were taken from farms, tobacco from warehouses, and Negroes from plantations; and what could not be borne away was frequently set on fire. Desperate patriot troops contributed to civilian distress, by despoiling not only the property of Tories but on occasion that of their own people.

Patriots suffered in addition from the interruption of their occupations by the presence of British troops and ships. Farmers and merchants were unable to make their customary purchases and to reach their usual markets. Familiar channels of trade were closed or impeded. Hardest hit of all were the New England fishermen, who were kept ashore by the British naval blockade and forced to seek other means of livelihood.

Ultimately farmers found new markets and fishermen discovered new employment, but a scarcity of finished products caused by patriot refusal to buy them from the British and by British efforts to prevent their importation from other countries brought far more complex problems. Before the war the colonists had purchased large quantities of such goods from Britain. Importation substantially ceased through the labors of the Continental Association, and the patriots continued, so far as it was within their power, to bar British manufacturers from American markets throughout the war. There followed a great shortage in clothing, linen, glass, ironware, paper, wines, and many other commodities. Goods obtained from non-British sources in spite of naval blockade helped to fill civilian needs from time to time and in one place or another; and American manufacturing sprang up. But the shortage was never generally relieved until after the close of hostilities. Civilian demand did not diminish with supply. In consequence merchants raised their prices again and again, profiting hugely. The requirements of the army—uniforms, shoes, blankets, tents in vast quantities—aggravated the situation. The result was soaring prices and an inflationary spiral.

Generous printing of paper currency by all the thirteen states and particularly by the Continental Congress augmented the evils of inflation. Hard money, British, French, and Spanish, was scarce in the early years of the conflict, although much French and Spanish cash circulated toward its end. There was never any lack of the patriot paper variety. In 1777 the Congress asked the states to cease their issues. Had they complied, the amount of paper in circulation would have been limited and that put out by the Congress would have been more acceptable. The states refused to co-operate, however, and the presses everywhere continued to print money. Eventually the currencies of the states were restricted to local use, since each strove to bar the paper, save for its own and that of Congress. Nevertheless, large quantities of paper money, notoriously the ever increasing Continental currency, were placed in circulation. Before the end of 1779, 200 million Continental dollars had been put out. Buying power, even though these dollars soon depreciated, was thus enormously enhanced when goods were scanty.[2]

Inflation was early recognized as a danger, and strenuous efforts were made to deal with it. In 1776 the New England states found a corrective in the fixing of prices and wages. At a convention which opened at Providence near the close of the year representatives of the four states called for rigid controls, and all four states responded by passing legislation for the purpose.[3] On February 15, 1777, Congress, although several members doubted both the wisdom and the feasibility of such controls, gave measured applause to the Yankee scheme and suggested that other states participate in similar gatherings to consider its adoption. Nine months later Congress urged the establishment of a grand program of price and wage regulation; and New York, New Jersey, and Pennsylvania copied the example of the Yankees in 1778.[4] Many states also turned to the panacea of laws which required that their paper currencies be accepted as legal tender. There was powerful opposition to both remedies, especially from merchants who professed to believe it "inconsistent with the principles of liberty to prevent a man from the free disposal of his property on such terms and for such considerations as he may think fit."[5] Legal tender provisions were

---

[2] Ralph V. Harlow, "Aspects of Revolutionary Finance, 1775–1783," *American Historical Review*, XXXV (1929), 52, asserts that the cause of inflation was excessive printing of paper money. But the shortage of goods was a basic difficulty, a fact emphasized in Oscar and Mary F. Handlin, "Revolutionary Economic Policy in Massachusetts," *William and Mary Quarterly*, Third Series, IV (1947), 11.

[3] Richard B. Morris, "Labor and Mercantilism in the Revolutionary Era," in Richard B. Morris (ed.), *The Era of the American Revolution: Studies Ascribed to Evarts Boutelle Greene* (New York, 1939), pp. 94–97.

[4] *Ibid.*, pp. 98–109.

[5] J. T. Scharf and Thompson Westcott, *History of Philadelphia* (3 vols., Philadelphia, 1884), I, 417.

unjust to the seller and to the creditor when they required the acceptance at par of depreciated paper currency; and public opinion was finally forced to admit the fact. Merchants, some of them, "profiteers," "forestallers," and "monopolizers," evaded or defied the restrictions and indulged in "black market" operations. They frequently put profit and personal liberty ahead of patriotism. Both the overwhelming public opinion and the machinery needed to enforce the laws were lacking, and the two remedies failed. In June, 1778, Congress, reversing its earlier stand, recommended that attempts to set prices be abandoned. In 1779–80 there was another spate of state legislation regarding wages and prices, but it quickly came to an end.[6]

There were other weapons with which to fight inflation. Taxation and public loans would drain off purchasing power. But taxes had come to be associated in patriot thinking with British tyranny, and in any event Congress lacked authority to collect them. Most of the state legislatures neither fully recognized the need for large levies—both to finance the war and to strike at inflation—nor had the courage to impose them, until the end of the war was in sight. At the beginning of the war taxes were low and they remained so, except in Massachusetts and Connecticut. They were often paid in depreciated currency. There was strong opposition even to payment in cheap money, and defiance of the collector was not unknown. Moreover, neither Congress nor the states were able to borrow from citizens in sums sufficient to reduce their buying power materially. Certificates of credit issued by the national government and the states had no great appeal, in part because they bore interest at no more than 6 per cent when the investor could easily double and triple his capital in commerce. Inflation with respect to imported goods accordingly ran on almost unrestrained. In 1778 an interstate convention at New Haven recommended that prices be set at a point 75 per cent above those existing before the war.[7]

[6] Morris, "Labor and Mercantilism," pp. 110–122.

[7] Robert A. East, *Business Enterprise in the American Revolutionary Era* (New York, 1938), p. 205. Prices were estimated to have risen 50 per cent in hard money in Philadelphia by July, 1780. Julian P. Boyd *et al.* (eds.), *The Papers of Thomas Jefferson* (4 vols. to date, Princeton, 1950———), III, 484. Anne Bezanson, *Prices and Inflation during the American Revolution: Pennsylvania, 1770–1790* (Philadelphia, 1951), p. 323, states that rises of 50 to 100 per cent occurred in Pennsylvania, but suggests that they were often temporary

Who profited by the war? First of all, the farmers, who formed more than 90 per cent of the American population. If their costs rose, so also did their income, for their products were in heavy demand by the armies. Secondly, many persons engaged in privateering, which was a business as well as a method of striking at Britain. Proprietors, officers, and seamen of privateers filled their pockets when fortune was favorable. The privateering ventures of John and Andrew Cabot of Beverly, Massachusetts, were remarkably lucrative. The Cabots began that rapid rise in the world which permitted them to restrict their earthly acquaintance to the Lowells. Richard and Elias Hasket Derby of Salem and Stephen Higginson of the same town similarly profited. Other investors in privateering in Newport, Rhode Island, Egg Harbor, New Jersey, Philadelphia, and Baltimore were extremely active and sometimes very successful in the business. It has frequently been remarked, perhaps without conclusive statistical data, that the number of men engaged in it was at times equal to the whole Continental army. To be sure, privateering involved great risks, and patriots devoting themselves to it were in the long run perhaps as likely to lose as to gain, while those who confined themselves to trade encountered fewer hazards.

All businessmen did not make money in the course of the War of Independence. Nevertheless, the times offered a golden opportunity for the merchant, the contractor, and their ally the lawyer. Goods imported from Europe and the West Indies sold at such remarkable advances in price that importers could afford rather frequent losses of ships to the British navy and privateers. The continuing demands of the Continentals and the patriot militia for meat, flour, clothing, weapons, horses, and military paraphernalia could be exploited to the trader's advantage. It was possible for the shrewd merchant to corner supplies urgently needed by troops and civilians and to extort excessive profit. Late in the war the contractors who undertook to supply the patriot and French armies made handsome gains.

Army commissaries and quartermasters were also in a position to profit. Their favor was sought by those with whom they dealt.

---

and restricted to scarce items. It would seem that inflation in terms of hard money occurred rather generally with reference to imported goods, that inflation in hard money in connection with other items was prevalent only in the vicinity of armed forces.

Moreover, commissaries commonly carried on private and public business simultaneously, perhaps emulating Robert Morris, the financial agent for the Continental Congress.[8] Morris and Jeremiah Wadsworth, Continental Commissary General, in public service and in personal operations turned small fortunes into large ones. The Englishman John Barker Church, who came to America at the beginning of the war as John Carter and who married a daughter of Philip Schuyler, similarly amassed great wealth. Another merchant who thus climbed the financial ladder was William Bingham of Philadelphia. While there were some "new" men in commerce who rose from poverty to property, the majority who acquired wealth were men of some means at the beginning of the war. Nevertheless, many of the leaders in the mercantile world of 1775, especially those who were Tories, were unable to cling to their top positions. The changes in individual rankings attributable to Revolutionary commerce were not marked by broad class upheavals.[9]

Those who suffered most from war inflation were the clergy, the public officials, the town laborers, and the soldiers and officers of the Continental army. The clergyman's fixed salary rose too slowly to keep pace with rising prices, and he was driven more than before the war to seek solace in things spiritual. The public functionary without private means or occupation was similarly hurt, and could find comfort only in the thought of patriotic duty done. National officials whose income consisted of salary in the form of Continental currency were especially heavy losers, and more than one member of Congress was personally embarrassed by the cost of food and lodging.

Town laborers, artisans, clerks, wagoners, dock workers formed only a small part of the American population, fortunately, for they and their families and poorer folk generally in the towns were victimized by inflation as was no other group save the Continentals. Wages increased, to be sure, as the war went on, but in Massachusetts they merely doubled while prices tripled and quad-

---

[8] East, *Business Enterprise*, pp. 86–88. This volume contains a balanced survey of the effects of the War of Independence upon commerce. The opportunities and complex problems which the war presented to merchants engaged in foreign and West Indian trade are thoroughly handled in James B. Hedges' illuminating study, *The Browns of Providence Plantations: Colonial Years* (Cambridge, Mass., 1952).

[9] East, *Business Enterprise*, p. 213.

rupled.[10] Although skilled labor had been scarce and consequently well paid before the war, the carpenter, the mason, and the printer soon were hard pressed. They fought for higher wages, in some cases even going on strike.[11] Employers who were not making large profits, and even those who were, looked upon their demands as exorbitant. The town workers quite naturally were ardent supporters of price fixing. They organized committees and even mobs to force merchants to reduce their prices. In October, 1779, a mob of desperate poor folk in Philadelphia actually besieged the house of James Wilson. Inside were Wilson himself, Robert Morris, David S. Franks, Thomas Mifflin, and others—lawyers, merchants, and commissaries—persons known or suspected of profiting in public service or private enterprise, or both. Shots were exchanged, and the siege was ended only when Philadelphia silk-stocking militia arrived in force. Such outbreaks—and physical violence was at most sporadic—brought at best temporary and partial relief. No check was ever devised which could permanently curb the profits which merchants and speculators considered their due.

Among all classes of patriots who suffered from inflation none were injured so much as those who deserved it least, the Continentals, officers and men. They could hardly have been rewarded beyond their deserts. Had they received their low wages in hard money, they would have been drubbed by rising prices. Since they were compensated in Continental paper, they were twice scourged, by soaring prices and by depreciating currency. Men in the ranks, where food, clothing, and lodging were furnished them after a fashion, could at best toward the close of the war buy inconsequential items with a month's pay. Officers were possibly worse off; given more dollars, they were required to feed and clothe themselves. And unhappily, pay, even in Continental paper, was often months in arrears. The families of both officers and men lacking private means shared some of the hardships of their heroes in arms.

After 1776 the presses putting out Continental currency worked overtime. By the end of that year $25 million had been put in circulation, perhaps as much as could be absorbed at the time.

[10] Morris, "Labor and Mercantilism," pp. 131–133.

[11] Several authorities assert that the first strike by American wage earners occurred in 1786. But see Richard B. Morris, *Government and Labor in Early America* (New York, 1946), pp. 200–201, n. 28.

Congress issued another $13 million in 1777, and its dollars by this date were rapidly losing their buying power. More than $63 million came from the presses in 1778, followed by fifty more early in the next year. In the summer of 1778 four Continental dollars were equal to one in gold; at the end of 1779 the ratio was fifty and even one hundred to one. Congress was well aware as early as 1776 that excessive issues would reduce the value of its money, but the Continental paper was its major financial resource. Since sufficient means to carry on the war could be obtained in no other way, Congress continued to put it forth for what it would bring. In September, 1779, the delegates resolved that no more than $200 million should be printed, but the downward march of the Continental dollar continued until it was almost worthless. On March 15, 1780, Congress announced repudiation, declaring forty Continental dollars equal to one in gold. Almost $200 million of debt were thus wiped out. But a simultaneous effort to set up a new paper currency supported by state taxation failed miserably. "Paper money," wrote Edmund Randolph in July, 1781, "is viler than the rags, on which it is printed." [12]

Continental soldiers paid in such paper eventually came to feel that there were perhaps no patriots outside the army. Washington again and again bewailed the cruel lot of the troops in the midst of a country filled with foodstuffs,[13] a nation flourishing and defaced by profiteers. "The long and great sufferings of this army is unexampled in history," [14] he wrote. Ebenezer Huntington, a loyal officer maddened by the hardships endured by his comrades and himself, wrote on July 7, 1780: "I despise my countrymen. I wish

[12] Edmund C. Burnett (ed.), *Letters of Members of the Continental Congress* (8 vols., Washington, 1921–36), VI, 51.

[13] Joseph Jones wrote on Nov. 5, 1780, "The states never were blessed with greater plenty or had it more in their power to lay up ample provisions for the army." *Letters of Joseph Jones of Virginia, 1777–1787* (Washington, 1889), p. 41.

[14] While it cannot be questioned that the Continentals underwent great hardships, every statement made by Washington concerning them is not to be taken at face value. In January, 1781, he wrote that they "seem to reach the bounds of human endurance." In the following month he mentioned "sufferings almost beyond human patience." On January 30, however, in general orders to his troops, he declared, "History is full of examples of armies suffering with patience extremities of distress which exceed those we have suffered. . . ." John C. Fitzpatrick (ed.), *The Writings of George Washington* . . . (39 vols., Washington, 1931–44), XXI, 121, 159, 208.

I could say I was not born in America. I once gloried in it but am now ashamed of it." [15] At times a prediction made by the Loyalist poet Jonathan Odell in 1778 seemed likely to be fulfilled:

> Mock-money and mock-states shall melt away,
> And the mock-troops disband for want of pay.

Lafayette declared that officers and men would receive their reward only in the next world. They did not receive it in this.

It was perhaps slight consolation to the Continentals and their families that equal if not greater sufferings were endured by the Tories, whose trials, proceeding from different causes, not only began before the war but continued after its close. They too were hurt by inflation, sometimes being forced to accept in exchange for goods Continental money which the patriots were permitted to refuse. The troubles which came from inflation, however, were doubtless the least of their lot. They suffered severely from persecution at the hands of the patriots. Some, to be sure, escaped maltreatment. Goldsbrow Banyar of New York lived unmolested on his estate at Rhinebeck, and Peter Kemble of New Jersey, father-in-law of General Gage, was not disturbed. Other Tories, prudently quiet on the subject of politics, not only eluded chastisement by the patriots but even made money as merchants and farmers. Many of them, the indiscreet, the socially and economically conspicuous, and the active supporters of the crown, underwent social ostracism, loss of civil rights, discriminatory taxation, confiscation of property, physical violence, and banishment.

In twentieth-century America it became rather fashionable to look with sympathy upon the Loyalists,[16] once the object of popular hatred. They are pitied for their sufferings and admired for their devotion to a lost cause. It is not now held against them that with Lord Tennyson they gave their allegiance to

> A land of settled government,
> A land of just and old renown,
> Where Freedom slowly broadens down
> From precedent to precedent. . . .

[15] *Letters Written by Ebenezer Huntington during the American Revolution* (New York, 1914), pp. 87–88.

[16] The trend in America toward a more favorable opinion of the Tories was given impetus by Claude H. Van Tyne's *Loyalists in the American Revolution* (New York, 1901). It was later possible for Kenneth Roberts to make a Tory the hero of his popular novel *Oliver Wiswell*.

Much has been said about the intellectual power, the character, the respect for law, and even the social grace which were lost to the United States as the result of the departure of Loyalist exiles. That the Tories were harshly treated cannot be denied. That they numbered men of ability and character is also true. Among them was Benjamin Thompson, Count Rumford, later distinguished as a scientist. Nevertheless, genius old and young—Franklin, Washington, Jefferson, and John Marshall—was on the side of the patriots, as was the bulk of the talent.[17] In censuring the patriots for their severity toward their enemies, it must be kept in mind that had the Tories been on the winning side, it is extremely doubtful whether either they or the London government would have exhibited any striking degree of forbearance toward their opponents.

The stakes for the Americans were high, and the Tories were a menace. They assisted the British armies and fleets in every way conceivable. They supplied the redcoats with food when Washington's men were half-starved, put forth propaganda favorable to Britain, and counterfeited Continental currency. They gave valuable military service to the British as spies, guides, and pilots. The Tories led Indians against the Western frontier settlements. They enlisted in redcoat regiments; they formed their own provincial battalions and their own militia; and they even engaged in privateering raids upon American commerce. Moreover, they were so numerous in certain areas that stern measures were required to keep them in check, particularly when British troops or ships were near. It is hardly surprising that the patriots dealt vigorously with these dangerous internal enemies, detested all the more because they had earlier been neighbors and friends. To be sure, the Americans erred when they accused the Loyalists of instigating the war—by giving false information and inflammatory advice to British officials—and when they used this charge and others without greater validity to justify expropriation of Tory property and banishment of its owners.

As war continued patriot feeling against the Tories, already high in 1775, steadily mounted, reaching a peak after the Loyalists began to take up arms. Washington, Franklin, and Governor William Livingston of New Jersey, men who were generally cool and mod-

---

[17] It must be admitted that the careers of those who went into exile were interrupted and that they had fewer opportunities to develop and to display their gifts.

erate, inveighed against them. The patriots even refused the services of schoolmasters, physicians, and merchants inactive in politics and warfare and inoffensive except for their Tory principles; and they continued to employ mob violence against the active Loyalists until after the end of the conflict. As early as January, 1776, the Continental Congress recommended that Tories be permitted neither to speak nor to write against the patriot regime; on November 27, 1777, it urged the states to seize and sell their property and to lend the proceeds to the central government.

The state legislatures needed no prodding from Congress. They placed upon the statute books and enforced hundreds of laws repressing and punishing the Loyalists. The states deprived them of citizenship by requiring oaths of allegiance which they could or would not take. Not citizens, they lost the right to vote. They were denied access to the courts, were stripped of freedom to speak and to print, and in some states were even barred from the legal and teaching professions. Heavy fines and special taxes were imposed upon them; and they were confined to their homes or moved from them as patriot authorities dictated. The most grievous penalties imposed upon them were confiscation of property and banishment.

Early in 1777 every state except South Carolina and Georgia undertook to chastise as traitors those who actively supported Britain. Acceptance of a royal commission, enlistment in the British army, or an attempt to persuade another to enlist, were proofs of treason. The penalties were death and forfeiture of property.[18] Thousands of trials followed, and many "caterpillars of the commonwealth" were found guilty and punished. It was impolitic, of course, to put to death captured Tories clad in royal uniforms, lest the British retaliate. Tory civilians were to a degree similarly protected, for their brethren were likely to exact life for life. Moreover, the infliction of the extreme penalty upon them, except for espionage, was regarded by many patriots as an atrocious injustice. In Philadelphia in 1778 the execution of two Loyalists, one of whom had guided Howe at Brandywine, called forth vigorous protests. That few Tory civilians were put to death is also explained in part by the flight of thousands of the more enterprising and the more conspicuous into the British lines.

If the Loyalists, except for those bearing arms, almost invariably

[18] Van Tyne, *Loyalists,* chap. 12.

preserved their lives, they frequently lost their property. Patriot leaders believed that they could finance the war, at least in part, by taking and selling their lands, homes, slaves, cattle, shops, and goods; and those same possessions caught the eyes of Americans who coveted them for themselves. Seizure and sale became commonplace. The state treasuries profited, and so did many patriot civilians, the clever and the unscrupulous among them finding splendid bargains. The value of the seized Tory property cannot be precisely ascertained, but it was several million pounds.

Forfeiture of lands and goods was often accompanied by banishment. After 1777 eight states formally expelled the active—and wealthy—Loyalists, with or without trial. In the other states the same end was achieved by indirect legal methods. And everywhere Tories unnerved by extralegal threats and violence sought safety in flight before official action could be taken against them. The exodus began before Lexington and continued throughout the war. They fled in every direction, north to Halifax, west to Niagara and Detroit, south to St. Augustine and the West Indies. Some went directly to England. Many first found refuge in towns of the thirteen states occupied by British troops—Boston, Newport, New York, and Charleston. Later these again moved to escape the patriots, thousands of them being evacuated with the redcoats from New York and Charleston at the end of the war.

The sorrows of the Loyalist exiles were many. Early in the war they expected to return triumphantly behind conquering British regiments. Without homes or means they subsisted as they could, in part through the bounty of British generals. They did not ordinarily enlist in British service, since they felt that the King did not need them. Often they were looked down upon by insular-minded Englishmen as unreliable colonials little better than the patriots themselves. Their British allies did not eagerly seek their help, yet censured them for failing to take up arms. As time went on, however, Loyalist refugees increasingly arrayed themselves for battle, especially after it had become apparent that the King's soldiers and sailors could hardly win without them. Some, perhaps not many, joined the British army and navy. Others, performing services not so useful, enrolled themselves as militiamen, doing temporary and occasional duty, especially in the vicinity of New York and in the far South. Thousands enlisted in "provincial" regiments officered by the Loyalists themselves and equipped like British regulars. These troops, acquiring discipline and experience, fought valiantly for their people and the empire in the later years of the war, especially in the South.

In the end the sufferings and sacrifices of the Loyalists were in vain. The majority, accepting the military verdict of the War of Independence as decisive, chose to remain in the United States and to share the destiny of their patriot neighbors. But perhaps 100,000 [19] became exiles, either because they were banished or because they refused to submit to the new order. Eleven hundred are reported to have accompanied the British when they evacuated Boston in 1776; nine thousand left Charleston and a similar number sailed from New York in 1783 with the departing redcoats. About half of the exiles eventually settled in Canada—especially Nova Scotia, New Brunswick, and Ontario—the remainder in the Bahamas, the British West Indies, and Great Britain.[20] In Canada they labored to build new homes as their ancestors had in the Thirteen Colonies. Because of them Canada became British as well as French, and Canadian loyalty to the empire was confirmed. The memory of their devotion to Britain, their sufferings, and their achievements, pridefully nourished by the society of the United Empire Loyalists, lives on in the Dominion.

Hard though their lot was, the Tories were generously treated by a grateful mother country. British commanders in America were unable to do much for them, but the home government opened its purse. The Treasury began to pay temporary pensions to needy Loyalists early in the war. By 1782 the annual appropriation for the Loyalists had mounted to more than £70,000. These grants were sometimes given to those who could exercise political influence rather than to the deserving. Permanent pensions were later created for those who had lost offices, and almost £3,300,000 was awarded to 4,118 persons as compensation for property losses.[21] As much again was spent to assist the Tories to establish themselves in Canada. Many were thus enabled to begin a new life. Loyalists

[19] The figure is commonly given. It is probably too large.
[20] Wilbur H. Siebert, "The Dispersion of the American Tories," *Mississippi Valley Historical Review*, I (1914), 185–197.
[21] Claims for property loss were presented to the British Loyalist commission by 5,072 persons. The claims of 954 were abandoned. The total amount asked by the Loyalists was £8 million.

were also given offices in the colonies; and those who had held commissions in Tory regiments at least occasionally obtained permanent rank in the British army.

The expatriates in Canada, largely from the Northern states, were stricken by homesickness and regretted losing the sweets of Canaan. Those who found refuge in England were often as not unhappy souls. The distant England to which in the days of prosperity they had offered devotion was not the England which they saw in adversity. There they were rather despised by thoughtless persons who looked upon them as inferior colonials. Some were exasperated by disparaging remarks about Americans, which they took as personal affronts. One such, Samuel Curwen, who was firmly opposed to American independence, was provoked to write in December, 1776:

It is my earnest wish the despised Americans may convince these conceited islanders, that . . . our continent can furnish brave soldiers and judicious and expert commanders, by some knock-down irrefragable argument; for then, and not till then, may we expect generous or fair treatment. It piques my pride . . . to hear us called *"our Colonies, our Plantations,"* . . . as if our property and persons were absolutely theirs, like the "villains" and their cottages in the old feudal system. . . .[22]

When Curwen learned after the war that he would not be molested in Salem, his former residence, he returned "home." Stephen Kemble, British army officer and brother-in-law of General Gage, came back to his native New Jersey to spend his last years. Joseph Stansbury, Loyalist poet, was unhappy in Nova Scotia. He wrote:

> Believe me, love, this vagrant life,
> O'er Nova Scotia's wilds to roam,
> While far from children, friends, or wife,
> Or place that I can call a home,
> Delights me not;—another way
> My treasures, pleasures, wishes lay.[23]

Stansbury, though not permitted to return to his former residence in Philadelphia because of patriot resentment there, was allowed to settle in New York. Other Tories came back to America. If she had misbehaved, they loved her nevertheless.

[22] George A. Ward (ed.), *Journal and Letters of Samuel Curwen* . . . (4th ed., Boston, 1864), p. 97.

[23] Winthrop Sargent (ed.), *Loyal Verses of Joseph Stansbury and Doctor Jonathan Odell* . . . (Albany, 1860), p. 90.

CHAPTER 15

Savannah to Yorktown

S POKESMEN for the Loyalists, insistent throughout the War of Independence that they formed the bulk of the population of the thirteen states, were stanch in asserting their eagerness to take up arms for Britain in areas as yet untouched by British troops. When the redcoats were in Boston, they were told they would be welcomed with open arms in New York; on Manhattan, they were informed that the Tories in New Jersey and Pennsylvania would rise as soon as they should appear; in Philadelphia, it was said that the supporters of the crown in Maryland and Delaware needed only minimal assistance to throw off the yoke imposed upon them by their patriot neighbors. Disillusioning experience had convinced British commanders in America by 1778 that the Loyalists exaggerated both their numbers and their will to fight. As they moved into the American interior they had found themselves surrounded by hostile militia rather than throngs of allies. In England, however, it was easier to accept Loyalist assertions at face value. At least Lord George Germain pretended to have faith in them. Such faith in part prompted the British invasion of the Southern states which began in the fall of that year. According to proponents of this plan, the Tories of the far South were both numerous and belligerent. Moreover, the states of Georgia and South Carolina were sparsely settled and so inaccessible by land routes from the north that the patriots would encounter serious difficulties in sending reinforcements to them. On the other hand, they could be easily reached by sea, there were British forces at St. Augustine which could be employed, and the British could expect some help from the Creek and Cherokee Indians. Accordingly, in March, 1778, when the British were forced to modify their immediate objectives in America, Sir Henry Clinton was instructed to mount an offensive in that area. In August Germain confirmed the order. Clinton was to assail Georgia, and if possible South Carolina.

There were risks, of course, in such a venture, greater risks than Germain knew. The patriots in the South might prove to be dangerous antagonists, and the French navy might cut off the British avenue of retreat. Nevertheless, in the fall of 1778, even though he was forced to send a large detachment to the West Indies to attack the French colony of St. Lucia, Clinton undertook the Southern campaign. When all was quiet at New York because of the approach of winter and the departure of D'Estaing, he ordered Lieutenant Colonel Archibald Campbell to lead 3,500 men to Georgia. There he was to join General Augustine Prevost, who was to move northward from St. Augustine with two thousand troops. On December 23 Campbell landed near Savannah, which was weakly held by Major General Robert Howe, who commanded under Congress in the South. Howe had available South Carolina and Georgia Continentals and militia less numerous than Campbell's force. Without waiting for Prevost, Campbell attacked the city and easily captured it on December 29. Shortly afterward Prevost made his appearance from Florida, and Augusta fell to the British on January 29, 1779. Within little more than a month Georgia had passed under British control. This stunning success was so impressive in London that Sir James Wright, the last royal governor of Georgia, was sent back to Savannah to resume his duties. He was able to maintain a British civil regime there for about three years.

General Benjamin Lincoln, sent south by Congress to replace Howe, did his best to deprive Governor Wright of territory to govern. Virginia and North Carolina rushed militia to join him. Gathering in South Carolina some six thousand men, of whom one thousand were Continentals, he made two attempts to reconquer Georgia. The first ended in defeat at Briar Creek, fifty miles above Savannah; the second was interrupted by a swift counterstroke of Prevost. As Lincoln crossed the Savannah River and marched against Augusta, Prevost moved northward to Charleston. On May

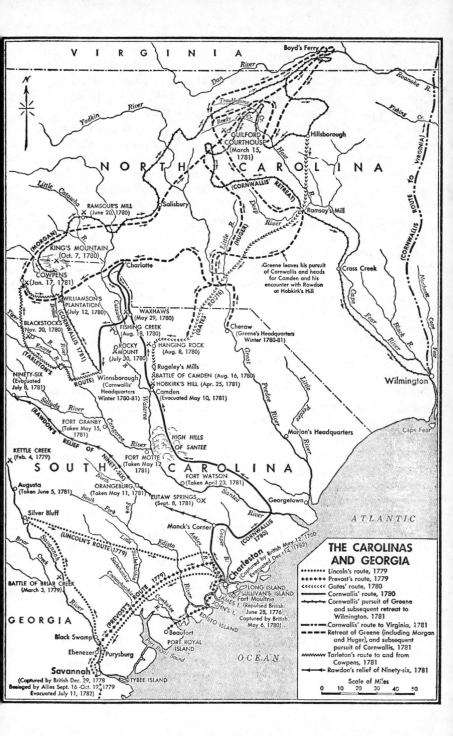

12 the British General demanded the surrender of that town. The civil authorities were disposed to treat with him, hoping to make Charleston neutral ground, its fate to be determined eventually by the progress of the war elsewhere. This course was favored despite the fact that the city was then rather well fortified, despite the presence within it of three thousand armed men—as many as the British without. The approach of Lincoln, hurrying back to the rescue, saved Charleston. Prevost withdrew to Savannah before superior numbers. By June, 1779, summer heat had ended all military activity. Prevost had not conquered Charleston, but he firmly dominated Georgia.

That summer the Southern situation was viewed with alarm by the more intransigent patriots. Lincoln, Governor John Rutledge of South Carolina, and other patriots besought D'Estaing to come from the West Indies to their assistance. Although Washington was counting on the French Admiral's joining forces with him for a major stroke in the North, D'Estaing chose to respond to the pleas from Charleston. Early in September he appeared off Savannah with his fleet and about four thousand troops. With Lincoln he undertook to besiege the town, since Prevost had strongly fortified it. Prevost made a stout defense. Finally, on October 9, because part of D'Estaing's fleet was needed in the West Indies, the Franco-American allies determined to force a quick decision and attacked the British entrenchments. They were beaten back, suffering more than eight hundred casualties. Eleven days later the siege was abandoned and D'Estaing sailed for France.[1] Successful in the West Indies, he had participated in three Franco-American joint operations, all of which were miserable failures.

Now began the great trials of the Southern patriots. The appearance of D'Estaing in American waters led Clinton to evacuate Rhode Island; the news of D'Estaing's defeat and departure enabled him to attack South Carolina in great force. Entrusting the defense of New York to the veteran soldier Baron Knyphausen, Clinton sailed southward in December with eight thousand troops. He was accompanied by a fleet under Admiral Marriot Arbuthnot. A Cape Hatteras storm scattered the transports and warships and compelled the destruction of all cavalry horses, but the army and

[1] There is an excellent account of the siege in Alexander A. Lawrence, *Storm over Savannah* . . . (Athens, Ga., 1951).

the fleet gathered south of Charleston early in February, 1780, and began a leisurely and orderly advance against it. Meanwhile Clinton secured reinforcements from New York, and Lincoln gathered at Charleston more than five thousand men, including two thousand Continentals, among whom were North Carolina and Virginia troops sent to help him by Washington. The city was fortified against attack either by land or by sea. However, on April 1 Clinton began formal siege operations from the land side against patriot fortifications between the Ashley and Cooper rivers, and steadily pushed forward; and Arbuthnot's fleet, sailing past Fort Moultrie on April 8 with very small loss, anchored within cannon shot of the shore. From the moment of Clinton's appearance Lincoln had doubted the wisdom of trying to defend the city. It was now apparent that it could not be held. He had kept open an avenue of escape across the Cooper River to the northward, by which a part of his forces might have escaped. Stirred by pleas of the civilian authorities that the defense be continued, he delayed his withdrawal. On April 14 Banastre Tarleton executed his first great exploit of the war, surprising and driving off patriot militia protecting Lincoln's escape route. Ten days later the British captured Haddrell's Point opposite Sullivan's Island. The fall of Charleston became then almost inevitable. On May 7 Fort Moultrie surrendered, followed five days afterward by Lincoln and all his forces.

The loss of Charleston, over five thousand men, and three hundred cannon was a heavy blow to the patriots, one of the most severe strokes they had suffered in the war. At the end of May Clinton was forced to return to New York because of the approach toward Newport of a French fleet and army under Admiral du Ternay and the Comte de Rochambeau, but he left behind Lord Cornwallis, eight thousand men, and a South Carolina seemingly subjugated. After the surrender of Charleston Tories in the interior of the state flocked to the British colors, most of them, to be sure, eager to fight against the French and Spanish rather than against their neighbors.[2] Downcast patriots, offered a choice between spoliation and taking an oath of allegiance to the King, pledged their loyalty to him by hundreds. British troops occupied forts

[2] Bernhard A. Uhlendorf (ed.), *The Siege of Charleston . . .* , *University of Michigan Publications in History and Political Science,* XII (Ann Arbor, 1938), 419.

throughout the state without meeting serious resistance. For a moment a joyful Clinton counted South Carolina and Georgia as securely regained for the crown. Arrangements were even made to send back to Charleston, as royal governor, William Bull, a respected Carolinian and Loyalist. Indeed, Clinton before his departure declared, "In short if a French or Spanish fleet does not interfere I think a few works if properly reinforced, will give us all between this and Hudson's River. . . . I leave Lord Cornwallis here in sufficient force to keep it against the world, without a superior fleet shews itself, in which case I despair of ever seeing peace restored to this miserable country." [3]

Many patriots were inclined to agree that they had lost at least the far South. In June there was a widely spread rumor that the Continental Congress was about to make peace, abandoning to Britain the two southernmost of the thirteen states. But the Congress resolved on June 23 unanimously "That this Confederacy is most sacredly pledged to support the liberty and independence of every one of its members; and . . . will unremittingly persevere in their exertions . . . for the recovery and preservation of any and every part of these United States that has been or may hereafter be invaded or possessed by the common enemy." [4] It became evident before long that the British would find it extremely difficult to hold Southern areas they had not fully conquered.

If two hundred Charleston men congratulated Clinton upon his capture of the city, if there were Tories in numbers in the South Carolina back country eager to fight for the crown, if there were many in the state seeking to be neutral, still there was in it a very hard core of patriot resistance. The patriots of both South Carolina and Georgia turned to guerrilla warfare. Under the leadership of the astute and courageous Francis Marion, Thomas Sumter, Andrew Pickens, and other partisan leaders they soon were bedeviling British and Tory detachments by attacks in dark, dawn, and daylight. Before long many who had been disposed to accept British victory were so angered by the depredations of the Tories that they allied themselves to the patriots. Moreover, help continued to come

---

[3] Clinton to William Eden, May 30, 1780, Sir Henry Clinton Papers, in William L. Clements Library, University of Michigan.

[4] Worthington C. Ford et al. (eds.), The Journals of the Continental Congress, 1774–1789 (34 vols., Washington, 1904–37), XVII, 554.

to them from the northward. In April Washington and the Continental Congress put in motion from New Jersey the Maryland and Delaware Continentals, about fourteen hundred men, and a small force of artillery. Led by the Baron de Kalb, these forces reached North Carolina in June. On July 25 they were joined by Horatio Gates, who had been appointed by the Congress to Lincoln's post, without Washington's approval.

Although his army was suffering from lack of food—Gates said it was in "inconceivable" distress [5]—he immediately ordered an advance by the most direct route through poor, ravaged, and hostile country against a British post at Camden, South Carolina. His officers protested, urging a circuitous march to the westward through rich territory dominated by the patriots. Gates insisted, for he hoped to capture Camden before it could be reinforced. His command, punished by both hunger and dysentery, moved sullenly southward. It was reinforced on the march by eight hundred Virginia and twelve hundred North Carolina militia. It was somewhat weakened, however, when Gates sent out one hundred Continentals and part of his militia on August 13 to assist Sumter in an attack on a British supply train approaching Camden from Charleston. Gates was then encamped thirteen miles north of Camden. Simultaneously Lord Cornwallis, summoned to his aid by Lord Rawdon, commander at Camden, arrived there with British reinforcements.

At ten o'clock on the night of August 15 Gates began a forced march toward Camden; at ten o'clock on the night of August 15 Cornwallis set out from that place to attempt a surprise attack. To their mutual astonishment they met on Saunder's Creek early in the following morning. Gates then discovered that Cornwallis had joined Rawdon. Cornwallis had more than 2,200 men, about two-thirds of them regulars; Gates could muster over three thousand, but of these no more than one-third were Continentals. The two armies, after preliminary firing, faced each other in an open forest with swamps at both sides. The British were at a disadvantage in position because Saunder's Creek lay directly in their rear and cut off their retreat. A council of war called by Gates decided to fight. After daylight, as the British began to advance toward his right

[5] Julian P. Boyd *et al.* (eds.), *The Papers of Thomas Jefferson* (6 vols. to date, Princeton, 1950———), III, 524.

wing, composed of Continentals, Gates ordered the Virginians on his left wing, made up of militia, to attack. The Virginians moved forward hesitatingly and in disarray. Cornwallis saw his opportunity, assailed them, and quickly drove them back. They fled in wild disorder, carrying with them most of the North Carolinians, along with Gates. Cornwallis then turned most of his forces against the Continentals. These fought desperately, and very effectively for a few minutes, but soon were outflanked on their exposed left and overwhelmed by numbers. Finally they fled, leaving behind them De Kalb mortally wounded. Riding rapidly, Gates reached Charlotte, North Carolina, sixty miles distant, the following night. His men, followed by cavalry under Tarleton, trailed on behind. Ten days afterward Gates was able to muster at Hillsborough only seven hundred men. In the battle the British had suffered more than three hundred casualties; but those of the Americans, chiefly among the precious Continentals, were possibly twice as great.[6]

It has been said that Camden was "the most disastrous defeat ever inflicted upon an American army"[7] and that Gates lost as the result of it North Carolina—if not Virginia—and his whole army.[8] That the triumph of Cornwallis was a jarring blow to the patriots is not to be questioned; yet its importance has frequently been inflated. It did, however, make possible a British invasion of North Carolina in much the same fashion that the capture of Fort Washington in 1776 exposed New Jersey. Cornwallis pushed on into North Carolina as he had across New Jersey almost four years earlier, and again in the end met failure. Upon leaving Charleston Clinton had instructed his venturesome subordinate above all to hold that city. Clinton wished to retain the recent conquests and to avoid expensive operations which might lead to the collapse of British power in the South. Cornwallis, however, believed that North Carolina might easily be overrun and that the cost of such an invasion would not endanger Charleston. Even before Camden he was planning this step.[9] He had asked Clinton to assist him by

[6] For a good account of the battle of Camden and of events immediately preceding see Christopher L. Ward, *The Delaware Continentals 1776–1783* (Wilmington, 1941), pp. 332–355, 531–535. The author is, however, too severe in his condemnation of Gates. Useful contemporary descriptions of the battle are published in *Jefferson Papers*, III, 558–559, 594–597.

[7] John Fiske, *The American Revolution* (2 vols., Boston, 1891), II, 197.

[8] Ward, *Delaware Continentals*, p. 364.

[9] William B. Willcox, "The British Road to Yorktown: A Study in Divided Command," *American Historical Review*, LII (1946), 6–7.

sending a force to the James River in Virginia to create a diversion.[10] Camden, and a smashing defeat inflicted by Tarleton upon Sumter two days later, confirmed his resolution.

On September 7 Cornwallis marched northward toward Charlotte, reaching that town without encountering opposition, but the North Carolina Tories, whose support he had sought, appeared only in small numbers to help him. Before a month had passed he must have doubted that he could break down American opposition and establish contact with British troops in Virginia. In any case, he was soon compelled to retreat. At Charlotte on October 7 he learned that an auxiliary force of eleven hundred New York and South Carolina Tories advancing parallel to his own army was hard pressed; shortly afterward he learned it had been destroyed. Major Patrick Ferguson, leading the Tories and pursuing patriot militia, suddenly became the pursued. Riflemen of the Virginia and North Carolina backwoods, including detachments from the new settlements in East Tennessee, nine hundred in all, followed him to King's Mountain in northern South Carolina. There on the seventh the riflemen surrounded him. They swarmed up the lofty hill. Three times Ferguson's men drove them back with bayonet charges. Then Ferguson fell, the resistance of the Tories crumbled, and they surrendered. In little more than an hour 224 had been slain and the remainder wounded or captured. On learning the news Cornwallis retraced his steps southward, his men plagued by hunger and patriot militia. He took post south of Camden, remaining there almost three months, an interval punctuated by strokes of the South Carolina patriot guerrillas.

Cornwallis might well have avoided further excursions into the interior of North Carolina, but he was joined early in January, 1781, by 2,500 regulars under General Alexander Leslie sent to his aid by Clinton. As a result, Cornwallis had perhaps four thousand men available for an offensive movement. About the same time the British General learned that Clinton had sent Benedict Arnold with another British force of twelve hundred men to Virginia. Once again the patriot line of communications to the northward was to be threatened. Undaunted by his recent failure, Cornwallis resolved to return to North Carolina.

[10] Benjamin Franklin Stevens (ed.), *The Campaign in Virginia, 1781* . . . (2 vols., London, 1888), I, 237–239.

Meanwhile the American army in the South had reoccupied Charlotte and had acquired a new leader, the fourth within two years. The new commander was Nathanael Greene. Reports of Camden caused the Continental Congress to recall Gates and to ask Washington to appoint his successor. Washington immediately chose Greene, who accepted the appointment and assumed command at Charlotte on December 4, 1780.[11] He had hitherto won no great battles, and he was to win none. Courageous, sanguine, active, and ingenious by nature, he had acquired through experience caution and steadiness in the face of adversity. He has occasionally been described as superior in both strategy and tactics to Washington; it is unlikely that any other American general could have surpassed his achievements in the South.[12] When he accepted his new post, he expressed a hope that he might check the British in that area. At Charlotte he found only fifteen hundred troops, more than a third of them militia. He also found there, however, General Daniel Morgan, who had recently re-entered the Continental service; and Light-Horse Harry Lee and his raiding corps were about to join him.

Greene could not stand against Cornwallis in battle but nevertheless took the offensive. Dividing his men, he sent one part under Morgan to the southwest and the other to the southeast. He planned to harass Cornwallis' flanks and communications. Well aware that Cornwallis might turn against and destroy either part or both, he relied on the quickness of movement of the patriots to avoid destruction. To make possible a rapid retreat, even to Virginia, he had Colonel Edward Carrington and Thaddeus Kosciuszko collect boats and otherwise prepare for speedy crossings of the major streams of North Carolina. This novel strategy puzzled Cornwallis. He sent Tarleton with one thousand men after Morgan. Tarleton caught him at the Cowpens on January 16, 1781, in an open wood with unprotected flanks and the Broad River at his back. Morgan's position was bad, but his numbers were equal to those of his op-

[11] Gates drew the appropriate conclusion from his defeat at Camden. He wrote to Jefferson, "Slow, and I hope sure, will be our next attempt." *Jefferson Papers*, III, 650. He was left without command for many months and was not again given an independent one.

[12] Although Greene has been the subject of several biographies, his career has not been closely and impartially examined. It is difficult, if not impossible, to weigh his talents against those of Washington.

ponent and his troops were superbly arranged. On the following morning Tarleton attacked and pushed back two lines of American riflemen, not without suffering losses. But the militia fled by a prearranged route, and when Tarleton advanced to complete his victory he was driven back by a steady line of Maryland and Delaware Continentals supported by William Washington's cavalry. The Americans, including the militia, who returned to the field, then counterattacked and routed the British. At least six hundred of Tarleton's command were killed, wounded, or captured. Morgan's losses were relatively small.

Had Cornwallis been a cautious man, the British defeat at the Cowpens, "a very unexpected and severe blow," as he described it,[13] would have led him to abandon all thought of invading North Carolina. Instead he hurried after Morgan, who retreated northward. Determined that the Americans should not escape, Cornwallis destroyed all his heavy baggage in order to move the faster. However, Greene managed to draw back both of his contingents beyond Cornwallis' reach and to effect a junction at Guilford Court House. With Cornwallis in hot pursuit, he then fled across the Dan River into Virginia. There he was reinforced by four hundred Continentals and by large bodies of militia who gathered to meet the pressing danger. Further help for Greene was near at hand. But the British prospects seemed less favorable. Arnold had made little progress into Virginia. Accordingly Cornwallis chose not to follow. He retired to Hillsborough, where he rested his army and called the North Carolina Tories to his aid. Some three hundred joined him. His regulars now numbered hardly more than two thousand.

From Virginia Green promptly took the offensive, moving back into North Carolina. At Guilford Court House on March 15 he offered battle on ground he had carefully chosen. Cornwallis accepted the challenge, perhaps gladly, even though he was faced by more than 1,700 Continentals and at least 2,800 militia.[14] Greene's arrangements were much like those of Morgan at Cowpens, two lines of militia with the bulk of his Continentals in their rear. Cornwallis, like Tarleton, attacked; and again the militia fled. But

[13] *Campaign in Virginia*, I, 355.
[14] Estimates of the number of Greene's militia range as high as 3,900. David Schenck, *North Carolina, 1780–1781* (Raleigh, 1889), p. 312.

they continued their flight far beyond the field. Moreover, Cornwallis had better fortune against the Continentals than his subordinate. Though unable to drive them from their positions, he withstood American counter-assaults and finally forced the Continentals to retreat.

At Guilford Cornwallis won another victory, at the expense of 93 killed and 413 wounded. It was now apparent even to that bold soldier that his triumphs in the Carolinas were empty. He could not safely remain in the interior of North Carolina; his depleted army was too weak even to risk defensive warfare there. He must move elsewhere, and he did, not toward Camden and Charleston, but rather to Wilmington. Unmolested by Greene, he reached that port and thence marched off to Virginia and a meeting with destiny at Yorktown.

Setting out for Virginia, Cornwallis did not leave South Carolina and Georgia uncovered, for there were about eight thousand British troops of one sort or another under Lord Rawdon in those two states. Nevertheless, the British army in the far South had been weakened by Cornwallis' operations. After his departure it consisted largely of Tory "provincials" and militia, and was not strong enough to hold more than seacoast bases. Greene saw his opportunity. Leaving to the patriots in Virginia and to the northward the task of dealing with Cornwallis, he attacked the British in South Carolina and Georgia. Marion, Sumter, Pickens, and Colonel Elijah Clark of Georgia, working with Greene and also independently, inspired the patriots of the two states to great efforts. On April 23 Fort Watson, one of seven British posts and forts ringing Charleston and Savannah, was captured by Marion and Light-Horse Harry Lee. Rawdon took the field to support his scattered garrisons, and he attacked Greene near Camden, at Hobkirk's Hill, two days later. The armies were equal in size, about fifteen hundred men in each. Again Greene was defeated. Rawdon withstood the American onslaught and after a slugging match forced the Americans to retreat. But, like Cornwallis after Guilford Court House, he failed to follow, instead cautiously falling back toward Charleston. It was impossible for him to maintain a long communication line. The patriots then swarmed about and surrounded the British garrisons at Forts Motte,[15] Granby,[16] Orangeburg,

---

[15] At the junction of the Congaree and Wateree rivers.
[16] At modern Columbia.

Augusta, and Georgetown, all of which were compelled to surrender by June 20. Greene himself undertook to seize the British post at Ninety-Six and as usual was repulsed. A Loyalist garrison there fought desperately and was finally relieved after a month's siege on June 20 by the approach of Rawdon, who had received reinforcements from Ireland. Once more Greene fell back, and Rawdon also. On July 3 Rawdon withdrew the Tories from Ninety-Six and concentrated the bulk of his forces about Charleston. Within three months after Cornwallis' departure for Virginia the British holdings in the far South were reduced to Charleston, Savannah, and small adjacent areas.

The tireless Greene was not yet content. In August, after receiving new troops from North Carolina—men condemned to twelve months' service as Continentals because they had misbehaved as militia—he advanced toward the South Carolina capital. At Eutaw Springs on September 8 he was opposed by Colonel Alexander Stuart, who had succeeded Rawdon. Each of the armies contained about 2,300 men. Greene attacked, the battle swayed back and forth, the British began to fall back, even abandoning their camp. The tide turned against the patriots, however, when thirsty Continentals stopped to drink British rum to celebrate their victory. The royal troops re-formed, counterattacked, and forced Greene to retire. A fourth time defeated in the open field, he again profited. The losses on both sides were heavy, but Stuart's reached almost 40 per cent. Thenceforth the British commander confined himself to the defense of Charleston. Not strong enough to try to carry the city, Greene hovered about it until the war came to a close. To the end of the war the British clung to Charleston, Savannah, and St. Augustine, but to no great purpose, since they were all abandoned to the United States and Spain at the peace.

While the conquests of the British in Georgia and the Carolinas waxed and waned, they were driven from West Florida by Bernardo de Galvez, the Spanish Governor of Louisiana, who consummated the capture of the province by the seizure of Pensacola in May, 1781. Nor did the Southern Indian allies of the British have cause at the conclusion of the conflict to celebrate their many scalpings. Some of the warlike Creeks refused to fight against the Americans; the others accomplished little; and their great chief Emistisiguo fell in battle in 1782 at the hands of the patriots near Savannah. The Cherokee were even less effective. Late in 1780 their country was overrun by backwoodsmen, and their military power virtually destroyed.[17] Below the southern boundary of Virginia the war terminated disastrously for Britain. Had Cornwallis pursued the cautious policy ordered by Clinton, the result in the Carolinas and Georgia would scarcely have been altered, for the British could not prevail against the combined forces of local patriots and Continentals. South Carolinians and Continentals contested for the credit of their common triumph, which neither could have won without the other.[18] The men of the line who held the British in check in the open field and the men of the swamps and woods who interrupted their communications and their sleep were equally indispensable. There was sufficient glory for both.

While British dreams of victory below the Dan River faded, Cornwallis brought the war to a decision in Virginia. On April 10, 1781, after retreating to Wilmington, he considered a plan to return to the interior of North Carolina as soon as he could secure reinforcements, but his heart was not in the project. Such an offensive would probably end in failure. Moreover, he could not quickly gather additional troops needed for the venture. Simultaneously, he was contemplating the conquest of Virginia, and urged Clinton to concentrate his forces there, if necessary even to abandon New York to accomplish this objective.[19] Two weeks later he set off for Virginia with the remains of his army. By May 20 he was at Petersburg. There he came into contact with Benedict Arnold's army, recently enlarged by reinforcements sent by Clinton to Virginia under Major General William Phillips.[20] Cornwallis was the senior officer, and he had been earlier given authority to issue commands to the British contingents in the Old Dominion. Adding the Phillips-Arnold forces to his own, and also three regiments from New York which reached Petersburg on May 23, he had under him more than seven thousand men.

[17] Elby Boosinger, "The Cherokees in the Revolutionary War," Master's thesis, in Love Library, University of Nebraska.

[18] The Continentals were inclined to look down upon their comrades. Otho Holland Williams, a Maryland officer, declared that the bulk of the inhabitants of South Carolina and Georgia were "the most unprincipled, abandoned vicious vagrants that ever inhabited the earth." *Calendar of the General Otho Holland Williams Papers* . . . (Baltimore, 1940), p. 46.

[19] *Campaign in Virginia*, I, 399.

[20] Phillips superseded Arnold in command in Virginia, but died shortly before the appearance of Cornwallis.

The news of Cornwallis' march to Virginia astounded Clinton. He would have been pleased had Cornwallis appeared on the James River after subjugating the Carolinas. He was unhappy because Cornwallis had abandoned his troops in the far South and also because he had concentrated an important part of the British army in Virginia. The British commander in chief had undertaken operations on the Chesapeake for the purpose of carrying on raids, interrupting American communications, and relieving the pressure on Cornwallis in the Carolinas. He had also hoped eventually to use the troops in Virginia as one arm of a pincers movement into the valley of the lower Susquehanna and the peninsula between Delaware and Chesapeake bays.[21] He had feared risking large forces in Virginia which might be cut off by a French fleet in the Chesapeake Bay,[22] and that fear had doubtless been increased in the preceding February when the French Newport squadron and American forces in the Old Dominion attempted to trap Arnold. The British navy had driven the French ships from the Chesapeake,[23] but it was possible that the French would return to the bay and in greater strength.

Facing awkward problems posed for him in part by his aggressive subordinate, Clinton resolved to do his best to meet them. However, he was not on good terms with Germain; he had quarreled with Admiral Arbuthnot; and he was expecting to be relieved of his command at any moment.[24] He failed to take a strong hand with Cornwallis, who would in all probability succeed him. He

[21] *Campaign in Virginia*, I, 439–440, 444, 451–452, 454–455, 460–462.

[22] On April 23 Clinton described operations in Virginia as "attended with great risk, unless we are sure of a permanent superiority at sea." He thought it safer to hazard large forces north and east of Chesapeake Bay. *Ibid.*, p. 459.

[23] On this preview of the Franco-American Yorktown strategy see Louis R. Gottschalk, *Lafayette and the Close of the American Revolution* (Chicago, 1942), chap. 9; and William Willcox, "Rhode Island in British Strategy 1780–1781," *Journal of Modern History*, XVII (1945), 318–321.

[24] In the spring of 1778, soon after Clinton became commander in chief, Cornwallis was given a "dormant" commission which authorized him to assume the supreme command if Clinton resigned or was unable to serve. The importance of this "dormant" commission has sometimes been exaggerated. It was intended to ward off a claim to inherit Clinton's authority by a German officer superior in rank to Cornwallis. Charles Ross (ed.), *Correspondence of Charles, First Marquis Cornwallis* (3 vols., London, 1859), I, 33. The commission merely made certain that the American command would be held by the senior British officer.

repeatedly suggested to Cornwallis that he act offensively, preferably in conjunction with Clinton himself, against Pennsylvania; alternatively, he should occupy a few posts in Virginia and send the bulk of his men to New York.[25] He warned Cornwallis that French ships might appear in major force in the Chesapeake. The General in Virginia, given opportunity to debate with the General in New York, did not fail to seize the opportunity. He refused to move northward by land; and when Clinton ordered him to establish a base on the bay and to send troops not needed for its defense to New York by water, he insisted that the base could not be held with less than his whole army. Clinton, deferring to the judgment of his subordinate, permitted him to keep his entire force.[26]

For weeks strategy was debated. In the meantime Cornwallis tried and failed to deal with the patriots in Virginia. Before his arrival British commanders in the state had inflicted heavy punishment with small forces. Jefferson as Governor had been unable to mobilize the militia and to drive the invaders back to their ships. Vigorous action on the part of Cornwallis might have crushed American resistance there, at least temporarily. Steuben was near Charlottesville collecting troops; Lafayette, sent with twelve hundred men to the aid of Virginia by Washington, was at Richmond; and Anthony Wayne with another one thousand men dispatched by Washington was moving across Pennsylvania. Cornwallis drove back Lafayette but did not, perhaps could not, prevent Wayne and then Steuben from joining him. At Jamestown the British General checked the combined patriot divisions under the Marquis. Raiding parties which he sent out under Tarleton and John Graves Simcoe penetrated far into the interior of the state. But Lafayette's army was still in the field when Cornwallis began to erect fortifications at Yorktown near the end of July, and it remained unmolested in the field throughout August and into September while the British General labored to build his base. Then Cornwallis was suddenly besieged by almost overwhelming Franco-American forces.

While Clinton worried lest a great French fleet appear on the

[25] Clinton's strategy and his attitude toward Cornwallis are ably defended in William Willcox, "The British Road to Yorktown: A Study in Divided Command," *American Historical Review*, LII (1946), 10–15.

[26] Clinton later claimed that Germain had ordered him not to weaken Cornwallis' army. His assertion was widely accepted. It has been recently proved that it is without basis in fact. *Ibid.*, pp. 19–20.

American coasts, Washington, Franklin, and John Laurens, who had been sent to Paris as a special emissary, urged the French to dispatch such a fleet. Accordingly, Admiral de Grasse sailed from Brest for the West Indies in the spring of 1781 with twenty warships and orders to move in summer to the mainland, there to co-operate with Washington and the French stationed at Newport. Receiving the news, Washington and Rochambeau met in May at Wethersfield, Connecticut, to lay plans for joint operations with De Grasse. They decided to assail New York by land and sea. Accordingly, Rochambeau's troops, about five thousand in number, joined Washington's in positions opposite Clinton's fortifications early in July. The American commander also made arrangements to call out the New England militia. However, Rochambeau, realizing that an attack upon the British in Virginia might have a better chance for success than one upon New York, pressed Washington to alter his objective. At length the American General permitted himself to be persuaded. Washington and Rochambeau, together with the Chevalier de la Luzerne, French Minister to the United States, urged De Grasse to bring troops from the West Indies, and to come to the Chesapeake. Washington kept in mind the alternatives of joint operations against New York and Charleston. From Haiti De Grasse promptly replied that he would proceed to the Chesapeake in August and that he would carry with him more than three thousand French regulars from the West Indies. As good as his word, he arrived at the entrance to the bay on the thirtieth of that month.

Washington learned of De Grasse' plans on August 14 and boldly decided to transfer the bulk of the Franco-American army encamped in the environs of New York to Virginia in the hope of trapping Cornwallis. He informed De Grasse and Lafayette of his plan, warning the Marquis not to let the British General flee southward. On August 21, leaving on the Hudson only ten regiments of Continentals and some militia under General Heath to occupy the attention of the British at New York, he put in motion seven thousand men, of whom five thousand were French troops. Almost simultaneously the French squadron at Newport set out for the Chesapeake. Most of Washington's command was beyond Philadelphia before Clinton could ascertain its destination. He wrote to

Cornwallis on September 2: "By intelligence I have this day received, it would seem that Mr. Washington is moving an army to the southward." [27] He might then have assailed Heath, might have secured control of the Hudson, but the advantages gained would probably be only temporary should Cornwallis' army be lost.[28] He turned to thoughts of rescuing Cornwallis.

The land operations of the Franco-American plan were superbly executed. Cornwallis remained immobile at Yorktown until September 7, when the troops carried by De Grasse joined Lafayette and took positions covering the British base on the land side. The British General was then confronted by a superior army. Knowing that retreat by sea was doubtful, he might have made a desperate attempt to cut his way either to New York or to Charleston and safety; he did not. A week later it was probably too late even to try, for Washington and his army, transported from Baltimore and Annapolis down Chesapeake Bay, had reached Williamsburg. Cornwallis was then effectively penned against salt water by sixteen thousand troops, half French and largely veterans. Behind these were detachments of militia covering the roads in every direction. If he was to be saved, he must be reinforced or evacuated by sea.

The French navy functioned with efficiency, and was assisted by British bungling. As early as April Germain was aware that De Grasse might appear off the coasts of the thirteen states; before the end of June he knew that the French Admiral was scheduled to reach those coasts in August. Yet he gave Clinton no explicit warning. Instead he assured him that the British fleet in the West Indies under Admiral Sir George Rodney would counter De Grasse and would if necessary follow him to the mainland. The burden of maintaining British control of American continental waters thus fell upon Rodney, who proved unequal to the task. Before the end of July he knew De Grasse was about to sail for the Chesapeake, but gambled that the French Admiral would leave some of his ships in the Caribbean to protect the Bourbon island possessions. He was

[27] *Campaign in Virginia,* II, 193.

[28] Francis Vinton Greene, in *The Revolutionary War and the Military Policy of the United States* (New York, 1911), p. 271, contends that Clinton, had he possessed the vigor of U. S. Grant or Robert E. Lee, would have attacked Heath and that the result might have been disastrous for the patriots. He overestimates the value to the British of control of the Hudson and minimizes the opposition which Clinton would have met.

outguessed, for De Grasse boldly took his entire fleet of twenty-eight vessels. On August 1 Rodney ordered Admiral Sir Samuel Hood to the northward; he himself, in ill health, set out for England, taking with him three ships of the line. He sent two more on convoy duty to Jamaica, requesting Sir Peter Parker, in command there, to put them in motion after Hood. He also suggested to Parker that four ships of the line stationed at Jamaica be dispatched northward. Without positive orders Parker did not act until too late. Hood reached New York on August 28 with only fourteen warships; he might then or soon afterward have had twenty or more.[29]

At New York Sir Thomas Graves, successor to Arbuthnot, had seven ships of the line; with those of Hood fit for service, the number mounted to nineteen. Ignorant of De Grasse' strength, Graves, with Hood as second in command, hurried to the Chesapeake, hoping to intercept the Newport squadron before it could join De Grasse. On September 5 he encountered De Grasse at the mouth of the bay. The French Admiral attacked. The resulting action was indecisive, but Graves felt forced to return to New York eight days later. Meanwhile the Newport squadron slipped around him and entered the bay, which thus came positively under French control. The doom of Cornwallis was virtually sealed.

Clinton realized as early as September 7 that a crisis had arrived, and he resolved to exert himself "to the utmost to save Lord Cornwallis."[30] He prepared to embark four thousand men for Virginia, these to depart as soon as Graves had opened the Chesapeake. A week later he received the news that the French could not be driven from the bay. On September 23 he heard from Cornwallis: "If you cannot relieve me very soon, you must be prepared to hear the worst."[31] Through September and into October Clinton and British officers at New York considered various plans to relieve him. After returning from the Chesapeake Graves was gloomy about

[29] William B. Willcox, "The British Road to Yorktown: A Study in Divided Command," *American Historical Review*, LII (1946), 1–35, particularly pp. 21–23, 34–35, ascribes the British disaster at Yorktown in considerable part to the shortcomings of Rodney, but especially censures Cornwallis for getting himself and a large army into a position where they were dependent for their safety upon the navy. Professor Willcox sees Clinton's conduct as less open to criticism.

[30] Clinton to Germain, Sept. 12, 1781, Clinton Papers.

[31] *Campaign in Virginia*, II, 158.

projects of forcing a passage into it and even more so about the possibilities of giving continued and adequate support to British land forces pinned down on the peninsula. Finally, after much

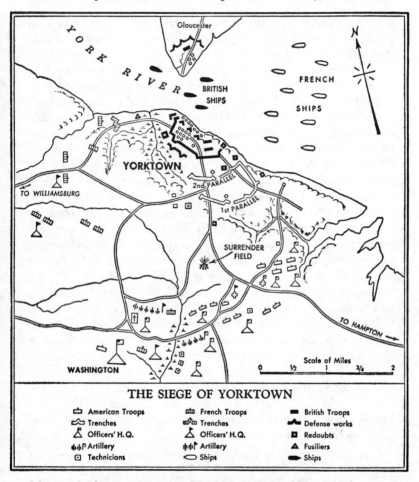

THE SIEGE OF YORKTOWN

⏚ American Troops	ᗕ French Troops	▬ British Troops
⏛ Trenches	⏛ Trenches	ᗒ Defense works
⏶ Officers' H.Q.	⏶ Officers' H.Q.	◨ Redoubts
⏛P Artillery	⏛P Artillery	⏶ Fusiliers
◨ Technicians	⬭ Ships	⬭ Ships

delay and after receiving naval reinforcements, Graves set sail on October 17 with a fleet no more than two-thirds the strength of that of De Grasse. Accompanying him were Clinton and some seven thousand troops. There was little chance that they could save Cornwallis, a big risk that they themselves would be defeated. As events

turned out, they were to learn before reaching the bay that Cornwallis had surrendered on October 19. Disheartened, they turned
the fleet about and sailed back to New York.[32]

Cornwallis' position on the York River was weak. Part of his
men were at Gloucester, north of the river, the bulk at Yorktown
opposite. His fortifications were not strong, and many of his men
were unable to do duty because of sickness. On September 28 the
Franco-American army, well supplied with siege guns and engineers, surrounded him on the land side. On October 6 the allies
opened a parallel against his works at Yorktown, five days later
another. In a night attack on the fifteenth they captured two British
redoubts, driving Cornwallis within his inner fortifications. Cornwallis had made only one sally. Now he planned an attempt to cut
his way out to the north through Gloucester. A storm intervened.
In any case it would doubtless have failed. He might have held out
for a week or ten days, until Graves and Clinton should appear; his
entrenchments might have been stormed before they could help
him. On October 17, four years to a day after the capitulation of
Burgoyne, he asked for terms. The surrender of all his forces was
demanded. He despondently agreed, and two days later he and
more than seven thousand men formally laid down their arms.

The war then virtually came to an end. Washington urged De
Grasse to join him in an attack upon New York, or upon Charleston, but the French Admiral was needed in the Caribbean, and he
soon departed. He had done enough. Few besides George III believed after Yorktown that the thirteen states could be conquered
by Britain. A British officer at New York hardly exaggerated when
he described the news of the surrender as "some of the blackest
tidings ever received from this country." [33]

[32] Clinton afterward perfectly described the situation in a few words: ". . .
All depended on a fleet. S H Clinton was promised one Washington had one."
Ibid., p. 157.

[33] Mrs. E. S. Wortley (ed.), *A Prime Minister and His Son* (New York,
1925), p. 173.

CHAPTER 16

The Path to Peace

ALTHOUGH the surrender of Cornwallis decisively put an end to major offensive efforts on the part of the British in North America and so insured a victory for the patriots, the task of collecting its fruits still lay before them. Would they insist upon and could they achieve recognition of absolute independence? What would they seek and obtain in the way of boundaries, fishing rights off Nova Scotia and Newfoundland, privileges in trade with the British Empire? The destiny of the United States was shaped in part by soldiers in the field, in part by diplomats at the conference table. The patriots proved to be as competent and fortunate in the conflict of words as they had been in the contest of arms.

Had it been within the power of George III to prevent American independence, the struggles and sacrifices of the patriots would have been in vain. During the two years which followed the beginning of hostilities with France Britain was threatened by invasion, by revolt in Ireland, and even by national bankruptcy as the costs of the war continued to mount;[1] meanwhile no progress was made in the American war, and British possessions and bases in the West Indies, the Mediterranean, Africa, and India were seized or endangered. The discouraging outlook for England, combined with high land taxes, whittled away the support which the King had long received in the House of Commons from the independent country gentlemen. In December, 1779, the leaders of the Opposi-

[1] The British debt doubled as the consequence of the war.

tion agreed to sink their differences.[2] In April, 1780, they were able to push through the Commons by a vote of 233 to 215 a trenchant declaration "that the influence of the crown has increased, is increasing, and ought to be diminished." [3] County associations and committees of Whigs and Radicals, engines like those employed so potently before 1775 by the Americans, were then springing up in England.

Yet George did not despair. Previously he had offered to accept some of the Whigs as members of the ministry, provided that they undertook to fight for the preservation of the empire. Now he repeated that offer. In June the Lord George Gordon riots, which were inspired by anti-Catholic fanaticism and which brought mob rule to London for almost a week, made it possible for him to abandon negotiations with his internal foes. Reacting against the violence of the religious zealots and released criminals who joined them, impressed by the firmness of the King, who finally restored order by military force, the public turned toward the camp of the monarch. The news of the capture of Charleston and the victory of Camden gave added impulse to the changing tide of opinion. The King and his supporters exploited the favorable news and called a general election for the autumn. George spent more than £100,000 in behalf of friendly candidates and the ministry won a majority of more than one hundred. Until the arrival of the news of Yorktown on November 25 the Opposition made little progress in the new Parliament.

Lord North, who had for years lacked faith in the King's policies and his own administration, at first assumed that Yorktown was the final blow.[4] The King, however, displayed a stubborn determination which in another cause would have inspired admiration. The war must be carried on, he insisted, "though the mode of it may require alteration." [5] Once more North steeled himself to do his master's bidding and sought to breast the storm which rose at Westminster.

[2] H. Butterfield, *George III, Lord North, and the People, 1779–80* (London, 1949), p. 168.

[3] William Cobbett (ed.), *The Parliamentary History of England, 1780–1781* (36 vols., London, 1806–20), XXI, 347, 367.

[4] Sir Nathanael William Wraxall, *The Historical and Posthumous Memoirs of* . . . (5 vols., London, 1884, Henry B. Wheatley, ed.), II, 139, reports that when he heard the news North exclaimed, "O God! it is all over!" It is at least doubtful that these exact words were uttered by North.

[5] Sir John Fortescue (ed.), *The Correspondence of King George the Third from 1760 to December, 1783* (6 vols., London, 1927–28), V, 304.

To no purpose. The supporters of the King were downcast, the Opposition was vehement, and the independent country gentlemen under the leadership of Thomas Powis clamored for an end to the American war. On December 12 Powis delivered a stunning blow, a speech comparing the British Empire under George III to the Roman Empire under Valentinian III and Honorius. Edward Gibbon had the ironic experience of hearing the regime which he himself supported witheringly castigated in his own majestic periods. The ministerial majority sank to forty-one. With the reports of new disasters early in 1782, it fell to nineteen. On February 11 the resignation of Germain was announced. For his services to the King he was made Viscount Sackville. Eleven days later a motion to abandon efforts to coerce America was defeated by one vote; on March 4 another to the same purpose was passed without a division. The resignation of the North ministry was made known on March 20.

When George III failed in efforts to form a coalition government, he prepared to abdicate.[6] But after sober second thought he reluctantly accepted a ministry drawn almost entirely from the Opposition. Rockingham became Prime Minister, Charles James Fox and Shelburne the Secretaries of State. Both Secretaries had diplomatic duties and powers, since Fox was placed in charge of relations with Europe and Shelburne was given the responsibility of dealing with America.[7] The new Cabinet promptly dispatched Sir Guy Carleton to New York to replace Clinton. He was instructed to avoid offensive measures and to capitulate rather than to defend himself against major attack. He was to conciliate rather than to fight; he was to try to persuade the Americans to let him peacefully withdraw the British forces from the thirteen states for service elsewhere against the French and Spanish. Since the patriots could not permit an undisturbed evacuation of the British army without arousing France and Spain, it is clear that the Cabinet hoped not only to create good will among them toward Britain but also to insert a wedge between them and the Bourbons. At the same time Shelburne sent Richard Oswald to Paris to open peace negotiations with Benjamin Franklin, to foster Anglo-American amity, and to

[6] *Ibid.*, p. 425.
[7] The Colonial Secretaryship held by Hillsborough, Dartmouth, and Germain was abolished.

try to wean the patriots away from France. These measures were not intended merely to divide Britain's enemies. Rockingham, Shelburne, and Fox still hoped that the Americans could be saved to the empire, that they could be persuaded to accept some sort of union with Britain. Carleton's maneuvers at New York deceived no one, and he was not allowed tranquilly to embark his soldiers; British diplomacy at Paris achieved a greater measure of success.

Certainly British hopes in 1782 of prying asunder the patriots and the Bourbons were not without foundation, for the Americans were quarreling with Spain and some of them distrusted France.

It will be recalled that the government of Charles III refused in 1778 to enter into an alliance with the United States and even to recognize their independence. Spanish politicians had then feared American republicanism and future American expansionism.[8] After 1778 Spanish officials in both the New World and the Old became increasingly alarmed lest the patriots encroach upon the empire of Castile. They saw Louisiana endangered; suspected American designs upon the British colonies of East and West Florida which they intended to secure for Spain; and perceived in the Mississippi River an avenue of American aggression.[9] They therefore sought to limit the United States on the west and the south, and if possible to confine them to the territory east of the Appalachian Mountains. In 1780–81 Spanish troops occupied West Florida, seizing its ports and penetrating into its hinterland;[10] and Spanish militia from St. Louis captured the British post of St. Joseph in southwestern Michigan, holding it for twenty-four hours, long enough for Madrid to assert a claim by the right of conquest to the entire eastern bank of the Mississippi.[11] Charles III persisted in refusing to recognize the United States until Britain had done so, and his ministers used all the arts of diplomacy to contain America and to keep her weak.

In fairness, it must be conceded that the Continental Congress

[8] See pp. 182–186.
[9] Samuel F. Bemis, *Diplomacy of the American Revolution* (New York, 1935), pp. 94–97, 99.
[10] Lawrence Kinnaird (ed.), *Spain in the Mississippi Valley, 1765–1794, Annual Report of the American Historical Association* (1945), II (Washington, 1949), 401.
[11] *Ibid.*, p. 418; Bemis, *Diplomacy*, p. 102, note 17. For the military role played by Spanish Louisiana in the war see John W. Caughey, *Bernardo de Galvez in Louisiana, 1776–1783* (Berkeley, 1934), pp. 85–242.

gave Spain cause for worry. In 1779, when the delegates prepared to send one emissary to Europe to negotiate a peace treaty and another to bid for a Spanish alliance, they debated at length the terms to be proposed. It was suggested that the territory of the United States should comprise the eastern third of North America, including the Floridas as well as Canada, and that Americans be guaranteed free use of the Mississippi. It was obvious, however, that such objectives were incompatible with a Spanish alliance. In August of that year the Congress determined to accept nothing less than the Mississippi as a western boundary and to insist that American territory extend on the south to the line of latitude 31° between the Father of Waters and the Chattahoochee River.[12] On September 17 it also resolved to offer to Spain a guarantee of the Floridas, if Spain should acquire them in the war, in exchange for an alliance and a pledge for the free navigation of the lower Mississippi.[13] When, early in the following year, John Jay appeared at Madrid to push these proposals, along with a loan and a commercial treaty, he was coolly received. Count Floridablanca conferred with him informally, but patronizingly regarded him as something of a beggar and a nuisance. He gave the American small loans which supported him at Madrid for more than two years and which helped Congress to carry on the war.

Throughout 1780 Floridablanca refused to come to terms with the United States, while at the same time he carried on long and extended secret negotiations with Richard Cumberland, a British agent. To Cumberland the Spanish Minister proposed as part of a general peace settlement, not independence for the United States, but a long-term truce between Britain and America, with the parties maintaining control of the territories occupied by their armed forces. According to this proposal, New York, Long Island, Wilmington, Charleston, and Savannah would have been left in British hands.[14] In 1781, in accordance with new instructions from Philadelphia, Jay expanded the American offer for an alliance to included renunciation of the right of navigation on the lower Missis-

[12] Worthington C. Ford *et al.* (eds.) *The Journals of the Continental Congress, 1774–1789* (34 vols., Washington, 1904–37), XIV, 920–921.

[13] *Ibid.*, XV, 1084.

[14] Samuel Bemis, *The Hussey-Cumberland Negotiation and American Independence* . . . (Princeton, 1931), chap. 7.

sippi; [15] but Floridablanca failed to seize what was actually a grand opportunity for Spain, and Jay quickly withdrew the renunciation. By that time he realized that the price of a Spanish alliance was far greater than it was worth. Before he left Spain in May, 1782, he also knew that the government of Charles III desired neither a strong America nor American friendship; and he had learned that France would lend little support to the patriots in disputes with the dons.

The patriot leaders at home were also well aware long before 1782 that they could not count on the backing of France when their interests clashed with those of Spain. Vergennes sought to reconcile the conflicting aims of France's allies rather than to favor either party. When he sent Conrad-Alexandre Gérard across the Atlantic as the first French Minister to the United States—before the entrance of Spain into the war—he told the Spanish court that Gérard would defend the interests of Spain in the New World as if they were those of France. He instructed Gérard to avoid the appearance of supporting that country but to do what he could toward bringing to Spain the Floridas, Jamaica, and a share in the Newfoundland fisheries. At the same time he assured the patriots that the sole reason for French participation in the war was zeal for the United States. In America Gérard, a trusted agent, undertook, without orders from Versailles, but undoubtedly with full knowledge of Vergennes's policies, to encourage Spain to come into the war by holding out as bait for Spain a barrier region along the eastern banks of the Mississippi to protect Louisiana. Ignoring the presence of patriots on and near those banks, he proposed that Spanish forces in Louisiana move eastward and sought to persuade the Continental Congress to accept a western boundary short of the Mississippi, a sacrifice he urged on the patriots in order to strengthen the common enemies of Britain. It was a source of embarrassment to Gérard that in the Franco-American alliance France had guaranteed the integrity of the possessions of the United States. He met that difficulty by asserting that the guarantee did not apply *before*

---

[15] Franklin, with that insight into the future which he so frequently displayed, vigorously opposed this step. "Poor as we are, yet, as I know we shall be rich, I would rather agree with them [the Spanish] to buy at a great price the whole of their right on the Mississippi, than sell a drop of its waters. A neighbour might as well ask me to sell my street door." Albert H. Smyth (ed.), *The Writings of Benjamin Franklin* (10 vols., New York, 1905–07), VIII, 144.

British recognition of American independence, a convenient interpretation of the treaty not pleasing to all members of the Congress.[16]

After Spain had come into the conflict Vergennes himself took
up the cudgels in behalf of her pretensions in America. He ordered
the Chevalier de la Luzerne, Gérard's successor, to insist that the
Floridas go to Spain at the peace and to push Spanish claims to
territory east of the Mississippi.[17] The Continental Congress,
although many of its members were desirous of placating France,
would settle for nothing less than the great river as a western boundary, and the interference of France in behalf of her Bourbon ally
was keenly resented. A French request that the Americans moderate
their demands upon Britain for Newfoundland fishing rights also
irritated the patriots, especially since France was deeply interested
in securing similar rights for her own fishermen.

In the winter of 1780–81, at a time when Vergennes was plagued
by a dearth of French victories and a shortage of cash, he even considered a peace in which the patriots would receive no more than
Spain proposed for them—a long-term truce between America and
Britain, with the latter holding the areas then occupied by her
forces. Such arrangements were clearly inconsistent with the provisions of the Franco-American alliance; Vergennes would have
defended them on the basis of the necessities of France. That winter
Catherine the Great and Count Kaunitz, the Austrian Foreign
Minister, offered to mediate between the various combatants in
order to bring the war to an end, and to call a peace conference at
Vienna. Vergennes appreciated the fact that France could not
decently suggest "so painful" terms to the patriots; but once the
mediators brought them forward, France could accept them. In
the summer of 1781 the French Minister at Paris sounded out John
Adams, whom Congress had authorized to negotiate a peace.
Adams refused to go to Vienna unless the governments tendering
their "good offices" recognized American independence; nor would

---

[16] Edward S. Corwin, *French Policy and the American Alliance of 1778*
(Princeton, 1916), pp. 233–242, maintains that the guarantee, at least by implication, went into effect when France entered the war, that France was
bound after 1778 not only to support the western boundary of the United
States at the Mississippi but also to defend American rights to navigation on
that stream below parallel 31°. The terms of the treaty are rather ambiguous.

[17] Henri Doniol, *Histoire de la participation de la France à l'établissement
des États-Unis d'Amérique* (6 vols., Paris, 1884–92), IV, 224–357.

he consent to a truce with Britain until the redcoats had been withdrawn from the thirteen states. Since Britain regarded such inter-
cession as meddlesome interference in her domestic affairs and since
Vergennes was not yet driven to extreme concessions, the attempted
mediation was abandoned. Adams had plumbed Vergennes's
thought; not trustful by nature, thenceforth he was to be highly
suspicious of the maneuvers of the artful French Minister.[18]

Though some members of Congress were disappointed that
France failed to uphold the claims of the United States against
those of Spain, to support the American stand on the fisheries and
the American designs upon Canada,[19] most patriot leaders stead-
fastly clung to the alliance of 1778 as a cornerstone of foreign policy.
Indeed, until the very end of the war the majority in Congress,
unlike some of its representatives in Europe, put great faith in the
friendship and altruism of "the great and good ally." Even the fact
that Vergennes looked upon the United States as a client failed to
arouse strong resentment. In August, 1779, when Adams was appointed as peace negotiator, he was instructed to govern his actions
in part "by the advice of our allies." In June, 1781, when Adams
was replaced by a commission consisting of Franklin, Jay, Henry
Laurens, Jefferson, and Adams himself, the commissioners were
ordered to insist only upon independence; as the result of pressure
from Vergennes and Luzerne they were told "to make the most
candid and confidential communications, upon all subjects to the
ministers" of France," to undertake nothing . . . without their
knowledge and concurrence; and ultimately to govern yourselves by
their advice and opinion . . ." [20]

When Lord Shelburne sent Richard Oswald to Paris he acted
in response to a suggestion from Franklin; and it was Franklin who
acted for America in the early stages of the discussions which led to
the peace of 1783. Jefferson was distracted by the last illness and
death of his wife and declined to serve on the American commission; Jay did not reach Paris from Spain until June 23; and
Adams, busily occupied in his efforts to secure a loan and in other
affairs at The Hague, did not arrive until October 26. Laurens, a
prisoner in the Tower of London at the beginning of the negotia-

[18] Bemis, *Diplomacy*, pp. 178–188.
[19] Vergennes preferred that Canada remain in British hands.
[20] *Continental Congress Journals*, XX, pp. 651–652.

tions, offered little assistance to his colleagues. He was sent by Shelburne under parole to Holland to confer with Adams when Oswald set out for Paris; soon afterward freed at the request of Franklin, he pleaded illness and the death of his son John Laurens in battle as reasons for failing to serve. He was not active on the commission until its labors were almost at an end.[21] It was perhaps to the advantage of the American people that the Sage of Philadelphia and Passy was for a time their sole negotiator; indeed, although much has been said about the later contributions of Jay and Adams to the success of the commission, it might have been just as well had Franklin conducted all its business. Despite his age Franklin's powers were undiminished, his vision was unclouded, his personality was pleasing to the French and British as those of Adams, Jay, and Laurens could never be. Shelburne was his long-time friend; so also was Oswald, an elderly and rich merchant who had profited from the African slave trade but who was nevertheless liberal and catholic in viewpoint.

With respect to achieving agreement toward specific peace terms Franklin and Oswald made no progress for many weeks. In part this fact is explained by rivalry in the British Cabinet between Shelburne and Fox which retarded action in London; in part it arose from the efforts of the British to isolate their enemies. While Franklin and Oswald carried on their discussions, Thomas Grenville, agent for Fox, dealt with Vergennes and also with Franklin. The British representatives, attempting to revive Anglo-American ties of friendship, strove to convince him that France did not have the interests of the patriots at heart and to persuade him that America would gain by bargaining separately and independently with the mother country. Franklin did not bite at the bait. He displayed a willingness to talk in confidence with the British, without the knowledge of Vergennes, and in spite of the explicit instructions of Congress. He insisted, however, as did Vergennes, that Anglo-American and Anglo-French negotiations, though carried on separately, should proceed simultaneously to a general peace settlement. Clinging

[21] Laurens had been captured en route to Europe. Shelburne hoped to exploit Laurens' awkward position as a prisoner to British advantage. Although the South Carolinian was discouraged and sick and did not devote himself to business, he seems to have remained faithful to American interests. *George III Corr.*, V, 487; David D. Wallace, *The Life of Henry Laurens . . .* (New York, 1915), pp. 390–419.

firmly to the French alliance, Franklin hinted to the British that they would find it to their own advantage to be generous to the patriots. Conceding his ancient attachment to Britain, he suggested that somehow or other at some vague time America and Britain might be reunited, and intimated that the mother country could smooth the way toward that end by making liberal concessions to an independent America. This approach genuinely influenced Oswald and his master Shelburne. It was the more effective because it was not insincere; because Franklin sought the welfare of America first, but also enduring peace and friendship between the United States and Britain; because his supernational views did not bar eventual Anglo-American reunion or an even broader federation of peoples.

The death of Rockingham on July 1 made possible more rapid progress in the Anglo-American negotiations. Shelburne became Prime Minister, and Fox resigned his post in a fit of jealousy. To a degree America may have been the loser by the shake-up, since Fox had been less averse to conceding independence than Shelburne. However, the new Prime Minister, less circumscribed by serious conflict in the Cabinet, had more authority behind him. His rise to leadership resulted in a change in British representation at Paris, Alleyne Fitzherbert replacing Grenville. Oswald, of course, continued his labors. Although Oswald lacked full powers and despite the fact that Parliament had failed to pass an act permitting a final agreement, Franklin orally and informally proposed to him in July terms which he personally felt Britain should offer to the patriots. Among them must be independence, a generously drawn American boundary on the north, and "a freedom of fishing on the banks of Newfoundland and elsewhere." Britain would do well also to admit responsibility for the war, to give indemnity for destroyed patriot property, to cede to the United States all of Canada, and to propose freedom of trade between America and the British Isles. Franklin's price for Anglo-American reconciliation and possible eventual federal union was high, though not shocking to the broad-minded Shelburne.[22] But the Prime Minister, clinging to a forlorn hope of reconciliation within the British Empire, refused to recognize American independence before the signing of a peace treaty and brought discussion of terms at Paris almost to a halt.

[22] Gerald S. Graham, *British Policy and Canada 1774–1791* . . . (New York, 1930), pp. 41–52.

Early in August Franklin—and Jay, now working with him—learned that Oswald's formal commission would give him power merely to deal with "any commissioner or commissioners" of the "colonies or plantations" and that recognition of independence, if it came, would be included in the treaty. This information disturbed the Americans, who on August 10 consulted Vergennes. That diplomat commented that the form of Oswald's papers meant nothing and that recognition in the articles of peace ought to be sufficient. Jay was then in the midst of discussions with Aranda, the Spanish Ambassador at Versailles, concerning the conflict of American and Spanish interests west of the Appalachians. Long hostile to Spanish aggrandizement in the Mississippi Valley and suspecting Vergennes of favoring the interests of Spain against those of the United States, Jay had found in the course of his talks with Aranda that Spanish pretensions were vast and that Vergennes gave them some support. Jay now became alarmed. He concluded that Vergennes's advice was dictated solely by the interests of France and Spain and that the French Minister was not even disposed to insist upon American independence. In anger he immediately told Oswald he would take part in no further negotiations until Britain had officially conceded independence.

Continuing his talks with Aranda through August and into September, Jay became ever more distrustful of France and Spain and more and more eager to push American interests against those of the Bourbons by dealing separately with Britain. Aranda at first claimed for Spain not only the Floridas but the great bulk of the territory between the Great Lakes, the Appalachians, and the Mississippi. He would even have put some of the new American settlements in Kentucky and Tennessee under the Spanish flag; American dominion would have been limited by a zigzag line running southward from the western end of Lake Erie.[23] When Jay asserted the claim of the United States to the eastern bank of the Mississippi above latitude 31° and also to free navigation below that line, Aranda sought support from Vergennes, who offered him the services of his secretary, M. de Rayneval. Rayneval and Aranda then worked out a "compromise" which they presented to Jay as the ideas of the French Minister. By this proposal the region between the Ohio and the Great Lakes was to remain British, and the

[23] See Bemis, *Diplomacy,* map opp. p. 216.

area west of a staggered line running from the mouth of the Cumberland River to the eastern boundary of West Florida was to be an Indian reservation under Spanish protection. Such arrangements would have barred the United States from the "Old Northwest" and the Mississippi and would have put under Spanish control the state of Mississippi, most of Alabama, and large parts of Tennessee and Kentucky.[24]

Jay was not deceived by the maneuvers of Aranda and Rayneval. When he learned on September 9 that Vergennes's secretary had departed on a secret mission to London he concluded, correctly, that Rayneval would urge French and Spanish interests at the expense of those of the United States. He broke off discussions with Aranda on the ground that the Ambassador lacked power to act; and he told Franklin that an immediate and drastic countermeasure was necessary. Franklin, though less fearful than his colleague of the possible duplicity of Vergennes, had earlier agreed with Jay to demand quick British recognition of independence in order to improve the American bargaining position. He now joined Jay in an offer to Britain which was not communicated to Vergennes and which would hardly have received his approval. The two Americans indicated to Oswald and to Shelburne that they would abandon their demand for acknowledgment of independence forthwith—if American freedom were constructively admitted by a change in Oswald's orders authorizing him to deal with the commissioners, not of the colonies, but of "the United States of America." They made it clear that the patriots would not remain in the war to win advantages for Spain, that they must have their share in the fisheries regardless of the wishes of France; they argued that it was to Britain's benefit that the United States extend to the Mississippi—Britain could have free commercial entry into the trans-Allegheny West by way of the great river and also the St. Lawrence; they hinted that they might accept a separate peace, that Britain had an opportunity to weaken the Franco-American alliance. To bring

[24] See *ibid.*, map opp. p. 218. It was once contended by American historians that Clark's conquest of the Illinois country gave the United States a claim to the "Old Northwest." When it was pointed out that there were no American military establishments north of the Ohio in 1782, it was argued that the United States possessed a claim because they exercised at least a measure of strategic control by reason of their forts on the south bank of the Ohio, particularly one at the mouth of the river built and defended by Clark. Both contentions are assailable; Jay apparently made no use of either.

pressure on Shelburne, Jay sent to England the young British agent Benjamin Vaughan, then in Paris.

In the meantime, on August 29, the Shelburne Cabinet had reluctantly decided, if necessary, to ask Parliament for permission to grant immediate American independence. Shelburne was gratified by the American offer and impressed by arguments in its behalf advanced by Vaughan.[25] He believed that the patriots could now be wedged apart from France, an end he had so long sought; he preferred to make concessions, if any, to the Americans rather than to Britain's other enemies, in order to further the restoration of Anglo-American friendship; and he valued the commercial privilege held out by the American commissioners. He gave little heed to hints from Rayneval that France would approve British retention of the "Old Northwest" and that France did not intend to support American claims to the fisheries. On September 19 the Cabinet resolved to empower Oswald to treat with "the commissioners appointed by the colonys, under the title of Thirteen United States."[26] Before the end of the month Oswald presented his new credentials to Franklin and Jay. It was widely believed in Europe and America that the United States then became independent, but their position was actually ambiguous, since the phrases employed by the Cabinet were not equivalent to formal and precise recognition.

That the United States did not become technically free in September, 1782, was a matter of little moment, since Franklin and Jay had only to insist upon an unquestionable acknowledgment to secure it. That the American representatives had chosen to be neither the clients nor the dupes of the subtle Vergennes was of greater significance. That they had resolved to secure the trans-Appalachian West and free access to the Gulf of Mexico, even at the price of concessions to Britain, was of the first consequence. Without these gains the whole history of our westward expansion might well have been altered.

On October 5, eight days after Oswald received his revised commission, he, Jay, and Franklin gave their approval to a draft of a peace treaty which would take effect when France and Britain came to terms. The negotiations moved with almost startling speed. Vergennes was informed of them, not about them. It was agreed

[25] *Ibid.*, p. 225.
[26] *George III Corr.*, VI, 131.

that the boundaries of an independent America should be drawn, save for Canada, substantially as the American representatives desired. On the north the limits of the United States were laid down in much the same fashion as they were afterward finally established, except that the peninsula of Ontario was included in the United States. The patriot dream—it had been no more than that since the spring of 1776—of a fourteenth state of Canada came to an end. It was abandoned in order to gain the empire of trans-Appalachia. Other provisions called for the evacuation of British forces "with all convenient speed," protected American access to the fisheries, and permitted the British freedom of navigation and trade on the Mississippi. It was also stipulated that American and British nationals were to possess equal rights in commerce and navigation throughout *the dominions of both countries.*

And still the American diplomats had not finished their labors. Shelburne refused to ratify the draft treaty. He believed in freedom of trade, but he knew that Parliament did not share his view. He therefore proposed that the clauses concerning trade and navigation be replaced by a mere statement that navigation of the Mississippi was to be unrestricted, a change which the Americans were compelled to accept. Stiffened by recent British military successes, including the decisive repulse of the final Franco-Spanish attack on Gibraltar in September, he now sought other alterations favorable to Britain. He sent Sir Henry Strachey to Paris to join Oswald, telling Strachey to try to persuade the Americans to accept for their country narrower limits on the north and west. The new British representative was also instructed to attempt to secure promises that the private debts of Americans to British citizens created before 1775 would be paid, and that the Loyalists would be compensated for their losses.

At Paris on October 26 Strachey and Oswald resumed the peace discussions with Franklin, Jay, and Adams, who had just finished his business in Holland. Since the New Englander fully shared Jay's distrust of the French and Spanish courts, the American agents continued to avoid giving information to and seeking advice from Vergennes. They felt compelled to make territorial concessions to Britain, doubtless minor ones in their opinion. They accepted as a boundary between the United States and Canada a line following the St. Croix River, the height of land between the St. Lawrence and New England to latitude 45°, and thence that latitude to the St. Lawrence, and either the line of 45° westward from that river to the Lake of the Woods and the Mississippi or the present river-and-lake demarcation. They also approved, if Britain did not cede West Florida to Spain, a line running eastward from the mouth of the Yazoo River to the Chattahoochee as part of the American southern boundary—this stipulation to be inserted in a secret article. They consented to validate American private debts. The patriot emissaries would not, however, promise to compensate the Loyalists. After pressing the point in order to satisfy the Loyalists that their interests had not been neglected, the British representatives consented to a clause according to which Congress would "recommend" to the states that they revise their confiscation laws. By November 5 the treaty draft was accordingly changed. The British Cabinet chose to accept for Canada the river-and-lake line instead of latitude 45°; a few minor modifications were made in the draft in the course of November; on the last day of that month the document was formally signed.[27]

Sending home the result of their labors, the American commissioners were exceptionally modest in their appraisal. True, they asserted that the boundary lines of the United States left "little to complain of and not much to desire," [28] but in view of the fact that both Britain and Spain attempted to "coop up" the Americans on the west, it would seem that the limits of the United States could hardly have been expanded. Happily for the new nation, the concessions made to Britain in the Mississippi Valley in order to thwart Spain proved to be of little importance. Had Britain kept West Florida with its northern boundary at the Yazoo line, the future growth of the United States might have been seriously checked. When West Florida was returned to Spain in the general peace, the Americans acquired a weak neighbor on the south and were able to push immediately for the line of latitude 31°, and later for possession of both Floridas. It has often been said that the American commissioners were both able and fortunate. So they were.

When Vergennes was told by Franklin that the American ally of

[27] For the text of the preliminary treaty see David Hunter Miller (ed.), *Treaties and Other International Acts of the United States of America* (8 vols., Washington, 1931–48), II, 96–101.

[28] Francis Wharton (ed.), *Revolutionary Diplomatic Correspondence of the United States* (6 vols., Washington, 1889), VI, 132.

France, without seeking his advice and without even informing him, had agreed upon terms with Britain, he had grounds for bitter reproaches, particularly since Franklin picked that moment to ask for assistance in securing a new loan. In part his disappointment stemmed from his ambition to serve as general manager of all the peace negotiations; and he was chagrined because Jay and Adams did not bother to conceal their personal coolness toward France. He sent off a polite and gentle remonstrance to Congress and addressed another directly to Franklin, who offered a deft apology, suggesting that France and America as friends should conceal their differences from their enemies. Vergennes gracefully accepted Franklin's explanation and even secured six million livres for the empty American treasury.

Within a few weeks after the signature of the Anglo-American agreement France and Spain came to terms with Britain. On January 20, 1783, Britain entered into preliminary treaties with the two allies. A general armistice was then established, but the final treaties were not signed until the following September. During the intervening months Charles James Fox and Lord North joined forces and overthrew the Shelburne ministry, which had suffered a loss in popularity for having made peace on the best terms possible to end a war for which it was in no way responsible. There was further time and opportunity to discuss Anglo-American problems, and Fox sent to Paris for that purpose David Hartley, who strove to reunite America and Britain. With Fox's approval he proposed freedom of trade between the two countries—with the exception that American ships be forbidden to carry to the British Isles goods not produced in the United States, a concession to those in England who clung to the Navigation Acts—and a defensive military alliance. Upon such foundations might have been built an Anglo-American federation, a new empire. It was a little too late or perhaps much too early for such arrangements. Fox, like Shelburne, was unable to persuade either the Cabinet or Parliament to tear down the barriers erected to defend British commerce; the British West Indies were closed to American ships in the very midst of Hartley's discussions with the American commissioners. The Americans could not abandon the alliance with France for one with Britain, and they could not have both. Hartley's efforts, though long continued, were fruitless.[29] As a liberal-minded Briton he might have found consolation in the thought that Britain remained the parent of America, that

> . . . the single note
> From that deep chord which Hampden smote
> Will vibrate to the doom.

On September 3 the Anglo-American preliminary treaty became, without change,[30] final. Early in the next year Congress unanimously ratified it at Annapolis. The United States, recognized as independent by France since 1778 and by Holland since 1782, was no longer to be denied full membership among the nations.

[29] The Hartley mission is discussed in detail in G. H. Guttridge, *David Hartley, M. P., an Advocate of Conciliation, 1774–1783* (Berkeley, Calif., 1926), pp. 294–317; Samuel F. Bemis (ed.), *The American Secretaries of State and Their Diplomacy* (10 vols., New York, 1927–36), I, 212–222.

[30] The secret article respecting West Florida was, of course, dropped.

CHAPTER 17

Conclusion

THE MILITARY triumph of the patriots and their allies led not only to independence but also to the firm establishment of republican government in the United States. After Yorktown there was very little chance for the Hanoverian dynasty either to maintain or to regain sovereignty over the thirteen states. Nor was there any danger that they would come under French domination. The fear entertained by some patriots that the defeat of Britain would be followed by a French attempt to assert authority over America proved to be groundless. Had France entertained such a design, she lacked the power to execute it. Moreover, France steadily clung to actual or virtual independence of the United States as the major objective of the conflict. Admiral de Grasse' fleet left the Chesapeake soon after Yorktown, and the last of the French troops departed from Virginia in the summer of 1782.

There was perhaps a greater risk that after Yorktown the Americans would find themselves under the rule of George Washington, either as monarch or as dictator. Some patriots familiar with history had long dreaded that the Revolution would bring one-man rule. That fear had given impetus to the movement to replace Washington in the winter of 1777–78. Before the close of 1778 Dr. Benjamin Rush gave forceful expression to that concern lest a struggle begun for liberty should bring merely independence, and asserted that there was no longer serious danger of tyranny from Britain, that such tyranny now could come "only in the shape of a Whig." [1]

[1] Rush to Rev. William Gordon, Dec. 10, 1778, *Pennsylvania Magazine of History and Biography*, XXIX (1905), 21–22.

In England the worldly-wise Horace Walpole, who had "no great faith in virtue tempted by power," had indicated his belief "that the American leaders will not easily part with dictatorships and consulships to retire to their private ploughs."

In certain respects conditions were not unfavorable after York-town for a seizure of power in America comparable to the coup engineered by Napoleon in 1799. Had Washington sought to wield the supreme authority, he would not have been opposed by all the patriots. He would probably have obtained some support among those who were suffering heavily from inflation and economic dis-location, and from Conservatives alarmed both by the weakness of the American governments and by the recent trend toward political and social democracy. He would have received assistance from a part of the Continentals, whose idol he had become. He might even have been aided by some Tories. Moreover, the state governments were relatively feeble and the national government under the Articles of Confederation was seemingly almost helpless.

There were indubitably individuals in the forces under Washing-ton's command, stationed near the Hudson after Yorktown, who would have helped him to stage a *coup d'état*. In the period 1782-83 his men were better clothed and fed than they had been since the spring of 1778, the state governments supplying their needs with some efficiency through a newly organized system of requisitions. Yet dissatisfaction continued in his army, partly because of long-standing arrears in pay, partly because of the officers' desire of assurance of half pay when discharged. Both officers and men were alarmed lest they be dismissed from the service without funds or prospects. A delegation of officers who came to Philadelphia in the winter of 1782-83 to appeal to Congress for action secured nothing but soothing words. Some members of Congress would even have referred their demands to the states. Resentment in the army mounted ever higher, and led to the anonymous Newburgh Ad-dresses [2] of March, 1783, which urged the army to take justice into its own hands. Washington managed to soothe the discontented, and a few days later Congress voted full compensation for five years to the officers, in lieu of half pay for life as it had earlier promised. Arrangements were also made by Robert Morris to forward three

---

[2] Commonly ascribed to Major John Armstrong, Jr.

months' pay, and the army finally went home peacefully. Before that event some Pennsylvania troops who had done little or no fighting so insulted and badgered the Congress that it withdrew from Philadelphia to Trenton.[3]

In the spring of 1782, when it had become apparent that the central government under the Articles of Confederation could not function efficiently, when it had become almost equally clear that they could not be amended so as to strengthen that government,[4] Colonel Lewis Nicola, an army supply officer, proposed to Washington a solution for the troubles of the army and the nation: the establishment of an American limited monarchy, with Washington ascending the throne. Apparently Nicola's scheme had some small support among the officers stationed at Newburgh. The General was shocked, and vigorously condemned the project. "Let me conjure you, then," he wrote to Nicola, "if you have any regard for your country, concern for yourself or posterity, or respect for me, to banish these thoughts from your mind . . ."[5] The scheme was thus scotched. Had it been attempted, there must have been armed conflict among the patriots. In all likelihood most of the patriots would have fought as vigorously against George I of Mount Vernon as they had against George III of Windsor Castle. But Washington was as firmly attached to republican principles as the overwhelming bulk of his fellow patriots, and the Nicola incident actually signifies the death of the monarchical idea in the United States and the total triumph of representative government.

Washington returned to the Potomac and gracefully retired to private life. Before leaving Continental service, he bade farewell to his army, issuing an appeal for the creation of a stronger national government.[6] It was needed. There was, however, little chance that the United States of America would collapse. In the fall of 1783 Franklin saw in America only "little discontents" and "domestic misunderstandings . . . of small extent." These "spots in the sun"

[3] This paragraph is largely based upon Edmund C. Burnett, *The Continental Congress* (New York, 1941), pp. 551–580.

[4] An amendment which would have permitted Congress to levy 5 per cent ad valorem import duties and thus to deal with its financial problems had been defeated by the negative vote of the Rhode Island legislature.

[5] John C. Fitzpatrick (ed.), *The Writings of George Washington* (39 vols., Washington, 1931–44), XXIV, 273.

[6] *Ibid.*, XXVII, 226.

did not mean "that the whole disk would soon be overspread with them. . . . The great body of intelligence among our people surrounds and overpowers our petty dissensions as the sun's great mass of fire diminishes and destroys his spots." [7] John Montgomery, a lesser figure in the Continental Congress, commenting upon the news that peace was near and also using solar metaphor, was hardly guilty of absurdity when he asserted that "the day is now come when the sun will raise on amirrica never to set. I look forward with pleasure to the happey days that our children will see." [8]

The homely wisdom of John Montgomery appeared also among the British and patriot troops who waited out the peace negotiations at New York. Reconciliation between America and Britain came very slowly and haltingly during many generations. However, at the lines about New York in December, 1782, redcoats and Continentals grounded their arms and drank in comradeship.[9] Before the signing of the peace both the diplomats and the common folk of Britain and America had taken steps toward the restoration of friendship.

The successful rebellion of the patriots profoundly affected the course of the future, not only for the Americans, but for all other peoples. The American Revolution brought the first break in the European colonial system. It inspired and continues to inspire colonials of all colors to seek freedom from European domination. It also brought into existence for the first time in modern history a republican system of government in a large nation. The example of republicanism successful over the vast territory of the United States constituted a threat to monarchism everywhere, stimulated revolt against kings and emperors. The proclamation in the Declaration of Independence of the equality of men in the sight of the Creator continues to serve as a battle cry for social and political justice. The patriots won independence; they also made a good start on the long road toward establishing and securing "the rights of mankind."

[7] Francis Wharton (ed.), *Revolutionary Diplomatic Correspondence of the United States* (6 vols., Washington, 1889), VI, 678.

[8] Edmund C. Burnett (ed.), *Letters of Members of the Continental Congress* (8 vols., Washington, 1921–36), VII, 43.

[9] Katharine Roof, *Colonel William Smith and Lady* . . . (Boston, 1929), p. 40.

Bibliography

Major Manuscript Collections and Guides

In the study of the American Revolution the British official records are obviously of the first importance. The British Public Record Office contains a vast store of documents dealing with America in the period 1775–83, a large part of which remains unpublished. Included among its holdings are official reports of military, naval, and civil officers, and copies of instructions sent to them. Charles M. Andrews published a very useful *Guide to the Materials for American History to 1783, in the Public Record Office of Great Britain* (2 vols., Washington, 1912). Of importance also are the holdings of the British Museum, described in Charles M. Andrews and Frances C. Davenport, *Guide to the Manuscript Materials for the History of the United States to 1783, in the British Museum, in Minor London Archives, and in the Libraries of Oxford and Cambridge* (Washington, 1908). These guides were sponsored by the Carnegie Institution of Washington, which also was responsible for the appearance of several other volumes analyzing documents concerning American history in various foreign archives. Waldo G. Leland reported upon the French archives and others upon the Spanish, providing helpful introductions to document collections essential to the writing of the diplomatic history of the period.

Of prime value in the study of the Revolution are the magnificent holdings of the Library of Congress, particularly the Papers of the Continental Congress, the George Washington Papers, and the copies of documents from European archives. The *Handbook of Manuscripts in the Library of Congress* (Washington, 1918), though it does not cover recent acquisitions, is still very useful. The library's immense collection of copies of papers from British archives, which usually serve as adequate substitutes for their originals, is described in Grace Gardner Griffin, *A Guide to Manuscripts Relating to American History in British Repositories Reproduced for the Division of Manuscripts of the Library of Congress* (Washington, 1946). Also of great value are the papers of Thomas Jefferson, Benjamin Franklin, and Alexander Hamilton.

The Archives of the United States of America, which offer so much to the student of later American history, do not contain vast quantities of documents upon the Revolution, although the student of that era will often find it necessary to examine particular items and collections there. A useful description of their holdings is to be found in *Guide to the Records in the National Archives* (Washington, 1948).

The Revolutionary records of the original thirteen states, specially important for regional and local history, but of great worth also for the history of the nation, are very generally preserved in the capitals of those states. They have sometimes escaped publication and, at least occasionally, intensive exploration by scholars.

Various historical societies and historical libraries shelter papers of the first magnitude for an understanding of the period 1775-83. Among these is the William L. Clements Library of the University of Michigan, which is remarkably rich in documents dealing with the British side of the War of Independence, and which also houses a valuable collection of General Nathanael Greene Papers. Included in its holdings are the General Thomas Gage Papers, especially important for the first year of the War of Independence as well as for the twelve years preceding the outbreak of hostilities. These are the headquarters records of the British army in America during the era 1763-75. The Sir Henry Clinton Papers, also preserved in that library, contain the headquarters records of the period 1778-82, many documents pertaining to the first years of the war, and other postwar items indited by Clinton concerning the conflict, among them his still unpublished history of the Revolution.[1] The Clements treasures likewise embrace the Papers of Lord George Germain, partly calendared by the *Royal Historical Manuscripts Commission*,[2] Lord Shelburne, Sir John Vaughan, William Knox, and David Hartley, important for military, political, and diplomatic aspects of the conflict. Mr. Howard H. Peckham has published a detailed and very helpful *Guide to the Manuscript Collections in the William L. Clements Library* (Ann Arbor, 1942).

Similar to the Gage and Clinton MSS are the General Sir Guy Carleton Papers, now in the possession of Colonial Williamsburg, Inc. These are the British headquarters records for the period 1782-83. They have been calendared by the *Royal Historical Manuscripts Commission*.[3]

---

[1] The headquarters papers for the period when General William Howe was commander in chief, 1775-78, have, alas, disappeared. It is said that they were destroyed by fire in Ireland. If unearthed they would unquestionably throw much new light on the Revolution.

[2] *Report on the Manuscripts of Mrs. Stopford-Sackville* (2 vols., London, 1904-10).

[3] *Report on American Manuscripts in the Royal Institution of Great Britain* (4 vols., London, 1904-09).

New York City is rich in manuscript materials dealing with the Revolution. The New York City Public Library houses several collections, including papers of Samuel Adams, Philip Schuyler, and the Livingstons, the still unpublished Revolutionary diary of William Smith, and the Bancroft transcripts, which contain a very large body of documents concerning the Loyalists from the British Public Record Office. Evarts B. Greene and Richard B. Morris, *Guide to the Principal Sources for Early American History (1600–1800) in the City of New York* (rev. ed., New York, 1952), is helpful with respect to the holdings of that library as well as other repositories in New York City. The New-York Historical Society also preserves several collections valuable for the Revolution, among them the papers of General John Lamb and especially those of General Horatio Gates. The latter, bulky as they are, do not, unfortunately, contain the letters written by Gates. In the Long Island Historical Society is a body of letters of Henry and John Laurens.

Philadelphia, the first national capital, does not lack manuscript treasures for the period 1775–83. The American Philosophical Society has a very important collection of Benjamin Franklin MSS, analyzed in J. Minis Hays (ed.), *Calendar of the Papers of Benjamin Franklin in the Library of the American Philosophical Society* (5 vols., Philadelphia, 1906–08), the Nathanael Greene-George Weedon Papers, and a body of manuscripts of Arthur and Richard Henry Lee. The Historical Society of Pennsylvania is similarly wealthy. Among its holdings, described in *Guide to the Manuscript Collections of the Historical Society of Pennsylvania* (2nd ed., Philadelphia, 1949), are the General Anthony Wayne Papers. In the Ridgeway Branch of the Philadelphia Free Library are the Dr. Benjamin Rush MSS.

The Massachusetts Historical Society has in its possession many Revolutionary documents, including the papers of Governor Jonathan Trumbull and a collection of General Henry Knox MSS. Its treasures are listed in *Handbook of the Massachusetts Historical Society, 1791–1948* (Boston, 1949). The General Otho Holland Williams Papers, analyzed in the *Calendar of the General Otho Holland Williams Papers . . .* (Baltimore, 1940), are preserved in the Maryland Historical Society. In the State Historical Society of Wisconsin are the Lyman Draper Papers, valuable for the history of the Revolutionary West. These and other holdings of that organization are described in Reuben G. Thwaites, *Descriptive List of Manuscript Collections of the State Historical Society of Wisconsin . . .* (Madison, 1906). A large collection of Henry Laurens Papers is preserved in the South Carolina Historical Society.

Newspapers

The American newspapers of the Revolutionary era are, of course, basic sources. They have not been very thoroughly explored. Fairly complete files of most of them have been preserved, but they are scattered among various repositories. The largest collection is in the American Antiquarian Society. The Library of Congress, the Historical Society of Pennsylvania, the New-York Historical Society, and the William L. Clements Library, among others, have substantial holdings. As a guide for research in the American newspapers Clarence L. Brigham's *History and Bibliography of American Newspapers, 1690–1820* (2 vols., Worcester, Mass., 1947), is almost indispensable.

The British newspapers of the period of the War of Independence have been little used, although they contain many items of importance. Quite complete files of *The London Chronicle* are available in the United States, but most of the British newspapers can be examined only in England. Ronald S. Crane and F. B. Kaye have published a very useful inventory of them in *A Census of British Newspapers and Periodicals, 1620–1800* (Chapel Hill, N. C., 1927).

Maps

Contemporary maps are to be found in many repositories. The splendid collection in the Library of Congress is described in Philip L. Phillips, *List of Maps in America in the Library of Congress* (Washington, 1901). A useful introduction to the "Manuscript Maps in the William L. Clements Library" was published by Lloyd A. Brown in *The American Neptune,* I (1941), 141–148. Randolph G. Adams, *British Headquarters Maps and Sketches* (Ann Arbor, 1928), supplies a complete list of the very large and valuable set of maps in the Sir Henry Clinton Papers in that institution.

Guides to Printed Documents

Documents emanating from the period of the American Revolution and printed at the time or later would, if gathered together, be enormous in both numbers and bulk. It is impossible to list more than a fraction of the more important published collections. There is no one complete guide to them. The notes in Justin Winsor's *Narrative and Critical History of America,* Vol. VI (Boston, 1889), are helpful in finding the older source publications sometimes neglected. *Writings on American History, 1902——* (Princeton and Washington, 1904——, ed. from 1906 for many years by Grace G. Griffin) gives an indispensable annual survey of printed documents and articles. Moses Coit Tyler, *Literary History of the American Revolution* (2 vols., New York, 1897), is still a very useful reference work. William Matthews (ed.), *American Diaries; an Annotated Bibliography . . . to the Year 1861* (Berkeley and Los Angeles, 1945), offers a guide to the numerous printed diaries and journals.

Public Documents

Among the basic printed collections of public documents is Worthington C. Ford *et al.* (eds.), *The Journals of the Continental Congress, 1774–1789* (34 vols., Washington, 1904–37), indispensable for the activities of the American central government. Edmund C. Burnett (ed.), *Letters of Members of the Continental Congress* (8 vols., Washington, 1921–36), a very convenient compilation both of diaries and of letters written by the delegates, is also of prime importance. Francis Wharton's *Revolutionary Diplomatic Correspondence of the United States* (6 vols., Washington, 1889) and David Hunter Miller, *Treaties and Other International Acts of the United States of America* (8 vols., Washington, 1931–48), are standard collections.

William Cobbett (ed.), *The Parliamentary History of England* . . . (36 vols., London, 1806–20), offering the best and the most complete record of the debates in the British Parliament during the American Revolution, is basic, though notoriously inadequate. British legislation concerning America may be found in Danby Pickering *et al.* (eds.), *Statutes at Large from Magna Charter* . . . (46 vols., Cambridge and London, 1762–1814). Sir John Fortescue has published *The Correspondence of King George the Third from 1760 to December, 1783* (6 vols., London, 1927–28), incomplete and not too carefully edited, but nevertheless valuable. Benjamin Franklin Stevens (ed.), *Facsimiles of Manuscripts in European Archives Relating to America, 1773–1783* (26 vols., London, 1889–95), offers a wide variety of documents especially useful for diplomatic and military history. Peter Force (ed.), *American Archives* . . . , Fourth Series (6 vols., Washington, 1837–46), and Fifth Series (3 vols., Washington, 1848–53) contains a vast quantity of documents gathered from many American sources and dealing with almost every phase of the Revolution during the years 1774–76. Other smaller collections of documents are to be found in Hezekiah Niles (ed.), *Principles and Acts of the Revolution in America* (New York, 1876), and Samuel E. Morison (ed.), *Sources and Documents Illustrating the American Revolution, 1764–1788* . . . (2nd ed., Oxford, 1929), Francis N. Thorpe (ed.), *Federal and State Constitutions* . . . (7 vols., Washington, 1909), gives the state constitutions made during the years 1775–83.

Several American states have published generously from their Revolutionary manuscripts, among them New Hampshire, Connecticut, Pennsylvania, and Maryland.

Works

The published papers of American and British leaders dealing with the American Revolution are both rich and revealing. Jared Sparks (ed.), *Correspondence of the American Revolution: Being Letters of Eminent Men to George Washington* (4 vols., Washington, 1853), is an old but still useful collection. Charles Francis Adams (ed.), *The Works of John Adams* . . . (10 vols., Boston, 1856), and Charles Francis Adams (ed.), *Familiar Letters of John Adams and His Wife Abigail Adams during the Revolution* (New York, 1876), are basic. *The Writings of Samuel Adams* (4 vols., New York, 1904–08) was edited by Harry A. Cushing. Also valuable is *The Warren-Adams Letters, Collections of the Massachusetts Historical Society* (2 vols., Boston, 1917–25). *The Manuscripts of the Earl of Carlisle* appear in rather complete form in *Royal Historical Manuscripts Commission, Fifteenth Report*, Pt. VI (London, 1897). Charles Ross edited the *Correspondence of Charles, First Marquis Cornwallis* (3 vols., London, 1859). James A. James edited the *George Rogers Clark Papers, 1771–1784, Collections of the Illinois State Historical Library*, VIII and XIX (Springfield, Ill., 1912–26). A large body of Silas Deane papers was published in the *Collections of the New-York Historical Society for the·Year 1886, . . . 1887, . . . 1888, . . . 1889, . . . 1890* (5 vols., New York, 1887–91), and in *The Deane Papers, Collections of the Connecticut Historical Society*, XXIII (1930). Paul L. Ford edited the *Writings of John Dickinson, Memoirs of the Pennsylvania Historical Society*, XIV (Philadelphia, 1895). The best edition of the works of Benjamin Franklin is Albert H. Smyth (ed.), *The Writings of Benjamin Franklin* (10 vols., New York, 1905–07). Important Franklin items concerning the onset of the War of Independence not included in Smyth are published in Verner W. Crane (comp. and ed.), *Benjamin Franklin's Letters to the Press, 1758–1775* (Chapel Hill, N. C., 1950). Clarence E. Carter edited *Correspondence of General Thomas Gage with the Secretaries of State* . . . , *1763–1775* (2 vols., New Haven, 1931–33). Many letters of Nathanael Greene are contained in George Washington Greene, *Life of Nathanael Greene* (3 vols., New York, 1871). Henry Cabot Lodge (ed.), *Works of Alexander Hamilton* (11 vols., New York, 1904), is useful. Many of the papers of Patrick Henry are printed in William Wirt Henry, *Patrick Henry: Life, Correspondence, and Speeches* (3 vols., New York, 1891). Valuable for military topics is the *Letters Written by Ebenezer Huntington during the American Revolution* (New York, 1914). The *Correspondence of Mr. Ralph Izard of South Carolina, from the Year 1774 to 1804* . . . (New York, 1844) offers some interesting letters. Henry P. Johnston edited *The Correspondence and Public Papers of John Jay* (4 vols., New York, 1890–93). Of the first importance is Julian P. Boyd *et al.* (eds.), *The Papers of Thomas Jefferson* (6 vols. to date, Princeton, 1950——), which supersedes the earlier collections of Jefferson's writings. The *Letters of Joseph Jones of Virginia, 1777–1787* (Washington, 1889) is useful, also William G. Simms (ed.), *Army Correspondence of Colonel John Laurens in the Years 1777–8* (New York, 1867). Richard Henry Lee, *Life of Arthur Lee* (2 vols., Boston, 1829), contains a number of documents. Of great value is *The Lee Papers, Collections of the New-York Historical Society for the Year 1871, . . . 1872, . . .*

1873, . . . 1874 (4 vols., New York, 1872–75), in which is published a mass of Charles Lee documents, many of them unavailable in manuscript. James C. Ballagh has edited the *Letters of Richard Henry Lee* (2 vols., New York, 1911–14), and Worthington C. Ford the *Letters of William Lee* (3 vols., Brooklyn, 1891). Kate M. Rowland, *The Life of George Mason* (2 vols., New York, 1892), contains many documents. Philip S. Foner's edition of *The Complete Writings of Thomas Paine* (2 vols., New York, 1945) supplements the earlier collection published by Moncure Conway. Charles K. Bolton edited the *Letters of Hugh Earl Percy* (Boston, 1902). Many of the papers of George Read appear in William T. Read, *Life and Correspondence of George Read* (Philadelphia, 1870), and of Joseph Reed in William B. Reed, *Life and Correspondence of Joseph Reed* (2 vols., Philadelphia, 1847). George H. Ryden (ed.), *Letters to and from Caesar Rodney, 1756–1784* (Philadelphia, 1933), is valuable. L. H. Butterfield (ed.), *Letters of Benjamin Rush* (2 vols., Princeton, 1951), is a splendid collection. G. R. Barnes and J. H. Owens, *Private Papers of the Earl of Sandwich* (London, 1932), and John H. Jesse, *George Selwyn and His Contemporaries . . .* (4 vols., London, 1843), are helpful with respect to the British side. *The Letters and Papers of Major General John Sullivan* (3 vols., Concord, N. H. 1930–39) is in the *Collections of the New Hampshire Historical Society,* Vols. XIII-XV. *The Trumbull Papers, Collections of the Massachusetts Historical Society* (Boston, 1885), is useful. Mrs. Paget Toynbee's edition of the *Letters of Horace Walpole* (16 vols., Oxford, 1903–05) and G. F. R. Barker's edition of Walpole's *Memoirs of the Reign of George the Third* (4 vols., London, 1894) offer comments by a civilized Englishman. By far the best edition of George Washington's papers is that by John C. Fitzpatrick, *The Writings of George Washington . . .* (39 vols., Washington, 1931–44). Jared Sparks' edition, *The Writings of George Washington* (12 vols., Boston, 1834–37), retains some value because it includes many documents received by Washington.

Diaries, Journals, and Memoirs

The printed personal accounts of the American Revolution would in themselves form a small library, and only a few of the more important can be mentioned here. The famous diary of John Adams may be found in his *Works,* listed above. Ethan Allen's experiences during the period 1775–78 are described by him in *A Narrative of Colonel Ethan Allen's Captivity . . .* (Boston, 1779). Henry Cabot Lodge edited [John] *André's Journal* (2 vols., Boston, 1903), covering the years 1777–78. Elias Boudinot's *Historical Recollections of American Events during the Revolutionary War* (Philadelphia, 1894) contains valuable extracts from Boudinot's journal and later recollections. John Burgoyne, *A State of the Expedition from Canada . . .* (2nd ed., London, 1780), contains Burgoyne's defense. *The Journal of Nicholas Cress-*

well, 1774–1777 (New York, 1924) offers interesting comments on the American scene by a young English civilian. G. A. Ward (ed.), *Journal and Letters of the Late Samuel Curwen, 1775–1784* (New York, 1842), is a basic piece of Tory literature. The best edition of Henry Dearborn's journals for the period 1775–83 is that of Howard H. Peckham and Lloyd A. Brown, *Revolutionary War Journals of Henry Dearborn, 1775–1783* (Chicago, 1939). One of the most useful journals dealing with the Burgoyne campaign is that of William Digby, published in James P. Baxter (ed.), *The British Invasion from the North . . .* (Albany, 1887). Alexander Garden's *Anecdotes of the American Revolution* (3 vols., Brooklyn, 1865, T. W. Field, ed.) retains interest and value. Alexander Graydon, *Memoirs of His Own Time . . .* (Philadelphia, 1846, J. S. Littell, ed.) is highly informative upon various phases of the Revolution. Horatio Rogers (ed.), *Hadden's Journal and Orderly Books* (Albany, 1884), is useful for the Burgoyne campaign. A fascinating journal for 1778–79 kept by Henry Hamilton is published in John D. Barnhart, *Henry Hamilton and George Rogers Clark in the American Revolution . . .* (Crawfordsville, Ind., 1951). Rufus R. Wilson (ed.), *Heath's Memoirs of the American War* (New York, 1904), offers records by General William Heath. Jacob C. Parsons (ed.), *Extracts from the Diary of Jacob Hiltzheimer* (Philadelphia, 1893, is informative in connection with social history. Peter O. Hutchinson (ed.), *Diary and Letters of . . . Thomas Hutchinson . . .* (2 vols., London, 1883–86), is a Tory classic. *The Kemble Papers, Collections of the New-York Historical Society for the Year 1883, . . . 1884* (2 vols., New York, 1884–85) is helpful for military history. Lafayette's memoirs may be consulted in *Mémoires, Correspondances et Manuscrits du Général Lafayette . . .* (2 vols., Brussels, 1837–38). R. Lamb, *An Original and Authentic Journal of Occurrences during the Late American War* (Dublin, 1809), and the *Diary of Frederick Mackenzie* (2 vols., Cambridge, Mass., 1930) are records of British soldiers. Henry Lee, *Memoirs of the War in the Southern Department of the United States* (2 vols., Philadelphia and New York, 1812), is of the first importance. William Duane (ed.), *Extracts from the Diary of Christopher Marshall . . . , 1774–1781* (Albany, 1877), deals with public affairs generally. *The Montresor Journals, Collections of the New-York Historical Society for the Year 1881* (New York, 1882) offers comment by a British officer. William Moultrie, *Memoirs of the American Revolution . . .* (2 vols., New York, 1802), is an account of the war as its author saw it. Theodore W. Tappert and John W. Doberstein are now publishing the *Journals of Henry Melchior Muhlenberg* (2 vols. to date, Philadelphia, 1942———). The fascinating diary of Baroness von Riedesel, covering the Burgoyne adventure, may be found in *Letters and Memoirs Relating to the American War of Independence* (New York, 1827). Thomas Rodney's diary, of special value for the Trenton-Princeton campaign, is in *Papers of the Historical Society of Delaware*, I (Wilmington,

1879). *The Journal of Isaac Senter* (Philadelphia, 1846) is one of the many accounts of the Arnold expedition against Quebec. E. H. Tatum (ed.), *The American Journal of Ambrose Serle* (San Marino, Calif., 1940), covers the period 1776–78 from the viewpoint of an arrogant secretary of Lord Howe. Josiah Quincy (ed.), *The Journals of Major Samuel Shaw* . . . (Boston, 1847), is an important record kept by a Continental officer and covering public affairs generally. Franklin B. Dexter (ed.), *The Literary Diary of Ezra Stiles* . . . (3 vols., New York, 1901), gives valuable comment by a cultured Yankee. Banastre Tarleton, or his ghost writers, tells his tale in *History of the Campaigns of 1780 and 1781* (Dublin, 1787). James Thacher, *A Military Journal during the American Revolutionary War* (Boston, 1823), offers detailed pictures of army life and of public figures. James Wilkinson, *Memoirs of My Own Times* (3 vols., Philadelphia, 1816), though often cited, is a highly dubious source.

Special Collections

Robert W. Gibbes, *Documentary History of the American Revolution* . . . (3 vols., Columbia, S.C., and New York, 1853–57). Franklin B. Hough (ed.), *Siege of Charleston* . . . (Albany, 1867) and *Siege of Savannah* . . . (Albany, 1866). John J. Meng (ed.), *Dispatches and Instructions of Conrad Alexandre Gerard, 1778–1780* . . . (Baltimore, 1939). Frank Moore (ed.), *Diary of the American Revolution* (New York, 1863). Roy W. Pettengill (ed.), *Letters from America, 1776–1779* . . . (Boston, 1924). Kenneth Roberts (ed.), *March to Quebec* (New York, 1938). Benjamin Franklin Stevens (ed.), *Campaign in Virginia, 1781* . . . (2 vols., London, 1888). Bernhard A. Uhlendorf (ed.), *Siege of Charleston* . . . , *University of Michigan Publications in History and Political Science*, XII (Ann Arbor, 1938). Margaret W. Willard (ed.), *Letters on the American Revolution, 1774–1776* (Boston, 1925).

General Accounts

Many of the narratives dealing with the American Revolution in general works are of comparatively little value to the student. George Bancroft, *History of the United States* (6 vols., New York, 1883–85), opinionated and partisan, cannot be ignored. Henry Belcher, *The First American Civil War* (2 vols., London, 1911), offers a British version. Edward Channing, *A History of the United States* (6 vols., New York, 1905–25), is instructive and suggestive. H. E. Egerton, *Causes and Character of the American Revolution* (Oxford, 1923), is useful. Sydney G. Fisher's *True History of the American Revolution* (Philadelphia, 1902) and his fuller and revised narrative, *Struggle for American Independence* (2 vols., Philadelphia, 1908), are thought provoking. William Gordon, *History of the Rise, Progress, and Establishment of the Independence of the United States of America* (3 vols., 3rd ed., New York, 1901), though not entirely original, retains value as a contemporary account. Evarts B. Greene, *The Revolutionary Generation, 1763–1790* (New York, 1943), is indispensable for social history. George Guttridge, *English Whiggism and the American Revolution* (Berkeley, Calif., 1942), analyzes the English background. Richard Hildreth, *History of the United States of America* (6 vols., New York, 1849–56), is remarkable for its accuracy. W. E. H. Lecky, *History of England in the Eighteenth Century* (8 vols., London, 1878–1900), is standard. The portions of it dealing with the Revolution have been published as *The American Revolution, 1763–1783* (New York, 1898, J. A. Woodburn, ed.). Mary M. Marks, *England and America, 1763 to 1783* (2 vols., New York, 1907) often inaccurate, is of some use because of its extensive analysis of Parliamentary debates. John C. Miller, *Triumph of Freedom, 1775–1783* (Boston, 1948), is recent and sound. Charles Stedman, *History of the Origin, Progress, and Termination of the American War* (2 vols., London, 1794), an account by a participant, remains worthy of study. Sir George O. Trevelyan, *The American Revolution* (4 vols., New York, 1899–1907), though Whiggish and outmoded in certain respects, remains the classic work. Claude H. Van Tyne, *The American Revolution, 1776–1783* (New York, 1905), is brief and standard. Professor Van Tyne's *Causes of the War of Independence* and his *War of Independence* (Boston, 1929), parts of his unfinished *History of the Founding of the American Republic,* are also useful.

Biographical Studies

Catherine D. Bowen, *John Adams and the American Revolution* (Boston, 1950). Gilbert Chinard, *Honest John Adams* (Boston, 1933). Ralph V. Harlow, *Samuel Adams* (New York, 1923). John C. Miller, *Sam Adams . . .* (Boston, 1936). John Pell, *Ethan Allen* (Boston, 1939). Isaac N. Arnold, *The Life of Benedict Arnold . . .* (Chicago, 1880). Malcolm Decker, *Benedict Arnold . . .* (Tarrytown, N.Y., 1932). Carl Van Doren, *Secret History of the American Revolution* (New York, 1941), dealing principally with the Arnold-André conspiracy. Kate M. Rowland, *Life of Charles Carroll . . .* (2 vols., New York, 1898). Peter Guilday, *Life and Times of John Carroll . . .* (2 vols., New York, 1922). John D. Barnhart, *Henry Hamilton and George Rogers Clark in the American Revolution . . .* (Crawfordsville, Ind., 1951). E. W. Spaulding, *His Excellency George Clinton* (New York, 1938). Charles J. Stillé, *Life and Times of John Dickinson . . .* (Philadelphia, 1891). Edward P. Alexander, *James Duane . . .* (New York, 1938). Verner W. Crane, *Benjamin Franklin, Englishman and American* (Baltimore, 1936). Carl Van Doren, *Benjamin Franklin* (New York, 1938). J. R. Alden, *General Gage in America* (Baton Rouge, 1948). Samuel W. Patterson, *Horatio Gates . . .* (New York, 1941). George Washington Greene, *Life of Nathanael Greene* (3 vols., New York, 1867–71). Francis V. Greene, *General*

Greene (New York, 1893). Nathan Schachner, *Alexander Hamilton* (New York, 1946). Herbert L. Allen, *John Hancock, Patriot in Purple* (New York, 1948). William W. Henry, *Patrick Henry* . . . (3 vols., New York, 1891). Frank Monaghan, *John Jay* (New York, 1935). Marie Kimball, *Jefferson* . . . (3 vols. to date, New York, 1943——). Dumas Malone, *Jefferson* . . . (2 vols. to date, Boston, 1948——). Henry S. Randall, *Life of Thomas Jefferson* (3 vols., New York, 1858). Anna F. De Koven, *Life and Letters of John Paul Jones* (2 vols., New York, 1913). Friedrich Kapp, *Life of John Kalb* (New York, 1870). M. Haiman, *Kosciuszko in the American Revolution* (New York, 1943). Louis Gottschalk, *Lafayette Comes to America* and *Lafayette and the Close of the American Revolution* (Chicago, 1935, 1942). David D. Wallace, *Life of Henry Laurens* . . . (New York, 1915). J. R. Alden, *General Charles Lee* . . . (Baton Rouge, 1951). Burton J. Hendrick, *The Lees of Virginia* (Boston, 1935). Irving Brant, *James Madison* . . . (3 vols. to date, Indianapolis, 1941——). Kate M. Rowland, *Life of George Mason* . . . (2 vols., New York, 1892). Ellis P. Oberholtzer, *Robert Morris* (New York, 1903). William G. Sumner, *Financier and the Finances of the Revolution* (2 vols., New York, 1891). Paul A. W. Wallace, *The Muhlenbergs of Pennsylvania* (Philadelphia, 1950). Reginald Lucas, *Lord North* (2 vols., London, 1913). Moncure D. Conway, *Life of Thomas Paine* (2 vols., New York, 1892). Robert L. Hilldrup, *Life and Times of Edmund Pendleton* (Chapel Hill, N.C., 1939). David John Mays, *Edmund Pendleton* (2 vols., Cambridge, Mass., 1952). Albert von Ruville, *William Pitt, Earl of Chatham* (3 vols., London, 1907). Basil Williams, *Life of William Pitt* (2 vols., London, 1913). H. J. Eckenrode, *The Randolphs* . . . (Indianapolis, 1946). W. B. Reed, *Life and Correspondence of Joseph Reed* (2 vols., Philadelphia, 1847). Esther Forbes, *Paul Revere and the World He Lived In* (Boston, 1942). George T. Keppel, Earl of Albemarle, *Memoirs of the Marquis of Rockingham* (2 vols., London, 1852). Nathan G. Goodman, *Benjamin Rush* . . . (Philadelphia, 1934). Benson J. Lossing, *Life and Times of Philip Schuyler* (2 vols., New York, 1872–73). Lord Edmond Fitzmaurice, *Life of William, Earl of Shelburne* . . . (3 vols., London, 1875–76). Roger S. Boardman, *Roger Sherman* (Philadelphia, 1938). Friedrich Kapp, *Life of Major General Frederick William Von Steuben* (2 pts., New York, 1859). John M. Palmer, *General von Steuben* (New Haven, 1937). Anne K. Gregorie, *Thomas Sumter* (Columbia, S.C., 1931). Charles Martyn, *Life of Artemas Ward* (New York, 1921). Charles H. Ambler, *Washington and the West* (Chapel Hill, N.C., 1936). John C. Fitzpatrick, *George Washington Himself* (Indianapolis, 1933). Paul L. Ford, *The True George Washington* (Philadelphia, 1896). Douglas S. Freeman, *George Washington* . . . (5 vols. to date, New York, 1948——). Rupert Hughes, *George Washington* (3 vols., New York, 1926–30). Dudley W. Knox, *The Naval Genius of George Washington* (Boston, 1932). Curtis P. Nettels,

George Washington and American Independence (Boston, 1951). Nathaniel
W. Stephenson and Waldo H. Dunn, *George Washington* (2 vols., New York,
1940). L. S. Mayo, *John Wentworth* (Cambridge, Mass., 1921). Burton A.
Konkle, *James Wilson* (Philadelphia, 1907).

Military Studies

Charles Francis Adams, *Studies, Military and Diplomatic* (Boston, 1911).
Gardner W. Allen, *Naval History of the American Revolution* (2 vols.,
Boston, 1913). Troyer S. Anderson, *Command of the Howe Brothers during
the American Revolution* (New York, 1936). Alfred H. Bill, *Campaign of
Princeton, 1776–1777* (Princeton, 1948), and *Valley Forge: The Making of
an Army* (New York, 1952). Charles K. Bolton, *Private Soldier Under
Washington* (New York, 1902). Allen Bowman, *Morale of the American
Revolutionary Army* (Washington, 1943). H. B. Carrington, *Battles of the
American Revolution, 1775–1783* (New York, 1888). John Codman, *Arnold's
Expedition to Quebec* (New York, 1902). Edward Curtis, *Organization of
the British Army in the American Revolution* (New Haven, 1926). Henry B.
Dawson, *Battles of the United States* (2 vols., New York, 1858). Max von
Eelking, *German Allied Troops in the North American War of Independence,
1775–1783* (Albany, 1893, J. G. Rosengarten, tr.). T. W. Field, *Battle of
Long Island, Long Island Historical Society Memoirs*, II (Brooklyn, 1869).
Sir John W. Fortescue, *History of the British Army* (13 vols., New York,
1899–1930). Allen French, *Day of Concord and Lexington* (Boston, 1925),
and *First Year of the American Revolution* (Boston, 1934). T. G. Frothing-
ham, *Washington, Commander-in-Chief* (Boston, 1930). Francis V. Greene,
Revolutionary War and the Military Policy of the United States (New York,
1911). Louis C. Hatch, *Administration of the American Army* (New York,
1904). William M. James, *British Navy in Adversity* (New York, 1926).
Victor L. Johnson, *Administration of the American Commissariat during
the Revolutionary War* (Philadelphia, 1941). Henry P. Johnston, *Campaign
of 1776 around New York, Long Island Historical Society Memoirs*, III
(Brooklyn, 1878), and *Battle of Harlem Heights* (New York, 1897). Bernhard Knollenberg, *Washington and the Revolution . . .* (New York, 1940).
Alexander A. Lawrence, *Storm over Savannah . . .* (Athens, Ga., 1951).
Benson J. Lossing, *Pictorial Field Book of the Revolution* (2 vols., New
York, 1859). Edward J. Lowell, *Hessians and the Other German Auxiliaries
. . .* (New York, 1884). C. H. Lundin, *Cockpit of the Revolution: the War
for Independence in New Jersey* (Princeton, 1940). Edward McCrady, *His-
tory of South Carolina in the Revolution . . .* (2 vols., New York, 1901–02).
Edward S. Maclay, *History of American Privateers* (New York, 1899). Alfred
T. Mahan, *Major Operations of the Navies in the War of Independence*
(Boston, 1913). Lynn Montross, *Rag, Tag, and Bobtail: the Story of the
Continental Army, 1775–1783* (New York, 1951). Hoffman Nickerson, *Turn-*

ing Point of the Revolution, or Burgoyne in America (Boston, 1928). Charles O. Paullin, *Navy of the American Revolution* (Cleveland, 1906). David Schenck, *North Carolina, 1780–81* (Raleigh, 1889). Justin Smith, *Our Struggle for the Fourteenth Colony* (2 vols., New York, 1907). William S. Stryker, *Battles of Trenton and Princeton* (Boston, 1898) and (with William S. Myers) *Battle of Monmouth* (Princeton, 1927). Howard Swiggett, *War out of Niagara* . . . (New York, 1933). Carl Van Doren, *Mutiny in January* (New York, 1943). Willard Wallace, *Appeal to Arms: A Military History of the American Revolution* (New York, 1950). Christopher Ward, *Delaware Continentals, 1776–1783* (Wilmington, 1941) and *War of the Revolution* (2 vols., New York, 1952, J. R. Alden, ed.). William B. Willcox, "British Strategy in America, 1778," *Journal of Modern History,* XIX (1947), 97–121, "Rhode Island in British Strategy, 1780–1781," *ibid.,* XVII (1945), 304–331, and "British Road to Yorktown: A Study in Divided Command," *American Historical Review,* LII (1946), 1–35.

Political and Social Change

Wilbur C. Abbott, *New York in the American Revolution* (New York, 1929). Thomas B. Abernethy, *Western Lands and the American Revolution* (New York, 1937). Herbert B. Adams, *Maryland's Influence upon Land Cessions to the United States* . . . (Baltimore, 1885). Randolph G. Adams, *Political Ideas of the American Revolution* . . . (Durham, N.C., 1922). Clarence W. Alvord, *Mississippi Valley in British Politics* (2 vols., Cleveland, 1917), Alice M. Baldwin, *New England Clergy and the American Revolution* Durham, N.C., 1928). Oscar T. Barck, *New York City during the War for Independence* . . . (New York, 1931). Carl Becker, *Declaration of Independence* . . . (New York, 1922). Anne Bezanson, *Prices and Inflation during the American Revolution: Pennsylvania, 1770–1790* (Philadelphia, 1951). Julian P. Boyd, *Declaration of Independence* . . . (Princeton, 1945). Carl and Jessica Bridenbaugh, *Rebels and Gentlemen* . . . (New York, 1942). C. J. Bullock, *Finances of the United States from 1775–1789* (Madison, Wis., 1895). Edmund C. Burnett, *The Continental Congress* (New York, 1941). A. L. Burt, *Old Province of Quebec* (Minneapolis, 1933). R. Coupland, *American Revolution and the British Empire* (New York, 1930). Philip A. Crowl, *Maryland during and after the Revolution* . . . , *The Johns Hopkins Studies in Historical and Political Science,* Series LXI, No. 1 (1943). Harry A. Cushing, *History of the Transition from Provincial to Commonwealth Government in Massachusetts* (New York, 1896). Robert A. East, *Business Enterprise in the American Revolutionary Era* (New York, 1938). H. J. Eckenrode, *Separation of Church and State in Virginia* . . . (Richmond, 1910) and *Revolution in Virginia* . . . (Boston, 1916). Bernard Fay, *Revolutionary Spirit in France and America* (New York, 1927). Herbert Friedenwald, *Declaration of Independence* (New York, 1906). Hugh B.

Grigsby, *Virginia Convention of 1776* (Richmond, 1855). Oscar and Mary F. Handlin, "Revolutionary Economic Policy in Massachusetts," *William and Mary Quarterly,* Third Series, IV (1947), 3–26. John H. Hazelton, *Declaration of Independence* . . . (New York, 1906). William H. Hoyt, *Mecklenburg Declaration of Independence* (New York, 1907). Edward F. Humphreys, *Nationalism and Religion in America, 1774–1789* (Boston, 1924). John Franklin Jameson, *American Revolution Considered as a Social Movement* (Princeton, 1926). Merrill Jensen, *Articles of Confederation* . . . (Madison, Wis., 1940). Gustav A. Koch, *Republican Religion* . . . (New York, 1933). James M. Leake, *Virginia Committee System and the American Revolution* (Baltimore, 1917). Charles H. Lincoln, *Revolutionary Movement in Pennsylvania* (Philadelphia, 1901). Charles L. Lingley, *Transition in Virginia from Colony to Commonwealth* (New York, 1910). Mary S. Locke, *Anti-Slavery in America* . . . (Boston, 1901). Charles H. McIlwain, *American Revolution: A Constitutional Interpretation* (New York, 1923). Richard B. Morris (ed.), *Era of the American Revolution* . . . (New York, 1939), several essays, and *Government and Labor in America* (New York, 1946). L. B. Namier, *Structure of British Politics at the Accession of George III* (2 vols., London, 1929) and *England in the Age of the American Revolution* (London, 1930). Allan Nevins, *American States during and after the Revolution, 1775–1789* (New York, 1924). Richard J. Purcell, *Connecticut in Transition* (Washington, 1918). Clinton Rossiter, *Seedtime of the Republic* (New York, 1953). Robert L. Schuyler, *Parliament and the British Empire* . . . (New York, 1929). J. Paul Selsam, *Pennsylvania Constitution of 1776* (Philadelphia, 1936). E. W. Sikes, *Transition of North Carolina from Colony to Commonwealth* (Baltimore, 1898). Richard F. Upton, *Revolutionary New Hampshire* (Hanover, 1936). Thomas J. Wertenbaker, *Father Knickerbocker Rebels: New York City during the Revolution* (New York, 1948). Otto Zeichner, *Connecticut's Years of Controversy, 1750–1776* (Chapel Hill, N.C., 1949).

Diplomacy

Samuel F. Bemis, *Diplomacy of the American Revolution* (New York, 1935) and *Hussey-Cumberland Negotiation and American Independence* (Princeton, 1931). Weldon A. Brown, *Empire or Independence,* . . . *1774–1783* (Baton Rouge, 1941). Edward S. Corwin, *French Policy and the American Alliance of 1778* (Princeton, 1916). Henri Doniol, *Histoire de la participation de la France à l'établissement des États-Unis d'Amérique* (6 vols., Paris, 1884–92). Gerald S. Graham, *British Policy and Canada, 1774–1791* . . . (New York, 1930). George H. Guttridge, *David Hartley, M. P., an Advocate of Conciliation, 1774–1783* (Berkeley, Calif., 1926). John Franklin Jameson, "St. Eustatius in the American Revolution," *American Historical Review,* VIII (1903), 683–708. Elizabeth S. Kite, *Beaumarchais and the War of Independence* (2 vols., Boston, 1918). Carl L. Lokke, *France and the Colonial Question . . . 1763–1801* (New York, 1932). John J. Meng, *Comte de Vergennes; European Phases of His American Diplomacy . . .* (Washington, 1932). James B. Perkins, *France in the American Revolution* (Boston, 1911). Paul C. Phillips, *The West in the Diplomacy of the American Revolution* (Urbana, 1913). Charles J. Stillé, "Beaumarchais and the Lost Million," *Pennsylvania Magazine of History and Biography,* XI (1887), 1–36. Kathryn Sullivan, *Maryland and France, 1774–1789* (Philadelphia, 1936). Claude H. Van Tyne, "French Aid before the Alliance of 1778," *American Historical Review,* XXXI (1925), 20–40.

The Loyalists

Julian P. Boyd, *Anglo-American Union: Joseph Galloway's Plans to Preserve the British Empire, 1774–1788* (Philadelphia, 1941). Arthur G. Bradley, *United Empire Loyalists . . .* (London, 1932). Robert O. DeMond, *Loyalists in North Carolina during the Revolution* (Durham, N.C., 1940). Lewis Einstein, *Divided Loyalties: Americans in England during the War of Independence* (Boston, 1933). Alexander C. Flick, *Loyalism in New York during the American Revolution* (New York, 1901). Harold B. Hancock, *Delaware Loyalists, Papers of the Historical Society of Delaware,* New Series, III (Wilmington, 1940). Isaac S. Harrell, *Loyalism in Virginia . . .* (Durham, N.C., 1926). Edward Alfred Jones, *Loyalists of New Jersey in the American Revolution, Collections of the New Jersey Historical Society,* X (1927). Thomas Jones, *History of New York during the Revolutionary War . . .* (2 vols., New York, 1879). George W. Kyte, "Some Plans for a Loyalist Stronghold in the Middle Colonies," *Pennsylvania History,* XVI (1949), 3–16. Leonard Labaree, "Nature of American Loyalism," *Proceedings of the American Antiquarian Society,* New Series, LIV (1944), 15–58, and *Conservatism in Early American History* (New York, 1948). Adolphus E. Ryerson, *Loyalists of America and Their Times . . .* (Toronto, 1880). Lorenzo Sabine, *Biographical Sketches of Loyalists of the American Revolution* (2 vols., Boston, 1864). Wilbur H. Siebert, "Dispersion of the American Tories," *Mississippi Valley Historical Review,* I (1914), 185–197, *Loyalists of Pennsylvania* (Columbus, Ohio, 1920), and *Loyalists in East Florida, 1774–1785* (2 vols., Deland, Fla., 1929). Claude H. Van Tyne, *Loyalists in the American Revolution* (New York, 1902). Harry B. Yoshpe, *Disposition of Loyalist Estates in the Southern District of the State of New York* (New York, 1939). Oscar Zeichner, "Rehabilitation of Loyalists in Connecticut," *New England Quarterly,* XI (1938), 308–330, and "Loyalist Problem in New York after the Revolution," *New York History,* XXI (1940), 284–302.

Index

hARPER ⚜ ꓔoRchBOOKS

American Studies: General

HENRY ADAMS Degradation of the Democratic Dogma. ‡ *Introduction by Charles Hirschfeld.* TB/1450

LOUIS D. BRANDEIS: Other People's Money, *and How the Bankers Use It. Ed. with Intro. by Richard M. Abrams* TB/3081

HENRY STEELE COMMAGER, Ed.: The Struggle for Racial Equality TB/1300

CARL N. DEGLER: Out of Our Past: *The Forces that Shaped Modern America* CN/2

CARL N. DEGLER, Ed.: Pivotal Interpretations of American History
Vol. I TB/1240; Vol. II TB/1241

A. S. EISENSTADT, Ed.: The Craft of American History: *Selected Essays*
Vol. I TB/1255; Vol. II TB/1256

LAWRENCE H. FUCHS, Ed.: American Ethnic Politics TB/1368

MARCUS LEE HANSEN: The Atlantic Migration: 1607-1860. *Edited by Arthur M. Schlesinger. Introduction by Oscar Handlin* TB/1052

MARCUS LEE HANSEN: The Immigrant in American History. *Edited with a Foreword by Arthur M. Schlesinger* TB/1120

ROBERT L. HEILBRONER: The Limits of American Capitalism TB/1305

JOHN HIGHAM, Ed.: The Reconstruction of American History TB/1068

ROBERT H. JACKSON: The Supreme Court in the American System of Government TB/1106

JOHN F. KENNEDY: A Nation of Immigrants. *Illus. Revised and Enlarged. Introduction by Robert F. Kennedy* TB/1118

LEONARD W. LEVY, Ed.: American Constitutional Law: *Historical Essays* TB/1285

LEONARD W. LEVY, Ed.: Judicial Review and the Supreme Court TB/1296

LEONARD W. LEVY: The Law of the Commonwealth and Chief Justice Shaw: *The Evolution of American Law, 1830-1860* TB/1309

GORDON K. LEWIS: Puerto Rico: *Freedom and Power in the Caribbean. Abridged edition* TB/1371

RICHARD B. MORRIS: Fair Trial: *Fourteen Who Stood Accused, from Anne Hutchinson to Alger Hiss* TB/1335

GUNNAR MYRDAL: An American Dilemma: *The Negro Problem and Modern Democracy. Introduction by the Author.*
Vol. I TB/1443; Vol. II TB/1444

GILBERT OSOFSKY, Ed.: The Burden of Race: *A Documentary History of Negro-White Relations in America* TB/1405

CONYERS READ, Ed.: The Constitution Reconsidered. *Revised Edition. Preface by Richrd B. Morris* TB/1384

ARNOLD ROSE: The Negro in America: *The Condensed Version of Gunnar Myrdal's* An American Dilemma. *Second Edition* TB/3048

JOHN E. SMITH: Themes in American Philosophy: *Purpose, Experience and Community* TB/1466

WILLIAM R. TAYLOR: Cavalier and Yankee: *The Old South and American National Character* TB/1474

American Studies: Colonial

BERNARD BAILYN: The New England Merchants in the Seventeenth Century TB/1149

ROBERT E. BROWN: Middle-Class Democracy and Revolution in Massachusetts, 1691–1780. *New Introduction by Author* TB/1413

JOSEPH CHARLES: The Origins of the American Party System TB/1049

HENRY STEELE COMMAGER & ELMO GIORDANETTI, Eds.: Was America a Mistake? *An Eighteenth Century Controversy* TB/1329

WESLEY FRANK CRAVEN: The Colonies in Transition: 1660-1712† TB/3084

CHARLES GIBSON: Spain in America † TB/3077

CHARLES GIBSON, Ed.: The Spanish Tradition in America + HR/1351

LAWRENCE HENRY GIPSON: The Coming of the Revolution: 1763-1775. † *Illus.* TB/3007

JACK P. GREENE, Ed.: Great Britain and the American Colonies: 1606-1763. + *Introduction by the Author* HR/1477

AUBREY C. LAND, Ed.: Bases of the Plantation Society + HR/1429

JOHN LANKFORD, Ed.: Captain John Smith's America: *Selections from his Writings* ‡ TB/3078

LEONARD W. LEVY: Freedom of Speech and Press in Early American History: *Legacy of Suppression* TB/1109

PERRY MILLER: Errand Into the Wilderness TB/1139

PERRY MILLER T. H. JOHNSON, Eds.: The Puritans: *A Sourcebook of Their Writings*
Vol. I TB/1093; Vol. II TB/1094

---

† The New American Nation Series, edited by Henry Steele Commager and Richard B. Morris.
‡ American Perspectives series, edited by Bernard Wishy and William E. Leuchtenburg.
a History of Europe series, edited by J. H. Plumb.
§ The Library of Religion and Culture, edited by Benjamin Nelson.
‖ Researches in the Social, Cultural, and Behavioral Sciences, edited by Benjamin Nelson.
Σ Harper Modern Science Series, edited by James A. Newman.
° Not for sale in Canada.
+ Documentary History of the United States series, edited by Richard B. Morris.
# Documentary History of Western Civilization series, edited by Eugene C. Black and Leonard W. Levy.
Λ The Economic History of the United States series, edited by Henry David et al.
¶ European Perspectives series, edited by Eugene C. Black.
** Contemporary Essays series, edited by Leonard W. Levy.
* The Stratum Series, edited by John Hale.

EDMUND S. MORGAN: The Puritan Family: *Religion and Domestic Relations in Seventeenth Century New England* TB/1227
RICHARD B. MORRIS: Government and Labor in Early America TB/1244
WALLACE NOTESTEIN: The English People on the Eve of Colonization: 1603-1630. † *Illus.* TB/3006
FRANCIS PARKMAN: The Seven Years War: *A Narrative Taken from Montcalm and Wolfe, The Conspiracy of Pontiac, and* A Half-Century of Conflict. *Edited by John H. McCallum* TB/3083
LOUIS B. WRIGHT: The Cultural Life of the American Colonies: 1607-1763. † *Illus.* TB/3005
YVES F. ZOLTVANY, Ed.: The French Tradition in America + HR/1425

American Studies: The Revolution to 1860

JOHN R. ALDEN: The American Revolution: 1775-1783. † *Illus.* TB/3011
MAX BELOFF, Ed.: The Debate on the American Revolution, 1761-1783: *A Sourcebook* TB/1225
RAY A. BILLINGTON: The Far Western Frontier: 1830-1860. † *Illus.* TB/3012
STUART BRUCHEY: The Roots of American Economic Growth, 1607-1861: *An Essay in Social Causation. New Introduction by the Author.* TB/1350
WHITNEY R. CROSS: The Burned-Over District: *The Social and Intellectual History of Enthusiastic Religion in Western New York, 1800-1850* TB/1242
NOBLE E. CUNNINGHAM, JR., Ed.: The Early Republic, 1789-1828 + HR/1394
GEORGE DANGERFIELD: The Awakening of American Nationalism, 1815-1828. † *Illus.* TB/3061
CLEMENT EATON: The Freedom-of-Thought Struggle in the Old South. *Revised and Enlarged. Illus.* TB/1150
CLEMENT EATON: The Growth of Southern Civilization, 1790-1860. † *Illus.* TB/3040
ROBERT H. FERRELL, Ed.: Foundations of American Diplomacy, 1775-1872 HR/1393
LOUIS FILLER: The Crusade against Slavery: 1830-1860. † *Illus.* TB/3029
DAVID H. FISCHER: The Revolution of American Conservatism: *The Federalist Party in the Era of Jeffersonian Democracy* TB/1449
WILLIAM W. FREEHLING, Ed.: The Nullification Era: *A Documentary Record* ‡ TB/3079
WILLIM W. FREEHLING: Prelude to Civil War: *The Nullification Controversy in South Carolina, 1816-1836* TB/1359
PAUL W. GATES: The Farmer's Age: *Agriculture, 1815-1860* Δ TB/1398
FELIX GILBERT: The Beginnings of American Foreign Policy: *To the Farewell Address* TB/1200
ALEXANDER HAMILTON: The Reports of Alexander Hamilton. ‡ *Edited by Jacob E. Cooke* TB/3060
THOMAS JEFFERSON: Notes on the State of Virginia. ‡ *Edited by Thomas P. Abernethy* TB/3052
FORREST MCDONALD, Ed.: Confederation and Constitution, 1781-1789 + HR/1396
BERNARD MAYO: Myths and Men: *Patrick Henry, George Washington, Thomas Jefferson* TB/1108
JOHN C. MILLER: Alexander Hamilton and the Growth of the New Nation TB/3057
JOHN C. MILLER: The Federalist Era: 1789-1801. † *Illus.* TB/3027

RICHARD B. MORRIS, Ed.: Alexander Hamilton and the Founding of the Nation. *New Introduction by the Editor* TB/1448
RICHARD B. MORRIS: The American Revolution Reconsidered TB/1363
CURTIS P. NETTELS: The Emergence of a National Economy, 1775-1815 Δ TB/1438
DOUGLASS C. NORTH & ROBERT PAUL THOMAS, Eds.: *The Growth of the American Economy to 1860* + HR/1352
R. B. NYE: The Cultural Life of the New Nation: 1776-1830. † *Illus.* TB/3026
GILBERT OSOFSKY, Ed.: Puttin' On Ole Massa: *The Slave Narratives of Henry Bibb, William Wells Brown, and Solomon Northup* ‡ TB/1432
JAMES PARTON: The Presidency of Andrew Jackson. *From Volume III of the* Life of Andrew Jackson. *Ed. with Intro. by Robert V. Remini* TB/3080
FRANCIS S. PHILBRICK: The Rise of the West, 1754-1830. † *Illus.* TB/3067
MARSHALL SMELSER: The Democratic Republic, 1801-1815 † TB/1406
TIMOTHY L. SMITH: Revivalism and Social Reform: *American Protestantism on the Eve of the Civil War* TB/1229
JACK M. SOSIN, Ed.: The Opening of the West + HR/1424
GEORGE ROGERS TAYLOR: The Transportation Revolution, 1815-1860 Δ TB/1347
A. F. TYLER: Freedom's Ferment: *Phases of American Social History from the Revolution to the Outbreak of the Civil War. Illus.* TB/1074
GLYNDON G. VAN DEUSEN: The Jacksonian Era: 1828-1848. † *Illus.* TB/3028
LOUIS B. WRIGHT: Culture on the Moving Frontier TB/1053

American Studies: The Civil War to 1900

W. R. BROCK: An American Crisis: *Congress and Reconstruction, 1865-67* ° TB/1283
T. C. COCHRAN & WILLIAM MILLER: The Age of Enterprise: *A Social History of Industrial America* TB/1054
W. A. DUNNING: Reconstruction, Political and Economic: 1865-1877 TB/1073
HAROLD U. FAULKNER: Politics, Reform and Expansion: 1890-1900. † *Illus.* TB/3020
GEORGE M. FREDRICKSON: The Inner Civil War: *Northern Intellectuals and the Crisis of the Union* TB/1358
JOHN A. GARRATY: The New Commonwealth, 1877-1890 † TB/1410
JOHN A. GARRATY, Ed.: The Transformation of American Society, 1870-1890 + HR/1395
HELEN HUNT JACKSON: A Century of Dishonor: *The Early Crusade for Indian Reform.* † *Edited by Andrew F. Rolle* TB/3063
ALBERT D. KIRWAN: Revolt of the Rednecks: *Mississippi Politics, 1876-1925* TB/1199
ARTHUR MANN: Yankee Reforms in the Urban Age: *Social Reform in Boston, 1800-1900* TB/1247
ARNOLD M. PAUL: Conservative Crisis and the Rule of Law: *Attitudes of Bar and Bench, 1887-1895. New Introduction by Author* TB/1415
JAMES S. PIKE: The Prostrate State: *South Carolina under Negro Government.* ‡ *Intro. by Robert F. Durden* TB/3085
WHITELAW REID: After the War: *A Tour of the Southern States, 1865-1866.* ‡ *Edited by C. Vann Woodward* TB/3066
FRED A. SHANNON: The Farmer's Last Frontier: *Agriculture, 1860-1897* TB/1348

2

History: Renaissance & Reformation

JACOB BURCKHARDT: The Civilization of the Renaissance in Italy. *Introduction by Benjamin Nelson and Charles Trinkaus. Illus.* Vol. I TB/40; Vol. II TB/41

JOHN CALVIN & JACOPO SADOLETO: A Reformation Debate. *Edited by John C. Olin* TB/1239

FEDERICO CHABOD: Machiavelli and the Renaissance TB/1193

THOMAS CROMWELL: Thomas Cromwell. *Selected Letters on Church and Commonwealth, 1523-1540. ¶ Ed. with an Intro. by Arthur J. Slavin* TB/1462

R. TREVOR DAVIES: The Golden Century of Spain, 1501-1621 ° TB/1194

J. H. ELLIOTT: Europe Divided, 1559-1598 *a* ° TB/1414

G. R. ELTON: Reformation Europe, 1517-1559 ° *a* TB/1270

DESIDERIUS ERASMUS: Christian Humanism and the Reformation: *Selected Writings. Edited and Translated by John C. Olin* TB/1166

DESIDERIUS ERASMUS: Erasmus and His Age: *Selected Letters. Edited with an Introduction by Hans J. Hillerbrand. Translated by Marcus A. Haworth* TB/1461

WALLACE K. FERGUSON et al.: Facets of the Renaissance TB/1098

WALLACE K. FERGUSON et al.: The Renaissance: *Six Essays. Illus.* TB/1084

FRANCESCO GUICCIARDINI: History of Florence. *Translated with an Introduction and Notes by Mario Domandi* TB/1470

WERNER L. GUNDERSHEIMER, Ed.: French Humanism, 1470-1600. * *Illus.* TB/1473

MARIE BOAS HALL, Ed.: Nature and Nature's Laws: *Documents of the Scientific Revolution #* HR/1420

HANS J. HILLERBRAND, Ed., The Protestant Reformation HR/1342

JOHAN HUIZINGA: Erasmus and the Age of Reformation. *Illus.* TB/19

JOEL HURSTFIELD: The Elizabethan Nation TB/1312

JOEL HURSTFIELD, Ed.: The Reformation Crisis TB/1267

PAUL OSKAR KRISTELLER: Renaissance Thought: *The Classic, Scholastic, and Humanist Strains* TB/1048

PAUL OSKAR KRISTELLER: Renaissance Thought II: *Papers on Humanism and the Arts* TB/1163

PAUL O. KRISTELLER & PHILIP P. WIENER, Eds.: Renaissance Essays TB/1392

DAVID LITTLE: Religion, Order and Law: *A Study in Pre-Revolutionary England. § Preface by R. Bellah* TB/1418

NICCOLO MACHIAVELLI: History of Florence and of the Affairs of Italy: *From the Earliest Times to the Death of Lorenzo the Magnificent. Introduction by Felix Gilbert* TB/1027

ALFRED VON MARTIN: Sociology of the Renaissance. ° *Introduction by W. K. Ferguson* TB/1099

GARRETT MATTINGLY et al.: Renaissance Profiles. *Edited by J. H. Plumb* TB/1162

J. E. NEALE: The Age of Catherine de Medici ° TB/1085

J. H. PARRY: The Establishment of the European Hegemony: 1415-1715: *Trade and Exploration in the Age of the Renaissance* TB/1045

J. H. PARRY, Ed.: The European Reconnaissance: *Selected Documents #* HR/1345

BUONACCORSO PITTI & GREGORIO DATI: TWO Memoirs of Renaissance Florence: *The Diaries of Buonaccorso Pitti and Gregorio Dati. Edited with Intro. by Gene Brucker. Trans. by Julia Martines* TB/1333

J. H. PLUMB: The Italian Renaissance: *A Concise Survey of Its History and Culture* TB/1161

A. F. POLLARD: Henry VIII. *Introduction by A. G. Dickens.* ° TB/1249

RICHARD H. POPKIN: The History of Scepticism from Erasmus to Descartes TB/1391

PAOLO ROSSI: Philosophy, Technology, and the Arts, in the Early Modern Era 1400-1700. || *Edited by Benjamin Nelson. Translated by Salvator Attanasio* TB/1458

FERDINAND SCHEVILL: The Medici. *Illus.* TB/1010

FERDINAND SCHEVILL: Medieval and Renaissance Florence. *Illus.* Vol. I: *Medieval Florence* TB/1090

Vol. II: The Coming of Humanism and the Age of the Medici TB/1091

R. H. TAWNEY: The Agrarian Problem in the Sixteenth Century. *Intro. by Lawrence Stone* TB/1315

H. R. TREVOR-ROPER: The European Witch-craze of the Sixteenth and Seventeenth Centuries and Other Essays ° TB/1416

VESPASIANO: Rennaissance Princes, Popes, and *XVth Century: The Vespasiano Memoirs. Introduction by Myron P. Gilmore. Illus.* TB/1111

History: Modern European

RENE ALBRECHT-CARRIE, Ed.: The Concert of Europe # HR/1341

MAX BELOFF: The Age of Absolutism, 1660-1815 TB/1062

OTTO VON BISMARCK: Reflections and Reminiscences. *Ed. with Intro. by Theodore S. Hamerow* ¶ TB/1357

EUGENE C. BLACK, Ed.: British Politics in the Nineteenth Century # HR/1427

EUGENE C. BLACK, Ed.: European Political History, 1815-1870: *Aspects of Liberalism* ¶ TB/1331

ASA BRIGGS: The Making of Modern England, 1783-1867: *The Age of Improvement* ° TB/1203

ALAN BULLOCK: Hitler, A Study in Tyranny. ° *Revised Edition. Illus.* TB/1123

EDMUND BURKE: On Revolution. *Ed. by Robert A. Smith* TB/1401

E. R. CARR: International Relations Between the Two World Wars. 1919-1939 ° TB/1279

E. H. CARR: The Twenty Years' Crisis, 1919-1939: *An Introduction to the Study of International Relations* ° TB/1122

GORDON A. CRAIG: From Bismarck to Adenauer: *Aspects of German Statecraft. Revised Edition* TB/1171

LESTER G. CROCKER, Ed.: The Age of Enlightenment # HR/1423

DENIS DIDEROT: The Encyclopedia: *Selections. Edited and Translated with Introduction by Stephen Gendzier* TB/1299

JACQUES DROZ: Europe between Revolutions, 1815-1848. ° *a Trans. by Robert Baldick* TB/1346

JOHANN GOTTLIEB FICHTE: Addresses to the German Nation. *Ed. with Intro. by George A. Kelly* ¶ TB/1366

ROBERT & ELBORG FORSTER, Eds.: European Society in the Eighteenth Century # HR/1404

C. C. GILLISPIE: Genesis and Geology: *The Decades before Darwin* § TB/51

5

ALBERT GOODWIN, Ed.: The European Nobility in the Enghteenth Century TB/1313
ALBERT GOODWIN: The French Revolution TB/1064
ALBERT GUERARD: France in the Classical Age: The Life and Death of an Ideal TB/1183
JOHN B. HALSTED, Ed.: Romanticism # HR/1387
J. H. HEXTER: Reappraisals in History: New Views on History and Society in Early Modern Europe ° TB/1100
STANLEY HOFFMANN et al.: In Search of France: The Economy, Society and Political System In the Twentieth Century TB/1219
H. STUART HUGHES: The Obstructed Path: French Social Thought in the Years of Desperation TB/1451
JOHAN HUIZINGA: Dutch Civilisation in the 17th Century and Other Essays TB/1453
LIONAL KOCHAN: The Struggle for Germany: 1914-45 TB/1304
HANS KOHN: The Mind of Germany: The Education of a Nation TB/1204
HANS KOHN, Ed.: The Mind of Modern Russia: Historical and Political Thought of Russia's Great Age TB/1065
WALTER LAQUEUR & GEORGE L. MOSSE, Eds.: Education and Social Structure in the 20th Century. ° Volume 6 of the Journal of Contemporary History TB/1339
WALTER LAQUEUR & GEORGE L. MOSSE, Ed.: International Fascism, 1920-1945. ° Volume 1 of the Journal of Contemporary History TB/1276
WALTER LAQUEUR & GEORGE L. MOSSE, Eds.: Literature and Politics in the 20th Century. ° Volume 5 of the Journal of Contemporary History. TB/1328
WALTER LAQUEUR & GEORGE L. MOSSE, Eds.: The New History: Trends in Historical Research and Writing Since World War II. ° Volume 4 of the Journal of Contemporary History TB/1327
WALTER LAQUEUR & GEORGE L. MOSSE, Eds.: 1914: The Coming of the First World War. ° Volume3 of the Journal of Contemporary History TB/1306
C. A. MACARTNEY, Ed.: The Habsburg and Hohenzollern Dynasties in the Seventeenth and Eighteenth Centuries # HR/1400
JOHN MCMANNERS: European History, 1789-1914: Men, Machines and Freedom TB/1419
PAUL MANTOUX: The Industrial Revolution in the Eighteenth Century: An Outline of the Beginnings of the Modern Factory System in England TB/1079
FRANK E. MANUEL: The Prophets of Paris: Turgot, Condorcet, Saint-Simon, Fourier, and Comte TB/1218
KINGSLEY MARTIN: French Liberal Thought in the Eighteenth Century: A Study of Political Ideas from Bayle to Condorcet TB/1114
NAPOLEON III: Napoleonic Ideas: Des Idées Napoléoniennes, par le Prince Napoléon-Louis Bonaparte. Ed. by Brison D. Gooch ¶ TB/1336
FRANZ NEUMANN: Behemoth: The Structure and Practice of National Socialism, 1933-1944 TB/1289
DAVID OGG: Europe of the Ancien Régime, 1715-1783 ° a TB/1271
GEORGE RUDE: Revolutionary Europe, 1783-1815 ° a TB/1272
MASSIMO SALVADORI, Ed.: Modern Socialism # TB/1374
HUGH SETON-WATSON: Eastern Europe Between the Wars, 1918-1941 TB/1330

DENIS MACK SMITH, Ed.: The Making of Italy, 1796-1870 # HR/1356
ALBERT SOREL: Europe Under the Old Regime. Translated by Francis H. Herrick TB/1121
ROLAND N. STROMBERG, Ed.: Realism, Naturalism, and Symbolism: Modes of Thought and Expression in Europe, 1848-1914 # HR/1355
A. J. P. TAYLOR: From Napoleon to Lenin: Historical Essays ° TB/1268
A. J. P. TAYLOR: The Habsburg Monarchy, 1809-1918: A History of the Austrian Empire and Austria-Hungary ° TB/1187
J. M. THOMPSON: European History, 1494-1789 TB/1431
DAVID THOMSON, Ed.: France: Empire and Republic, 1850-1940 # HR/1387
ALEXIS DE TOCQUEVILLE & GUSTAVE DE BEAUMONT: Tocqueville and Beaumont on Social Reform. Ed. and trans. with Intro. by Seymour Drescher TB/1343
G. M. TREVELYAN: British History in the Nineteenth Century and After: 1792-1919 ° TB/1251
H. R. TREVOR-ROPER: Historical Essays TB/1269
W. WARREN WAGAR, Ed.: Science, Faith, and MAN: European Thought Since 1914 # HR/1362
MACK WALKER, Ed.: Metternich's Europe, 1813-1848 # HR/1361
ELIZABETH WISKEMANN: Europe of the Dictators, 1919-1945 ° a TB/1273
JOHN B. WOLF: France: 1814-1919: The Rise of a Liberal-Democratic Society TB/3019

Literature & Literary Criticism

JACQUES BARZUN: The House of Intellect TB/1051
W. J. BATE: From Classic to Romantic: Premises of Taste in Eighteenth Century England TB/1036
VAN WYCK BROOKS: Van Wyck Brooks: The Early Years: A Selection from his Works, 1908-1921 Ed. with Intro. by Claire Sprague TB/3082
ERNST R. CURTIUS: European Literature and the Latin Middle Ages. Trans. by Willard Trask TB/2015
RICHMOND LATTIMORE, Translator: The Odyssey of Homer TB/1389
SAMUEL PEPYS: The Diary of Samual Pepys. ° Edited by O. F. Morshead. 60 illus. by Ernest Shepard TB/1007
ROBERT PREYER, Ed.: Victorian Literature ** TB/1302
ALBION W. TOURGEE: A Fool's Errand: A Novel of the South during Reconstruction. Intro. by George Fredrickson TB/3074
BASIL WILEY: Nineteenth Century Studies: Coleridge to Matthew Arnold ° TB/1261

Philosophy

HENRI BERGSON: Time and Free Will: An Essay on the Immediate Data of Consciousness ° TB/1021
LUDWIG BINSWANGER: Being-in-the-World: Selected Papers. Trans. with Intro. by Jacob Needleman TB/1365
H. J. BLACKHAM: Six Existentialist Thinkers: Kierkegaard, Nietzsche, Jaspers, Marcel, Heidegger, Sartre ° TB/1002
J. M. BOCHENSKI: The Methods of Contemporary Thought. Trans. by Peter Caws TB/1377
CRANE BRINTON: Nietzsche. Preface, Bibliography, and Epilogue by the Author TB/1197

ERNST CASSIRER: Rousseau, Kant and Goethe. *Intro. by Peter Gay* TB/1092
FREDERICK COPLESTON, S. J.: Medieval Philosophy TB/376
F. M. CORNFORD: From Religion to Philosophy: *A Study in the Origins of Western Speculation §* TB/20
WILFRID DESAN: The Tragic Finale: *An Essay on the Philosophy of Jean-Paul Sartre* TB/1030
MARVIN FARBER: The Aims of Phenomenology: *The Motives, Methods, and Impact of Husserl's Thought* TB/1291
MARVIN FARBER: Basic Issues of Philosophy: *Experience, Reality, and Human Values* TB/1344
MARVIN FARBERS: Phenomenology and Existence: *Towards a Philosophy within Nature* TB/1295
PAUL FRIEDLANDER: 'Plato: *An Introduction* TB/2017
MICHAEL GELVEN: A Commentary on Heidegger's "Being and Time" TB/1464
J. GLENN GRAY: Hegel and Greek Thought TB/1409
W. K. C. GUTHRIE: The Greek Philosophers: *From Thales to Aristotle* ° TB/1008
G. W. F. HEGEL: On Art, Religion Philosophy: *Introductory Lectures to the Realm of Absolute Spirit.* ‖ *Edited with an Introduction by J. Glenn Gray* TB/1463
G. W. F. HEGEL: Phenomenology of Mind. ° ‖ *Introduction by George Lichtheim* TB/1303
MARTIN HEIDEGGER: Discourse on Thinking. *Translated with a Preface by John M. Anderson and E. Hans Freund. Introduction by John M. Anderson* TB/1459
F. H. HEINEMANN: Existentialism and the Modern Predicament TB/28
WERER HEISENBERG: Physics and Philosophy: *The Revolution in Modern Science. Intro. by F. S. C. Northrop* TB/549
EDMUND HUSSERL: Phenomenology and the Crisis of Philosophy. § *Translated with an Introduction by Quentin Lauer* TB/1170
IMMANUEL KANT: Groundwork of the Metaphysic of Morals. *Translated and Analyzed by H. J. Paton* TB/1159
IMMANUEL KANT: Lectures on Ethics. § *Introduction by Lewis White Beck* TB/105
WALTER KAUFMANN, Ed.: Religion From Tolstoy to Camus: *Basic Writings on Religious Truth and Morals* TB/123
QUENTIN LAUER: Phenomenology: *Its Genesis and Prospect. Preface by Aron Gurwitsch* TB/1169
MAURICE MANDELBAUM: The Problem of Historical Knowledge: *An Answer to Relativism* TB/1198
H. J. PATON: The Categorical Imperative: *A Study in Kant's Moral Philosophy* TB/1325
MICHAEL POLANYI: Personal Knowledge: *Towards a Post-Critical Philosophy* TB/1158
KARL R. POPPER: Conjectures and Refutations: *The Growth of Scientific Knowledge* TB/1376
WILLARD VAN ORMAN QUINE: Elementary Logic *Revised Edition* TB/577
WILLARD VAN ORMAN QUINE: From a Logical Point of View: *Logico-Philosophical Essays* TB/566
JOHN E. SMITH: Themes in American Philosophy: *Purpose, Experience and Community* TB/1466
MORTON WHITE: Foundations of Historical Knowledge TB/1440
WILHELM WINDELBAND: A History of Philosophy *Vol. I: Greek, Roman, Medieval* TB/38
Vol. II: Renaissance, Enlightenment, Modern TB/39

LUDWIG WITTGENSTEIN: The Blue and Brown Books ° TB/1211
LUDWIG WITTGENSTEIN: Notebooks, 1914-1916 TB/1441

Political Science & Government

C. E. BLACK: The Dynamics of Modernization: *A Study in Comparative History* TB/1321
DENIS W. BROGAN: Politics in America. *New Introduction by the Author* TB/1469
CRANE BRINTON: English Political Thought in the Nineteenth Century TB/1071
ROBERT CONQUEST: Power and Policy in the USSR: *The Study of Soviet Dynastics* ° TB/1307
ROBERT A. DAHL & CHARLES E. LINDBLOM: Politics, Economics, and Welfare: *Planning and Politico-Economic Systems Resolved into Basic Social Processes* TB/1277
HANS KOHN: Political Ideologies of the 20th Century TB/1277
ROY C. MACRIDIS, Ed.: Political Parties: *Contemporary Trends and Ideas* ** TB/1322
ROBERT GREEN MC CLOSKEY: American Conservatism in the Age of Enterprise, 1865-1910 TB/1137
MARSILIUS OF PADUA: The Defender of Peace. *The Defensor Pacis. Translated with an Introduction by Alan Gewirth* TB/1310
KINGSLEY MARTIN: French Liberal Thought in the Eighteenth Century: *A Study of Political Ideas from Bayle to Condorcet* TB/1114
BARRINGTON MOORE, JR.: Political Power and Social Theory: *Seven Studies* ‖ TB/1221
BARRINGTON MOORE, JR.: Soviet Politics—The Dilemma of Power: *The Role of Ideas in Social Change* ‖ TB/1222
BARRINGTON MOORE, JR.: Terror and Progress—USSR: *Some Sources of Change and Stability* TB/1266
JOHN B. MORRALL: Political Thought in Medieval Times TB/1076
KARL R. POPPER: The Open Society and Its Enemies *Vol. I: The Spell of Plato* TB/1101
Vol. II: The High Tide of Prophecy: Hegel, Marx, and the Aftermath TB/1102
CONYERS READ, Ed.: The Constitution Reconsidered. *Revised Edition, Preface by Richard B. Morris* TB/1384
JOHN P. ROCHE, Ed.: Origins of American Political Thought: *Selected Readings* TB/1301
JOHN P. ROCHE, Ed.: American Political Thought: *From Jefferson to Progressivism* TB/1332
HENRI DE SAINT-SIMON: Social Organization, The Science of Man, and Other Writings. ‖ *Edited and Translated with an Introduction by Felix Markham* TB/1152
CHARLES SCHOTTLAND, Ed.: The Welfare State ** TB/1323
JOSEPH A. SCHUMPETER: Capitalism, Socialism and Democracy TB/3008

Psychology

ALFRED ADLER: The Individual Psychology of Alfred Adler: *A Systematic Presentation in Selections from His Writings. Edited by Heinz L. & Rowena R. Ansbacher* TB/1154
LUDWIG BINSWANGER: Being-in-the-World: *Selected Papers.* ‖ *Trans. with Intro. by Jacob Needleman* TB/1365
HADLEY CANTRIL: The Invasion from Mars: *A Study in the Psychology of Panic* ‖ TB/1282
MIRCEA ELIADE: Cosmos and History: *The Myth of the Eternal Return* § TB/2050
MIRCEA ELIADE: Myth and Reality TB/1369

MIRCEA ELIADE: Myths, Dreams and Mysteries: *The Encounter Between Contemporary Faiths and Archaic Realities* § TB/1320
MIRCEA ELIADE: Rites and Symbols of Initiation: *The Mysteries of Birth and Rebirth* § TB/1236
HERBERT FINGARETTE: The Self in Transformation: *Psychoanalysis, Philosophy and the Life of the Spirit* || TB/1177
SIGMUND FREUD: On Creativity and the Unconscious: *Papers on the Psychology of Art, Literature, Love, Religion.* § Intro. by Benjamin Nelson TB/45
J. GLENN GRAY: The Warriors: *Reflections on Men in Battle. Introduction by Hannah Arendt* TB/1294
WILLIAM JAMES: Psychology: *The Briefer Course. Edited with an Intro. by Gordon Allport* TB/1034
C. G. JUNG: Psychological Reflections. *Ed. by J. Jacobi* TB/2001
KARL MENNINGER, M.D.: Theory of Psychoanalytic Technique TB/1144
JOHN H. SCHAAR: Escape from Authority: *The Perspectives of Erich Fromm* TB/1155
MUZAFER SHERIF: The Psychology of Social Norms. *Introduction by Gardner Murphy* TB/3072
HELLMUT WILHELM: Change: *Eight Lectures on the I Ching* TB/2019

Religion: Ancient and Classical, Biblical and Judaic Traditions

W. F. ALBRIGHT: The Biblical Period from Abraham to Ezra TB/102
SALO W. BARON: Modern Nationalism and Religion TB/818
C. K. BARRETT, Ed.: The New Testament Background: *Selected Documents* TB/86
MARTIN BUBER: Eclipse of God: *Studies in the Relation Between Religion and Philosophy* TB/12
MARTIN BUBER: Hasidism and Modern Man. *Edited and Translated by Maurice Friedman* TB/839
MARTIN BUBER: The Knowledge of Man. *Edited with an Introduction by Maurice Friedman. Translated by Maurice Friedman and Ronald Gregor Smith* TB/135
MARTIN BUBER: Moses. *The Revelation and the Covenant* TB/837
MARTIN BUBER: The Origin and Meaning of Hasidism. *Edited and Translated by Maurice Friedman* TB/835
MARTIN BUBER: The Prophetic Faith TB/73
MARTIN BUBER: Two Types of Faith: *Interpenetration of Judaism and Christianity* ° TB/75
MALCOLM L. DIAMOND: Martin Buber: *Jewish Existentialist* TB/840
M. S. ENSLIN: Christian Beginnings TB/5
M. S. ENSLIN: The Literature of the Christian Movement TB/6
ERNST LUDWIG EHRLICH: A Concise History of Israel: *From the Earliest Times to the Destruction of the Temple in A.D. 70* ° TB/128
HENRI FRANKFORT: Ancient Egyptian Religion: *An Interpretation* TB/77
ABRAHAM HESCHEL: The Earth Is the Lord's & The Sabbath. *Two Essays* TB/828
ABRAHAM HESCHEL: God in Search of Man: *A Philosophy of Judaism* TB/807
ABRAHAM HESCHEL: Man Is not Alone: *A Philosophy of Religion* TB/838
ABRAHAM HESCHEL: The Prophets: *An Introduction* TB/1421

T. J. MEEK: Hebrew Origins TB/69
JAMES MUILENBURG: The Way of Israel: *Biblical Faith and Ethics* TB/133
H. J. ROSE: Religion in Greece and Rome TB/55
H. H. ROWLEY: The Growth of the Old Testament TB/107
D. WINTON THOMAS, Ed.: Documents from Old Testament Times TB/85

Religion: General Christianity

ROLAND H. BAINTON: Christendom: *A Short History of Christianity and Its Impact on Western Civilization. Illus.* Vol. I TB/131; Vol. II TB/132
JOHN T. MCNEILL: Modern Christian Movements. *Revised Edition* TB/1402
ERNST TROELTSCH: The Social Teaching of the Christian Churches. *Intro. by H. Richard Niebuhr* Vol. TB/71; Vol. II TB/72

Religion: Early Christianity Through Reformation

ANSELM OF CANTERBURY: Truth, Freedom, and Evil: *Three Philosophical Dialogues. Edited and Translated by Jasper Hopkins and Herbert Richardson* TB/317
MARSHALL W. BALDWIN, Ed.: Christianity through the 13th Century # HR/1468
W. D. DAVIES: Paul and Rabbinic Judaism: *Some Rabbinic Elements in Pauline Theology. Revised Edition* ° TB/146
ADOLF DEISSMAN: Paul: *A Study in Social and Religious History* TB/15
JOHANNES ECKHART: Meister Eckhart: *A Modern Translation by R. Blakney* TB/8
EDGAR J. GOODSPEED: A Life of Jesus TB/1
ROBERT M. GRANT: Gnosticism and Early Christianity TB/136
WILLIAM HALLER: The Rise of Puritanism TB/22
GERHART B. LADNER: The Idea of Reform: *Its Impact on Christian Thought and Action in the Age of the Fathers* TB/149
ARTHUR DARBY NOCK: Early Gentile Christianity and Its Hellenistic Background TB/111
ARTHUR DARBY NOCK: St. Paul ° TR/104
GORDON RUPP: Luther's Progress to the Diet of Worms ° TB/120

Religion: The Protestant Tradition

KARL BARTH: Church Dogmatics: *A Selection. Intro. by H. Gollwitzer. Ed. by G. W. Bromiley* TB/95
KARL BARTH: Dogmatics in Outline TB/56
KARL BARTH: The Word of God and the Word of Man TB/13
HERBERT BRAUN, et al.: God and Christ: *Existence and Province. Volume 5 of Journal for Theology and the Church, edited by Robert W. Funk and Gerhard Ebeling* TB/255
WHITNEY R. CROSS: The Burned-Over District: *The Social and Intellectual History of Enthusiastic Religion in Western New York, 1800-1850* TB/1242
NELS F. S. FERRE: Swedish Contributions to Modern Theology. *New Chapter by William A. Johnson* TB/147
WILLIAM R. HUTCHISON, Ed.: American Protestant Thought: *The Liberal Era* ‡ TB/1385
ERNST KASEMANN, et al.: Distinctive Protestant and Catholic Themes Reconsidered. *Volume 3 of Journal for Theology and the Church,*

edited by Robert W. Funk and Gerhard
Ebeling TB/253
SOREN KIERKEGAARD: On Authority and Revela-
tion: *The Book on Adler, or a Cycle of
Ethico-Religious Essays. Introduction by F.
Sontag* TB/139
SOREN KIERKEGAARD: Crisis in the Life of an
Actress, *and Other Essays on Drama. Trans-
lated with an Introduction by Stephen Crites*
TB/145
SOREN KIERKEGAARD: Edifying Discourses. *Edited
with an Intro. by Paul Holmer* TB/32
SOREN KIERKEGAARD: The Journals of Kierke-
gaard. ° *Edited with an Intro. by Alexander
Dru* TB/52
SOREN KIERKEGAARD: The Point of View for My
Work as an Author: *A Report to History.* §
Preface by Benjamin Nelson TB/88
SOREN KIERKEGAARD: The Present Age. § *Trans-
lated and edited by Alexander Dru. Intro-
duction by Walter Kaufmann* TB/94
SOREN KIERKEGAARD: Purity of Heart. *Trans. by
Douglas Steere* TB/4
SOREN KIERKEGAARD: Repetition: *An Essay in
Experimental Psychology* § TB/117
SOREN KIERKEGAARD: Works of Love: *Some
Christian Reflections in the Form of Dis-
courses* TB/122
WILLIAM G. MCLOUGHLIN, Ed.: The American
Evangelicals: 1800-1900: *An Anthology*
TB/1382
WOLFHART PANNENBERG, et al.: History and Her-
meneutic. *Volume 4 of* Journal for Theol-
ogy and the Church, *edited by Robert W.
Funk and Gerhard Ebeling* TB/254
JAMES M. ROBINSON, et al.: The Bultmann
School of Biblical Interpretation: New Direc-
tions? *Volume 1 of* Journal for Theology
and the Church, *edited by Robert W. Funk
and Gerhard Ebeling* TB/251
F. SCHLEIERMACHER: The Christian Faith. *Intro-
duction by Richard R. Niebuhr.*
Vol. I TB/108; Vol. II TB/109
F. SCHLEIERMACHER: On Religion: *Speeches to
Its Cultured Despisers. Intro. by Rudolf
Otto* TB/36
TIMOTHY L. SMITH: Revivalism and Social Re-
form: *American Protestantism on the Eve
of the Civil War* TB/1229
PAUL TILLICH: Dynamics of Faith TB/42
PAUL TILLICH: Morality and Beyond TB/142
EVELYN UNDERHILL: Worship TB/10

*Religion: The Roman & Eastern Christian
Traditions*

A. ROBERT CAPONIGRI, Ed.: Modern Catholic
Thinkers II: *The Church and the Political
Order* TB/307
G. P. FEDOTOV: The Russian Religious Mind:
*Kievan Christianity, the tenth to the thir-
teenth Centuries* TB/370
GABRIEL MARCEL: Being and Having: *An Ex-
istential Diary. Introduction by James Col-
lins* TB/310
GABRIEL MARCEL: Homo Viator: *Introduction to
a Metaphysic of Hope* TB/397

Religion: Oriental Religions

TOR ANDRAE: Mohammed: *The Man and His
Faith* § TB/62

EDWARD CONZE: Buddhism: *Its Essence and De-
velopment.* ° *Foreword by Arthur Waley*
TB/58
EDWARD CONZE: Buddhist Meditation TB/1442
EDWARD CONZE et al, Editors: Buddhist Texts
through the Ages TB/113
ANANDA COOMARASWAMY: Buddha and the Gos-
pel of Buddhism TB/119
H. G. CREEL: Confucius and the Chinese Way
TB/63
FRANKLIN EDGERTON, Trans. & Ed.: The Bhaga-
vad Gita TB/115
SWAMI NIKHILANANDA, Trans. & Ed.: The
Upanishads TB/114
D. T. SUZUKI: On Indian Mahayana Buddhism.
° *Ed. with Intro. by Edward Conze.* TB/1403

Religion: Philosophy, Culture, and Society

NICOLAS BERDYAEV: The Destiny of Man TB/61
RUDOLF BULTMANN: History and Eschatology:
The Presence of Eternity ° TB/91
RUDOLF BULTMANN AND FIVE CRITICS: Kerygma
and Myth: *A Theological Debate* TB/80
RUDOLF BULTMANN and KARL KUNDSIN: Form
Criticism: *Two Essays on New Testament Re-
search. Trans. by F. C. Grant* TB/96
WILLIAM A. CLEBSCH & CHARLES R. JAEKLE: Pas-
toral Care in Historical Perspective: *An
Essay with Exhibits* TB/148
FREDERICK FERRE: Language, Logic and God.
New Preface by the Author TB/1407
LUDWIG FEUERBACH: The Essence of Christianity.
§ *Introduction by Karl Barth. Foreword by
H. Richard Niebuhr* TB/11
ADOLF HARNACK: What Is Christianity? § *Intro-
duction by Rudolf Bultmann* TB/17
KYLE HASELDEN: The Racial Problem in Chris-
tian Perspective TB/116
MARTIN HEIDEGGER: Discourse on Thinking.
*Translated with a Preface by John M. Ander-
son and E. Hans Freund. Introduction by
John M. Anderson* TB/1459
IMMANUEL KANT: Religion Within the Limits of
Reason Alone. § *Introduction by Theodore
M. Greene and John Silber* TB/FG
WALTER KAUFMANN, Ed.: Religion from Tol-
stoy to Camus: *Basic Writings on Religious
Truth and Morals. Enlarged Edition* TB/123
H. RICHARD NIEBUHR: Christ and Culture TB/3
H. RICHARD NIEBUHR: The Kingdom of God in
America TB/49
ANDERS NYGREN: Agape and Eros. *Translated by
Philip S. Watson* ° TB/1430
JOHN H. RANDALL, JR.: The Meaning of Reli-
gion for Man. *Revised with New Intro. by
the Author* TB/1379
WALTER RAUSCHENBUSCHS Christianity and the
Social Crisis. ‡ *Edited by Robert D. Cross*
TB/3059

Science and Mathematics

JOHN TYLER BONNER: The Ideas of Biology. Σ
Illus. TB/570
W. E. LE GROS CLARK: The Antecedents of
Man: *An Introduction to the Evolution of
the Primates.* ° *Illus.* TB/559
ROBERT E. COKER: Streams, Lakes, Ponds. *Illus.*
TB/586
ROBERT E. COKER: This Great and Wide Sea: *An
Introduction to Oceanography and Marine
Biology. Illus.* TB/551
W. H. DOWDESWELL: Animal Ecology. *61 illus.*
TB/543

C. V. DURELL: Readable Relativity. *Foreword by Freeman J. Dyson* TB/530

GEORGE GAMOW: Biography of Physics. Σ *Illus.* TB/567

F. K. HARE: The Restless Atmosphere TB/560

J. R. PIERCE: Symbols, Signals and Noise: *The Nature and Process of Communication* Σ TB/574

WILLARD VAN ORMAN QUINE: Mathematical Logic TB/558

Science: History

MARIE BOAS: The Scientific Renaissance, 1450-1630 ° TB/583

STEPHEN TOULMIN & JUNE GOODFIELD: The Architecture of Matter: *The Physics, Chemistry and Physiology of Matter, Both Animate and Inanimate, as it has Evolved since the Beginnings of Science* TB/584

STEPHEN TOULMIN & JUNE GOODFIELD: The Discovery TB/576

STEPHEN TOULMIN & JUNE GOODFIELD: The Fabric of the Heavens: *The Development of Astronomy and Dynamics* TB/579

Science: Philosophy

J. M. BOCHENSKI: The Methods of Contemporary Thought. *Tr. by Peter Caws* TB/1377

J. BRONOWSKI: Science and Human Values. *Revised and Enlarged. Illus.* TB/505

WERNER HEISENBERG: Physics and Philosophy: *The Revolution in Modern Science. Introduction by F. S. C. Northrop* TB/549

KARL R. POPPER: Conjectures and Refutations: *The Growth of Scientific Knowledge* TB/1376

KARL R. POPPER: The Logic of Scientific Discovery TB/1376

STEPHEN TOULMIN: Foresight and Understanding: *An Enquiry into the Aims of Science. Foreword by Jacques Barzun* TB/564

STEPHEN TOULMIN: The Philosophy of Science: *An Introduction* TB/513

Sociology and Anthropology

REINHARD BENDIX: Work and Authority in Industry: *Ideologies of Management in the Course of Industrialization* TB/3035

BERNARD BERELSON, Ed.: The Behavioral Sciences Today TB/1127

JOSEPH B. CASAGRANDE, Ed.: In the Company of Man: *Twenty Portraits of Anthropological Informants. Illus.* TB/3047

KENNETH B. CLARK: Dark Ghetto: *Dilemmas of Social Power. Foreword by Gunnar Myrdal* TB/1317

KENNETH CLARK & JEANNETTE HOPKINS: A Relevant War Against Poverty: *A Study of Community Action Programs and Observable Social Change* TB/1480

LEWIS COSER, Ed.: Political Sociology TB/1293

ROSE L. COSER, Ed.: Life Cycle and Achievement in America ** TB/1434

ALLISON DAVIS & JOHN DOLLARD: Children of Bondage: *The Personality Development of Negro Youth in the Urban South* || TB/3049

PETER F. DRUCKER: The New Society: *The Anatomy of Industrial Order* TB/1082

CORA DU BOIS: The People of Alor. *With a Preface by the Author*
Vol. I *Illus.* TB/1042; Vol. II TB/1043

EMILE DURKHEIM et al.: Essays on Sociology and Philosophy: *with Appraisals of Durkheim's Life and Thought.* || *Edited by Kurt H. Wolff* TB/1151

LEON FESTINGER, HENRY W. RIECKEN, STANLEY SCHACHTER: When Prophecy Fails: *A Social and Psychological Study of a Modern Group that Predicted the Destruction of the World* || TB/1132

CHARLES Y. GLOCK & RODNEY STARK: Christian Beliefs and Anti-Semitism. *Introduction by the Authors* TB/1454

ALVIN W. GOULDNER: The Hellenic World TB/1479

ALVIN W. GOULDNER: Wildcat Strike: *A Study in Worker-Management Relationships* || TB/1176

CESAR GRANA: Modernity and Its Discontents: *French Society and the French Man of Letters in the Nineteenth Century* TB/1318

L. S. B. LEAKEY: Adam's Ancestors: *The Evolution of Man and His Culture. Illus.* TB/1019

KURT LEWIN: Field Theory in Social Science: *Selected Theoretical Papers.* || *Edited by Dorwin Cartwright* TB/1135

RITCHIE P. LOWRY: Who's Running This Town? *Community Leadership and Social Change* TB/1383

R. M. MACIVER: Social Causation TB/1153

GARY T. MARX: Protest and Prejudice: *A Study of Belief in the Black Community* TB/1435

ROBERT K. MERTON, LEONARD BROOM, LEONARD S. COTTRELL, JR., Editors: Sociology Today: *Problems and Prospects* ||
Vol. I TB/1173; Vol. II TB/1174

GILBERT OSOFSKY, Ed.: The Burden of Race: *A Documentary History of Negro-White Relations in America* TB/1405

GILBERT OSOFSKY: Harlem: The Making of a Ghetto: *Negro New York 1890-1930* TB/1381

TALCOTT PARSONS & EDWARD A. SHILS, Editors: Toward a General Theory of Action: *Theoretical Foundations for the Social Sciences* TB/1083

PHILIP RIEFF: The Triumph of the Therapeutic: *Uses of Faith After Freud* TB/1360

JOHN H. ROHRER & MUNRO S. EDMONSON, Eds.: The Eighth Generation Grows Up: *Cultures and Personalities of New Orleans Negroes* || TB/3050

ARNOLD ROSE: The Negro in America: *The Condensed Version of Gunnar Myrdal's* An American Dilemma. *Second Edition* TB/3048

GEORGE ROSEN: Madness in Society: *Chapters in the Historical Sociology of Mental Illness.* || *Preface by Benjamin Nelson* TB/1337

PHILIP SELZNICK: TVA and the Grass Roots: *A Study in the Sociology of Formal Organization* TB/1230

PITIRIM A. SOROKIN: Contemporary Sociological Theories: *Through the First Quarter of the Twentieth Century* TB/3046

MAURICE R. STEIN: The Eclipse of Community: *An Interpretation of American Studies* TB/1128

EDWARD A. TIRYAKIAN, Ed.: Sociological Theory, Values and Sociocultural Change: *Essays in Honor of Pitirim A. Sorokin* ° TB/1316

FERDINAND TONNIES: Community and Society: *Gemeinschaft und Gesellschaft. Translated and Edited by Charles P. Loomis* TB/1116

SAMUEL E. WALLACE: Skid Row as a Way of Life TB/1367

W. LLOYD WARNER: Social Class in America: *The Evaluation of Status* TB/1013

FLORIAN ZNANIECKI: The Social Role of the Man of Knowledge. *Introduction by Lewis A. Coser* TB/1372